HISTORY THROUGH HEADLINES

Published in 2010 by
World Publications Group, Inc.
140 Laurel Street,
East Bridgewater, MA 02333
www.wrldpub.com
Copyright © 2009 Igloo Books Ltd

10 9 8 7 6 5 4 3 2 1

ISBN: 978-1-57215-661-6

Printed and manufactured in China

The news stories featured here reflect the social attitudes of the day
and do not reflect the opinions of the publisher.

HISTORY THROUGH HEADLINES

Contents

Introduction

Read all about it! The past 100 years of world history are portrayed here, through dramatic newspaper headlines, vivid front-page images, detailed explanatory stories and timelines with important events, from atomic bombs and the sinking of the Titanic, to the fall of the Berlin Wall and the election of President Obama.

Events that shaped the 20th Century and, therefore, life as we know it, from major experiences such as the assassination of President John F. Kennedy, to the less crucial but life-changing flight of Charles Lindbergh, the first person to fly solo across the Atlantic, are chronicled here, by decade and by year.

This comprehensive reflection of the past 100 years encapsulates history from 1900 up to the present.

Right: Ethiopian refugees rest as they reach a camp in Sudan in 1985, having been forced out of their country by famine.

Crowds gather outside the New York Stock Exchange on Wall Street following news of the stock market crash on October 24, 1929.

American astronaut Bruce McCandless uses the Manned Maneuvering Unit to move around the space shuttle Challenger *in 1984.*

The wreck of the oil tanker Amoco Cadiz sinks off the coast of Brittany, France, in March 1978 releasing what was, at the time, the largest oil slick ever spilled.

AT SPA WHERE ARMISTICE COMMISSION IS SITTING

Major-General Kavanagh receives a bouquet on his arrival at Spa.

Lieutenant-General Sir R. Haking acknowledges the salute of a German sentry posted in Spa.

Lieutenant-General Sir R. Haking (A), General Nudan (B), and General Delobbe (C), photographed at Spa.

General von Winterfeldt, who was sent to receive armistice terms.

The Armistice Commission, consisting of military representatives of the Allies and of the enemy Army Command, is sitting at Spa in what was the German General Head- quarters. This was in the Grand-Hotel Britannique, which is now once more used for a purpose that does no dishonour to its name.—(Exclusive to *The Daily Mirror*.)

1900-1919

WHY WERE THERE ONLY TWENTY LIFEBOATS FOR 2,207 PEOPLE ON BOARD THE ILL-FATED TITANIC?

THE FINAL ACT OF THE WORLD DRAMA AT VERSAILLES

THE FIRST PHOTOGRAPHS OF CAPTAIN SCOTT'S DASH FOR THE SOUTH POLE: THE EXPLORER SEEN AT THE FOOT OF MOUNT EREBUS.

MISS FLORENCE NIGHTINGALE, "THE ANGEL OF THE CRIMEA," WHOSE DEATH IS ANNOUNCED, WITH SOME OF THE NURSES WHOSE PROFESSION SHE CREATED.

KUROKI IS COMING!

PRINCE ITO, THE BISMARCK OF JAPAN, ASSASSINATED BY A KOREAN AT HARBIN RAILWAY STATION.

The 20th century opened with the closing of an era, which had seen Britain transformed into a prosperous industrialized nation with an expanding empire. By the end of the First World War, faith in authority had been shattered and an entire generation of men had been all but wiped out. The war had brought Britain and America together against a common enemy, and U.S. President Woodrow Wilson was instrumental in trying to establish a lasting peace in the Treaty of Versailles.

In an age when science and engineering were at their peak, successful expeditions to the North and South Poles demonstrated the indomitable power of the human spirit, but there were demonstrations too of the fallibility and fragility of human endeavor, epitomized by the sinking of the supposedly 'unsinkable' ocean liner *Titanic*.

One of the defining moments of the century came in 1917 as a revolution saw Vladimir Lenin's Bolsheviks overthrow the old Tsarist regime in Russia. Weary of war, much of Europe came close to revolution, and for a time it looked likely that Germany would follow Russia's lead. The German revolution failed, but anti-Soviet forces, which fought on in Russia for another six years, would be defeated. The battle of ideologies that was to dominate much of the 20th century had begun in earnest.

1900–1906

1900
SIEGE OF MAFEKING

The Second Boer War was fought between the British Empire, of which South Africa was a part, and two independent Boer republics within South Africa. In May 1900, the Siege of Mafeking in South Africa ended in an overwhelming British victory against the Boers. Colonel Robert Baden-Powell, who later founded the Scouting movement, made his name by raising two regiments in Cape Colony and taking up a defensive position in the town of Mafeking. Although Baden-Powell's troops were greatly outnumbered, they managed to resist Boer forces. This was largely due to Baden-Powell's employment of skillful deceptions, including laying fake landmines and telling his troops to climb over imaginary barbed wire.

'The Siege of Mafeking in South Africa ended in an overwhelming British victory against the Boers.'

1901
QUEEN VICTORIA DIES

Queen Victoria reined for 63 years, overseeing an expanding British Empire, the technological advances of the Industrial Revolution, and increased literary and artistic output. She died of a cerebral hemorrhage on January 22, 1901, at the age of 82. Since the death of her husband, Prince Albert, in 1861, Victoria had taken on somber mourning, both in her dress and in her manner, an attitude that was reflected in national habits where mourning became lavish, ornate, and drawn out. Her death was to mark the end of such a somber fashion. Her funeral took place on February 2, 1901, and she was laid beside the body of her husband at the mausoleum in Great Windsor Park.

Above: The Albert Memorial was commissioned by Queen Victoria (right) in 1861.

1900
New Quantum Physics
German physicist Max Planck formulates new laws of physics, showing that energy comes in tiny packets called 'quanta.'

September 6, 1901
McKinley Assassinated
U.S. President William McKinley is shot as he meets the public in Buffalo, New York. He dies of his injuries a week later.

December 10, 1901
First Nobel Prizes Awarded
At a ceremony in Sweden the first annual nobel prizes, for Chemistry, Physics, Medicine, Literature, and Peace, are awarded. They were set up according to the will of the Swedish inventor Alfred Nobel.

1900-1906

1904
JAPAN AND RUSSIA AT WAR

In 1904, war broke out between Russia and Japan over control of Korea and Manchuria. In 1896, Russia had formed an alliance with China that allowed the country to extend the Trans-Siberian Railway across Chinese-held Manchuria to the Russian port of Vladivostock. The Japanese demanded that the Russians withdraw from Manchuria and threatened military action. On February 8, 1904, the Japanese fleet launched a surprise attack on the Russian Navy at Port Arthur in Southern Manchuria. On land, the two armies were fairly evenly matched, and despite mounting casualties, neither side was able to claim a victory. At sea, however, the Japanese had the upper hand, and when the Japanese Navy destroyed the entire Russian Baltic Fleet at the Battle of Tsushima in May 1905, the Russians were forced to sue for peace. The resultant deal saw the Russians withdraw from Southern Manchuria, which was returned to the Chinese, while Japan took control of the rest of Manchuria and Korea.

1906
SAN FRANCISCO DEVASTATED BY EARTHQUAKE AND FIRE

The earthquake that struck northern California on April 18, 1906 was one of the most severe in America's history. The quake itself caused significant loss of life, and started a fire in the city of San Francisco that raged out of control. At the time, it was estimated that 700 people were killed, but it is now thought that there were many more fatalities. The 1906 Californian earthquake also taught geologists a good deal about earthquake patterns. The tremor along the San Andreas Fault was 296 miles (480 km) long, and its horizontal displacements over such a large area baffled scientists of the day. In the years before the discovery of plate tectonics, analysts developed a theory of elastic-rebound at the quake's source, which today still stands as the clearest explanation of earthquake cycles.

February 23, 1903
U.S. Lease Guantanamo Bay
Cuba leases Guantanamo Bay, an area in the east of the island, to the U.S.A.

December 1, 1903
First Feature Film
The first full-length silent movie, *The Great Train Robbery*, goes on general release in the U.S.A.

1905
E=MC²
Albert Einstein publishes his Special Theory of Relativity, in which he formulates the relationship between energy and matter: $E=mc^2$.

February 19, 1906
Kellogg's Founded
Will Keith Kellogg founds the Toasted Corn Flake Company to sell the new breakfast cereal he developed with his brother John Harvey Kellogg.

1906
Finnish Women Granted the Vote
Finland is the first European country to give women the vote.

1909–1911

1909
PRINCE ITO ASSASSINATED

On October 26, 1909, Prince Itō Hirobumi, former Prime Minister of Japan and Resident-General of Korea since it became a Japanese Protectorate in 1905, was assassinated by a Korean nationalist. Prince Itō was shot three times on his way to a meeting with Russian representatives in Manchuria. As Resident-General, Itō's policy on Korea was to keep it as a protectorate rather than annexing it to Japan. Although he apparently supported the Japanese Annexation of Korea Treaty of 1907, his main motivation in doing so was to keep Korea out of Russian hands. Itō believed that only by working together and presenting a strong united front could East Asian nations avoid Western control, and he saw Japan's protectorship of Korea as a means of achieving this. Itō had, in fact, attempted to delay the annexation to Japan, making him the enemy of the Imperial Japanese Army, which forced his resignation in June 1909. The assassination of Prince Itō in October 1909 actually had the opposite effect to that intended by his assassin, as it allowed the Japanese annexation of Korea to go ahead without opposition in 1910.

1910
KIND EDWARD DIES

Edward VII, the son of Queen Victoria and Prince Albert, had a reputation as something of a libertine – keeping mistresses, gambling, and eating and drinking to excess. King Edward VII turned out to be conservative in many issues, however. He opposed women's suffrage, and rejected reforms of the House of Lords. King Edward died suddenly on May 6, 1910, leaving his son George V to take on the constitutional crisis caused by Liberal demands for the reform of the House of Lords.

Above: Edward VII died aged 68.

February 12, 1909
N.A.A.C.P. Founded
The National Association for the Advancement of Colored People is founded in New York City.

July 25, 1909
Plane Flown Across the English Channel
Frenchman Louis Bleriot is the first person to fly a heavier-than-air craft (as opposed to a hot-air balloon) across any large body of water as he crosses the English Channel.

November 20, 1910
Call to Arms in Mexico
Opposition leader Francisco Madero issues a statement declaring the re-election of Mexican president Porfirio Días null and void. His call for armed resistance marks the start of the Mexican Revolution.

1909–1911

1910
FLORENCE NIGHTINGALE DIES

MISS FLORENCE NIGHTINGALE, "THE ANGEL OF THE CRIMEA," WHOSE DEATH IS ANNOUNCED, WITH SOME OF THE NURSES WHOSE PROFESSION SHE CREATED.

'She found the hospitals overcrowded and filthy and the wounded soldiers unwashed and poorly treated.'

Florence Nightingale, a nurse who reformed the military nursing system during the Crimean War in the 1850s, died on August 13, 1910 at the age of 90. In 1853, reports reached England about the appalling conditions in the army hospital in Scutari barracks in Istanbul, where British soldiers injured in the Crimean War were being treated. Around 8,000 soldiers had already died of cholera, dysentery, typhoid, and malaria. The British government allowed Nightingale to take a group of 38 nurses to Scutari, where she found the hospitals overcrowded and filthy and the wounded soldiers unwashed and poorly treated. She set about improving sanitation and care, helped by a publicity campaign through *The Times* newspaper back home. Her campaigning led to the establishment of the Army Medical Hospital, and she also set up her own Nightingale School and Home for Nurses in St. Thomas's Hospital in London.

1911
CORONATION OF NEW BRITISH KING

Following the death of his father Edward VII, George V was crowned at Westminster Abbey in London on June 22, 1911, one year after he had ascended the throne. His wife, Victoria, chose 'Mary' as her royal name and was crowned Queen on the same day. The ceremony, which has followed roughly the same lines since the coronation of William the Conqueror nearly 1,000 years ago, kept with newer traditions in which the sovereign wears a series of royal robes, each one representing different aspects of kingship. After being administered an oath by the Archbishop of Canterbury, King George proceeded to King Edward's Chair, under which sits the Stone of Scone (or 'Coronation Stone'), brought from Scotland by King Edward I in the 13th century. After the crowning, the King was presented with the spurs, orb, ring, and two scepters, before the crown of St. Edward was placed on his head to shouts of 'God save the King!'

THE SYMBOL OF SOVEREIGNTY: THE PRICELESS CROWN WHICH THE KING WILL WEAR TO-DAY AS HE RIDES HOMEWARD AFTER THE CORONATION.

Above: George V and Queen Mary on a visit to India.

February 6, 1911
Fire in Instanbul
A huge fire destroys much of downtown Istanbul in Turkey.

May 23, 1911
New Public Library for New York
The main branch of the New York Public Library, one of the largest lending libraries in the world, is officially opened by President William Taft.

May 30, 1911
First Indy 500
The first Indianapolis 500 automobile race is held. It is won by Ray Harroun in his car the Marmon 'Wasp'.

July 24, 1911
'Lost City' Rediscovered
American explorer Hiram Bingham rediscovers the abandoned Inca city Machu Picchu high in the Andes mountains.

1911–1912

1911
AMUNDSEN REACHES SOUTH POLE BEFORE SCOTT

THE FIRST PHOTOGRAPHS OF CAPTAIN SCOTT'S DASH FOR THE SOUTH POLE: THE EXPLORER SEEN AT THE FOOT OF MOUNT EREBUS.

To-day we are able to reproduce the first photographs to reach England from the British Antarctic Expedition, which is under the leadership of Captain R. F. Scott. The struggle to reach the South Pole has now developed into a race, as Captain Amundsen, the Norwegian explorer, is also in the field. It was on November 29 of last year that the members of the expedition left Port Chalmers, New Zealand, on their dash to the Pole, where, it is hoped, the Union Jack will to be hoisted. Above, Captain Scott is seen just prior to his departing journey. Mount Erebus, the great active volcano, is seen in —(Photograph by Mr. H. G. Ponting, F.R.G.S., Camera Artist to arctic Expedition. Copyright in U.S.A. and Europe.)

In September 1909, while planning a voyage to the North Pole, Norwegian explorer Roald Amundsen received news that American explorer Robert Peary had already reached it before him. Although Amundsen continued to insist to his financial backers that his expedition was solely for scientific purposes and not concerned with breaking records, he secretly changed his plans and aimed for the South Pole in the Antarctic instead – a destination still yet to be reached. The British explorer Robert Scott was planning the same trip with the aim of being the first to the South Pole, but Amundsen afterwards claimed that he thought Scott's expedition was purely scientific. Amundsen's boat *Fram* left Norway on August 9, 1910, heading as if for the North Pole in the Arctic, but secretly heading south. Scott's *Terra Nova* had already left for the Antarctic eight weeks earlier. Amundsen sent a telegram to Scott announcing his intention, but only after it was too late for either man to turn back. Scott took dogs and ponies with him. Amundsen used only dogs. Amundsen's understanding of the value of dogs was to prove crucial.

On December 14, 1911, Amundsen's party reached the South Pole and planted a Norwegian flag. They also erected a tent and left a message inside for Scott. The announcement was made public on March 17, 1912. However, the news of Amundsen's achievement was not greeted with universal applause in the scientific world, where it was generally felt that he had been underhand in damaging Scott's mission.

Right: Robert Scott reached the South Pole on January 17, 1912. On the way back, he and four of his comrades died from hunger and cold.

December 12, 1911
New Emperor, New Capital
The day after British king George V has been crowned Emperor of India, New Delhi is named the country's new capital city, replacing Kolkata (Calcutta).

Jan 6, 1912
New Mexico Admitted to the Union
New Mexico is named the 47th state of the United States of America.

January 8, 1912
A.N.C. Founded
The South African Native National Congress is founded in Bloemfontein, South Africa, to fight for the rights of black South Africans. It changes its name to the African National Congress in 1923.

April 13, 1912
New Flying Corps
The precursor to the R.A.F., the Royal Flying Corps, is formed in the U.K.

1912
FIRST BALKAN WAR

Formed in 1912, the Balkan League consisted of an alliance between Bulgaria, Greece, Serbia, and Montenegro. When, on October 8, 1912, Montenegro declared war against Turkey, the other countries joined in the offensive, eager to exercise and extend their power in the region. Within weeks, the Turks had retreated to Constantinople, while the Balkan states took over Albania, Macedonia, Thrace, and Epirus. Once Adrianople, Scutari, and Janina had also fallen to the Balkan League, a treaty was signed in London in May 1913, in which Turkey was forced to hand over Crete to Greece, as well as give up control of its western states. The Treaty of London also triggered negotiations for a new Albanian state. However, the disputes over territory that followed this peace led to the Second Balkan War soon after.

1912
TITANIC HITS ICEBERG

Four days into its maiden voyage across the Atlantic Ocean, and with 2,200 people on board, the ocean liner R.M.S. *Titanic* hit an iceberg. The ship had been designed to be 'unsinkable' because its hull was divided into sixteen 'watertight' compartments, up to four of which could safely fill with water before the ship lost its buoyancy. However, when the ship hit an iceberg just before midnight on April 14, 1912, it tore through the hull, filling five of the compartments with water, and the ship began to sink. The *Titanic* did not have adequate emergency measures in place. A shortage of lifeboats meant that, although around 700 passengers were saved, the remaining 1,500 people on board drowned or froze to death in the ice-cold waters of the Atlantic. It took little more than two hours for the ship to sink.

'Although around 700 passengers were saved, the remaining 1,500 people on board drowned or froze to death'

March 30, 1912
French Take Control of Morocco
France establishes a protectorate over Morocco in North Africa.

May 5, 1912
Fifth Summer Olympics Begin
The Games of the V Olympiad begin in Stockholm, Sweden. For the first time, there are competitors from all five of the inhabited continents symbolized by the five Olympic rings.

November 5, 1912
Wilson New U.S. President
Democratic challenger Woodrow Wilson defeats the incumbent William Taft in the U.S. election, as the Republican vote is split between Taft and a third candidate, former president Theodore Roosevelt.

December 20, 1912
Fossil Hoax
The discovery of the remains of a form of early human is announced in the U.K. Known as Piltdown Man, it is later exposed as a hoax.

1913-1918

1913
SUFFRAGATE RUNS IN FRONT OF KING'S HORSE

WOMAN RUSHES ON THE DERBY COURSE AND SNATCHES AT THE BRIDLE OF THE KING'S HORSE, INJURING HERSELF AND THE JOCKEY.

The Epsom Derby was one of the highlights of the British racing calendar, and the royal family usually entered a horse in the race. The King's horse in June 4, 1913 was Anmer. Anmer was third from last at the final corner when Emily Davison ran out in front of the horse, and was thrown up into the air by impact with the animal. At first it was assumed that she had thought the race was over and was following the final horse to the finish, as was the tradition. However, there were claims from spectators that they had heard her shout 'Votes for women!' before dashing onto the track. She died four days later. Her gravestone was inscribed with the phrase: 'Deeds, not words.' In February 1918, women over the age of 30 were granted the vote.

1914-1918
POISON GAS IN BRUTAL NEW WARFARE

In August 1914, the French Army became the first to use poison gas in the First World War when they fired tear-gas grenades at the Germans. Up till then, gas had been viewed as uncivilized. The French used it in an effort to break the standoff that had arisen as a result of trench warfare – the immobile state in which neither side made any progress. Although it was the French who first used them, it was the Germans who began to develop chemical weapons on a mass scale. In April 22, 1915, during the Second Battle of Ypres, German troops deployed the poisonous gas chlorine against the French and Algerian troops manning the Ypres Salient. The yellow-green cloud of vapor destroyed the victims' respiratory organs moments after it was inhaled, triggering helpless choking fits. The French fled in panic, allowing the Germans to break the line, but the Allies managed to reform. The use of poison gas was widely condemned. Great Britain also condemned its use, but the British were already planning to use it themselves.

September 1, 1914
Last of the Passenger Pigeons
The last passenger pigeon in the world dies in Cincinatti Zoo. Just a few decades earlier, the species had been the most common bird in North America.

December 15, 1914
Mine Explosion in Japan
A gas explosion in a coal mine on Kyushu island kills 687 people, the worst coal mine disaster ever in Japan.

April 24, 1915
Armenian Leaders Arrested
250 Armenian intellectuals and leaders are arrested in Istanbul, marking the beginning of a campaign by the Ottoman Empire to murder all Christian Armenians within its borders. More than 1 million people are killed in the genocide.

September 6, 1915
New Tank Tested
A prototype tank is tested by the British army. Tanks are used in battle for the first time by the British during the Battle of Flers-Courcellette a year later.

1914–1918
LUSITANIA IS SUNK BY GERMAN U-BOAT

On May 1, 1915, R.M.S. *Lusitania* left port in New York, heading for England with 1,959 people on board. The British ocean liner was one of the most luxurious of its kind on the waters between Great Britain and the U.S., ferrying passengers and carrying goods. However, since the outbreak of war, ocean liners had become targets for German U-boats. On May 7, 1915, the *Lusitania* was 14 miles (22 km) off the coast of Ireland when it was torpedoed by a German U-boat. It sank within 18 minutes, taking the lives of 1,198 passengers, 128 of whom were American. The loss of so many civilian lives outraged public opinion in the U.S., as the country had maintained its neutrality up to that point. It is now thought that the *Lusitania* was, in fact, transporting war materials and that a second explosion, caused by ammunition on board, actually led to the sinking of the ship.

The Lusitania, *a luxury liner that was sunk on its way from New York to England.*

1914–1918
BATTLE OF VERDUN IN FRANCE

The Battle of Verdun, which lasted from February 21 to December 19, 1916, has gone down in history as the longest battle on the smallest piece of land, with the greatest loss of life. There were 700,000 casualties in total; lives lost over a patch of land no more than 7 sq miles (12 sq km), in a battle that had become more about pride and stubbornness than anything else. Both sides thought 1916 would be the year in which the two-year standoff would be broken, and the Germans poured everything into a victory

'There were 700,000 casualties in total; lives lost over a patch of land no more than seven sq miles (12 sq km)'

at Verdun. They wanted to get at the British by destroying their closest ally, the French, and they chose Verdun, to the east of Paris, as the most important French garrison strategically. The German army channeled a massive amount of ammunition into an artillery bombardment. Neither side was prepared to give in, even in the face of massive losses; food, water, and munitions shortages; terrible conditions; and troop exhaustion. The Germans captured several French garrisons but by December 19, they had been forced back to their original position. Neither side had achieved anything.

December 29, 1916
Rasputin Assassinated
Influential Russian mystic Grigoriy Rasputin, who is close to the Tsar, is murdered.

October 25, 1917
Revolution in Russia
The October Revolution in Russia, a series of events that will eventually lead to the overthrow of old Tsarist order and the establishment of a Communist regime, begins in earnest, as the Winter Palace in Petrograd, official residence of the Tsar, is captured by revolutionaries. The Bolsheviks, led by Lenin, quickly seize power, but a civil war rages in Russia for the next six years.

November 17, 1917
P.D.S.A. Founded
In the U.K., the People's Dispensary for Sick Animals is founded to provide veterinary care for the animals of the poor.

March 1, 1918
Russia Leaves War
The new Bolshevik regime in Russia signs a peacy treaty with Germany and Austria.

1914–1918

1914–1918
BATTLE OF THE SOMME

The Battle of the Somme, which started on July 1, 1916, summed up the horrors of the First World War. New British recruits were known as 'Kitchener's Volunteer Army', and they had responded to the military call-up as a reaction to posters of General Kitchener declaring 'Your Country Needs You!' Many new recruits were killed within weeks of signing up. The British offensive on the Somme was intended to provide relief for the French defending Verdun by drawing away the Germans. Many British and French generals believed that the attack was futile, but the order was given that it should go ahead. The Allies began by launching an artillery bombardment of the German trenches. Allied infantry then advanced straight into German machine-gun fire. In total, 420,000 British, 200,000 French, and 500,000 Germans were killed. In the end, the Allies advanced just 7 miles (12 km).

1914–1918
U.S.A. JOINS THE WAR

U.S. President Woodrow Wilson kept America out of the war for three years. U.S. isolationism and a significant German and Austrian population in the U.S. prevented their direct involvement. The German government had already announced their intention to strike any vessels traveling between Great Britain and America, so when a new German submarine offensive was announced in January 1917, the U.S. broke off diplomatic ties with Germany. The U.S. public was angered when it was revealed that the German government had offered to help Mexico regain territory in Arizona and Texas. On April 2, 1917, President Wilson sought Senate approval for war against Germany, and this was granted on April 4. The U.S. was still not officially taking sides: it was declaring a separate war against Germany. However, in reality the U.S. had joined the Allies.

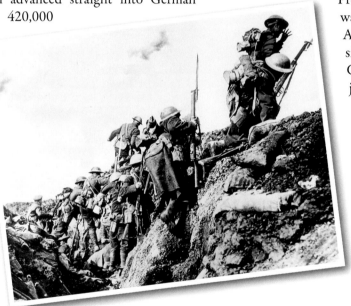

'The U.S. public was angered when it was revealed that the German government had offered to help Mexico regain territory in Arizona and Texas'

July 17, 1918
Tsar Executed
Tsar Nicholas II of Russia, his immediate family, and many of his staff are executed on the orders of the Bolsheviks.

August 1918
Flu Pandemic
A pandemic of Spanish Flu sweeps the world. Over the next six months, more than 25 million people die of the flu, more than twice as many as were killed during the First World War.

October 31, 1918
Hungary Ends Empire
The Hungarian government ends its union with Austria, bringing the Austro-Hungarian Empire to an end.

November 9, 1918
Kaiser Abdicates
Kaiser Wilhelm II of Germany abdicates and goes into exile in the Netherlands.

1914–1918
FIRST WORLD WAR ENDS

On November 11, 1918, at 5 a.m. the Allies and Central Powers agreed to end hostilities, signing an armistice that signaled the end of the war. The armistice came into effect six hours later at 11 a.m. – the eleventh hour of the eleventh day of the eleventh month of the year. Germany had first sued for a peace agreement in October, eager that U.S. President Wilson's 'Fourteen Points', which included an end to secret treaties and general military disarmament, should be implemented. Great Britain and France objected to various points, but they were persuaded by Wilson to agree to them. The armistice, which was signed in a railway carriage in France, demanded that Germany withdraw from all territories that it had occupied, while the Allies would occupy parts of Germany. The Germans were also instructed to give up the majority of their military equipment and the German Kaiser Wilhelm II was to abdicate. The exact nature of reparation payments to be made by Germany was not agreed in detail – the Treaty of Versailles in early 1919 would settle that.

1919
TREATY OF VERSAILLES SETS TERMS OF PEACE

The treaty that officially tied up the loose ends of the First World War was signed in the vast palace of Versailles near Paris. France, represented by Georges Clemenceau, pushed for harsher treatment of Germany, while Great Britain, represented by British Prime Minister David Lloyd George, urged caution. U.S. President Woodrow Wilson was also in favor of reconciliation, but Clemenceau reflected both French public opinion and his own feelings when he demanded the highest price possible. Germany's new leader, Friedrich Ebert, accepted responsibility for the war on behalf of his country and agreed to the terms outlined, which included the loss of German territories outside Germany, the occupation of Germany by the Allies, military disarmament, and heavy financial penalties. Russia, which had fought on the side of the Allies, had made peace with Germany separately in 1918.

January 1, 1919
Spartacist Uprising
Demonstrations in Berlin threaten a Communist revolution in Germany. The uprising fails.

May 19, 1919
Turks at War
Mustafa Kemal Ataturk lands on Turkish soil, marking the start of the Turkish War of Independence.

May 29, 1919
Einstein Is Right
Observations by Arthur Eddington of a total solar eclipse in Brazil confirm predictions made by Albert Einstien with his radical new Theory of Relativity.

August 11, 1919
Weimar Era Begins
The new Weimar Constitution marks the start of the Federal Republic of Germany.

October 28, 1919
Alcohol Outlawed
Prohibition begins in the United States as the sale of alcohol is banned by the Volstead Act.

A ROYAL RIVET | WALL STREET'S PANIC DAY

The Duke of York greets ex-Service men at Grindon Hall, Sunderland, where he opened a new sanatorium pavilion.

First pictures received of the worst crash in the history of Wall Street, when thousands of people were ruined. Anxious watchers in front of the Sub-Treasury, which is opposite the New York Stock Exchange. £7,000,000,000 is estimated as the total losses. A rally took place later.

The Duke of York inspects the last rivet which he inserted to complete the new bridge across the Wear at Sunderland yesterday.—(By " Daily Mirror " photo-telephony.)

Wall Street when shares were at their lowest. The New York Stock Exchange is to be closed to-day and to-morrow.

1920-1929

A forward-looking and progressive decade, the 1920s saw a great advance in women's rights in the form of the first birth control clinic, which opened in London in 1922. The decade was also a time for individual heroism, with Gertrude Ederle becoming the first woman to swim the English Channel, and Charles Lindbergh the first man to fly solo across the Atlantic Ocean. There was heroic self-sacrifice, too, in the form of Ghandi's personal struggle for India's freedom from British rule. There were great horrors and great discoveries: Japan was struck by a devastating earthquake, Smyrna in Greece was destroyed by a fire in which 100,000 people perished,

and Tutankhamen's tomb was finally uncovered in Egypt by British archaeologist Howard Carter.

The decade saw the beginning of world-changing regimes, historic births, and monumental deaths. In Britain, Princess Elizabeth was born, later to reign as Queen Elizabeth II. In Russia, the first leader of the Soviet Union, Vladimir Lenin, died. In Italy, Mussolini came to power, marking the beginning of the rise of fascism in Europe..

In the United States the crash of the New York Stock Exchange burst the bubble of post-war prosperity.

1920

SINN FEIN PRISONERS ON HUNGER STRIKE

SINN FEIN IRELAND PARALYSED BY GENERAL STRIKE

Mr. Philip Shanahan, M.P., one of the Sinn Fein hunger-strikers in Mountjoy Gaol, with his wife and family. A vain attempt was made to give him milk.

Sinn Feiners demonstrating outside Mountjoy Gaol, cheering prisoners at cell window.

One of the armoured cars engaged in patrolling the streets around Mountjoy Gaol.

Captain White, D.S.O., son of Sir George White, detained by police for addressing soldiers at Mountjoy Gaol.

Drawing a military cordon across Mountjoy-street, Dublin, in the vicinity of the prison.

Girls parading Dublin streets with placards calling for prayers for "Ireland's prisoners."

Mrs. Ellis, mother of a hunger-striker in Mountjoy Gaol.

Ireland, with the exception of Belfast and the north, is in the grip of a general strike. Trains have stopped running on the chief railways, shops have shut, and even schools have closed. The general strike is in response to the call of the Irish Trades Union Congress for a twenty-four-hour protest against the treatment of Sinn Fein hunger strikers.

In Mountjoy Gaol, many of whom are in a being witnessed in Dublin, where the mil parade the streets, and at nights searchlig side Mountjoy Gaol the crowds demonstrat

On April 4, 1920, more than 100 political prisoners belonging to the Irish republican party Sinn Féin went on hunger strike at Mountjoy Gaol in Dublin to protest at their treatment. Many of them were being held without charge. On April 12, the Irish Labour Executive called for a general strike among the workers of Dublin as an expression of sympathy with the prisoners' plight and outrage at their treatment. The 'manifesto' calling for the strike acknowledged that a general strike should only be used in dire circumstances when nothing else would work. On this occasion, it worked, and many of the hunger-striking prisoners were released two days later. In the north of Ireland, tension on the streets of Belfast between Protestant Unionists and Catholic Nationalists had reached a high by July 1920, and was concentrated around the shipyards on Queen's Island. The unity shown by the two sides in the Belfast General Strike of 1919, when workers had come together to demand a 44-hour working week, had broken down. On July 20, 1920, 'disloyal' workers – that is to say, Catholics and socialists – were violently driven out of the shipyards while the management turned a blind eye. The vigilante expulsion sparked riots throughout the city that lasted for three days, with fatalities on both sides.

> **'The vigilante expulsion sparked riots throughout the city that lasted for three days, with fatalities on both sides.'**

Left: Gerry Adams, leader of today's Sinn Fein party.

January 6
Babe Ruth Sold For Massive $125,000
Newspapers announce that the Boston Red Sox have sold Babe Ruth to the New York Yankees for $125,000.

February 17
Woman Claims She's Anastasia
A woman named Anna Anderson claims she is Anastasia, the Romanov princess who was murdered with the rest of the Russian royal family by the Bolsheviks in 1918.

May 17
France and Belgium Leave Germany
French and Belgian troops leave the German cities they have been occupying since the end of the First World War.

August 10
Powerful Pact Signed
Treaty of Sevres is signed between Turkey and the Allied Powers, abolishing the Ottoman Empire and limiting Turkish control in Africa, Asia, and Europe.

LEAGUE OF NATIONS ESTABLISHED

CLERGYMAN'S RESCUE WORK.

The wreckage-strewn beach on the morning after the wreck.

The Rev. H. M. Piercy, who helped the few survivors ashore.

The coastguard's house at Worth Matravers, where twenty bodies lie awaiting burial.

The wrecked steamer Treveal, broken in two, lying on the rocks in Dead Men's Pool.

Only seven members of the crew of forty-three of the steamship Treveal, a brand-new boat, which was dashed to pieces on the Kenmerridge Rocks, near St. Alban's Head, have survived. The Rev. H. M. Piercy, who showed the greatest pluck, was up to his neck for an hour in water and shingle, carrying some of the men ashore.

DEATH BEFORE ARREST

Mr. R. Harris, a Bromley (Kent) rate collector and ex-officer, who had been missing, was found at Felixstowe. A warrant had been issued and, when a constable called on him, he went into another room to get his coat. Later he was found fatally wounded, with a revolver by his side.

LEAGUE OF NATIONS' PRESIDENT?

Viscount Grey, who, it was noticed, was no longer wearing his dark glasses, after alighting from the train at Waterloo yesterday on his return from the States. His name has been mentioned in connection with the Presidency of the League of Nations.

In 1920, the League of Nations was established in response to the horror of the First World War. It was an agreement between nations, aimed at avoiding further conflict by finding diplomatic solutions to disputes. The League came into being as a result of the Treaty of Versailles, at which the chief victors of the war, Britain, France, and the United States, had set about restoring peace and order in the aftermath of the war. The initial council of the League included four permanent members: the United Kingdom, France, Japan, and Italy. The United States originally intended to make up the numbers as a fifth permanent member. Indeed the U.S. President, Democrat Woodrow Wilson, had first championed the idea of the League and had keenly supported its formation at the Treaty of Versailles. However, the shift to a Republican government in the States signaled a move toward isolationism, and the U.S. did not join. However, lacking its own army and reliant on the co-operation of opposing powers with vastly different agendas, the League failed to achieve its objective, as the outbreak of the Second World War two decades later demonstrated. It was replaced in 1946 by the United Nations, which inherited many of its agencies.

'The League of Nations was established in response to the horror of the First World War.'

Right: The Treaty of Versailles, signed in June 1919, formally ended the First World War six months after the fighting had ceased. The British and French prime ministers, Lloyd George and Clemenceau, pictured here at the negotiation table, demanded reparations from a defeated Germany.

Far right: The Palace of Nations in Geneva, Switzerland, where the League of Nations met.

August 26
Women's Suffrage Enshrined
Women's suffrage is enshrined in the U.S. constitution in the form of the Nineteenth Amendment.

September 20
Spain's Foreign Legion
The first soldier joins the Spanish Legion, an elite regiment in the Spanish Army, formed to control rebels in Morocco.

November 21
Bloody Sunday
The first Bloody Sunday in Ireland: the I.R.A. kills 12 suspected British spies, and British police retaliate by opening fire on crowds at a football match in Dublin.

1920

JOAN OF ARC CANONIZED BY CATHOLIC CHURCH

In May 1920, Joan of Arc followed in the footsteps of many other renowned religious martyrs when she was officially canonized by the same Church which had originally – in name at least – put her to death. Joan was a French peasant girl who claimed that she was instructed by divine voices to free her country from English rule. She led the French army in several successful attacks against the English during the Hundred Years War in the 15th century. She was eventually put to death at the age of 19 by an English Christian court which found her guilty of heresy. Although she was found innocent by a Catholic investigation some years later, it was not until 1909, when the work of 19th-century historians had popularized her cause, that she was eventually beatified, a necessary step on the path to canonization. Her official recognition as a saint may have been prompted in part by a report that Joan of Arc appeared in the night sky to French troops fighting in the First World War, spurring them on to victory. The ceremony to mark her canonization was held at St. Peter's in Rome and attended by many thousands.

Right: A statue of Joan of Arc in battle armor at the cathedral at Reims, France.

Above: The beatification of Joan of Arc at St. Peter's, in Rome.

November
Mexican Revolution Ends
The Mexican Revolution, which had begun in November 1910 with the overthrow of dictator Porfirio Díaz, ends in 1920, following the creation of a Mexican Constitution in 1917.

November
Russian Civil War Ends
The Russian Civil War between the Bolsheviks (Reds) and opposing factions (Whites) ends in Bolshevik victory for Lenin.

December
Mahatma Ghandi Initiates Boycott
Mahatma Ghandi organizes a boycott of British cotton as part of his policy of non-cooperation against British rule in India.

HOLLYWOOD STAR CLEARED OF ALL CHARGES

After two previous trials had failed to collect enough evidence to convict him, at a third trial in 1921 Hollywood actor Roscoe 'Fatty' Arbuckle was finally acquitted of the rape and manslaughter of Virginia Rappe. Although the jury went as far as to issue a statement of apology for Arbuckle's appalling mistreatment, the damage had been done. A comic actor who was something of a mentor to two other comic legends, Charlie Chaplain and Buster Keaton, Arbuckle was greatly respected in the business. He was a natural for slapstick comedy and his short films popularized the classic pie-in-the-face gag. However, Arbuckle's acting career has been entirely overshadowed by the trial, which tarnished him for life, and permanently connected his name to rape rather than films. It had all begun at a Hollywood party some months earlier when a woman named Virginia Rappe had died of a ruptured bladder. Her friend Maude Delpont later told police that Arbuckle had raped Virginia Rappe, though it was subsequently discovered that she frequently set Hollywood stars up with girls who would later cry rape in order to extort money from them. The newspapers did much to enhance the speculation and hype surrounding the trial. It was typical of the lack of evidence against Arbuckle that it was variously claimed that he crushed her with his weight while raping her and that he tore her bladder with a Coke bottle. After the trial, despite his acquittal, Arbuckle was banned from appearing on screen.

"FATTY" ARBUCKLE ON HIS TRIAL: FIRST PICTURES

Left: Comic legend Charlie Chaplin, who was mentored by Fatty Arbuckle.

January 21
Play Introduces Robots
Karel Capek's play *Rossum's Universal Robots* opens in Prague, coining the word 'robot' from the Czech for 'forced labor' and popularizing the concept of artificial life.

March 6
Portuguese Communist Party Founded
The Portuguese Communist Party is founded in Lisbon.

March
Soviet Union Allows Open Markets
Lenin introduces the New Economic Policy, allowing the operation of the open market, thus reviving the Soviet economy.

March
Games for Women
The first Women's Olympic Games are held in Monte Carlo to rival the male-only Olympic Games.

1921

MARIE STOPES OPENS FIRST BIRTH CONTROL CLINIC

The first birth control clinic, known as the Mothers' Clinic, was opened by Dr. Marie Stopes in London, England, in March 1921, to provide a free contraceptive service to married women. Originally an academic and the first ever female lecturer at Manchester University, Stopes caused a stir with the publication of her book *Married Love,* which openly addressed the subject of sexual enjoyment. Opening a birth control clinic only fueled the fires of disapproval, and Stopes faced fierce opposition from organizations such as the Catholic Church. But she continued to voice her views forcefully and campaign for methods of birth control to be more freely available to women. By bringing contraception into the public domain, Stopes paved the way for more open attitudes towards sex generally, which had the effect of improving sexual health and removing the taboo from the idea of sexual pleasure. A lesser-known aspect of Stopes' work was her support for the concept of eugenics, that is, the creation of a superior human breed via artificial selection. Her proposals included the forced sterilization of those she considered unfit to be parents, specifically those in the lower classes that produced large numbers of children who, she thought, then became a burden to society as a whole. She was in Berlin during the early days of Hitler's Third Reich and supported his proposals for breeding out defects in the human race. However, it is for her ground-breaking work in the female sexual revolution that she is best remembered, and the organization Marie Stopes International continues to provide its services across 38 countries today.

Right: Dr. Marie Stopes, a British campaigner for women's rights and birth control.

May 14–17
Violent Riots
Anti-European riots occur in Cairo and Alexandria in Egypt.

May 24
Ulster Elections
Elections are held for the first time for the new Northern Ireland Parliament, with the Ulster Unionist Party winning a majority.

May
New 'Coco' Perfume
Ernest Beaux creates Chanel No. 5 perfume for the Parisian fashion designer Gabrielle 'Coco' Chanel.

July 14
Guilty of Murder
Nicola Sacco and Bartolomeo Vanzetti, Italian immigrants who are part of the anarchist movement in the U.S., are found guilty of murder on patchy evidence and executed.

July 18
New Vaccine
The first B.C.G. vaccination against tuberculosis is given in France.

IRISH FREE STATE ESTABLISHED

The Anglo-Irish Treaty marked the end of the Irish War of Independence, and set up the Irish Free State as an independent nation incorporating 26 of the 32 counties of Ireland. Northern Ireland, which had been established as a separate entity in 1920, was given the choice to opt out of the Irish Free State, which it did. Though self-governing, the Irish Free State remained within the dominion of the British Empire, and consequently the British monarch remained head of state. The Irish would be 'free' but bound under an oath of loyalty to the British Crown. The treaty followed a truce on July 11, agreed between the leader of the Irish Dáil (parliament), Eamon de Valera, and British Prime Minster David Lloyd George. Michael Collins, the infamous freedom-fighter and ruthless leader of the Nationalists' underground army, had been forced out of hiding by de Valera to attend the negotiations in London. De Valera persuaded Collins to go in his place, ostensibly because it was not appropriate for de Valera himself, as head of state, to attend. It may also have been a strategy to avoid signing a treaty that de Valera knew would not grant complete independence and therefore would not please the Irish Nationalists. Although the treaty marked the end of a long road and seemed to suggest that an agreement had finally been reached between the Irish and the British, the Irish Nationalists were deeply divided over the terms of the treaty and their disagreement led to a long-lasting and bitter civil war.

Right: Laganside in Belfast, Northern Ireland, whose six counties opted out of the Irish Free State.

1922

IRISH REBELS CAPTURED IN DUBLIN

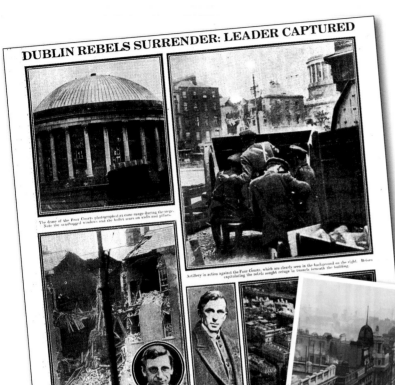

DUBLIN REBELS SURRENDER: LEADER CAPTURED

Right: O'Connell Street in Dublin, which was the scene of fierce fighting between government and rebel troops in June and July 1922.

The split within the Irish Nationalist movement over the terms of the Anglo-Irish Treaty, which had established the Irish Free State, erupted on June 28, 1922 into full-blown civil war. The key Irish negotiators had known that the partial autonomy that they had eventually wrenched from the British was never going to please the hardliners. Indeed, after signing the treaty, Michael Collins had announced, 'I have signed my own death warrant.' But even he did not realize how quickly things would fall apart. A rebel group opposed to the treaty, led by Rory O'Connor, took occupation of the Four Courts, an important building in Dublin that housed the National Archives, and made it their military headquarters. Michael Collins, in his new role as Commander-in-Chief of the Irish Army, ordered an attack on the Four Courts after a two-day siege. The rebels inside surrendered under fire, but before emerging they retaliated by letting off explosions within the building. In the process, a substantial amount of the nation's archive material was entirely destroyed. Eye-witnesses described being rained with ashen strips of paper. The complete loss of such valuable historical material was, and still is, seen as a national disaster. Inevitably, each side blamed the other for the outrage. The rebels blamed the artillery fire of the army, while the Irish newspaper *An Toglach* called the explosions a vindictive act of revenge. Rory O'Connor was immediately arrested and executed later that year.

February 6
New Naval Treaty Signed
The Five-Power Naval Limitation Treaty between the U.S., Britain, Japan, France, and Italy is signed in Washington, aimed at naval disarmament.

February 27
Challenge Rebuffed
A challenge to the Nineteenth Amendment to the United States Constitution, allowing women the right to vote, is rebuffed by the Supreme Court of the United States.

February 28
Egypt is Independent
The United Kingdom grants Egypt independence, with Sultan Fuad I as its first king.

April 3
Stalin for General Secretary
Joseph Stalin is appointed General Secretary of the Communist Party by Lenin.

GANDHI ARRESTED BY BRITISH

On March 10, 1922, the Indian resistance leader Mohandas Gandhi was arrested in Ahmedabad charged with encouraging civil disobedience through his writings. Gandhi had always recognized the power of words to force change. He began as a journalist whose mission it was to point out the truth of a situation, even if that meant displeasing the authorities. After fighting for the rights of the Indian community in South Africa, he subsequently took up the cause of freedom in his homeland. Ghandi edited various journals, using the written word as a weapon in his policy of *satyagraha*, or peaceful resistance. As editor of *Young India* he persistently spoke out against the indignities forced on the population by their British rulers. These articles prompted his arrest on the charge of spreading disaffection, a charge to which Gandhi replied: 'I hold it to be a virtue to be disaffected towards a government which in its totality has done more harm to India than any previous system.' Gandhi spent two years in prison.

Left: Gandhi, seen here during a tour of the cotton mills in Lancaster in northwest England during September 1931.

TURKISH ARMY ENTERS SMYRNA

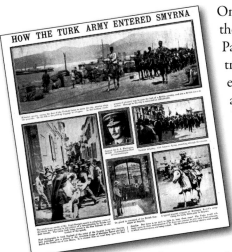

On September 9, 1922, the Turkish Army under Pasha Kemal regained control of the city of Smyrna, effectively bringing to an end the two-year war between the Turks and the Greeks. The thriving trading city set on the Aegean (now known as Izmir) was home to Greeks, Turks, and Armenians, all of whom had lived relatively harmoniously together with a common commercial aim. In the aftermath of the First World War, the problematic peace process opened old wounds and disputes over territory resurfaced. Three days after the Turks had taken the city, it was set alight. The fire entirely destroyed Smyrna and the majority of its inhabitants were killed. It has remained a matter of dispute who started the fire. Much of the killing and looting that followed the Turkish takeover was blamed on Turkish 'irregulars', or guerrillas, who had been hiding out in the hills for many months. Whoever was responsible, the massacre reached an appalling scale and it is thought that some 100,000 people were killed. Only those able to reach the American ships in the harbor were saved.

Above: The ancient agora, or marketplace, at Smyrna in western Turkey.

April 7
Mid-Air Collision
The first mid-air collision between two planes, one flying from London to Paris, the other from Paris to London, kills six people.

May 12
Meteorite Hits America
A 20-ton meteorite lands near Blackstone, Virginia, U.S.A.

May 30
Memorial Unveiled
The Lincoln Memorial building in Washington D.C., designed to represent the Union, is unveiled in a special dedication ceremony.

June 28
Civil War Breaks Out
The Irish Civil War, involving a dispute over the Anglo-Irish Treaty, begins.

1922

TUTANKHAMUN'S TOMB DISCOVERED

After searching for several years, on November 5, 1922, British archaeologist Howard Carter discovered the tomb of Pharaoh Tutankhamun in Egypt's Valley of the Kings. King Tutankhamun had only ruled for a short time as a boy king and had died at the age of 18. Given that most of the tombs in the area had already been discovered and looted, it was generally assumed that his had met a similar fate. But on November 26, Carter broke through to the inner section that had been closed by the tomb-builders 3,000 years earlier – their footprints were still visible in the dust on the ground. There he discovered, besides thousands of precious artefacts, the intact and mummified body of the boy king lying in his solid-gold coffin. The full excavation of the four-roomed tomb took several years, and in the process Carter unearthed countless objects, including a fleet of miniature ships intended to aid the king on his journey to the next world.

Above: The Tutankhamun gold mask at the British Museum in London.

MUSSOLINI BECOMES PRIME MINISTER OF ITALY

Italy felt that it had been given a raw deal at the Paris Peace Conference that followed the First World War. The general complaint was that the other Allied Powers were preventing Italy from becoming a great power by denying it the territorial advantages allowed to others. Post-war Italy was crippled by poverty and unemployment, which led to social unrest and a rise in organized crime. Benito Mussolini exploited this volatile situation and harnessed discontent by forming a paramilitary group called the Blackshirts. The Italian government, fearing a Communist revolution, welcomed Mussolini's strong-arm tactics, despite their profoundly undemocratic nature, and so the leader of the Fascist Party joined mainstream politics. The democratic government was viewed as weak and ineffective, and many of the Fascist party's proposals, which included a minimum wage, an eight-hour working day, and votes for women, were popular. The party had aligned itself with national pride, and appeared to represent both a strong economy and a return to law and order for those who feared revolution. In March 1922, Mussolini organized a march on Rome and forced King Victor Emmanuel III to make him Prime Minister. At first, under Mussolini's rule, Italy experienced economic revival while extensive public works provided much needed employment.

Above: Benito Mussolini taking his morning ride at the Villa Torlonia near Rome with his youngest son.

August 22
Michael Collins Assassinated
Michael Collins, Irish Republican leader, is assassinated in an exchange of fire when his car is ambushed by anti-treaty I.R.A. members.

October 25
End of Russian Civil War
The Bolshevik Red Army occupies Vladivostok, ending the Russian Civil War.

December 18
Helicopter Makes First Flight
The first helicopter, called the H-1, designed by Dr. George de Bothezat and Ivan Jerome, makes its first public flight, rising to an altitude of 6 ft (1.8 m) and remaining in the air for 1 minute 42 seconds.

First Snowmobile
Joseph Bombardier, a Canadian mechanic, designs and builds the first snowmobile in Quebec, which comes on the market in 1937.

HYPER-INFLATION HITS GERMANY

In 1923, the German economy went into hyper-inflation, and the exchange rate reached a point where U.S.$1 was worth 1 trillion marks (before the war it had been U.S.$1 to 5 marks) and a wheelbarrow full of money could not buy a loaf of bread. The reasons for this economic catastrophe were many, but chief among them were the facts that Germany had abandoned the gold-backing for its currency in 1914, and that it had subsequently financed the war with borrowed money. After the war there were monumental reparation payments to be made and a decision was taken to print more money in order to meet them. On the whole, business and industry welcomed the lowering value of the mark because it made German goods cheaper and therefore easier to export. However, the devaluation process soon got out of control. High-street prices multiplied by the hour; pensions and insurance policies, saved over twenty years, when cashed in could not even buy a newspaper. In order to halt this disastrous situation, a new currency was introduced at the end of 1923 called the rentenmark, which equaled 1 billion old marks.

Above: A 50-million mark bank note issued by the Weimar Republic.

FRENCH TROOPS ENTER GERMAN TERRITORY

In the aftermath of the First World War, the Germans were frequently unable to make their reparation payments. For the French these payments provided an opportunity to improve their economic position in Europe, so when payments were not forthcoming, they targeted the Ruhr, Germany's high-production industrial region. This was also territory right on the French border, and France had long held ambitions to annex it. On January 11, 1923, the French Prime Minister ordered troops into the Ruhr. The official justification was that the Germans were defaulting on their reparations, some of which took the form of goods, and since the Ruhr was the major coal-, iron-, and steel-producing region, the French were merely extracting goods owed to them. The occupation was not in direct breach of the Treaty of Versailles, since France was attempting to secure what it was owed by essentially peaceful means. But the Germans in the Ruhr region carried out a policy of passive resistance and industrial workers refused to cooperate. When the French finally left in 1925, it was partly in recognition that they could not extract their dues without the help of German labor.

February 10	March 2	July 20
Wilhelm Conrad Röntgen Dies	**New 'Time' Magazine**	**General Assassinated**
Wilhelm Conrad Röntgen, the Nobel Prize winner and discoverer of the X-ray, dies.	*Time* magazine hits newsstands in the U.S. for the first time.	Mexican revolutionary general Pancho Villa is assassinated.

33

1923

ITALY INVADES GREEK ISLAND OF CORFU

CORFU SEIZED BY ITALIANS

The Greek forts and harbour of Corfu, the chief of the Ionian Islands in the Adriatic, which was last night reported to have been seized by the Italians within a few hours of the rejection by the Italian Government of the Athens reply to their ultimatum.

WED IN LONDON

Sir David Dalrymple, of New Hailes, Midlothian, and his bride, Mrs. Dorothy Lewis, widow of Major H. M. Lewis, after their wedding, quietly, at the Marylebone register office yesterday. Three friends were present at the ceremony.

BROTHERS AS FINALISTS

C. G. Fletcher, left, and G. S. Fletcher, two brothers, singles finalists in the Surrey junior lawn tennis championship meeting at Surbiton yesterday. They play together in doubles final.

EARL OF KINNOULL FINED

The Earl of Kinnoull

MATHIESON NEW BOYS' GOLF CHAMPION

ITALIANS STILL HOLD CORFU AS A GUARANTEE

On August 27, 1923, four Italian officials including General Enrico Tellini were assassinated while driving through Greece as part of an international commission to establish the border between Greece and Albania. The assassin was never discovered. The Italian government of Benito Mussolini acted swiftly, demanding a hefty payment and the immediate execution of the assassin. Since the Greek government could not identify the killer, they ignored both demands. Mussolini's army stormed the island of Corfu in retaliation. It was generally thought that Mussolini was exploiting the chance assassination to seize a strategically placed island. When the two powers submitted their dispute to the arbitration committee at the Conference of Ambassadors, the arbitrators backed the Italians against the Greeks, who were forced to pay the reparation demanded. One month after invading the island, the Italians left.

Above: The Greek island of Corfu lies in the Ionian Sea, 2 miles (3 km) off the coast of Albania.

July
Revolutionary Design
Scottish inventor John Logie Baird files a patent for his television design.

October 13
Turkey Has New Capital
Angora (later Ankara) is named as the new capital of Turkey, replacing Istanbul.

October 16
Cartoon Studio Founded
Roy and Walt Disney found the Disney Brothers' Cartoon Studio, which later becomes the Walt Disney Company.

October 29
Turkey a Republic
Turkey becomes a republic under Mustafa Kemal Ataturk following the dissolution of the Ottoman Empire.

ETNA ERUPTS, LEAVING 60,000 HOMELESS

EARTHQUAKE SHAKES JAPAN

In June 1923, Mount Etna, an active volcano on the Mediterranean island of Sicily, began a prolonged eruption. After a few days of slow and steady rumbling, there was a series of violent explosions, which sent shock-waves throughout the surrounding region, and the area was flooded in molten lava. Ash showered down on the countryside and five streams of white-hot lava poured down the side of the mountain, destroying houses and forests in its wake. Numerous villages were thought to be at risk and around 50,000 local inhabitants were evacuated to the city of Catania on the east coast, where the Red Cross provided aid. Though no lives were lost, the damage to property was estimated to be about 100,000,000 lira (in the area of U.S.$5 million).

Just before noon on the morning of September 1, 1923, a massive earthquake shook the Kanto plain on the Japanese island of Honshu. The quake, which registered 7.9 to 8.4 on the Richter scale, lasted for more than 5 minutes and devastated Tokyo, Yokohama, and some surrounding areas, claiming around 100,000 lives. Most of the fatalities were caused by fire. The earthquake struck at the time when people were lighting fires to cook lunch, and this misfortune of timing was worsened by winds from a nearby typhoon, which caused the fire to spread rapidly. To make matters worse, the earthquake damaged the water mains, so it took two days to put the fires out. But the trouble did not end there. A state of panic ensued when rumors were put about exaggerating the extent of the disaster. It was widely believed that Tokyo had been entirely wiped out and the government killed. There were further casualties when wild rumors were used as an excuse for vigilante attacks on Koreans, who were said to be using the disaster to cause further destruction.

Above: Mount Etna continues to erupt regularly. It is one of Europe's most active volcanoes.

November 8
Hitler's Failed Coup
In Munich, Adolf Hitler leads the Nazis in an unsuccessful attempt to overthrow the German government. Police and troops crush the attemped coup the next day.

November 20
New Invention for Traffic
Garrett A. Morgan, the son of former slaves from Kentucky, patents his new traffic signal, which is the first to be manufactured in the U.S.

Hollywoodland is Born
The 'Hollywoodland' sign is erected in the Hollywood hills by property developer and *LA Times* publisher Harry Chandler to advertize his new development.

1924

LENIN DIES

MOSCOW MOURNS LENIN

Right to left, Kalinin (in spectacles), Tomsky and Kameneff, bearing Lenin's coffin.

Thousands of people accompany the coffin past the famous palace of the Kremlin, within which

Lenin's wife, Krupskaia (marked x), walking behind the coffin with the sisters of

These pictures are the first received in London of the ceremonies connected with the f Bolshevist leader. They show scenes from the great procession from the station of F miles through the snow into the centre of Moscow. One hundred thousand people f

FILM STARS WED

Lenin's death in 1924 after a series of major strokes came while he was still at the height of his power and an active leader. He had time during his illness, however, to consider his replacement and warned his party against electing Stalin as their leader, suggesting that he was not a man who knew how to handle absolute power responsibly, and citing his intolerance, lack of consideration, and treachery as unsuitable traits. Lenin was more in favor of Trotsky as his successor. But he judged neither of them truly fit to take his place, and would have preferred a collective government.

However, Stalin made sure that he handled the aftermath of Lenin's death in such a way that he was assumed to be the natural successor. Lenin was idolized in death as he had been in life. His corpse was embalmed and put on display, and slices of his brain were studied at a specially set up Brain Institute with the aim of discovering the secret to his genius as leader.

'Lenin was idolized in death as he had been in life.'

Left: Children line Red Square in Moscow to mark the anniversary of Lenin's birth in April, 1960.

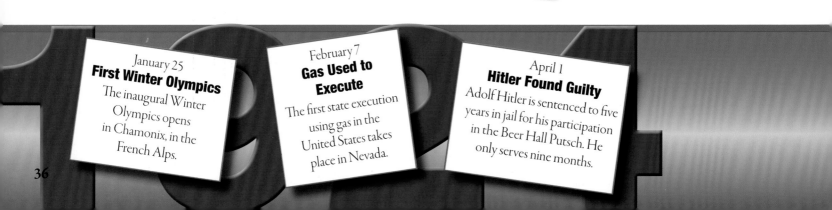

January 25
First Winter Olympics
The inaugural Winter Olympics opens in Chamonix, in the French Alps.

February 7
Gas Used to Execute
The first state execution using gas in the United States takes place in Nevada.

April 1
Hitler Found Guilty
Adolf Hitler is sentenced to five years in jail for his participation in the Beer Hall Putsch. He only serves nine months.

YOUTHS CHARGED WITH MURDER FOR SPORT

The 1924 trial of Nathan Leopold and Richard Loeb was the first of its kind to be dubbed 'the trial of the century'. The privileged teenagers, both students of the University of Chicago, had pleaded guilty to the kidnapping and murder of a 14-year-old boy, Bobby Franks, who lived in the same wealthy Jewish neighborhood. There was no trial-by-jury, since they had admitted guilt, so the trial involved renowned defense attorney Clarence Darrow pleading against the death penalty. After a lengthy speech on Darrow's part, which has gone down in legal history for its emotive power, the pair were sentenced to life imprisonment for murder. Clarence Darrow was an ardent campaigner against the death penalty and he argued in this case that the boys (who were 18 and 19) could not help being born intellectually gifted, nor that they had been taught the philosophy of Nietzsche at university – Loeb and Leopold had killed the boy simply to see if they could. They were obsessed with the Nietzschean idea that there was no such thing as moral good and evil, and were convinced that they themselves were 'supermen', above worldly responsibility for their actions. Leopold, in his turn, was obsessed by Loeb, and claimed that if he did have a motive, it was to please him. Loeb had his throat slit in jail by a fellow inmate who claimed that he had acted in self-defense to ward off a sexual assault. Leopold was released after 34 years and moved to Puerto Rico.

YOUTHS CHARGED WITH MURDER "FOR SPORT"

The two accused, Nathan Leopold, jun. (second from left), and Richard Loeb, between Loeb's uncle (left) and Leopold's father, in court.

Richard Loeb (extreme right) leading the search for the little victim's belt.

Nathan Leopold, jun., one of the accused students.

Mr. Jacob Franks, the multi-millionaire and father of the murdered boy, with his son Jacob.

found in a swamp, and later Nathan Leopold, jun., and Richard Loeb, two University students, were arrested. It is alleged that in their search for a victim to be murdered "for the experience" they drove round a school and through binoculars watched boys playing games. They selected Franks when he was umpiring a baseball match.

Left: Clarence Darrow, whose oratory pursuaded the court to spare the youths' lives.

April 6
First Round-the-World Flight
Four planes from the Douglas Aircraft Company leave Seattle, Washington, on the first round-the-world flight, which takes 175 days.

May 4
France Opens Summer Olympic Games
The opening ceremony of the Summer Olympic Games is held in Paris.

June 5
Message Sent Across Ocean
Ernst Alexanderson sends the first facsimile message across the Atlantic Ocean (to his father in Sweden).

1924

BRAZILIAN ARMY OFFICERS REVOLT

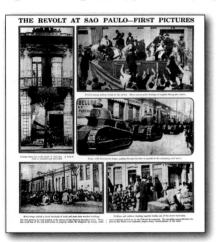

A revolt erupted in São Paulo in July 1924 in the form of a struggle for control of the army. The revolt was led by a group of young officers known as the *tenentes* (lieutenants), and was directed not only against central government but against the corruption within the ranks. The younger generation of officers believed that the senior ranks were too closely allied to the old order of the corrupt landed elite, which they believed was preventing the country from modernizing its economy. Among the *tenentes*' demands for reform were fairer election laws, including the introduction of a secret ballot, and measures to remedy the social ills suffered by the vast agrarian peasant population. The 1924 revolt ended in its leaders going into hiding, but it sparked further, more successful revolts. Six years later, the old order was overthrown in a military coup, and Brazil's new leader, Getúlio Vargas, restored the *tenentes* to the army, promoting many of them to the senior ranks.

Above: São Paulo, the largest city in Brazil, where the revolt began.

BRITAIN AND EGYPT AT LOGGERHEADS

On November 29, 1924, General Sir Oliver Lee Stack, the British Commander-General of the Egyptian Army, was assassinated by a criminal gang in Cairo. This act put an end to Egypt's first democratically elected government, the so-called 'People's Government' led by nationalist leader Saad Zaghlul, when it was less than a year old. Following the assassination, the British High-Commissioner Lord Allenby issued an ultimatum which included demands for an apology, bringing the criminals to justice, a hefty reparation payment, and the withdrawal of Egyptian troops from British-controlled Sudan. Though Zaghlul expressed 'profoundest distress at this atrocious crime', the British maintained that he had actively encouraged violence against them. When Zaghlul rejected the ultimatum on the grounds that the Egyptian government could accept no responsibility for the actions of the criminals, but would pay the reparation as a gesture of its sorrow, the British took action and instructed the Sudanese to expel all Egyptian troops. The end of the nationalist government made room for the royal family to seize back power, putting an end to the hard-won democratization process. 'This is the most horrendous calamity that has befallen us,' said Saad Zaghlul, 'and the most detrimental to the honor and reputation of the country.'

June 6
Huge Mountain to Climb

George Mallory, a British schoolteacher, and Andrew Irvine, a student at Cambridge University, attempt to reach the top of Mount Everest. Mallory's body was found on May 1, 1999, but Irvine's body has never been found.

July
Food to be Frozen

American inventor Clarence Birdseye founds his frozen-food company after discovering a method of flash-freezing food.

July
Ford Reaches 10 Million

The 10 millionth Ford car is built and goes on a victory tour from New York to San Francisco.

EVOLUTION ON TRIAL

In March 1925, the U.S. state of Tennessee passed a law making it a crime to teach Darwin's theory of evolution in public schools. It was known as the Butler Act and it had the vigorous support of the religious right for whom the Bible story of mankind's creation was the only possible truth. No sooner had the Butler Act been passed than the newly formed American Civil Liberties Union pounced on the chance to test whether it would stand up in court. In order to test the new act, they needed a teacher who would be willing to act as a defendant, who would agree to teach the theory of evolution to school children. It so happened that a young teacher had just arrived in the small town of Dayton, Tennessee. He was called John Thomas Scope, and it was his fate to be playing tennis alongside the town drugstore when two members of the American Civil Liberties Union approached him. Scope agreed to take part in their experiment and so became a guinea pig in what was to be known as the 'monkey trial'. It was a big-name trial – Scope was defended by Clarence Darrow, the hot-shot criminal lawyer of the day – and the country's media went to town. It was also the first live radio broadcast of a trial in American history and the American people were hooked. The paparazzi had a field day, feeding the national hunger for 'live' images of real trials. After evidence from two teenagers in Scope's class – one of whose comments, 'I lapped it up: all about monkeys and things,' gave the trial its name – Scopes was found guilty and fined. After his conviction, he declared: 'Your Honor, I feel that I have been convicted of violating an unjust statute. I will continue in the future, as I have in the past, to oppose this law in any way I can.' But in all likelihood, he was only playing his part well. In reality, the trial was a heated debate between the two sides – the evolutionists and creationists – with a hapless Scopes at the center of the stage.

> **'In order to test the new act, they needed a teacher who would be willing to act as a defendant, who would agree to teach the theory of evolution to school children.'**

FIRST COURT PICTURES OF THE "MONKEY TRIAL"

Left: Charles Darwin, whose theory of evolution holds that humans and other primates evolved from a common ancestor.

January 3
Benito in Control
Benito Mussolini announces he is taking dictatorial powers over Italy.

January 27–February 1
Dogs Fetch Antitoxin
In what becomes known as the 'Great Race of Mercy', dog sleds carry the diphtheria antitoxin across Alaska to combat an epidemic.

March 18
Deadliest Tornado Ever
The Tri-State Tornado, the deadliest on record to date, kills nearly 700 people across the states of Missouri, Illinois, and Indiana.

May 29
Final Letter from Explorer
Explorer Percy Harrison Fawcett writes his last letter home before disappearing during an expedition to find an ancient lost city in the jungles of Brazil.

1925

FRANCO-SPANISH ALLIANCE IN MOROCCO

SPAIN REJOICES THAT HER LONG WAR IS ENDING

The King of Spain and native troops from the victory of Kudia-Tahar.

Spaniards throng one of the principal streets of Madrid to cheer the homecoming of victorious troops.

ONLY A PUNCTURE!—JAPANESE LUCK

A Japanese air mechanic repairing a puncture to a tyre on the aeroplane in which Mr. Kawachi, the Japanese airman, crashed in landing near Farnborough, at the conclusion of his Tokio-London flight.

DECREE NISI AGAINST D.S.O. BARONET   **JOCKEY'S CENTURY**

SPANIARDS' GALLANT LANDING AGAINST RIFF FIRE

Spanish General Francisco Franco was placed in command of the Spanish troops when they joined forces with the French against Abd-el-Krim of Morocco. Abd-el-Krim had launched an offensive against the French in April of 1925, demanding full recognition of the Rif Republic in northern Morocco. During one bout of fighting on Monte Malmusi in Ajdir, the Spanish lost 700 men, but ultimately the Franco-Spanish alliance was victorious. The Riffians, though skilled in the art of killing, were not practiced in securing ground or gaining strategic positions. After the French and Spanish had followed them for some months, Abd-el-Krim surrendered. His surrender came too late to secure any of the claims for autonomy that he had previously been offered.

Right: the remote and rugged Rif Mountains of northern Morocco provided a stronghold for Abd-el-Krim's Berber rebels.

June 6
New Motor Company
The Chrysler Motor Company is founded by Walter P. Chrysler.

June 13
Pictures and Sound United
Charles Francis Jenkins achieves the first synchronized transmission of pictures and sound, sending a 10-minute film of a miniature windmill in motion across 5 miles (8 km) from Anacostia to Washington, D.C.

June 17
Chemical Weapons Banned
The Geneva Protocol banning the use of chemical and biological weapons is signed by most of the great powers except for Japan and the U.S., who join later.

July 7
Afrikaans Officially Recognized
Afrikaans is recognized as one of the official languages of South Africa, along with English and Dutch.

ZEEBRUGGE HEROES COMMEMORATED

During the First World War, as Britain and Germany engaged in intense submarine warfare, the German Army occupied Belgium. The port of Zeebrugge, which stands on the point where the city of Bruges meets the North Sea, became of vital strategic importance to Germany and they set up a heavily armed fortress along the man-made harbor wall that ran along the coast. From this new vantage point, the Germans attacked the British fleet mercilessly. By 1917, around 400 British ships were being sunk every month. When Admiral Roger Keyes took over as Director of Planning at the Admiralty office in England, he took a new approach: instead of keeping the navy defensively lying in wait, they would launch an attack on Zeebrugge. The plan was complex but inspired: it involved several redundant warships, filled either with concrete or explosives and with minimal crew on board. Two hundred volunteer sailors were recruited to take part in the highly dangerous plan. The raid was launched on St. George's Day, April 23, 1918, and though there was heavy loss of life, the main objective of blocking the mouth of the Brugge canal was achieved. More importantly, British morale was given a much needed boost. The paralyzed navy had joined the army in its offensive and the submarine attacks that had threatened to starve Britain out of the war had been halted. Winston Churchill said of the operation: 'The raid on Zeebrugge may well rank as the finest feat of arms in the Great War.' Seven years later, on St. George's Day in 1925, a memorial of St. George and the Dragon was unveiled on Zeebrugge harbor and a service held for all those who had died there.

HEROES' NEW RAID ON THE MOLE—1918-25
Special "Daily Mirror" Photographs Brought to London by Air

Left: Modern Zeebrugge. The Allies again blocked the canal to deter U-boats in 1940. The sunken ships were not removed until 1954.

July 18
Hitler Publishes Mein Kampf
Adolf Hitler publishes his personal manifesto, *Mein Kampf.*

November 11
Cosmic Rays Detected
U.S. physicist Robert Milliken announces the discovery of rays hitting Earth from space.

November
Roads to be Painted
The painting of white lines on the road is approved by the Ministry of Transport in the U.K. in an attempt to improve road safety.

December 1
Locarno Treaty Signed
The Locarno Treaty is signed in London, England, establishing the post-war territorial settlement.

December 26
Sphinx is Uncovered
The Great Sphinx of Giza in Egypt is revealed after extensive excavation work.

1926

GENERAL STRIKE IN THE U.K.

NO COAL SETTLEMENT ARRIVED AT LAST NIGHT

Mr. Arthur Henderson, Miss Bondfield (centre) and Miss Quaile at Eccleston-square. The Misses Bondfield and Quaile are on the T.U.C. General Council.

Left to right, Mr. Thomas, Mr. MacDonald and Mr. Henderson after a T.U.C. conference.

Lord Balfour (left) and Mr. W. C. Bridgeman leaving a Cabinet meeting.

The Sunday evening crowd which assembled outside 10, Downing-street, waiting for the latest news of the negotiations.

Following a day of inconclusive meetings, negotiations continued at 10, Downing-street until the small hours of this morning with the object of finding a solution of the coal deadlock and thus avoiding the general strike called for midnight to-night. First the Trades Union Congress Negotiating Committee, who are dealing with the crisis on behalf of the miners, and then the full General Council of the Congress were summoned to Downing-street. At 11.45 members of the Miners' Executive arrived. Later the Cabinet declared that constitutional rights had been challenged, and no negotiations proceeded until the trade unions withdrew the instructions for a general strike.

The coal industry in Britain went into decline at the end of the First World War. Various factors, including the exhaustion of reserves during the war, a fall in exports, and a fall in prices, contributed to the decline. The mine owners responded to these conditions by cutting jobs and wages. The Conservative government under Stanley Baldwin offered a subsidy to the mines, but it was only delaying the inevitable industrial dispute. The Trade Union Congress (T.U.C.) rejected government proposals for down-scaling the industry and called a general strike to begin on May 3, 1926. Around 1.75 million workers from the railway, transport, printers, docks, iron- and steel-work industries went on strike. The government went to great lengths to portray the strikers as anarchists and revolutionaries trying to bring the country to its knees, and the strike divided the nation's sympathies. There was individual sympathy for the strikers, however, most notably in the person of King George V of England, who said 'try living on their wages before judging them'. The strike lasted nine days, during which time the government deployed emergency measures to keep the country running, sending brigades of volunteers to perform essential services such as driving buses and trams. By this time, the individual unions had turned against the Trade Union Congress and took them to court. The judge, Justice Astbury, ruled the strike illegal and the T.U.C. was forced to back down, but ill-feeling remained and the coal industry in Britain was deeply troubled for some time to come.

Left: Crowds gather on the streets of London during the general strike of May 1926.

January 26
Television Demonstration
Scottish inventor John Logie Baird demonstrates a television system.

February 7
Look to History
Negro History Week, originated by Carter G. Woodson, is celebrated for the first time in the U.S. It later becomes Black History Month.

February 11
Church Property Nationalized
The Mexican government nationalizes all Church property in an attempt to suppress the Church, prompting the Cristero War, three years of religious rebellion.

March 16
Rocket Lands Safely
Robert Goddard, American space pioneer, successfully launches the first liquid-fueled rocket in Massachusetts.

April 25
Iran Crowns New Shah
Reza Khan is crowned the new Shah of Iran, founding the Pahlavi Dynasty.

PRINCESS ELIZABETH BORN

On April 21, 1926, a new member of the British royal family was born. Princess Elizabeth was the daughter of Prince Albert, Duke of York, and Elizabeth, Duchess of York. She was born in London and baptized by the Archbishop of York in a private chapel in Buckingham Palace. The first grandchild of King George V, to whom she was particularly close, Elizabeth would become Queen of the United Kingdom 27 years later in 1952, following the abdication of her uncle, King Edward VIII, and subsequent death of her father, King George VI.

BRITISH HERO OF CHINA FIGHT

Lieut.-Commander L. S. Acheson, D.S.C., commander of H.M.S. Cockchafer, in hospital at Hankow, suffering from a wound received in river fighting at Wanhsien, in the interior of China For two hours after he had been shot through the side he lay on the deck and directed the operations. Three officers and four men of another naval vessel were killed.—(Exclusive.)

THE ROYAL BABY

Princess Elizabeth, the baby daughter of the Duke and Duchess of York, out for an airing in London, where she is remaining while her parents are in Scotland.

GERMAN INDUSTRIALISTS' VISIT TO ENGLAND FOR MEETING WITH BRITISH BUSINESS CHIEFS

Carl von Weinberg, Dr. Sorge, Dr. Elster, Dr. Ephraim and Dr. Kastl, leaving the German Em...

...trialists have arrived in England to meet British ...at the German Embassy yesterday the visitors ...here they are to be the guests for the week-end of

Colonel Wilfrid Ashley, Minister of Tr... their host. Herr von Weinberg state... official one, but it was hoped that it w...

Above: Street parties, such as this one in Deptford, London, were held throughout the U.K. to celebrate the Queen's silver jubilee in 1977.

DAUGHTER BORN TO THE DUCHESS OF YORK

April 30
Pioneering Woman Pilot Dies
Bessie Coleman, the first African-American woman to get her pilot's license, is killed after falling 2,000 ft (600 m) from an airplane.

May
Eat Your Liver
Drs. George R. Minot, William P. Murphy, and George H. Whipple discover that eating liver is a cure for pernicious anemia. They go on to win the 1934 Nobel Prize in Medicine and Physiology.

May 11
Mercedes-Benz Car Company Founded
German company Mercedes-Benz is formed by merging companies owned by Gottlieb Daimler and Karl Benz.

May 12
Flight Over North Pole
Roald Amundsen is part of a team that successfully flies over the North Pole.

1926

MUSSOLINI SHOT BY IRISHWOMAN

On April 7, 1926, there was an assassination attempt on Italian dictator 'Il Duce' Benito Mussolini, as he was leaving a gathering of doctors whom he had been addressing. The bullet merely grazed his nose, and after having the wound bandaged, he continued with his official visit. The shot was fired by Violet Gibson, an Irish woman in her fifties, who was believed to be mentally unstable. She gave no reason for her actions and at the request of the Duce was deported without charge to Great Britain, where she spent the rest of her life in a mental institution. It was widely assumed that the idea had been put into her head by an enemy of the Fascist leader.

GERTRUDE EDERLE FIRST WOMAN TO SWIM THE ENGLISH CHANNEL

The daughter of a German immigrant butcher in Manhattan, Gertrude – known as 'Trudy' – joined the Women's Swimming Association when she was 15, reportedly because her father said he would let her bob her hair if she did. After winning a gold medal at the 1924 Olympics, she went on to undertake long-distance open-water swims. At the time, the 21-mile-wide (34-km) stretch of water separating England and France, the English Channel, had only been crossed by five men and the record time was 16 hours 39 minutes. On August 6, 1926, Ederle, aged 20, swam from Cap Gris-Nez in France to Kingsdown in England. The feat took her 14 hours and 33 minutes and she held the record for 24 years until Florence Chadwick shaved an hour off her time in 1950. In an interview after the event, Gertrude described how her boat full of relatives and supporters had sung constantly to keep her spirits up during the swim, but had actually needed cheering up themselves during some of the more stormy weather.

Above: Gertrude Ederle, who became the first woman to swim the English Channel in August 1926.

July 16
First Color Underwater Photos
A *National Geographic* photographer takes the first natural-color underwater photos – of a hogfish in the Gulf of Mexico.

September 1
Lebanon Becomes Republic
Charles Debbas is elected the first president of the new Republic of Lebanon.

September 8
Germany Allowed In
Germany is admitted to the League of Nations, which was formed after the First World War.

September 25
New Eight-Hour Day
Henry Ford announces that all of his staff will work an eight-hour day (instead of the usual ten) and a five-day week (instead of the usual six).

FIRST NON-STOP SOLO FLIGHT ACROSS ATLANTIC

In 1927, Charles Lindbergh, a Minnesota mail pilot, became the first person to fly a plane non-stop from New York to Paris. As soon as Lindbergh heard about a competition to cross the Atlantic with a prize of $25,000, he secured sponsorship and set about having a plane built to his own specifications. The result was the *Spirit of St. Louis*. Lindbergh set out from Long Island on the morning of May 20, 1927, carrying on board four sandwiches and two canteens of water.

'Lindbergh set out from Long Island on the morning of May 20, 1927, carrying on board four sandwiches and two canteens of water.'

Around 33 hours later, on the evening of May 21, he touched down in Paris to be met by thousands upon thousands of well-wishers. Lindbergh's achievement sparked an overnight enthusiasm for aviation and the man himself became a hero. There was something in his spirit of adventure and endeavor that captured the hearts of the American people. On his return home, he was treated to parade after parade, and lauded in high places wherever he went. Charles Lindbergh then embarked on tours all over America, and devoted the rest of his life to advancing aviation – a mission which he fulfilled ably. He received a number of accolades in the course of his career, culminating in the Congressional Medal of Honor, the highest honor the U.S.A. awards its people.

Above: Today, thousands of people cross the Atlantic daily on passenger air liners.

September 25
Slavery Abolished
A treaty signed at the League of Nations Slavery Convention abolishes all types of slavery.

January 7
First Transatlantic Phone Call Made
The first transatlantic telephone call is made using radio, from New York to London.

April 12
New Name
The Royal and Parliamentary Titles Act renames the 'United Kingdom of Great Britain and Ireland' the 'United Kingdom of Great Britain and Northern Ireland', acknowledging that the Irish Free State is no longer part of the Kingdom.

1927

GAS EXPLOSION IN PITTSBURGH, U.S.A.

RUIN WROUGHT BY THE PITTSBURG GAS EXPLOSION

A workman, injured by the explosion, being assisted through ruins flooded by burst water mains.

A battered car beside the twisted remains of the gasometer, one of the largest in the world.

The scene of devastation as v

Pictures received in London yesterday of the fearful and widespread destruction caused at Pittsburg, U.S.A., by the explosion of a huge gasometer, containing 5,000,000ft. of natural gas. More than twenty people were killed outright, and hundreds were injured.

On November 14, 1927, three huge gas storage tanks belonging to Equitable Gas exploded in Pittsburgh, Pennsylvania, wrecking much of the city and killing 28 people. In what felt to residents of the city like a great earthquake, the tanks, each with a capacity of around 5 million cubic ft (150,000 m³), exploded when engineers called to the site to investigate a leak did so using a naked flame. A ball of fire shot high up into the air and showered the area for miles around with glass and steel. Damage to property was estimated to be in the region of $5 million and camps had to be set up to house the homeless all around the city.

'A ball of fire shot high up into the air and showered the area for miles around with glass and steel.'

Left: Even today, explosions of gas appliances and heating systems can cause massive amounts of damage to homes and offices.

May 20
Saudi Arabia is Independant
Saudi Arabia becomes independent of the United Kingdom according to the Treaty of Jeddah.

May 23
Massive Earthquake Hits China
An earthquake in China's Qinghai Province measuring 8.3 on the Richter scale kills around 200,000 people dead.

August 22
Protest Against Execution
In Hyde Park, London, 200 people demonstrate against the sentence of Sacco and Vanzetti, a day before their execution.

September 7
Image is Transmitted
American Philo T. Farnsworth transmits an image of a woman to a receiver in another room using his invention of an early television.

September 18
CBS Founded
American broadcaster the Columbia Phonographic Broadcasting Service (CBS) is formed and takes to the airwaves with 47 radio stations.

GREAT MISSISSIPPI FLOOD DISPLACES 700,000 PEOPLE

During the winter of 1926–7, the rains were so heavy in the southern states of America that the Mississippi River broke its banks, flooding parts of Oklahoma, Kansas, Illinois, and Kentucky. Some years previously, U.S. Army engineers had built a levee to prevent the banks of the river from being broken, and the army reassured residents that the levee would hold. Then on Good Friday, April 15, 1927, the banks broke, flooding an area of 27,000 miles (70,000 km²). Around 700,000 people were displaced by the flood, 330,000 of them African Americans. Later, there were reports of appalling treatment of African Americans, both in the refugee camps and during the rescue operation, when plantation workers were forced at gunpoint to carry on working.

Right: Today the Mississippi has hundreds of miles of levees to prevent a repeat flood. of Mississippi or levee?

RIOTS IN VIENNA

'Around 100 people were killed in the course of the rioting'

In Austria during the 1920s, conflicts between Nationalists and Social Democrats were not unusual, but when two Nationalists in Bergenland were acquitted of killing a man and child during a street fight, Social Democrats in Vienna took to the streets rioting in protest. It was widely believed that the government had intervened to prevent a conviction, fearing Nationalist riots. In Vienna, mobs marched, crying for 'Justice,' and before long were burning papers ransacked from the Justiz-Palast, inadvertently setting light to the building itself. The riots were eventually quelled when the Chancellor of Austria and Burgomaster of Vienna united to bring in troops from elsewhere. Around 100 people had been killed in the course of the rioting, and although violence was brought to a halt, a general strike continued.

October 4
Mountain Will Have Faces
Carving begins on the face of Mount Rushmore in South Dakota of the faces of four past U.S. presidents: Lincoln, Washington, Jefferson, and Teddy Roosevelt.

October 6
Movie with Sound
The Jazz Singer, the first feature-length movie with synchronized dialogue, opens to great acclaim, signaling the end of the silent film era and the start of the 'talkies.'

October 28
Mail Sent by Plane
Pan Am, whose aim is 'to provide mass air transportation for the average man,' launches its first scheduled flight delivering mail between Key West and Havana.

November 12
Stalin Solo
Trotsky, Zinoviev, and their followers are expelled from the Communist Party in the U.S.S.R., leaving Stalin in full control.

November 13
Holland Tunnel Opens
The Holland Tunnel, a vehicular route under the Hudson River linking New Jersey and New York City, opens to traffic for the first time.

1928

NORTH POLE MISADVENTURE

POLAR AIRSHIP AT SPITZBERGEN: FIRST PICTURES

The Polar airship Italia being held down in a high wind by the crew of her supply ship on her arrival at King's Bay, Spitzbergen, from Vadso, Norway.

The crew of the supply ship, the Citta di Milano, clearing snow from the canvas hangar in readiness for the arrival of the Italia at Spitzbergen

First and exclusive pictures of the arrival at King's Bay, Spitzbergen, of the Italian airship Italia, in which General Nobile intends to fly to the North Pole. The airship had an anxious voyage from Vadso, Norway, through a snowstorm and in high winds.

In May 1928, Umberto Nobile, an Italian aeronautical engineer, failed in his second attempt to cross the North Pole in an airship he had built himself. He had already successfully crossed the North Pole in 1926 as part of a joint Italian-American-Norwegian expedition, but although Nobile had built the airship, public acclaim fell to the Norwegian Roald Amundsen. Nobile, bitter that he had not received more credit, decided to go it alone. He set out on May 22, 1928 and successfully reached the North Pole in his airship *Italia*, but disaster struck when he crashed over ice on the return journey. Nobile himself, along with nine crew members, was thrown from the airship and eventually rescued from the ice-floe. In a cruel twist to the story, Roald Amundsen was killed while helping with the rescue mission. The last survivors were only rescued after a Russian ice-breaker reached them seven weeks after the crash. Nobile was criticized at the time for saving himself first, but he continued to insist that though he had begged to be left, the rescue party had insisted on his coming first.

NEW SENSATION IN THE POLAR AIRSHIP DRAMA

Above: Umberto Nobile before the mission

April
First Dictionary
The *Oxford English Dictionary* (*O.E.D.*), a project launched in 1879, is published with over 414,000 entries.

April 12
First Transatlantic Flight East to West
The first ever east–west transatlantic flight leaves Dublin for New York.

May 15
Flying Doctor Service Takes Off
The Royal Flying Doctor Service, the brainchild of Reverend John Flynn, is launched in Australia to provide medical aid to remote rural areas of Queensland.

May 17
Women Compete for First Time
The opening ceremony takes place in Amsterdam for the ninth Olympic Games, during which women compete in track and field events for the first time, despite opposition from the Vatican.

June 17
Earhart Flies Over the Atlantic
Commander Amelia Earhart departs on a flight from Newfoundland to the British Isles, becoming the first woman to fly across the Atlantic.

KELLOGG-BRIAND PACT SIGNED

On August 27, 1928, an agreement was signed between France and the United States, renouncing war as a valid means of resolving international disputes. The leaders who had brought the deal to the table – U.S. Secretary of State Frank D. Kellogg and French Foreign Minister Aristide Briand – gave the pact its name. The agreement was originally intended to be a pledge between the two countries, but Kellogg transformed it into a general agreement with a wider application. Cynics later claimed that he did this in order to slip out of the net of committing the U.S. to a specific non-aggression pact by creating instead an idealistic manifesto which would have no direct accountability. America significantly included a clause discounting self-defense. In the event, 61 nations signed up to the Kellogg-Briand Pact. The pact itself had no direct influence on subsequent events and certainly did not prevent war from breaking out between the various countries who signed it in the coming years, but it did help to define future ideas in international law regarding conflict.

'In the event, 61 nations signed up to the Kellogg-Briand Pact.'

NATIONS SIGN WITH GOLDEN PEN PACT AGAINST WAR

Mr. Kellogg, author of the world's first treaty to outlaw war, signing it with a golden pen in Paris yesterday on behalf of the United States.

...ch Foreign Office in Paris. M. Briand, who presided, is talking to secretaries. ...speech—a welcome by M. Briand, who described the Pact as the awakening of a great hope. The actual signing occupied but a few minutes. Lord Cushendun signed twice, once for Great Britain and then for India. See also page 32.—(*Daily Mirror* photographs received by air.)

Left: Paris, where the Kellog-Briand Pact was signed.

September 18
Airship Returns Safely
German airship *Graf Zeppelin* completes a return flight to the U.S.

September 28
Penicillin Discovered
Alexander Fleming makes the first breakthrough in his discovery of penicillin.

October 1
Stalin's Five-Year Plan
Stalin launches his first Five-Year Plan for the economy of Soviet Russia, forcing rapid industrialization.

October 12
New Iron Lung
An iron lung respirator is used for the first time at the Children's Hospital in Boston, U.S.A.

November 6
Shaving Made Easy
Jacob Schick, an ex-colonel in the U.S. Army, patents the first electric shaver.

1928

HIROHITO ENTHRONED AS EMPEROR OF JAPAN

SOLEMN ENTHRONEMENT OF THE EMPEROR OF JAPAN

Japanese Ministers awaiting the arrival of the Emperor at Kyoto.

The Empress Nagako in the robes she wore at the enthronement ceremony.

The Emperor in his enthronement robes and holding the shaku.

M. Mitsuchi, Japanese Minister of Finance, and his wife.

Nobles and high dignitaries assemble outside the ment Hall, from which the Emperor proclaimed h

Solemn pageantry marked the Great Announcement, the principal rite of the enthrone ment of the Emperor Hirohito of Japan. The ceremony took place at Kyoto, the ancient capital. The Emperor and Empress wore the elaborate robes traditionally associated with the great occasion and formal Japanese dress was ordained for all wor After seating himself on the throne the Emperor was presented with the shab baton symbolising his authority—and read a rescript announcing his accessi

On November 10, 1928, Michinomiya Hirohito was enthroned as the 124th Emperor of Japan, in a line stretching back 2,000 years. The ceremony took place in the throne room of the royal palace, and the crowds who had thronged to see it were delighted when, after days of murky weather, the sky outside was lit by a bright sun and a rainbow appeared, boding well for the future. In taking up his position as divinely ordained absolute monarch, Hirohito adopted the name Shiwoo, which means 'Enlightened Peace' but the name would be a far from accurate description of his reign. He came to the throne at a time when Japan was in the throes of massive military expansion and charged almost inevitably into war with China. Hirohito was to remain Emperor of Japan through some of its most difficult times, including the Pearl Harbor attack, defeat by the Allies in the Second World War, and the atomic bomb attacks on Hiroshima and Nagasaki. Although Hirohito was stripped of his title by the post-war occupying forces, he remained Emperor in the hearts and minds of his people until his death in 1989.

> '**In taking up his position as divinely ordained absolute monarch, he adopted the name Shiwoo, which means "Enlightened Peace".**'

Right: Hirohito saw many changes in Japan during his reign, as Tokyo was transformed into a world center of commerce.

November 18
First Cartoon with Sound
Steamboat Willie, the first cartoon with sound, starring Mickey Mouse, is released.

November
Building Begins
Building begins on the art deco Chrysler Building in New York, designed by William Van Alen to house the Chrysler Corporation.

1928
New Seven Member Rule
The Seven Member Rule is enacted in the United States, specifying that government agencies must turn over information if it is requested by seven members of the House Government Reform Committee.

January 2
Niagra Falls to be Saved
The United States and Canada reach an agreement on joint action to preserve the Niagara Falls.

WALL STREET CRASH HERALDS THE GREAT DEPRESSION

On Thursday October 24, 1929 (known thereafter as Black Thursday), a massive slide in the price of shares on the New York Stock Exchange prompted a complete loss of confidence in the value of stocks, which in turn led to an unprecedented collapse in the U.S. financial market, known as the Wall Street Crash. The crash came at the end of the 1920s, which in America had been a decade of prosperity, excess, and extravagance. The feel-good factor was so high that President Hoover felt moved to comment in 1928: 'We in America today are nearer to the final triumph over poverty than ever before in the history of any land.' The crash followed a period of ever-rising stock prices, when everyone wanted a piece of the pie. More people than ever bought stock, assuming that it would continue to rise, and this forced prices up even higher. The problem was that much of the money used to buy stock was borrowed, so the situation was entirely false. All it took for the bubble to burst was a moment of doubt. As soon as prices took a downturn, worried investors sold up, which created a sense of panic as more and more investors sold up and prices continued to drop. The Wall Street Crash forced the closure of around 100,000 businesses across America. The consequent unemployment meant that consumers could not afford to spend, which in turn led to more business closures and further unemployment. Thus began the Great Depression of the 1930s.

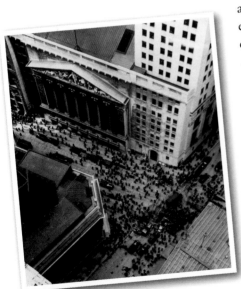

Left: Crowds take to the streets outside Wall Street on hearing news of the crash.

January 10 — Julio Assassinated — Julio Antonio Mella, the founder of Cuba's Communist Party, is assassinated in Mexico.

January 10 — Meet Tintin — Tintin, a comic book character created by Hergé, makes his debut in *Tintin in the Land of the Soviets*.

January 15 — Future Pioneer — Martin Luther King Jr. is born in Atlanta, Georgia.

January 17 — Meet Popeye — Popeye first appears in the comic strip 'Thimble Theater.'

1929

TREATY ESTABLISHES VATICAN CITY AS INDEPENDENT STATE

MORE VATICAN PHOTOGRAPHS BY TELEPHONE

The Lateran Treaty was a pact signed by Italian leader Benito Mussolini and representative of the Catholic Church, Cardinal Gasparri, in Rome on June 7, 1929. Under the terms of the treaty, the papacy agreed to recognize Italy as a state, and the Italian state agreed to recognize the Vatican City as an independent sovereign state within its capital city. However, further conditions were laid down by the papacy: the treaty established Roman Catholicism as the official state religion of Italy, made religious education compulsory in public schools, and banned divorce. There was mutual agreement that the Italian government would punish crimes committed within Vatican City if the papacy so required, and for its part, the Vatican would extradite to Italy those whom both deemed criminals. Significantly, however, the person of the Pope would be recognized by the state as sacred and one who cannot be removed. The Lateran Treaty would remain in place even after the abolition of the monarchy in Italy, and was incorporated into the constitution of the new republic in 1947. It has been weakened in recent years, however. Roman Catholicism ceased to be the state religion of Italy in 1985, and in 2008, the Vatican announced that it would no longer immediately adopt all Italian laws, a response to Italy's abortion laws.

CIVIL WAR IN AFGHANISTAN

Following large-scale revolt in November 1928 between rival factions within Afghanistan, the emir Amanullah Khan, who had ruled as sovereign since 1919 and had successfully achieved independence for his country, abdicated in favor of his brother. Habibullah Ghazi, a rebel leader, took advantage of the newly weak leadership and captured Kabul, thus seizing power and proclaiming himself emir. Thereafter, there were several attempts on behalf of Amanullah Khan's relatives to regain the throne and eventually, with British help, they succeeded.

February 14
Al Capone's Rivals Massacred
In the 'St. Valentine's Day Massacre,' seven gangster-rivals of Al Capone are murdered in Chicago.

May 16
First Academy Awards
The First Academy Awards are presented in a quiet private ceremony.

June 21
Cristero War Ends
An agreement brokered by U.S. ambassador Dwight Whitney Morrow ends the Cristero War in Mexico.

June 27
Color Television Demonstrated
The first public demonstration of color television is given by H. E. Ives at Bell Telephone Laboratories in New York.

September 21
Fighting Along Manchurian Border
Fighting between China and the Soviet Union breaks out along the Manchurian border.

PALESTINE RIOTS

In the summer of 1929, after several years of relatively peaceful relations between Arabs and Jews in Palestine, a dispute broke out over rights to pray at the Western Wall (also known as the Wailing Wall) in Jerusalem. The original incident which sparked the riots involved a common Jewish practice of putting up a screen of chairs to separate men and women during prayers at the wall. The situation was exploited by the Mufti (interpreter of Islamic law) of Jerusalem who fueled the fires of hatred by claiming that Jews were violating Muslim sites and planning to take over a mosque. On August 23, 1929, a new wave of Arab violence erupted when the Mufti allegedly called for Arabs to 'slaughter Jews'. Jewish leaders had already warned British authorities that they feared an outbreak of violence, but they were assured of their safety. During seven days of rioting, hundreds were killed on both sides. British police were later criticized for their apparent lack of intervention. In what was viewed as one of the worst atrocities ever in the area, the 1929 riot also involved many instances of Arabs helping to shelter their Jewish neighbors from the massacres, which were led by extremists and did not represent majority feeling in Palestine.

RHINELAND EVACUATION AGREEMENT

The signing of the Rhineland Evacuation Agreement in 1929 was the final result of two years of difficult negotiations between Britain, France, and Germany. After lengthy talks, all three powers eventually agreed to pull British and French troops out of the Rhineland in the west of Germany, where they had been on guard since the end of the First World War. The Treaty of Versailles, the peace agreement signed at the end of the First World War, had demanded the demilitarization of the Rhineland, and Allied troops had occupied the region ever since. For the Germans, the Treaty of Versailles was nothing short of national humiliation and a 'violation of honor'. It required them to accept full responsibility for the war and made various demands in terms of territory and financial compensation for the victors, as well as forbidding any further military growth. The signing of the Rhineland Evacuation Agreement was seen as the final gesture of renewed trust in Germany. At a meeting at The Hague in August of 1929, it was agreed that the Allied troops would pull out of the Rhineland, even though the Treaty of Versailles had stated that they should remain until 1935. German Foreign Minister Gustav Stresemann boldly suggested that they could be out by Christmas, and when the French foreign minister, Briand, replied, 'I fear it would be a great hardship to move our troops in the cold winter months,' Stresemann came back with: 'Your troops could be spared the inhumane experience of a winter evacuation by leaving now.' The significance of this occasion for the future of Europe was immense, as Germany began to rearm and remobilize its troops, to a greater extent than ever before.

November
Farms Jointly Run
'Collectivization' begins in Russia, resulting in the holdings of several farmers being run as a joint enterprise.

December 28
Police Kill Unarmed Demonstrators
Named 'Black Saturday' in Samoa, New Zealand colonial police kill 11 unarmed demonstrators, an event which leads the Mau movement to demand independence for Samoa.

There is More Out There
Edwin Hubble sees a vast universe beyond the Milky Way and first proposes that there are other galaxies out there.

New Radio in Your Car
American Paul Galvin invents the first car radio, known as the Motorola.

Take Color Photograhs
George Eastman, founder of the Eastman Kodak Company, first markets color film.

HINDENBURG EXPLODES —NEARLY 100 DEAD

The German airship, Hindenburg, in flight.

FLAMING WRECK FALLS ON AIRFIELD: CHILDREN VICTIMS

From Our Own Correspondent

Lakehurst, New Jersey, Thursday

Hindenburg, biggest airship in the world, exploded and crashed in flames with the loss of 96 lives—eight women and three children among them—as she was about to moor in a thunderstorm here to-day.

Only four people escaped—by jumping from a window—while the rest of the passengers and crew were trapped in the blaze.

BUFFETED BY A GALE AND WITH LIGHTNING FLICKERING AROUND HER, THE HINDENBURG APPROACHED THE AERODROME AND TOSSED HER NOSELINES TO THE GROUND READY TO BE MADE FAST, WHEN THERE WAS A TERRIFIC ROAR.

Flames burst from the stern, the giant ship hovered for a moment, then crashed to the ground from 300ft., shaking the whole neighbourhood. Within a few minutes her steel frame had collapsed into a twisted mass.

According to ground watchers, passengers were laughing and waving from the observation windows when a bomb-like explosion sent out clouds of red and black billowing smoke. Within a few seconds screams filled the air.

For half her length her girders lay bare while the other half was hidden by clouds of smoke. Flames lighted up the wreckage.

Spectators stood sobbing, many of them hysterical, as army trucks, with screaming sirens, sped to the still blazing wreckage.

The Hindenburg, making her first flight over the Atlantic this season,

Mr. Ira Nelson Morris, Chicago meat packer millionaire, one of the dead passengers.

was carrying thirty-nine passengers in addition to a crew of sixty-one. Captain Max Pruss was in command with Captain Lehmann, acting in an advisory capacity. Among the passengers, most of them Germans or Americans, were:—

Mr. Charles Seymour Higgens, of London.

Mr. J. Grant, assistant manager of the Hamburg-America Line, London.

Colonel Nelson Morris, Chicago meat packer millionaire and former U.S. Minister to Sweden.

Caught like rats in a trap, with the only exit from the airship barred by flames, not one passenger is believed to have escaped.

Four members of the crew, two of them cabin boys and one a steward, saved themselves by jumping from a window as the airship neared the ground. They are Clifford Osburn, Joseph Spahs, Philip Mungun and Herbert O'Laughlin.

"Flames were leaping round me, and I saw the only thing for it was to jump," said O'Laughlin. "I waited till the ship was ten feet above the ground."

Harry Wellbrook, a member of the ground crew, said:

"We got three bodies from the stern of the ship.

"All were burned beyond recognition, but one, whose features were unrecognisable, was still breathing. The clothing on all three was burned to a cinder and their skin had been scorched off."

A photographer on the spot told me: "I ran towards the ship and saw it enveloped in flames.

"I saw a man walking towards me assisted by two other men. He had no clothes on."

Louis Krantz, another witness, said: "I have seen hell. Hindenburg exploded in the air and

(Continued on back page)

1930-1939

TRIUMPHANT RETURN OF AMY JOHNSON

LINDBERGH BABY FOUND DEAD

GIRL BANDIT SHOT IN 85 MILE-AN-HOUR FIGHT

HITLER NOW MASTER OF GERMANY
Decree an Hour After Death of Hindenburg

SOLDIERS' OATH OF "LOYALTY TO DEATH" TO NEW PRESIDENT

KING EDWARD WILL BROADCAST TO-NIGHT

GERMAN TROOPS MARCH ON AS CAROL MANS FRONTIER

During the 1930s, economic depression hung over Britain and America. Unemployment soared, food and fuel were scarce, and a spirit of gloom descended. In Britain, hunger-marchers highlighted the plight of the unemployed, while the Labour government urged its people to 'Buy British'. In America, a growing criminal underworld preyed on people's desperation with a ruthlessness that was typified by the reckless violence of notorious criminals Bonnie and Clyde.

Meanwhile, as Germany began to re-arm in violation of the 1919 Treaty of Versailles, it became clear that nothing would stop new Chancellor Adolf Hitler's personal ambition for Germany's relentless expansion across Europe and beyond.

The course of history was altered in Britain when King Edward VII decided to give up his throne to marry the divorced American Mrs. Wallis Simpson, thrusting the title on his unprepared brother, who became King George VI, a diversion from the royal line that gave Britain Queen Elizabeth II two decades later.

Two tragic airship explosions, which took the lives of scores of adventurous passengers, ended this new style of leisure travel. Amy Johnson made her solo flight from Britain to Australia and this demonstration of individual heroism not only lifted British national pride but signaled a viable future form of passenger transportation.

1930

R101 AIRSHIP EXPLODES IN FRANCE ON MAIDEN VOYAGE

BISHOP'S DEATH NEAR PARLIAMENT

DISCLOSURES AT R101 INQUIRY

The Bishop of Worcester, Dr. E. H. Pearce, who collapsed and died in a few minutes in Parliament-square yesterday when walking with a friend to attend the opening of Parliament.

Sir William Jowitt, the Attorney-General, speaking at the R101 inquiry which opened yesterday at the Institute of Civil Engineers, Westminster. Right: Sir John Simon, the president, sitting between Lieutenant-Colonel Moore-Brabazon (profile) and Professor Ing...

In the years following the First World War, there was still a fascination with airships, which to date had been seen chiefly as the most effective means of mass-transporting troops and military equipment. Airships were based on the principle of being lighter than air (rather than heavier, as with airplanes) and as a result they required a massive volume of hydrogen gas to be kept aloft. In 1929, the government set up the Imperial Airship Scheme, which launched an initiative to design an airship with a capacity of 5 million ft³ (150,000 m³). This was far beyond the capacity of any existing design. There were two teams of designers: one within the Air Ministry and one in a private firm, Vickers. The *R101* was the final outcome of the Air Ministry effort, but there had been significant pressures along the way, tests had been hurried, and designers were felt to be insufficiently experienced. The

'She was badly designed and heavily overloaded, and members of the technical crew predicted before take-off that she wouldn't make it.'

function of such a high-capacity airship was still of a military nature, but when the *R101* was built, the potential for leisure travel became apparent. After two slightly shaky trial runs, the *R101* took off for her maiden voyage on October 4, 1930 carrying 54 passengers. She was badly designed and heavily overloaded, and members of the technical crew predicted before take-off that she wouldn't make it. On route from London to Karachi, the *R101* took a nose-dive over Beauvais in France and hit the ground at 13 mph (21 kph), killing 48 of the passengers on board.

Right: French rescue workers and police among the wreckage of the R101 airship after it crashed near Beauvais, France.

January 13
Mickey Mouse Appears in Comic Strip
Mickey Mouse appears in a comic strip for the first time. The early strips are written by Walt Disney himself.

January 16
Jet Engine Invented
Frank Whittle registers a patent for the turbojet engine in 1930. Hans von Ohain is granted a patent for a turbojet engine in 1936. Both are recognized as the co-inventors of the jet engine.

February 18
New Planet Discovered
Clyde Tombaugh discovers Pluto while studying photographs. Pluto is considered a planet until 2006. Pluto is now considered to be a dwarf planet.

March 31
Rules Applied to Film Production
The Motion Picture Production Code is adopted. This imposes strict guidelines on the treatment of sex, crime, religion, and violence in motion pictures for the next forty years.

AMY JOHNSON FLIES SOLO FROM BRITAIN TO AUSTRALIA

The daughter of a fish merchant from the north of England, Amy Johnson took up flying as a hobby in 1928 at the age of 25, while working at a London solicitor's firm. After taking lessons at the London Aeroplane Club, she became the first British woman to hold a ground engineer's license. Johnson planned her solo trip to Australia for months, but she didn't manage to get hold of a plane until two months before take-off, when her father helped her to buy a secondhand de Havilland Gipsy Moth, which she named *Jason*. Johnson's flight to Australia took 20 days, and when she landed in Darwin on May 24 after only a few minor glitches, she was greeted by rapturous applause and received a telegram reading 'Bravo' from French aviator Louis Bleriot. During the 1930s, Johnson went on to establish various long-distance flying records, until, while on a flying mission for the British government during the Second World War, she died when her plane went down over the sea. Her body was never recovered.

TRIUMPHANT RETURN OF AMY JOHNSON

is Amy Johnson, the air heroine of the Empire, on her dramatic arrival soon after 5 o'clock—some three hours late owing to a gale—at Croydon aerodrome yesterday evening. In the upper picture she is seen (marked with a cross) in front of the liner City of Glasgow, which brought her through terrific winds. Below, Miss Johnson is speaking to the crowd through microphones without showing a sign of nervousness. Behind her stands Lord Thomson, the Air Minister. Miss Bondfield, Minister of Labour, Sir Sefton Brancker and her parents were among those who greeted her. See also page 20.—("Daily Mirror" photographs.)

Above: A de Havilland Gypsy Moth, similar to the one flown by Amy Johnson.

'After taking lessons at the London Aeroplane Club, she became the first British woman to hold a ground engineer's license.'

April 18
No News to Report
The BBC Radio Service from London reports that 'There is no news' and then piano music follows.

May 6
Deadly Quake
The Great Salmas Earthquake in Iran measures 7.3 on the Richter scale and kills 4,000 people.

May 15
First Flight with Stewardess
Ellen Church becomes the first airline stewardess, aboard a Boeing tri-motor on a flight from Oakland, California, to Chicago, Illinois.

May 28
Chrysler Building Opens its Doors
The Chrysler Building opens in New York City after two years of work to construct it.

1930

BURMESE REBEL AGAINST BRITISH RULE

In 1930, Saya San, a Buddhist monk and doctor who was part of the extreme nationalist movement in Burma intent on restoring the Burmese monarchy, organized peasant discontent into an uprising against the British 'invaders'. Burmese peasants had been left poverty stricken by heavy taxes and a recent fall in the price of rice, and their uprising, though political in name, was largely economically driven. Saya San's peasant followers became the 'Galon' army, named after a bird from Hindu mythology. Though skilled fighters, their primitive weapons gave them little chance against their British rulers. On the night of December 22, 1930, an uprising broke out in Tharrawaddy, which quickly spread to surrounding districts. Around 10,000 peasants were killed by British gunfire. Though their leader Saya San escaped, he was later captured and sentenced to death in March 1931.

Above: Golden pagodas at Shwedagon, the most sacred pagoda for the Burmese.

ANGLO-INDIAN REGIMENT CLASHES WITH AFRIDI TRIBESMEN

For decades, the inhabitants of the treacherous mountainous regions on the borders of Afghanistan had posed an almost constant threat to British India. The native tribes were skilled fighters and their relentless sallies into British-Indian territory occupied the Anglo-Indian army for longer than any other revolutionary movement. Chief among the tribes were the Punjabi Pathan, who were well armed and determined. These skirmishes took a massive toll on the Anglo-Indian army, who weren't used to conditions in the hilly tribal regions. Vast amounts of army resources were poured into special training and equipment, but the elusive tribal groups consistently retained the upper hand. In 1931, the Anglo-Indian regiment the Bengal Lancers led an attack on horseback against Afridi tribesmen near the Khyber Pass. The clash, which became known as the Battle of Karawal, was the last time that the British Army would attempt to put down Indian tribes – and the last time they would fight on horseback with swords.

July 7
Work Begins on Dam
Building of the Boulder Dam (now known as the Hoover Dam) is started.

July 13
World Cup Kicks Off!
The first Football World Cup begins with a match between France and Mexico. Lucien Laurent for France scores the first goal.

December 2
Hoover Pleas for Money
During the Great Depression, U.S. President Herbert Hoover goes before Congress and asks for a $150 million public works program to help generate jobs and stimulate the economy.

Machine Solves Equations!
Vannevar Bush invents the 'differential analyzer', or analog computer, at MIT in Boston. It is designed to solve differential equations.

INDIA'S FUTURE DEBATED

The Round Table Conferences, held in London between 1930 and 1932, were aimed at resolving the difficult issue of Indian self-rule and bringing some resolution to the differences between Muslims and Hindus. The first conference, held at Westminster, had failed to include a representative from the Indian National Congress, the party that was leading the fight for independence. This was largely because most of the party leadership were in jail for their participation in acts of civil disobedience. This absence was widely felt to indicate a lack of real commitment on the side of the British, since the very people who represented independence could not present their case. On March 5, 1931, Gandhi and Lord Irwin, British Viceroy of India, signed a pact which promised the release of political prisoners in exchange for Gandhi calling an end to the civil disobedience movement. As a result, Mohandas Gandhi was released from prison early so that he could attend the second Round Table Conference in September 1931 as the Indian National Congress representative. The specific aim of the conference was to bring about some agreement between Hindus and Muslims in India so that they could form an effective united government together, but there was no clear outcome. Muslim leaders continued to push for separate status and conditions, while Gandhi refused to accept that those in the 'untouchable' caste be treated as a separate minority group.

'Muslim leaders continued to push for separate status and conditions, while Gandhi refused to accept that those in the "untouchable" caste be treated as a separate minority group.'

GANDHI'S DEFIANCE

Reginald Reynolds, a British follower of Gandhi.   Mahatma Gandhi, the Indian Nationalist leader.

What Gandhi expected to be the first law-breaking move of his anti-British campaign in India has been made. He and his followers filled pots with sea water and obtained salt residue. The authorities take the view that as the salt was unfit for human consumption no infringement of Salt Laws took place.

BLAZING ROOF THRILLS

A big crowd, many from Hyde Park, watch the outbreak.

VETERAN M.P. TO MARRY FOURTH WIFE

Right: Gandhi emerges from the Round Table conference of 1931, held at Westminster, London.

February 5
Campbell Breaks Speed Record
Sir Malcolm Campbell breaks the land speed record in his car *Bluebird*. He reaches 246.09 mph (396.04 kph), which makes him the first to travel faster than 4 miles (6.4 km) a minute.

February 10
India's New Capital
New Delhi becomes the new capital of India.

March 3
National Anthem for US
'The Star-Spangled Banner' becomes the U.S. official national anthem.

March 19
Gambling Legalized
Nevada legalizes gambling as a way of lifting the state out of the hard times of the Great Depression.

1931

BRITISH GOVERNMENT FIGHTS RECESSION WITH 'BUY BRITISH' CAMPAIGN

BUY — *BUT BUY* BRITISH

Placing experimental steel sleepers on the G.W.R. line at Twyford. If successful, they will replace wooden ones largely imported from abroad and will help to end the depression in South Wales.

BUY BRITISH

Setting up a huge sign on the side of a new building facing Trafalgar-square, in connection with the great Buy British campaign launched by the Empire Marketing Board. The letters are some of the biggest ever used and when illuminated at night will form one of the most gigantic electric signs in the world. The Prince of Wales is to inaugurate the campaign in a broadcast appeal to the nation from the B.B.C. studio at Birmingham this evening. Supporters of the Tudor Rose League, which numbers 59,000 associate members, proclaim by wearing a little enamel rose, that they give first consideration to British products.

The emblem of the Tudor Rose League.

Right: Stephen Tallents. Following his success with the Buy British campaign he became head of public relations at the General Post Office.

By 1930, the British government knew their nation was heading towards serious recession. So in 1931, the government established the Empire Marketing Board with the aim of boosting the economy by encouraging spending on home-grown products. The Empire Marketing Board was headed by Stephen Tallents, who was known as 'the imaginative civil servant'. This was an early example of a massive public relations exercise. The aim of the board's 'Buy British' campaign was to make consumers aware of how they could spend their money to strengthen the British economy. From neon signs in London's Trafalgar Square to curry-and-yoga nights, via a variety of stunts including a fly-past by aviator Amy Johnson trailing a banner with the 'Buy British' slogan, and commissioning Girl Guides to deliver posters, the board used imaginative and creative methods to rein consumer spending back into the home territory. The success of the campaign was not necessarily seen in terms of an upturn in sales, but it was claimed that the £12,000 spent on it had been put to invaluable use in changing the mindset of the nation. Stephen Tallents was renowned in his day for successful advertising campaigns – he was even credited with the idea for 'rebranding' the British Empire as the Commonwealth.

> **'From neon signs in London's Trafalgar Square to curry-and-yoga nights … the board used imaginative and creative methods to rein consumer spending back into the home territory.'**

May 1
Empire State Building Opened
Construction of the Empire State Building in New York is completed and it is officially opened.

July
Iron Lung Finished
John Haven Emerson perfects the iron lung, which is an early respirator.

July 31–August 1
Matterhorn Conquered!
The northern face of the Matterhorn Mountain in Switzerland is climbed for the first time by Toni and Franz Schmid.

August 19
Devastating Floods
The second in a series of three devastating floods hits China. The floods are caused by the overflowing of the Huang He (Yellow River) and are thought to be the most deadly natural disaster in history.

KING ALFONSO OF SPAIN ABDICATES

King Alfonso XIII had ruled as monarch of Spain throughout the troubled period of the early 20th century. During his reign he faced demands for autonomy from the Basque and Catalan peoples, the loss of Cuba, the Philippines and Puerto Rico to the United States, and general political instability in Spain, with eight prime ministers passing through in four years. By the time Miguel Primo de Rivera declared himself military dictator in 1923, Alfonso was just glad to have someone in control and accepted de Rivera's dictatorship, proudly calling him 'my Mussolini'. Rivera's dictatorship was unpopular, however, and soon even his own army would not support him. In the subsequent elections, Alfonso's association with him had sullied his standing among his people and the republican party won majorities in all the main urban centers. Spain became a republic in April 1931 and on April 14 King Alfonso was forced to flee into exile, eventually settling in Rome. Although he abdicated the exercise of his powers in Spain, he nevertheless passed the title of King to his son Juan on his deathbed in 1941.

Above: De Rivera (left) with King Alfonso XIII.

JAPANESE TROOPS INVADE MANCHURIA

On September 18, 1931, a section of the Japanese-controlled South Manchuria Railway in China was blown up. The Japanese Imperial Army responded by invading Manchuria, claiming that the explosion, near Mukden, was caused by Chinese dissidents. In fact, documentary evidence now points to Japanese sabotage. They had blown up their own railway as a means of justifying an invasion of China. In the event, the explosion was not sufficient to cause much harm and a train managed to pass over the damaged rail even after the dynamite had gone off. Nonetheless, the next morning, around 500 Japanese soldiers attacked the Chinese garrison of 7,000 soldiers at Beidayang. Though outnumbered, the Japanese troops were more highly trained and the attack resulted in the loss of 5,000 Chinese lives, alongside only two Japanese lives. The 'Mukden Incident' which prompted the invasion of Manchuria was a significant step on the path to the Second Sino-Japanese War (1937–45) and the Second World War.

Above: The South Manchuria Railway was a source of friction between China, Japan and Russia.

October 18
Thomas Edison Dies
Thomas Edison, inventor of the first practical lightbulb, dies after a series of ailments.

October 22
Al Capone Imprisoned
Gangster Al Capone is sentenced to 11 years in prison for tax avoidance.

Stop-Action Photography Invented
Harold 'Doc' Edgerton invents a way to stop motion with his camera with a specially designed flashing light called a stroboscope.

Electron Microscope Invented
In Germany, Max Knott and Ernst Ruska co-invent the electron microscope.

1932

CHARLES LINDBERGH JR. KIDNAPPED

LINDBERGH BABY FOUND DEAD

Colonel Lindbergh's twenty-months-old son, Charles, dead by neighbours near Lindbergh's house at Hopkidnapped from his nursery on March 1. The ann

'BIRDMEN' HUNT FOR LINDBERGH BABY

On March 1, 1932, the infant son of famous aviator Charles Lindbergh was found to be missing from his crib at the family home in Princeton, New Jersey. A ransom note left on the windowsill – demanding $50,000 – indicated that he had been abducted. The New Jersey Police Department immediately launched a previously unprecedented search that involved the entire force of 19,000 personnel working around the clock to find the child. A week later, a second ransom note appeared, demanding $70,000. There followed further ransom notes, increasing the money and changing the arrangements. A retired school principal, who had offered to be the go-between, acted on behalf of the family and carried out all of the kidnapper's instructions. He handed over the money and was told that they would find the boy in a boat named 'Nellie' on Martha's Vineyard. The boat was never discovered, however, and on May 12, ten weeks after he had been abducted, the toddler was found dead by a passer-by, some 4 miles (6 km) from the family home. His body had been mutilated and was badly decomposed. A lengthy and thorough nationwide investigation led eventually to the arrest of German immigrant Bruno Richard Hauptmann in 1934. In February 1935, Hauptmann was found guilty of first-degree murder, sentenced to death, and electrocuted in April 1936. A clear motive for the murder was never established, and though evidence clearly identified the ladder used in the kidnapping as belonging to Hauptmann, his widow continued to protest his innocence.

> **'He handed over the money and was told that they would find the boy in a boat named "Nellie" on Martha's Vineyard.'**

March 19
Sydney Bridge Opened
Sydney Harbour Bridge is opened by Premier Jack Lang, after eight years of construction.

April 5
Poisoned Racehorse
Australian wonder racehorse Phar Lap is poisoned with arsenic in California and dies.

April 4
Vitamin C Isolated
Chemist C.C. King isolates vitamin C.

April 19
Art Dealer Sentenced
German art dealer Otto Wacker is sentenced to 19 months for fraudulent paintings attributed to Van Gogh.

FRENCH PRESIDENT ASSASSINATED

On May 6, 1932, while attending a book fair, the French President Paul Doumer was assassinated by a Russian émigré called Paul Gorgulov. Doumer had been President of France since May 13, 1931. The President, who lost four of his five sons during the First World War, had been a guest at a book fair for work by French war veterans. He had just signed a book when the Russian man raised a gun and shot. He shouted, 'Die for the Fatherland,' as he shot. The assassin was violent and difficult to overpower, but when he was eventually wrestled to the ground he was attacked by many of the women present. Though he claimed to be the president of a Communist group called the 'Green Fascists' whose purpose in killing the President was to get France to invade Russia so that he could take over the government there, no such group appeared to exist and he was later deemed to be mentally unstable. This prognosis was reversed at his trial, however, probably so that he could be executed. Gorgulov had twice been expelled from France for practicing medicine without a license, which prompted a serious investigation into how he had managed to get back into the country. President Doumer came from a very underprivileged background and had worked long and hard to achieve his political position: somewhat naively, he assumed that everyone must know that he was a good, industrious family man who had the nation's best interest at heart and, since no one would want to kill such a man, he consistently refused police protection while in office. The chief press photographer on the scene of the assassination used his camera to hit the assassin over the head rather than take a photograph of the momentous event.

ROAD TO WAR BETWEEN CHINA AND JAPAN

The January 28 Incident, also known as the 'Shanghai Incident', was one more example of deliberate provocation on the road that led to the Second Sino-Japanese War. Following the Mukden Incident, which had enabled Japanese forces to occupy much of the northeastern territories of China, the Japanese were looking for opportunities to antagonize the Chinese further in order to force a conflict. On January 18, some Japanese Buddhist monks were beaten by agitated Chinese workers. In retaliation, instigated Japanese agents burnt down their factory. The antagonistic atmosphere prompted outbursts of anti-Japanese protest, which gave the Japanese a justification for moving their troops into strategic defense positions around Shanghai, in case riots should break out. Along with other foreign powers, Japan held extraterritorial concessions, or territory, in the city. On January 28, the Japanese went as far as to bomb Shanghai from the air, instigating the Shanghai War (January 28–March 3) over control of the city.

June
Polaroid Photography Invented
Edwin Herbert Land and George Wheelwright drop out of university in June to work on their production of the 'polarizer' – a material to eliminate glare which is now known as Polaroid film. They successfully complete the invention in August.

June 6
Gas Taxed
The first gas tax in the United States is enacted at 1 cent per US gallon (0.26 ¢/L) sold.

September 1
Balloon Tire Invented
The balloon tire is demonstrated for the first time. This is the first low-pressure tire for farm tractors.

1932

BRITISH UNEMPLOYED ORGANIZE MASS HUNGER MARCH

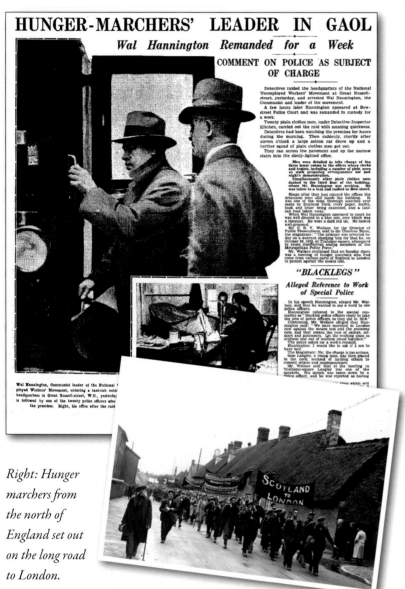

HUNGER-MARCHERS' LEADER IN GAOL

Wal Hannington Remanded for a Week

COMMENT ON POLICE AS SUBJECT OF CHARGE

Detectives raided the headquarters of the National Unemployed Workers' Movement at Great Russell-street, yesterday, and arrested Wal Hannington, the Communist and leader of the movement.

A few hours later Hannington appeared at Bow-street Police Court and was remanded in custody for a week.

Twenty plain clothes men, under Detective-Inspector Kitchen, carried out the raid with amazing quickness. Detectives had been watching the premises for hours during the morning. Then suddenly, shortly after eleven o'clock a large saloon car drove up and a further squad of plain clothes men got out.

They ran across the pavement and up the narrow stairs into the dimly-lighted office.

Wal Hannington, Communist leader of the National Unemployed Workers' Movement, entering a taxi-cab outside headquarters in Great Russell-street, W.C., yesterday, is followed by one of the twenty police officers who raided the premises. Right, his office after the raid.

Right: Hunger marchers from the north of England set out on the long road to London.

In October 1932, with unemployment in Britain at an all-time high and 2,750,000 people out of work, the National Unemployed Workers Movement organized a Hunger March to force public recognition of the plight of the jobless. The march was also a protest against the introduction of means-testing in state benefits whereby applicants had to prove their poverty. The Labour government under Ramsay MacDonald had cut state benefits in order to fund public borrowing, which it hoped would stop the value of the pound from sliding even further. On October 28, 3,000 men from the North of England, Scotland, and South Wales marched to London and converged on Hyde Park in Kensington. The marchers were fed and housed by charitable organizations along their route and received welcoming support from crowds of London workers on their arrival. The police presence was high because violence was anticipated. In the event, the police used their batons in response to stone-throwing, and soon rioters were using broken-off tree branches from the park as clubs. There were scores of arrests, but it was later discovered that most of those arrested were Londoners who had joined in, rather than the hunger marchers themselves. The marchers intended to present a petition to Westminster with over 1 million signatures, calling for action to support the unemployed and an end to means-testing, but it never reached its intended destination. On the day of the proposed march on the House of Commons at Westminster, the headquarters of the National Unemployed Workers Movement were stormed by police and its National Organizer Wal Hannington was arrested for inciting a mutiny. He was jailed for three months and the N.U.W.M.'s chairman Sid Elias for two years.

> 'The Labour government ... had cut state benefits in order to fund public borrowing, which it hoped would stop the value of the pound from sliding even further.'

October 3
Iraq Independent
Iraq gains independence from Britain and is admitted to the League of Nations as an independent state.

November 8
America's New President
Franklin Delano Roosevelt is elected as the new president of the United States.

Parking Meter is Invented
Carl Cole Magee invents the first parking meter in response to the increasing problem of parking congestion. He files for a patent on May 13, 1935.

November 9 (1933)
Nobel Prize for Heisenberg
The 1932 Nobel Prize for Physics is awarded to Werner Heisenberg for the creation of the matrix theory of quantum mechanics. The announcement is delayed and made the following year on November 9.

KING FAISAL OF IRAQ DIES

TRAGIC DEATH OF KING FEISAL

Broken by Anxiety Over Assyrian Trouble

FORMER HARROW BOY AS THE NEW RULER

Worry and anxiety over the Assyrian trouble which led to the massacres of Christians is believed to have hastened the end of King Feisal of Iraq, who died suddenly yesterday in a Switzerland hotel from a heart attack.

His son, Crown Prince Ghazi, a former Harrow boy, was crowned yesterday at Bagdad as King of Iraq.

By a tragic coincidence the manager of the hotel also died yesterday morning.

BERNE, Friday.

The King of Iraq, "Feisal the Fearless," as he was called by his Arab people, died shortly after midnight in the hotel here where he had been staying.

It was only four days before that he had arrived from Bagdad, a tired man, to complete the cure which he had been forced to abandon earlier in the summer owing to the Assyrian trouble.

His death came as a terrible shock to those in his entourage. Pan Bin Kadry Bey, Chief Master of Ceremonies, gave the following account of King Feisal's last hours.

A Very Tired Man

"King Feisal, on his first visit to Berne in July, felt much better. He returned here by air from Bagdad on August 2, but he had lost between 10lb and 12lb in weight, due to worry and anxiety.

"Yesterday morning he went by motor-car to Interlaken, where he had lunch. He returned to the Hotel Bellevue in the afternoon. He appeared to be overtired and complained of a headache, saying he wished to retire early.

He went to bed shortly after 7 p.m., and at eight o'clock, putting his hands on his heart, he complained of palpitation.

"King Feisal had an attack of breathlessness and Dr. Kocher was called, but did not consider the patient was seriously ill.

"Towards midnight King Feisal suddenly collapsed and died within three minutes."

"I Have Done My Duty"

A Bagdad Reuter message states that the last words of the King were: "I am satisfied. I have done my duty. I have served the nation with all my power. My hope is that after I have gone, my nation will be happy, strong and united."

All Bagdad is mourning the King, says the message, by chants and processions in the streets.

King Feisal's embalmed body will be conveyed by a British cruiser from an Italian port to Haifa, probably on Sunday. From Haifa it will be taken by a R.A.F. aeroplane to Bagdad, where the funeral is expected to take place next Thursday or Friday.—Reuter.

THE KING'S REGRET

The following message has been sent from Balmoral to the new King of Iraq:—

"The Queen and I have learnt with profound regret of the sudden and unexpected death of your illustrious father, his Majesty King Feisal, whom we so recently had the pleasure of welcoming as our guest.

"We would ask your Majesty to accept our heartfelt condolences on the grievous loss which you and your royal house and people have sustained through this melancholy event.

"At the same time I take pleasure in offering to your Majesty my cordial congratulations on your accession to the throne, together with my heartiest good wishes for the happiness and prosperity of your reign.—(Sgd.) George, R.I."

King Feisal was the third son of Hussein, the late King of the Hedjaz, and became ruler of Iraq on August 23, 1921.

In the Great War he raised an Arab army which helped Lord Allenby to defeat the Turks.

The Assyrian trouble which caused King Feisal overwhelming anxiety blazed up in August.

King Fuad of Egypt's master of ceremonies greeting King Feisal when he arrived at Cairo by air recently en route for Switzerland.

King Feisal driving from Victoria Station to Buckingham arrival for his state visit to England.

The Crown Prince Ghazi, King Feisal's son, who was proclaimed King of Iraq yesterday at Bagdad, where he was acting as Regent. He was educated at Harrow and is twenty-one.

King Feisal of Iraq, who died at Berne, Switzerland, photographed in London this summer.

King Faisal I of Iraq died of a heart attack while staying in Switzerland on September 8, 1933. Faisal was an Arab nationalist who, even before he became king, worked tirelessly to establish Arab independence from foreign rule in the form of autonomous emirates. He was instrumental in supporting the Allies against the Ottoman Empire during the First World War, working alongside T.E. Lawrence to bring an end to the Caliphate – or Muslim rule – there. He also supported the Allies in taking over Greater Syria and as a result became head of an Arab government in Damascus. Faisal became King of Syria in March 1920, but only a few months later occupying French forces expelled him and he fled to England. There it was decided that establishing a monarchy in the troubled British colony of Iraq might be the best way forward, and Faisal was offered the position, becoming King of Iraq in August 1921. King Faisal died in what some deemed to be mysterious circumstances: though the cause of death was given as a heart attack, he was not yet 50 years old, there was no official autopsy, and the member of hotel staff who found him dead also died the same day. His son Ghazi, who was 20 years old and inexperienced, succeeded him as King of Iraq.

> **'King Faisal died in what some deemed to be mysterious circumstances ... though the cause of death was given as a heart attack'**

March 20
Concentration Camp
The first Nazi concentration camp is opened in Dachau, Germany.

May 2
Nessie Spotted
The first modern sighting of the Loch Ness Monster is reported in a newspaper.

June 23
Hitler's Power
Hitler bans all political parties in Germany except the Nazi Party.

1933

FRENCH LUXURY LINER CATCHES FIRE

On January 5, 1933, the French-owned luxury liner *L'Atlantique*, one of the largest and certainly the most magnificent afloat at the time, caught fire. *L'Atlantique* was relatively new and shamelessly extravagant. When she caught fire, however, she was mercifully empty of passengers, making a trip to Le Havre, France, for maintenance work. The majority of the 200-strong crew were rescued as they jumped from the decks by Dutch, British, and German vessels also in the Channel at the time, but 17 people were killed. More than 24 hours after the liner had caught fire, a bizarre game of chase began. According to international law, if a ship has been abandoned she becomes the property of whoever catches her. Given the immense value of the ship and the goods on board, the company who owned her decided to reinstall their captain to ward off bounty-hunters. So Captain René Schoofs approached the blazing ship in a tug, only to enter into a contest with other European tugs as each tried to capture the ship by throwing lines aboard. Meanwhile, as the ship drifted towards the coast of England, British onlookers waited eagerly to see if she would land there, thus forfeiting a quarter of her value to the British crown. Eventually, two French men climbed aboard and hoisted a French flag, and three days after she first caught fire, the still burning ship was docked in Cherbourg, France. Despite extensive damage, hull and engines alone were still estimated to be worth around $2 million. The French government suspected sabotage, since three other French liners had also been damaged or destroyed in as many years, but although they investigated, their findings were never revealed.

REICHSTAG FIRE IN GERMANY

On February 27, 1933, the Reichstag, the building where the German parliament met, caught fire. A Communist Party leader, Marinus van der Lubbe, confessed under torture to starting the fire, although he denied that it was a Communist plot. Hitler, who had been made Chancellor by President Hindenburg earlier that year, tried to order the immediate hanging of all Communist leaders but was prevented by Hindenburg. However, this threat of a Communist takeover provided Hitler with the justification he needed for taking dictatorial powers. The fire also led to a ban on the German Communist Party; the Social Democratic Party followed soon after, until, by July 14 of the same year, the Nazi Party had become the only legal party. In September 1933, Marinus van der Lubbe was put on trial along with four other suspected Communist plotters. The Leipzig Trial, as it was called, was expected to be a foregone conclusion, but in the event only van der Lubbe was found guilty. He was executed for his part in the Reichstag Fire in January

1934. It is now widely proposed that Hitler's own people started the fire to provide a pretext for the suspension of civil liberties via the Reichstag Fire Decree. Using the Communist Party as a scapegoat also fed popular fears of a Communist takeover and allowed Hitler to crush his most powerful opposition.

July 22
Round-the-World Solo Flight
Wiley Post makes the first solo round-the-world flight in 7 days and 19 hours.

October 10
Sabotage Mid-air
The first proven case of air sabotage occurs when a United Airlines Boeing 247 is destroyed by a bomb.

October 12
Alcatraz Island Used for Imprisonment
Alcatraz is acquired by the United States Department of Justice with plans to use the land for prisons.

October 14
Germany Leaves League
Germany withdraws from the League of Nations.

HITLER BUILDS POWER IN GERMANY

Following a distinguished military career, Paul von Hindenburg was first elected President of Germany in 1925. He was a popular leader who attempted to quell the rise of Hitler's Nazi Party. However, by the time he was re-elected President in 1932, he was advancing in age and proved unable to stand up to Hitler's forceful personality. Though clearly disturbed

'Though clearly disturbed by Hitler's ideas and methods, he thought the safest plan was to keep him close.'

by Hitler's ideas and methods, he thought the safest plan was to keep him close. When he appointed Hitler Chancellor in January 1933, he was as wary as everyone else of a Communist threat and felt he had little choice but to go with the thrust of public opinion. Hindenburg's presence did act as a safeguard to some extent: he was so revered by the German people that Hitler could not entirely over-ride him. But his death in August 1934 removed that safeguard – and by then Hitler had been helped into a unique position of power.

The newspaper clipping reads:

HITLER MAY RULE AS DICTATOR
Fighting in Germany Last Night

Herr Adolf Hitler, the new German Chancellor, receiving the salute from National-Socialist followers. Right: Herr von Papen, Vice-Chancellor.

A studio portrait of Hitler. Right, the new Chancellor surrounded by a surging, cheering crowd as he left his Berlin hotel to go to his official residence after his appointment yesterday.

TWO KILLED AND MANY INJURED AT MUNICH
NAZIS' MARCH

Germany was last night in the grip of wild excitement following the appointment of Adolf Hitler one-time labourer, house-painter and army corporal—as Chancellor.

Communists and Nazis (Hitler's followers) came to blows at Munich, when "Reds" evaded the police and attacked the guard at the Nazi headquarters.

A Communist was killed and several combatants on both sides were wounded.

Fighting also took place in the suburbs of Munich, where a Communist was stabbed to death. Fifty arrests were made.

The streets were filled with cheering and hissing crowds, says Reuter.

Serious trouble is also reported from several towns in Bavaria.

The atmosphere in the capital, says the Central News, is hourly growing more and more reminiscent of the heyday of Kaiserism, though without its glamour.

Great celebrations, including torchlight processions, are planned to mark the victory of the Nationalist movement.

From Doorn it is stated that the ex-Kaiser regards the change of Government as a step in the right direction, but the ex-Crown Prince is described as disappointed at Hitler's changed attitude towards the monarchy.

The entire storm troops of Berlin and the Brandenburg district, together with Steel Helmet detachments, last night marched down the Wilhelmstrasse. Some 15,000 men took part.

Earlier in the day it was stated that the procession was to be in honour of Hitler. But the new Chancellor made it known that he did not desire a personal demonstration. "Let it be in honour of President Hindenburg," he is reported to have said.

As, however, the President's Police and the Chancellor's residence practically face one another in the Wilhelmstrasse, the demonstrators, as they filed past, gave rousing cheers for the new Chancellor as well as the President.

The principal men in the new German Cabinet are:—

Chancellor—HERR HITLER.
Vice-Chancellor—HERR VON PAPEN.
Foreign Minister—BARON VON NEURATH.
Minister of the Interior—DR. FRICK.
Minister for Defence—HERR VON BLOMBERG (formerly Commander of the First Division in Koenigsberg).

This is virtually a Coalition Cabinet, and seems to provide a check on Hitler, although his men hold important key posts.

President's Future

"What is to be the future of President Hindenburg?" is the question being asked.

It is recalled that when, only last November, Hitler demanded the Chancellorship President Hindenburg turned him down, and in the course of the letter sent to the Nazi leader on the President's behalf Dr. Meissner wrote: "The President fears that a Presidential Cabinet led by you would necessarily develop into a party dictatorship with enormous aggravation of the antagonism in the German nation as its sequel."

(Continued on back page)

Left: Adolf Hitler addresses the state funeral of President Paul von Hindenburg in August 1934.

October 15
Modernism Banned
In Germany, modernism in art is suppressed in favor of superficial realism. Approximately 60,000 people in the arts leave Germany between 1933 and 1939.

December 1
Turkey's First Five-Year Plan
Turkey sets out to develop its chemical and textile industries and its banks.

December 5
Beer Legal Again
Prohibition ends in the U.S. and beer is legalized again.

December 26
FM Radio Invented
Edwin Howard Armstrong receives a patent for Wideband Frequency Modulation (FM). This enables much clearer radio broadcasting with less static.

1934

KING ALEXANDER OF YUGOSLAVIA ASSASSINATED IN FRANCE

When King Alexander of Yugoslavia embarked on a state visit to France in October 1934, it looked as if relations between the two countries were back on track. The Franco-Yugoslav alliance, formed after the First World War, was for France a means of navigating relations with Italy and Germany. With the threat that Germany posed to France looming ever closer, the French foreign minister Louis Barthou had made an official visit to Belgrade as a means of reassuring the Yugoslavian King that France's recent support of the Soviet Union would not endanger their relationship, despite the King's severe anti-Communist stance. When King Alexander made a return visit to France, however, he was shot dead while being driven through the streets of Marseille. The assassin was a member of a Bulgarian terrorist group, seeking to annex Macedonia, then part of Yugoslavia, to Bulgaria. It was later claimed that the terrorist group was linked with a fascist Croatian faction supported by Italian dictator Mussolini. During the confusion, French police accidentally shot the French foreign minister Barthou.

BONNIE AND CLYDE SHOT DEAD IN LOUISIANA

On May 20, 1933, the United States Bureau of Investigation had finally gathered enough evidence to issue a warrant for the arrest of Clyde Barrow and Bonnie Parker on the charge of stealing a car. By this time, Barrow and Parker were already suspected of various crimes, including around 13 murders, kidnappings, bank robberies, and numerous car thefts, but the police had found it impossible to pin any evidence on them, let alone catch them. Bonnie Parker had already been married to a convicted murderer when she met Clyde at the age of 19, in 1930. When he was jailed for burglary soon afterwards, she helped him to escape by smuggling a gun into jail. Though Clyde was later caught and returned to jail, when he came out they took up a life of crime together. What made the pair so notorious was the length of time for which they evaded capture. On January 6, 1934, they successfully freed five dangerous criminals from a prison in Texas, as always showering bullets around them and escaping. On April 1, 1934, they shot a further two highway patrolmen dead in Texas, and on May 6 two more. The Bureau finally narrowed their whereabouts down to a remote corner of Ruston, Louisiana, where a known criminal family, the Methvins, lived. On May 23, police from Texas and Louisiana, led by Texas Ranger Frank Hamer, hid in bushes surrounding the house and, when Bonnie and Clyde arrived in a car, shot them instantly.

January 17
Magnificent Diamond Found
The third largest diamond in the world is found in South Africa. It is 726 carats.

May 28
Quintuplets Born
The Dionne Quintuplets, the first quintuplets known to survive their infancy, are born.

June
Women Allowed to Wear Shorts at Wimbledon
Female tennis players at Wimbledon are allowed to wear shorts instead of skirts for the first time.

June 9
Donald Duck Takes to the Silver Screen
Donald Duck makes his debut in *The Wise Little Hen*. The bird is another of Walt Disney's characters.

NAZI UPRISINGS IN AUSTRIA

Engelbert Dollfuss became Chancellor of Austria in 1932, charged with lifting the country out of the Depression, at a time when it had lost much of its manufacturing industry via the territorial losses of the Treaty of Versailles. After a chaotic parliamentary dispute, which saw the President and two Vice-Presidents of the National Council resigning in order to cast votes, Dollfuss suspended parliament altogether. In order to counter the joint but opposing threats of National Socialism in Nazi Germany and Communism in Stalin's Soviet Union, Dollfuss formed the Christian Social Party with himself as dictatorial head, and refused to recognize any other political parties. Having

'Having narrowly escaped an assassination attempt in October 1933 by a disgruntled soldier, Dollfuss was faced with opposition from social democrats within Austria.'

narrowly escaped an assassination attempt in October 1933 by a disgruntled soldier, Dollfuss was faced with opposition from social democrats within Austria which, aided by Nazi agitators, erupted into a brief civil war in February 1934. Dollfuss forced through a new constitution in

May 1934 which did away with the last vestiges of democracy, but on July 25, 1934, he was shot dead by a group of Austrian Nazis. The intention had been a full-scale invasion of Austria by Nazi Germany, but Mussolini threatened war if they went ahead. Although the assassination prompted Nazi uprisings all over Austria, the army remained patriotic and put down insurrections, as well as seizing and executing the Nazi assassins.

Left: The state funeral of Engelbert Dollfuss. His death weakened Austria and opened the way to Hitler's takeover in 1938.

July 2
Hopeful President
Lázaro Cárdenas is elected the new President of Mexico having once been a soldier in the Mexican revolution. He is under pressure to deliver social change.

September 18
U.S.S.R. in League
The U.S.S.R. joins the League of Nations.

September 22
Worst Tragedy in Mining History
On the night shift at Gresford Colliery, Wales, there is a gas explosion that kills 266 people.

1934

ADOLF HITLER MADE FÜHRER OF GERMANY

HITLER NOW MASTER OF GERMANY

Decree an Hour After Death of Hindenburg

SOLDIERS' OATH OF "LOYALTY TO DEATH" TO NEW PRESIDENT

Within an hour of the death of Field-Marshal von Hindenburg, Germany's "Grand Old Man," at Neudeck yesterday, Herr Adolf Hitler, the Chancellor, had assumed both the offices of President and Chancellor.

Thus, an ex-bricklayer and war-time lance-corporal becomes Master of Germany at one swoop.

THE late President is to be given a State funeral next Tuesday at Tannenberg.

New laws decided upon by the Cabinet were issued soon after news of Hindenburg's death reached Berlin.

Orders issued by the Cabinet and broadcast to the nation stated :—

" The office of Reich President is to be united with that of Chancellor. Therefore the powers of the President pass to Herr Hitler, who will appoint his deputy."

In a letter to the Minister of the Interior yesterday Herr Hitler requests that he be referred to only as Leader and Chancellor.

'Holy Oath'

General von Blomberg, the Minister of Defence, issued an order that all soldiers are immediately to take an oath of loyalty to Hitler. The oath is:—

" I swear by God this holy oath that I will give absolute obedience to the leader of the German Reich and people, Adolf Hitler, the supreme head of the Army, and that I will be ready as a brave soldier to lay down my life on his behalf."

THE KING'S SYMPATHY

The King telegraphed to Colonel Oskar von Hindenburg, the dead President's son:—

"I have learned with profound regret of the death of your distinguished father, whose high qualities both as a soldier and statesman will ensure him a most honoured place in the annals of your country.

"I offer you my sincere condolences on the great loss which you have sustained."

By last evening all members of the Reichswehr had taken the oath.

Herr Hitler as President is ex-officio Commander-in-Chief of the Army and Navy.

Thus the man born in Austria of humble parentage, who worked as a builder's labourer, and was a war-time lance-corporal, takes over supreme power at the age of forty-five.

It was stated officially last night that a plebiscite will be held on Sunday, August 19, to confirm the appointment of Herr Hitler as President.

The Reichstag will meet on Monday at noon.

Germany's mourning is described on page 3

President von Hindenburg with Hitler, one-time corporal who now succeeds him.

Chancellor Hitler taking leave of Hindenburg's son at Neudeck after seeing the aged President alive for the last time. See also pages 14 and 15.

The death of President Hindenburg on August 2, 1934 cleared the way for Hitler's assumption of absolute power in Germany. Hitherto, Hindenburg's popularity had kept a check on Hitler's actions, but as soon as he was out of the way, Hitler prepared a referendum asking the German people to vote him in as leader of the country. On the eve of the referendum, Rudolf Hess delivered a speech broadcast to the German people which he opened by declaring, 'It is a challenge to attempt to prove the good of something as obvious as Hitler's assumption of Hindenburg's position,' and ended: 'To you, our Führer, we pledge our loyalty – Adolf Hitler, we believe in you.' In his assumption of Hindenburg's position, Hitler combined the roles of Chancellor and President in one new title, Führer, or absolute ruler. As a result of the overwhelming propaganda, including a forged letter from Hindenburg recommending Hitler, 90% of German voters agreed to Hitler's succession as Führer. The army subsequently swore an oath of allegiance, not to the nation but to Hitler himself, making it in effect Hitler's personal army.

> **'Hitler combined the roles of Chancellor and President in one new title, Führer, or absolute ruler.'**

Right: Hitler's home in the Obersalzberg of the Bavarian Alps, renamed the Berghof in 1935.

December
Monopoly launched
Monopoly is launched by Parker Brothers and proves to be a huge success.

December 5
Turkish Women's Suffrage
Turkish women are granted the right to vote and to be elected.

Cat's Eyes Invented
Englishman Percy Shaw invents 'cat's eyes' – or road reflectors – which are later used on British roads. His patent for them is accepted on October 3, 1935.

First Tape Recorder
German inventor Semi Joseph Begun invents the first tape recorder for broadcasting. This is later used in black box aircraft recorders.

ITALY INVADES ETHIOPIA

During the 1930s, Mussolini's Fascist Italy had been busy establishing colonies in Africa, including Eritrea and what became known as Italian Somaliland. Outbreaks of violence had been erupting throughout the African colonies towards the end of 1934, and Mussolini had reportedly called for 'the total conquest of Ethiopia'. Though the League of Nations made several attempts to prevent war by bargaining with Mussolini and offering Italy various freedoms within Ethiopia, their intervention proved ineffective. Mussolini pressed ahead and continued to send Italian forces to the region, ostensibly to protect Italian colonies from Ethiopian aggression. As soon as Ethiopia began to mobilize its own troops, Mussolini took his chance and invaded on October 3. The troops of Haille Selassie, Emperor of Ethiopia, realized that they were outnumbered and withdrew immediately.

'As soon as Ethiopia began to mobilize its own troops, Mussolini took his chance and invaded on October 3.'

SHIPS OF THE CINQUE PORTS

ITALY'S statement being read by Baron Aloisi (A), the Italian delegate, to the League of Nations Council at Geneva yesterday. Among those listening are M. Laval (B), the French Prime Minister, and Mr. Anthony Eden (C). The statement is that Italy reserved complete freedom of action.

LEAGUE CRISIS

CALAMITY IF WE FAIL

Grave Warning by Mr. Anthony Eden

(Continued from page one)

for the security of her colonies and the safeguarding of her own interests.

He surprised the Council when he gave a strong indication that Signor Mussolini no longer regards the 1928 treaty of friendship with Abyssinia as binding.

Baron Aloisi protested that Italy refuses to be treated on an equal footing with Ethiopia before the League because Ethiopia had violated her obligations as a member of the League.

While this attempt was being made to solve a dispute which has caused anxiety in all parts of the world, Mussolini was sending more troops to East Africa.

Two thousand Blackshirts and forty-five officers sailed from Naples last night.

To Save Mankind

After the opening of the public meeting of the League Council yesterday, Mr. Anthony Eden submitted a long report on the Paris Three-Power negotiations and the offer made to Italy.

The British Minister in solemn tones declared: "Great Britain will exert herself to reach a peaceful settlement. We have all tried to create a new international order which will save mankind from the scourge of war.

"If in the judgment of world opinion the League fails in this dispute, its authority will be seriously shaken and its influence seriously impaired.

"And the collapse of the League and of the new conception of international order for which it stands will be a world calamity.

"I need hardly repeat that there is in this dispute between Italy and Ethiopia no question of any political or economic conflict between the United Kingdom and Italy.

Britain's Only Concern

"The sole concern of his Majesty's Government in this dispute is as a member of the League and a signatory to the Pact of Paris."

M. Laval followed Mr. Eden and assured the Council of the truthful collaboration of France. Baron Aloisi followed with a very strong indictment of Abyssinia.

As, he concluded, it was a question of vital interest for Italy's security and civilisation, the Italian Government would be failing in its most elementary duty if it did not withdraw all its confidence with regard to Ethiopia and if it did not reserve all liberty of action in order to adopt all measures which might become necessary regarding of its colonies

NY AND ANTIQUATED WEAPONS ONLY

NCE OF ETHIOPIA
Y EQUIPPED WITH
LATEST BIG GUNS

ST AN INVADER

ITALY'S HEAVY MIGHT

JUST A MAKESHIFT

1935

GERMANY UNDERTAKES FULL RE-ARMAMENT

GERMANY ARMS: CABINET ACTS
Meeting To-day—Then Commons Statement
WILL SIR JOHN SIMON GO TO BERLIN?
Austria May Follow Lead on Conscription

BY OUR DIPLOMATIC CORRESPONDENT

THROUGHOUT LAST NIGHT EUROPE'S STATESMEN WERE DISCUSSING THE NEW ARMED GERMANY.

WITH conscription and the founding of an army of 500,000, proclaimed by Hitler on Saturday, the Treaty of Versailles had become a scrap of paper. As the statesmen saw before them a new chapter being written in world history they strived to piece together the Security Jig-saw.

And as minister talked with minister a new blow fell. Austria's intention to introduce conscription by autumn at the latest was reported—later "officially" denied—from Vienna.

Britain's attitude towards the week-end's developments will be made known by Sir John Simon in the House of Commons to-day. His pronouncement will follow a day of hurried consultations in London.

The Prime Minister dashed to London yesterday morning from Chequers, and had a long consultation with Mr. Stanley Baldwin, Sir John Simon, Mr. Anthony Eden, the Lord Privy Seal, and Sir Robert Vansittart.

Into the Open

They met again last night. A Cabinet meeting was called for this morning, when Sir John Simon's visit to Berlin next Sunday will be discussed. Geneva was saying last night that it will be his turn to have a cold, but at the moment there is no question of a postponement.

"The German proclamation, in the Government's view, adds to the importance of Sir John Simon's visit because Europe is now fully aware of the German Government's intentions. Unrealities have been shattered. It is Europe's chance to test Germany's sincerity in the open.

Meanwhile in Berlin—where as throughout Germany intense excitement prevails—Dr. Goebbels, Minister of Propaganda, has explained that the conscription law applies to army, navy and air force.

The new peace army will consist of thirty-six divisions split into twelve army corps—400,000 more men than allowed by the "hated" Versailles document. Already a military air force has been decided on—again in defiance of Versailles.

Three-Power Talks

While Hitler, who interrupted his "health" holiday to make the momentous announcement, was returning by air via Munich to his Bavarian mountain home, these were reactions in the capitals:—

PARIS.—London, Paris and Rome should join in protest or take the matter to the League of Nations.

ROME.—"Unrealistic" attitude of the Allies held in some measure responsible.

MOSCOW.—Not surprised.

The French point of view has already been presented to British Ministers in a Note. The need for immediate consultation is emphasised as Germany, having agreed to discussions with Britain, has now taken action which seems to cut away the whole foundation of the hoped-for system of agreements.

On page 5 David Walker describes Germany's Day of Mourning; on the same page our Paris correspondent tells how football was played with the best of good sportsmanship between France and Germany.

MYSTERY TAXI DASH AT HITLER

WHILE in Berlin, without even cabarets or dancing to mark the end of a day of ceremony, all was quiet last night, Munich watched Hitler figure in a drama of mystery and terror.

Thousands of people had gathered to welcome him, says Reuter, at a review of troops. For two hours Storm Troops and plain clothes men had kept the square before his hotel empty of all men and motor-cars.

Just as the Fuehrer re-emerged from his hotel to take up his position for the review a taxi shot into the square.

The crowd gasped. The car jammed on its brakes and, stopping dead just at the spot where Hitler was standing, its doors swung open.

For thirty seconds a terrorised silence ensued.

Then the door was slammed to and two of the Black Bodyguard leaped on to the running boards and escorted the taxi away. The Fuehrer crossed the street with steady step and proceeded to carry out the review.

THE KING'S SHAMROCK

As usual on St. Patrick's Day the King and Queen received many gifts of shamrock, sent to Eastbourne yesterday, from various parts of the country and from Ireland.

EUROPE'S LAND AND AIR FORCES

	Armies (Strength)	Air Forces (First line craft)
Russia	562,000	750
France	560,000	1,700
Italy	510,000	1,507
Germany	500,000	—
Britain	154,000	853

Herr Hitler, between Field-Marshal Von Mackensen (in full-dress uniform) and General Von Blomberg, Minister for Defence, ac... ...inutes as he left the Opera ... great d... many's ... Goering...

Hitler had withdrawn from the League of Nations in 1933 on the basis that if no other country in Europe was prepared to disarm then neither would Germany. On March 16, 1935, Hitler publicly announced that Germany would re-arm, safe in the knowledge that none of the other European powers would risk stopping him. The British, French, and Italians were all intent on safeguarding their own interests. Hitler reintroduced conscription into the German army and held a massive military parade. He then entered into a secret agreement with Britain, supposedly undertaking to limit the size and strength of the German navy. In reality, this agreement acted only as an acceptance that he was re-arming in the first place, and when the French and Italians found out about it they were furious. Thus Hitler succeeded in turning the other European powers against each other and temporarily distracting them from the fact that Germany was undertaking a full re-armament to return her to her former military glory.

> 'Hitler reintroduced conscription into the German army and held a massive military parade.'

February 27
Shirley Temple Wins an Oscar
Shirley Temple becomes the youngest person ever to win an Oscar at seven years old.

March 21
Persia becomes Iran
Persia is officially renamed Iran.

April 14
U.S. Suffers Dust Storms
The most severe in a series of dust storms hits the U.S., dumping tons of dust on western Kansas.

June 1
Drivers Tested
Compulsory driving tests are introduced in the U.K.

HITLER PASSES NUREMBERG LAWS

On September 15, 1935, Hitler passed the Nuremberg Laws, the first acts of racial policy to take effect in the Nazi regime. Their declared purpose was 'for the protection of German blood and German honor'. The laws forbade marriage or sexual relations between Jews and those of German blood. Furthermore, the Nuremberg Laws clarified exactly who counted as a citizen of the German Reich, thereby ridding the Jews of any rights as citizens. The laws were not unexpected, given that Hitler had made clear his determination to preserve the 'purity' of German blood. Violent assaults on Jewish people by the army had by that time become commonplace and were weakening the government's standing among the German public. Hitler had felt it necessary to create a firm anti-Jewish policy, stating the action that would be taken in the future, in order to avoid any accusation of underhand behavior.

'The Nuremberg Laws clarified exactly who counted as a citizen of the German Reich, thereby ridding the Jews of any rights as citizens.'

LAWRENCE OF ARABIA DIES

On May 18, 1935, Mr T.E. Shaw of Dorset, formerly Colonel T.E. Lawrence of the British Army and more popularly known as Lawrence of Arabia, died as the result of a motorcycle accident, at the age of 46. His career in the army had been long and distinguished. His special relationship with the Arabs, whom he helped to gain independence from the Ottoman Empire, was to be romanticized in the 1965 movie *Lawrence of Arabia*, which popularized the vision of Lawrence as heroic freedom fighter. In fact, though Lawrence was instrumental in negotiating with the Arab tribes and helped direct their uprising against their Ottoman rulers, his main role was to ensure that the uprising helped the Allies in their own battle against the Ottoman Empire. In short, he coordinated the insurgency so that it acted as a distraction and diverted Ottoman resources. The Arab revolt was successful and Lawrence was helping to establish an Arab kingdom with its capital in the city of Damascus when French occupation and the death of King Faisal of Iraq put an end to his plans, but he continued to campaign for Arab independence. When he left the army, he enlisted in the R.A.F. as T.E. Shaw. Lord Allenby, who had worked closely with Lawrence during the Palestine Campaign of 1917–18, said of him, 'He was the mainspring of the Arab movement and knew their language, their manners and their mentality.'

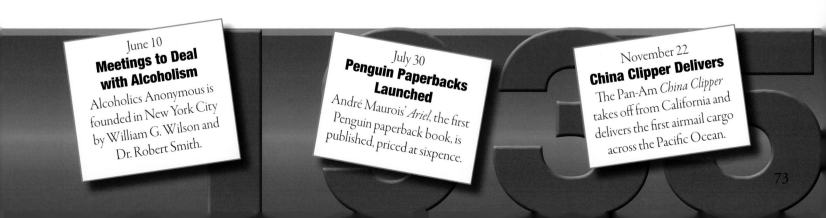

June 10
Meetings to Deal with Alcoholism
Alcoholics Anonymous is founded in New York City by William G. Wilson and Dr. Robert Smith.

July 30
Penguin Paperbacks Launched
André Maurois' *Ariel*, the first Penguin paperback book, is published, priced at sixpence.

November 22
China Clipper Delivers
The Pan-Am *China Clipper* takes off from California and delivers the first airmail cargo across the Pacific Ocean.

1936

BRITISH CARGO SHIP AND ITS MEN KIDNAPPED

SEIZED BRITISH SHIP— THEN APOLOGISED

Repulse Clears Decks for Action in Chase

PURSUED BY TWO BRITISH DE-STROYERS AND THE BATTLE CRUISER REPULSE WITH HER DECKS CLEARED FOR ACTION, THE SPANISH CRUISER, MIGUEL DE CERVANTES, WAS STOPPED AND HER CAPTAIN APOLOGISED LAST NIGHT FOR HAVING BOARDED AND SEIZED A BRITISH MERCHANTMAN.

THE captain of one of the destroyers, H.M.S. Codrington, boarded the cruiser and protested against interference with British shipping outside territorial waters.

While the discussion was going on the Repulse—with Captain J. H. Godfrey in command—steamed past, her crew standing by the guns.

After the apology had been made the ships went on their ways and the master of the seized British merchantman, the Gibel Zerjon (1,535 tons), was told that he could proceed as he thought fit.

PATROL'S ROUND-UP OF OFFICERS AND MEN ASHORE

Prompt action by the British Navy had followed the official reports that the Gibel Zerjon, which plies between Gibraltar and North Africa, had been stopped off Melilla (Spanish Morocco).

Within half an hour H.M.S. Repulse, accompanied by H.M. Flotilla Leader Codrington, were steaming out of Gibraltar.

Many of the officers and men of the Repulse were on shore when orders were given her to leave immediately. Naval patrols, assisted by civil police, "rounded up" those not on board, and told them to report immediately.

H.M. Destroyer Wolsey also sailed from Malaga.

Although the Spanish Government gave a categorical assurance to the British Government this week-end that such incidents would be avoided, it is recognised that instructions on the subject might not have reached the Miguel de Cervantes.

An official protest is likely to be made

Captain J. H. Godfrey.

In Germany, which has not yet made known her reply to the French appeal for non-intervention, the Spanish civil war is still being made the excuse for an elaborate newspaper campaign against Soviet Russia.

BARRACKS BOMBED IN MADRID AIR RAID

A renewed bombardment of the Government positions between San Sebastian and Irun by insurgent warships, an air raid on Madrid, and the gutting of a big petrol depot of Malaga, were features of the civil war over the week-end.

The petrol depot, which was hit by several incendiary bombs dropped by insurgent aircraft in a raid on the city yesterday, is understood to have held a million gallons of spirit.

Insurgent 'planes are said to have bombed heavily districts where the militia barracks are situated in their raid on Madrid.

British cargo steamer Gibel Zerjon.

THE QUEEN MARY IN FOG ON RECORD DASH

WITH a new Atlantic record for the westward crossing within her grasp, the Queen Mary early this morning was driving on through patches of fog.

Before reaching the fog she had touched 30.5 knots, her average speed for the first four days of the crossing being 30.66 knots, as against 29.94 knots averaged by the Normandie.

Speaking by telephone from the Queen Mary, Charles MacArthur, husband of Helen Hayes, told the Daily Mirror New York Correspondent:

"Officers seem optimistic that we shall reach Ambrose Light about midnight local time. This will surpass the Normandie's record by from two to three hours.

"We are planning all-night celebrations. Meanwhile the Union Castle liner Stirling Castle was ahead of schedule on her bid to reduce the England-South Africa voyage by three days.

On August 23, 1936, the Spanish ship *Miguel de Cervantes* seized a British cargo steamer, kidnapping a British merchantman. The incident took place in British territorial waters just off the coast of Morocco, when the Spanish ship stopped the British vessel, *The Gibel Zerjon*. The British ship raised the alarm and British Naval officers both on and off-shore were called up for the rescue mission. First on the scene was the destroyer, H.M.S. *Codrington*. The ship's captain boarded the Spanish vessel, demanding the release of British civilians. Steaming out from its Gibraltar base, H.M.S. *Repulse* was close behind. Commanded by Captain J. H. Godfrey, the decks were cleared and British Naval officers stood by their guns – prepared for the worst. The British government praised the Navy's quick response. The Spanish were quick to apologize, returning the captured merchantmen and their boat immediately. It was thought that the message given by the Spanish Government at the weekend that such incidents should not happen had not reached *Miguel de Cervantes*.

Right: British battlecruiser H.M.S. Repulse.

February 4
Manmade Radioactivity
Radium E. is the first radioactive element to be made synthetically.

February 26
Beetle Launched
Germany launches the VW Beetle, a small four-seater family car.

March 1
Hoover Dam Completed
The construction of the Hoover Dam is completed, creating Lake Mead, the largest reservoir in the world.

KING EDWARD VIII ABDICATES

On January 20, 1936, Edward, Prince of Wales, had become King of the United Kingdom and the British Dominions on the death of his father King George V. By this time, he was already deeply involved in a romantic relationship with Mrs. Wallis Simpson, who was still at the time married to her second husband, Ernest Simpson. King George V had been outraged by his son's relationship and had refused to meet Mrs. Simpson when she stayed at Buckingham Palace. During the course of the year, the King and Mrs. Simpson were photographed together on various outings and holidays. By October, despite

> **'King George V had been outraged by his son's relationship and had refused to meet Mrs Simpson when she stayed at Buckingham Palace.'**

pleas by the British Prime Minster Stanley Baldwin that the King conduct his affair more privately and urge Mrs. Simpson to put off divorcing, the Simpsons had been granted a divorce. A month later, the King told the Prime Minister of his intention to marry Wallis Simpson, even if public and government opposition to her becoming Queen forced him to abdicate. King Edward tried to resolve the issue in various ways, but in the end was told that he must either finish the relationship, lose his government ministers, or abdicate in favor of his brother. This he did in December, and while his brother (the father of Queen Elizabeth II) became King George VI, he became the Duke of Windsor and married Wallis Simpson in France soon afterwards.

March 7
Germans March into Rhineland
German troops march into the Rhineland in defiance of the Treaty of Versailles, which said that the Rhineland should remain a demilitarized area.

March 17–18
Major Floods Hit Pennsylvania
Pennsylvania suffers the worst flooding in its history, known as the 'St. Patrick's Day Flood'.

June 25
New Plane Takes Off
The popular Douglas DC3 airliner makes its first passenger flight for American Airlines.

August 16
Berlin Olympics Ends
The Summer Olympics in Berlin marks the first live television coverage of a sports event.

1936

SPAIN PLUNGES INTO CIVIL WAR

BRITON KILLED, WIFE INJURED WHEN REBELS SHELL YACHT

Destroyer Races to Rescue of Vessel After Bombardment

A BRITON killed and his wife seriously injured when a shell from a rebel warship hit their yacht off the north coast of Spain, and an attack on the United States Consul in Barcelona threatened an international flare-up in the Spanish civil war last night.

Captain Rupert Savile, a former R.A.F. officer, of Fowey, Cornwall, left England with his wife on a health cruise in their yacht, the Blue Shadow, last autumn.

BRITONS MUST LEAVE, OR—

Urgent appeal to all British subjects in Madrid to leave the capital as soon as possible has been issued, following the receipt of a cable from London last night from the British Foreign Office, says Reuter.

The appeal, which has been distributed to all the hundred or so members of the British colony who still remain at their posts, contains these paragraphs:—

"I am willing to be evacuated at once. (Space for signature).

"I do not wish to be evacuated, and hereby absolve his Britannic Majesty's Government of any responsibility for the safety of myself, my wife, family or property in Spain. (Space for signature).

Yesterday as they sailed near Gijon, in North Spain, a shell from the cruiser Almirante Cervera, which has been bombarding the town for several days, hit the yacht.

Captain Savile was killed outright and his wife was wounded in the legs. The yacht, although badly damaged, remained afloat.

First news of the incident reached the British Consul at Bayonne, and H.M.S. destroyer Comet, on its way from Gijon, raced to the scene and picked up Mrs. Savile with her husband's body.

Tried to Escape

The story was told to the Daily Mirror last night by an official of the British Embassy, which moved from Spain to Hendaye, on the Franco-Spanish frontier, last week.

"Captain Savile, with his wife and three members of the crew of the Blue Shadow had put into Gijon after the Blue Shadow had been aground off the harbour on a sandbank.

"Apparently this was to inspect possible damage to the vessel.

"Warned, however, that the Almirante Cervera was approaching and had threatened to bombard the town, it was decided to put out again to sea as quickly as possible in the hope of escaping before the bombing started.

"It seems that as she approached the mouth of the harbour the rebel cruiser, which had been firing at everything entering and leaving the harbour, dropped a shell right on to the yacht, killing Captain Savile and wounding his wife.

Flying Blue Ensign

"The Spanish Government authorities immediately sent a doctor on board, and then the Comet, which was on its way to St. Jean de Luz, took off the dead man and Mrs. Savile and the crew.

"The Blue Shadow was flying the Blue Ensign at the time, but visibility was very poor—about a mile.

"Sir Henry Chilton, the British Ambassador, who was near St. Jean de Lus at the time.

(Continued on back page)

Bicycle Made for Two . . .

. . . new style is this strange craft of the road seen in a Lincolnshire lane.

The Sermon on Wings . . . bare heads and bare backs were prominent among the Rev. Cecil Boulton, curate of

THE KING TRAVELS TO YACHT IN YUGOSLA

FROM OUR SPECIAL CORRESPONDENT
JESENICE, Sunday.

KING Edward reached the Yugoslav frontier this evening at six o'clock more than two hours behind scheduled time, after his journey across Europe.

On arrival at this little frontier station, he was greeted by Prince Paul, Senior Regent of Yugoslavia, and brother-in-law of the Duchess of Kent, and Mr. J. Balfour, British Chargé d'Affaires at Belgrade.

Prince Paul and the King—they were at Oxford together—chatted smilingly.

In the meantime the King's party transferred from the special Austrian train to the luxurious Yugoslav royal train, which had been waiting, with steam up, for several hours for the King's journey to the coast.

On July 17, 1936, rebel groups within the Spanish army rose against the Republican government, instigating a civil war which was to last for the next three years. The war was politically motivated: the Nationalists, as the rebels were termed, had the support of Fascist Italy, Nazi Germany, and Portugal, while the Republic was backed by Communist Russia and Mexico. In this sense, it was seen as a clash of ideologies which prefigured the Second World War. Spain had already undergone years of wrangling between conservatives and reformists, which had led to the abolition of the absolute monarchy. The anti-religious Constitution of 1931 had created much discontent and failed to please either side in the struggle for a church-state balance. The outcome of the civil war was the installation of General Franco as fascist dictator.

> **'Spain had already undergone years of wrangling between conservatives and reformists, which had led to the abolition of the absolute monarchy.'**

Right: A church bombed during the Spanish Civil War.

October 1
Broadcasts Become Regular
The BBC launches the world's first regular television broadcasts.

October 5
Jarrow Crusade
In Tyneside, northern England, 200 unemployed men begin a march demanding help from the government.

November 23
Life Magazine Launched
The first edition of *Life* magazine is published.

Your Voice Recognized
Scientist Homer Dudley at Bell Labs invents the voice-recognition machine, which he calls the 'voice coder' but becomes known as the 'Vocoder.' He later demonstrates his invention at the New York World's Fair in 1939.

36 DIE IN HINDENBURG AIRSHIP DISASTER

After one resoundingly successful year of transporting passengers across the Atlantic in style and luxury, the *Hindenburg* airship burst into flames while waiting to land at Lakehurst, New Jersey, and was entirely consumed by fire within 34 seconds. In the second year of its service, *Hindenburg* flights were proving less popular and so the airship was only half full, with 36 passengers on board. In the days before airplane passenger service between Europe and America, the *Hindenburg* represented the height of sophisticated travel, complete with cocktail lounge, library, and grand piano. The first flight of the year was scheduled to land in New Jersey on the morning of May 6, but stormy weather had delayed it until evening. Friends and family, who had been waiting all day for the passengers to arrive and disembark, looked up at 7.35 p.m. to see the airship burst into flames as its pilot was trying to attach to the mooring mast. The inferno only lasted moments and the entirety of the brief tragedy was broadcast by radio reporter Herbert Morrison, who was eventually too overcome with emotion to speak, as passengers either jumped, fell, or were engulfed by the fire. There were 97 people on board in total and of those, miraculously, 62 managed to survive. The *Hindenburg* disaster put an end to commercial passenger services in airships.

HINDENBURG EXPLODES —NEARLY 100 DEAD

FLAMING WRECK FALLS ON AIRFIELD: CHILDREN VICTIMS

The German airship, Hindenburg, in flight.

ZEPPELIN FACTS

THE Hindenburg was 803ft. long—nearly as long as Britain's crack liner Queen Mary—and as wide as Nelson's Column is high. She was constructed partly from the wreckage of the R 101.

Empty, she weighed 100 tons, 200 when loaded.

Flames on her crash were fed by the 7,062,800 cubic feet of gas in her envelope

She cost £500,000 and took two years to build.

A sister ship, almost a replica of the Hindenburg, is now under construction in Germany. It is to be completed by the end of this year.

From Our Own Correspondent
Lakehurst, New Jersey, Thursday

Hindenburg, biggest airship in the world, exploded and crashed in flames with the loss of 96 lives—eight women and three children among them—as she was about to moor in a thunderstorm here to-day.

Only four people escaped—by jumping from a window—while the rest of the passengers and crew were trapped in the blaze.

BUFFETED BY A GALE AND WITH LIGHTNING FLICKERING AROUND HER, THE HINDENBURG APPROACHED THE AERODROME AND TOSSED HER NOSELINES TO THE GROUND READY TO BE MADE FAST, WHEN THERE WAS A TERRIFIC ROAR.

Flames burst from the stern, the giant ship hovered for a moment, then crashed to the ground from 300ft., shaking the whole neighbourhood. Within a few minutes her steel frame had collapsed into a twist ed mass.

According to ground watchers, passengers were laughing and waving from the observation windows when a bomb-like explosion sent out clouds of red and black billowing smoke. Within a few seconds screams filled the air.

For half her length her girders lay bare while the other half was hidden by clouds of smoke. Flames lighted up the wreckage.

Spectators stood sobbing, many of them hysterical, as army trucks, with screaming sirens, sped to the still blazing wreckage.

The Hindenburg, making her first flight over the Atlantic this season,

Mr. Ira Nelson Morris, Chicago meat packer millionaire, one of the dead passengers.

was carrying thirty-nine passengers in addition to a crew of sixty-one. Captain Max Pruss was in command with Captain Lehmann, acting in an advisory capacity. Among the passengers, most of them Germans or Americans, were:—

Mr. Charles Seymour Higgens, of London.

Mr. J. Grant, assistant manager of the Hamburg-America Line, London.

Colonel Nelson Morris, Chicago meat packer millionaire and former U.S. Minister to Sweden.

Caught like rats in a trap, with the only

exit from the airship barred by flames, not one passenger is believed to have escaped.

Four members of the crew, two of them cabin boys and one a steward, saved themselves by jumping from a window as the airship neared the ground. They are Clifford Osburn, Joseph Spahs, Philip Mungun and Herbert O'Laughlin.

"Flames were leaping round me, and I saw the only thing for it was to jump," said O'Laughlin. "I waited till the ship was ten feet above the ground."

Harry Wellbrook, a member of the ground crew, said:

"We got three bodies from the stern of the ship.

"All were burned beyond recognition, but one, whose features were unrecognisable, was still breathing. The clothing on all three was burned to a cinder and their skin had been scorched off."

A photographer on the spot told me: "I ran towards the ship and saw it enveloped in flames.

"I saw a man walking towards me assisted by two other men. He had no clothes on."

Louis Krantz, another witness, said: "I have seen hell. Hindenburg exploded in the air and

(Continued on back page)

January 23
Trial in Moscow
In Moscow, 17 men go on trial, accused of participating in a plot led by Leon Trotsky to overthrow Joseph Stalin's regime and assassinate its leaders.

April 26
Spain Bombed
Germans bomb Guernica, the ancient capital of the Basques, and then machine gun the streets, killing about a third of the population.

May 27
Golden Gate Bridge Opened
In California, the Golden Gate Bridge is opened to pedestrian traffic.

June 8
Total Eclipse of the Sun
The first total eclipse to exceed 7 minutes in over 800 years takes place.

77

1937

GEORGE VI IS CROWNED KING OF UNITED KINGDOM

May 12, 1937 saw the coronation of the king who had never expected to be king. Christened Albert Frederick Arthur George (the Albert to please his great-grandmother Queen Victoria), the second son of King George V was timid as a child: he was shy by nature and developed a speech impediment which continued to trouble him in adult life, although he eventually overcame it with the support of his wife. Prince Albert had served in the Royal Navy during the First World War and seen action at sea, where he was known simply as Mr. Johnson. Since it was not expected that he would become King of England, Prince Albert was given relative freedom in his choice of a wife, and after a two-year courtship persuaded Lady Elizabeth Bowes-Lyon to marry him. Though the daughter of a Scottish earl, she was considered a 'commoner' in terms of royal marriage. When his brother, King Edward, gave up the throne in order to marry his mistress Wallis Simpson in 1936, Prince Albert had to face the inevitable. It was reluctantly that he took on the mantle of kingship. He called himself King George VI in order to suggest as strongly as possible a straight line between himself and his father King George V, bypassing the unfortunate year leading up to the abdication of his brother. By the time of his coronation, he had two daughters, Elizabeth and Margaret.

'It was reluctantly that he took on the mantle of kingship.'

AMELIA EARHART DISAPPEARS

On July 1, 1937, Amelia Earhart, who on May 20, 1932 had become the first woman to fly across the Atlantic alone, disappeared while flying across the Pacific. Over the course of her career, she had broken various flying records and become an inspiration to countless women. Earhart vanished in her plane *Electra* while attempting for a second time to fly round the world. She was over a month into her journey, which so far had gone smoothly, but when she set off from New Guinea for Howland Island in the Pacific she had embarked on the most challenging part of her trip. With the vast expanse of the Pacific Ocean to cover, a limited amount of fuel, and no sure means of navigation, reaching land safely was always going to be a gamble. On July 1, Earhart, who was flying with co-pilot Fred Noonan, managed to radio in that they knew they were near but could not see the island and were low on fuel. That was the last that was heard of them. It is presumed that the plane went down in the Pacific but no wreckage was ever discovered.

June 29
Snowmobile Invented
Joseph Bombardier is granted the patent for the first snow mobile.

October
Paper Copier
Chester Carlson is granted a patent for his invention of the first photocopier.

November 29
Dial 999 for Help
The emergency 999 telephone service is launched in the U.K.

WAR BETWEEN JAPAN AND CHINA

After years of violent outbreaks and barely disguised hostility, in August 1937 the Second Sino-Japanese War began in earnest when Chinese aircraft bombed Shanghai. The war was the result of decades of Japanese attempts to dominate China in order to secure its vast resources, with Chinese nationalism fanning the flames. The ostensible target of the Chinese bombers was the Japanese warships moored in the Huangpu River, but in the event they misfired and hit surrounding streets crowded with civilians. The bombs killed more than a thousand people within seconds. The Chinese bombers were known to be inexperienced and the massacre of innocents has generally been accepted as accidental. There followed a full-scale evacuation of Shanghai directed by the British consulate. Amid the turmoil, Japanese aircraft launched their own attacks from the air, including loosing machine gun fire on the car of the British Ambassador. The Union Jack flag was spread across the car and would have been plainly visible from the air, but the Japanese denied both the gun fire and subsequently bombing the area around the car, blaming the Chinese. The ambassador was wounded but there were no fatalities in this particular incident.

'The war was the result of decades of Japanese attempts to dominate China in order to secure its vast resources, with Chinese nationalism fanning the flames.'

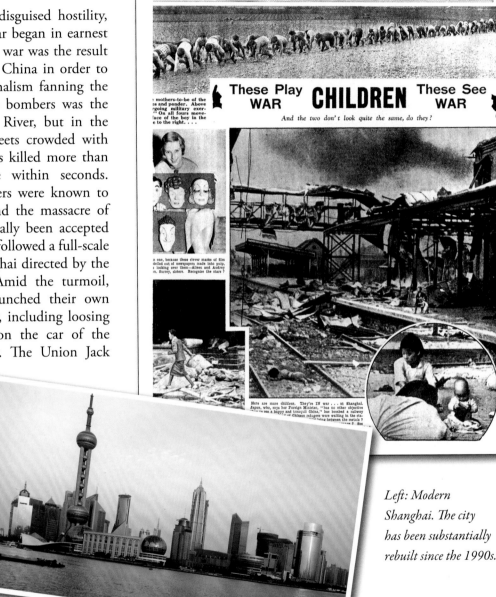

Left: Modern Shanghai. The city has been substantially rebuilt since the 1990s.

December 21
Disney Film Premieres
The first full-length cartoon, *Snow White and the Seven Dwarfs*, is released after three years' hard work for Walt Disney.

Toyota Motor Company Launches in Japan
The Toyota Motor Company is established as an independent company. The founding family name was 'Toyoda,' but to mark the company's beginning and simplify pronunciation the new company is given a different name.

Jet Engine Built
The first jet engine is built by Frank Whittle.

Nylon Invented
Wallace H. Carothers patents nylon – the world's first successful synthetic fiber.

1938

HITLER'S GERMANY ANNEXES AUSTRIA

OUR BRETHREN SHALL BE FREE, SAYS HITLER

"A great nation in the long run will not tolerate the oppression of millions of their brethren.

"The German nation desires peace, but it is ready to defend its existence and its honour. This is not a mere phrase."

HERR Hitler shouted these sentences to the Reichstag in Berlin last night when he told how he had conquered Austria.

That conquest, he claimed, saved the lives of tens of thousands who, because of their treatment of Nazis, did not deserve to live any longer. Nevertheless National Socialism had "magnanimously spared them."

"I took measures designed to spare Austria the fate of Spain. Bloodshed was imminent, so I determined to put an end to further oppression in my homeland.

"How right I was appeared when, three days later, the entire country came to me without a single shot being fired or a single fatality being caused."

If I Had Not Acted—

"Had I not acted then, intervention would have been necessary later."

Hitler then told of the negotiations with Dr. Von Schuschnigg.

"Dr. Schuschnigg did not think I would act. They ought to thank God that I did act."

He said that Austria's plight had been distressful and thundered: "I do not say this because I believe I could impress the self-righteous citizens of the world, for I know that their heart is completely without feeling towards such affairs.

"They can firmly look on while in Spain 500,000 people are butchered without being in the slightest moved thereby.

"And without going red in the face they can hypocritically display profound disgust when in Berlin or Vienna a Jewish provocateur is deprived of his business foundation."

Declaring that the "tragic democracies" failed to understand his action in Austria, Herr Hitler said that "their reaction is incomprehensible and partly insulting."

Pleased with Italy

He paid a tribute to the attitude of Italy, and said that the outcome of the Austrian crisis was confirmation of the "indissoluble friendship of Germany and Italy."

"I felt obliged, in a letter to Signor Mussolini, to explain the reasons for my action and also to assure him that relations between Italy and Germany remain unchanged following the anschluss, Germany recognising the Italian frontiers just as it recognises the French frontiers.

"The land and the frontiers of this friend of ours are inviolable. I repeat now what I have said, that I shall never forget Mussolini's attitude. The Italian nation may know that the entire German nation is behind my word."

Hitler announced that all Germany will vote on the Austrian plebiscite and that a new

(Continued on back page)

POUFF!
See page 3.

CHAMBERLAIN—BY HIMSELF

MR Neville Chamberlain quoted the proverb, "One decrepit camel still bears the burdens of many asses," when last night he was the guest of the Parliamentary Press Gallery.

Referring to the fact that it was his sixty-ninth birthday, he said:—

"All the old know what it is to be young and foolish, but none of the young know what it is to be old and wise.

"I remember that Mr. Gladstone used to say that the politician who entered the House of Commons after he was forty could no more make a success of his career than a lady of the same age who started to be a ballet dancer.

"But I know what is a really incredible thing, and that is that this 'I' this 'ego'—here Mr. Chamberlain pointed to himself—"should be occupying the office which at present I hold."

And by Cripps

Sir Stafford Cripps made a bitter attack on Mr. Neville Chamberlain when speaking at Birmingham—the Premier's native city—last night.

"The puny son of one who could be called courageous—however mistaken his views—has disgraced not only his native city and his country but the whole civilised world as well." he said

£350 FOR GIRL "LEFT LIKE DAMAGED GOODS"

She's Miss Clara Ball, of Ansdell-road, Blackpool, awarded £350 breach-of-promise damages at Manchester, yesterday, against Jack Gledhill Jones, of Lytham St. Annes (Lancs).

Counsel said Jones had left her like "damaged goods in the marriage market." (See story on page 3.)

Lithuanian Submission Reported

Authoritative Polish circles in London informed the Central News last night that Lithuania has accepted Poland's terms.

Normal diplomatic relations between the two countries are to be resumed. An official of the Lithuanian Legation in London told the "Daily Mirror": "We have received no communication regarding Lithuania accepting the ultimatum. Any report would be premature before Parliament meets to-morrow." At the Embassy it was received.

TIME AND THE CRUNDELLS—TO BED ALWAYS AT 7

BY A SPECIAL CORRESPONDENT

SECRET BOMB WARNING AFTER R.A.

AN old lady walked briskly to the scene of an R.A.F. bomber crash in which three men were killed in fog in the beautiful Swyre Valley, near Corfe Castle, Dorset, yesterday, and asked if she could help.

A R.A.F. official asked her to return to the nearby village of Kingston and warn mothers not to let their children play in their favourite haunt—Swyre Wood, overlooking the valley.

Hidden somewhere in the wood is a highly explosive bomb of a new type the R.A.F. is keeping secret, which the 'plane dropped after hitting the tree-tops.

Although police officers and R.A.F. men have combed the wood it has not yet been found.

Mothers called their children indoors, fearing that they might wander into the wood, where the bomb might easily be exploded.

To prevent any unauthorised person getting possession of the bomb an all-night guard patrolled the outskirts of the wood while air-

After several attempts by Austrian Nazis to take over the government under Chancellor Schuschnigg and unite Austria with Germany, the Chancellor eventually submitted to pressure from Adolf Hitler and resigned his post on March 11, 1938. The following day, Nazi troops invaded Austria and declared an Anschluss, or annexation, making Austria a federal state of Germany. Hitler believed that any areas of land inhabited by German-speaking people, such as Austria, should be a part of Germany. Hitler was already using the wounds inflicted on the German people by the 1919 Treaty of Versailles to justify his policy of territorial expansion, and the other European powers were reluctant to intervene in the hope that by leaving him alone they would somehow avoid large-scale conflict. Consequently, Hitler was allowed free rein for too long. None of the other European powers realized that he did not plan to limit his territorial conquest to German-speaking lands before it was too late.

> **'Nazi troops invaded Austria and declared an Anschluss, or annexation, making Austria a federal state of Germany.'**

January 27
Fallen Bridge Over the Falls
Niagara Bridge collapses at Niagara Falls due to an ice jam.

April 1
Coffee Goes Instant
After years of research, Nestlé launches an instant coffee.

June 15
Write with a Biro
The Biro, a ballpoint pen, is patented by László Bíró, a Hungarian journalist.

June 30
Superman Flies into Action
Action Comics publishes the first cartoon featuring Superman, considered to be the first comic-strip superhero.

RADIO BROADCAST OF 'WAR OF THE WORLDS' CAUSES PANIC

On October 30, 1938, for the Halloween episode of American radio network CBS's *Mercury Theater on the Air*, Orson Welles adapted for radio the novel *War of the Worlds* by H.G. Wells. The broadcast reportedly caused widespread panic on the east coast of America. The novel involves Martians invading the suburban streets of England, but it was adapted for radio in the form of news broadcasts which sounded alarmingly real. The action was transported to the streets of Grover's Mill, New Jersey, and produced in such a convincing style, without any commercial breaks, that after the first few minutes, listeners were already calling friends and neighbors to verify its accuracy. This in turn spread misunderstanding and panic, although whether there was any genuine 'mass hysteria', with people fleeing from their homes, has since been called into question.

Above: English writer Herbert George Wells.

MUNICH AGREEMENT ATTEMPTS TO AVERT SUDETENLAND CRISIS

The Munich Agreement, signed in September 1938 by Germany, France, Britain, and Italy, settled Germany's territorial claims to the Sudetenland in Czechoslovakia. The Sudetenland was inhabited largely by Germans who had previously fought for independent status and had never considered themselves a part of Czechoslovakia. It was widely anticipated in Western Europe that Hitler would imminently annex the Sudetenland as he had Austria, and although France had an alliance with Czechoslovakia, the French, like everyone else, wanted to avoid all-out war. The aim of the meeting in Munich, as far as Britain, France, and Italy were concerned, was to avert the crisis by giving Hitler some measure of his demands. Consequently, they agreed to support his annexation of the Sudetenland as long as he promised to leave it at that. Six months later, Hitler invaded the rest of Czechoslovakia from his strategic vantage point.

'It was widely anticipated in Western Europe that Hitler would imminently annex the Sudetenland as he had Austria.'

July 15
RAF Launches Spitfire Aircraft
The Spitfire is brought into service by the U.K.'s R.A.F.

July 18
Which Way?
Aviator Douglas 'Wrong Way' Corrigan takes off from New York heading for California, but lands in Ireland instead.

July 30
Beano Comic Strip
The first edition of the *Beano* is published.

September 27
Queen Launches Largest Ship
R.M.S. *Queen Elizabeth*, the largest transatlantic passenger ship yet built, is launched from John Brown's shipyard on Scotland's Clyde River.

1938

JAPANESE AND SOVIET ARMIES COME TO BLOWS

JAPAN MAKES ARMISTICE WITH RUSSIA AS TROOPS FALL BACK

588 Too Many Shades in Stockings

There are 588 too many shades of stockings, think the Dyers' Federation at Leicester. "Stocking fanatic" Elsie Randolph agrees with them.

The number of shades may be reduced from 600 to twelve standard types because of increased charges for dyeing.

"I'm stocking mad," Miss Randolph told the "Daily Mirror."

"But any woman who wants more than twelve shades is unnecessarily finicky."

Miss D. Rickards, a secretary, of Westbourne Park-road, "an average girl," said: "I use two shades. Few girls wear more than four."

WOMAN 'LOST' IN LUSITANIA COMES HOME

FROM A SPECIAL CORRESPONDENT

WHEN Mrs. Margaret O'Connell landed from an Atlantic liner at Liverpool last night, awaiting her on the quayside was her sister, who had mourned her as dead for twenty-three years—believing she had been drowned when a German submarine sank the Lusitania off the Irish coast on a still May morning in 1915.

Her sister, Mrs. Bird, ran eagerly to her, recognising her from a photograph. Then they went to the home of their mother, Mrs. Spinns, in Whitecote, Bramley.

"Mother, at Last!"

Mrs. O'Connell ran into the house, up to a bedroom where she found a frail, white-haired invalid. Flinging her arms around the old lady's neck, Mrs. O'Connell kissed her crying, "Mother! Mother! At last!"

Snuggling close to her mother, Mrs. O'Connell told me, "To stroke her hair as I

(Continued on back page)

WORLD tension was eased early this morning with the news that an armistice was declared at midnight between Soviet Russia and Japan, whose troops had been engaged for more than a week in pitched battles on the Soviet-Manchukuo frontier.

The armistice, announced in Moscow, came into effect at 4.0 this morning.

Agreement was reached on the basis of Japan's acceptance of the proposal that the Soviets should have representation on a border commission equal to that of Japan and Manchukuo (Japan's puppet State) combined.

Japanese troops had, it was announced yesterday, already been driven off Changkufeng, the strategic height, their occupation of which started hostilities.

The Russian and Japanese troops are to keep the territory as occupied by them yesterday. This is subject to a condition that both sides are to send representatives to arrange details for the cessation of hostilities.

THE TERMS OF THE ARMISTICE REPRESENT A CLIMB-DOWN BY JAPAN, SINCE ALL THE SOVIET CONDITIONS OF PEACE ARE FULFILLED.

Set-Back to Japan

Russia had claimed that Japan was violating her territory by her forceful occupation of the disputed hill. The hill was marked on an official map attached to a treaty with China in 1869. Manchukuo was then Chinese.

This set-back to Japan is the first she received since she began her conquest, three years ago, of China, with the dream of great empire in the Far East.

It is due to Russia's plain statement of continuation of the border battle meant-scale war, and to the fact that Germany, of Japan's partners in the anti-Communist angle, had warned her that she could only "moral support" from Hitler.

Opinion in London, Paris and New York that this check to one of the dictator will have a good effect throughout the The smaller countries—in particular Russia—will rejoice.

And it is plain notice to Japan cannot afford to ignore the vital interest other Powers in China and the Far This is of particular interest to whose huge interests in China have by the Japanese invasion.

(Messages: Daily Mirror, British Press and Reuter.)

Undressed by Car in High Street

THROUGH Sittingbourne's high street yesterday morning a slim brunette, clad only in brief panties, chased madly along the pavement, weeping, crimson with embarrassment.

A moment earlier she had alighted from a car dressed in a blue beach suit.

She had slammed the door of the car. As she did so the driver, a man, drove quickly off.

But the skirt of her dress had become fastened in the door. So as the car moved away, there was a tearing sound . . . and her dress went with the car.

The car went about thirty yards before the driver, hearing her shriek, turned and saw her plight. Then he stopped, flung open the door, pulled her in and sped off . . . with the dress still fluttering like an ensign.

"The whole thing happened very quickly," Mr. Frobert, of Canterbury-road, an eye-witness, told the "Daily Mirror."

"I felt very sorry for the girl—quite young and good-looking

"I saw a man blushing furiously."

ROAD TAX FOR PRAM

BY A SPECIAL CORRESPONDENT

BECAUSE his wife was tired out every time she took their two bonny children for an airing, by pushing the pram up steep hills, Mr. Vernon Mayer, young electrical engineer, of Doxey, near Stafford, got the idea of fitting a small electric motor on one of the wheels.

Mrs. Mayer breathed a sigh of relief, but they reckoned without the Ministry of Transport.

Mrs. Mayer has received a solemn letter from Whitehall stating that if she has a mechanical pram she must:—

PAY AN ANNUAL LICENCE DUTY OF £1 0s.

OBTAIN A DRIVING LICENCE.

INSURE AGAINST THIRD PARTY RISK.

CARRY PLATES BEARING A NUMBER AND REGISTRATION MARK.

TAKE THE PRAM OFF THE PAVEMENT WHEN THE MOTOR IS IN USE, AND FIT TWO BRAKES AND A HOOTER.

Boon to Thousands

Ministry are not insisting on a man before her.

By the beginning of 1938, Japan had taken over vast swathes of China in the course of the Second Sino-Japanese War. Nevertheless, Chinese forces fought on and refused to countenance any peace pact with the Japanese aggressor. The fact that, even while staring defeat in the face, China still seemed no closer to giving in, caused Japan to look elsewhere for a solution to the crisis. Meanwhile, the Russians had been covertly supplying China with fighter planes and sending their own pilots over to aid in the war against Japan. When challenged by Japan, Russia denied any involvement. Russo-Japanese relations were already troubled due to the fact that Japan had yet to finish paying for the Chinese Eastern Railway which they had bought from the Russians, and the Russians had in retaliation refused the Japanese fishing rights in Russian-controlled Siberian waters. Finally, the tension between the two erupted in the Changkufeng Incident in which Japanese forces invaded Soviet territory.

They were repelled and forced to plea for peace in the form of an armistice signed on August 11, 1938.

> 'Meanwhile, the Russians had been covertly supplying China with fighter planes and sending their own pilots over to aid in the war against Japan.'

Left: Chinese soldiers use a dirt embankment as protection from fire during a battle in the Sino-Japanese. War.

November 9
Kristallnacht in Germany
'The night of broken glass' begins in Germany as troops loot and burn Jewish businesses. Around 7,000 businesses and 200 synagogues are destroyed, and about 91 Jews are killed.

December 22
Fish Not So Extinct
A coelacanth fish thought to be extinct is caught off the coast of South Africa.

Oil from Saudi Arabia
The first oil is exported from Saudi Arabia.

Speed for Steam
The steam locomotive *Mallard* sets the world speed record for steam by reaching 126 mph (202 kph) on the London to Newcastle line.

GERMANY INVADES POLAND

In planning Germany's territorial expansion, Hitler made the assumption that, if he headed east towards the Soviet Union, the Western powers would leave him alone. Following his successful takeover of Czechoslovakia, therefore, he moved towards Poland, claming right of access through Poland to East Prussia, which was part of Germany. British Prime Minster Neville Chamberlain, however, had already lost face over the breaking of the Munich Agreement, and he was determined not to appear helpless a second time. As a warning to Hitler that he could not do as he pleased, Chamberlain declared in the House of Commons that Britain would support Poland if the Nazis invaded, and France agreed. When Hitler falsified an invasion of Germany by Polish soldiers, he had his pretext and invaded Poland on September 1, 1939 – the day that the Second World War is held to have begun. On September 3, Britain and France presented a united front and demanded that Hitler withdraw his troops from Poland immediately. Hitler did not consider the demand worthy of a response and continued as planned. British Prime Minister Neville Chamberlain had up until this point been pursuing a policy of appeasement, which involved giving in to Hitler's territorial demands in Eastern Europe in the hope that he would be satisfied. The overriding aim had been to avoid war with Germany at all costs, but the policy of appeasement did not take into account the sheer magnitude of Hitler's ambitions. For Poland, Western intervention came too late, however. The Soviet army had joined the invasion, and old-fashioned Polish cavalry horses had little hope against modern tanks. On September 27, Poland had no choice but to surrender to its invaders.

'[Britain's] aim had been to avoid war ... but the policy of appeasement did not take into account the sheer magnitude of Hitler's ambitions.'

January 1
Gone with the Wind
Starring Vivien Leigh and Clark Gable, the romantic drama *Gone with the Wind* is released and goes on to become a huge success.

January 13
'Black Friday' Fires
One of Australia's worst bushfires kills 71 people as it sweeps over Victoria.

March 3
Seaplane Takes Off
The first seaplane carries passengers across the Atlantic. The Pan American seaplane is named the *Yankee Clipper* by Mrs. Franklin D. Roosevelt.

1939

BRITAIN DECLARES WAR ON GERMANY

At 11.15 a.m. on September 3, 1939, British Prime Minister Neville Chamberlain made a radio broadcast to the nation announcing that Britain was at war with Germany. That same morning, an ultimatum had been issued to Germany stating that, if they did not withdraw their troops from Poland by 11 a.m., Britain would attack Germany in defense of Poland. Mr. Chamberlain reported in his broadcast: 'I have to tell you now that no such undertaking has been received, and that consequently this country is at war with Germany.' King George VI also addressed the nation, saying: 'There may be dark days ahead and war can no longer be confined to the battlefield. But we can only do the right as we see the right and reverently commit our cause to God.' France gave a similar ultimatum to Germany and declared war on the same day. In Britain, a National Service Act was immediately brought into effect requiring all men aged between 18 and 41 to sign up. Mr. Chamberlain's policy of appeasing Hitler was now generally viewed as a mistake – many felt that Britain should have acted earlier to halt Germany's ruthless advance.

SOVIETS INVADE POLAND

On September 17, 1939, Soviet troops invaded Poland, sixteen days after Nazi Germany began its attack on Poland. The path for this invasion started in early 1939, when the Soviet Union tried to join forces with the United Kingdom, France, Poland, and Romania against Nazi German, but Poland and Romania would not agree to let the Soviet troops through their countries. As a result of this failure to agree, the Soviets signed the Molotov-Ribbentrop Pact with Nazi Germany, leading to 1.25 million German soldiers invading an ill-equipped Poland from the west on September 1, and Soviet troops invading Poland from the east on September 17. The Soviets announced that, because Poland had collapsed when the Germans invaded, and Poland could not guarantee the safety of its own citizens, the Soviets were protecting the Ukranians and Belarusians living in eastern Poland. The Soviet Army hugely outnumbered any resistance from Poland. By the end of September, the Polish government had evacuated to Romania, some 60,000 Poles were dead, 200,000 were injured, and 700,000 were prisoners of war. The Soviet government annexed the territory of 76,000 square miles (196,800 square km) they had invaded and, in November, declared that the 12.8 million Polish citizens who lived there were now Soviet citizens. They arrested thousands of Polish people who disagreed, leading to executions. Many more dissidents were sent to camps in Siberia and other remote areas of the U.S.S.R., in deportations from 1939 to 1941.

April 1
Spanish Civil War Ends

The Spanish Civil War ends when the last Republican forces surrender.

June 26
France Ends Public Executions

France holds its last public execution with the guillotining of a murderer.

August
Cooler Cars

The Packard Motor Car Company becomes the first automobile manufacturer to put air conditioners into its cars.

August 23
Hitler and Stalin to be Partners

Hitler and Stalin agree to be partners in 'nonaggression' and not to attack each other.

GERMAN BATTLESHIP LOST IN BATTLE OF THE RIVER PLATE

The German battleship *Admiral Graf Spee*, named after a German hero of the First World War, was tasked at the outset of the war with causing havoc to the British navy. From September 1939, the mission of the *Graf Spee* had been to sink as many Allied merchant ships as possible with the aim of drawing Allied navy ships away from important posts elsewhere. In the space of three months, she had sunk nine ships in the Atlantic. In December 1939, the *Graf Spee* was finally hunted down by Allied forces. Faced with overwhelming odds, the *Graf Spee*'s captain, Hans Langsdorff, ordered the crew to sink their own ship rather than risk lives in a losing battle. Langsdorff himself committed suicide later.

MUSSOLINI'S ITALY OCCUPIES ALBANIA

In his attempt to rival Hitler's acquisition of territory, Italian leader Benito Mussolini occupied Albania on April 7, 1939. The move was intended to demonstrate Italian military strength but was also part of a larger attempt to reassert Italian control in the Balkans. The Albanians were unprepared for such an attack and their army could not compete with Mussolini's. Though they launched a counter-offensive, it was only sufficient to delay the occupation for a couple of days. Once the Italians had bombarded the coast with heavy fire, the occupation was inevitable. King Zog of Albania fled the country with his family.

September 14 — Helicopter Flies
Russian Igor Sikorsky makes the first successful helicopter – his VS-300 helicopter.

Fridges with Freezers
The first fridge with a freezer compartment is launched by the General Electric Company in the U.S.

D.D.T. Invented
D.D.T., the synthetic insecticide for pests such as fleas, mites, ticks, locusts, and caterpillars, is invented.

VE-DAY !

IT'S OVER IN THE WEST

TODAY is VE-Day—the day for which the British people have fought and endured five years, eight months and four days of war.

With unconditional surrender accepted by Germany's last remaining leaders, the war in Europe is over except for the actions of fanatical Nazis in isolated pockets, such as Prague.

The Prime Minister will make an official announcement—in accordance with arrangements between Britain, Russia and the U.S.—at 3 o'clock this afternoon. ALL TODAY AND TO-MORROW ARE PUBLIC HOLIDAYS IN BRITAIN, IN CELEBRATION OF OUR VICTORY.

We also remember and salute with gratitude and pride the men and women who suffered and died to make triumph possible — and the men still battling in the East against another cruel enemy who is still in the field.

War winners broadcast today

You will hear the voices of the King, Field-Marshals Montgomery and Alexander, and General Eisenhower when they broadcast over the B.B.C. Home Service tonight.

After the King's speech, at 9 p.m., and separated from it by the news bulletin, comes "Victory Report," a special programme which will contain the recorded voices of Ike and Monty, and other famous personalities of the war.

Additional features of the B.B.C. Home programme, which will end at 2 a.m. to-morrow, include, at 8 p.m., an address by the Archbishop of Canterbury at a Thanksgiving Service for Victory, and at 8.39 a tribute to the King.

★ VE-SCENE ★
TRAFALGAR SQUARE

It was a high old time in Trafalgar-square last night. Everybody wanted to climb something. This party of Wrens and Allied soldiers celebrated by clambering on to the lions. Army policemen present—like Nelson on his column—turned a blind eye.

London had joy night

"Daily Mirror" Reporter

PICCADILLY CIRCUS, VE-EVE.

THIS is IT—and we are all going nuts! There are thousands of us in Piccadilly-circus. The police say more than 10,000—and that's a conservative estimate.

We are dancing the Conga and the jig and "Knees up, Mother Brown," and we are singing and whistling, and blowing paper trumpets.

The idea is to make a noise. We are. Even above the roar of the motors of low-flying bombers "shooting up" the city.

We are dancing around Eros in the black-out, but there is a glow from a bonfire up Shaftesbury-avenue and a news reel cinema has lit its canopy lights for the first time in getting on for six years.

A huge V sign glares down over Leicester Square. And gangs of girls and soldiers of all the Allied nations are waving rattles and shouting and climbing lamp - posts and swarming over cars that have become bogged down in this struggling, swirling mass of celebrating Londoners.

We have been waiting from two o'clock to celebrate. We went home at six when it seemed that the news of VE-Day would never come, but we are back now.

And on a glorious night we are making the most of it. A paper-hatted throng is trying to pull me out of this telephone box now. I hold the door tight, but the din from Piccadilly Circus is drowning my voice.

It is past midnight. We are still singing. A group of men liberated from German prison camps are yelling—"Roll out the Barrel."

"We sang it when we went to France in 1939 and we sang it as we tried to get out in 1940," they told me. "Now we sing it for victory."

Amid terrific cheers a New Zealand sailor climbed on the bonnet of a bus and from there to the roof.

He stood there swaying above the crowds as the American army swarmed up

◆ Continued on Back Page

1940-1949

The 1940s were dominated by the Second World War and its aftermath. When Prime Minister Neville Chamberlain's failed negotiations with Adolf Hitler forced his resignation, Winston Churchill became the British leader, stamping the war with his 'bulldog' spirit. In 1941, the bombing of Pearl Harbor brought America into the war on the side of the Allies, greatly increasing their chance of victory. After many acts both heroic and horrific, Europe was finally liberated from Nazi terror, and Hitler committed suicide. Subsequently, Germany was occupied by both the Soviets and the Allies, and eventually divided into East and West.

Other nations were also undergoing history-changing experiences. Japan felt the full horror of scientific advance when America dropped the first atomic bombs on two of its cities, causing thousands of deaths and untold suffering for many of the survivors. A short time later, India took its first steps as an independent nation, although the man who had made it possible eventually sacrificed his life for the cause.

In Britain, meanwhile, where post-war rationing made life's pleasures harder to come by, there was the celebration of a royal wedding to lift spirits when Princess Elizabeth married Prince Philip.

1940

FRANCE SURRENDERS TO GERMAN OCCUPATION

PETAIN YIELDS FRANCE—LEADER HERE TO FIGHT ON

GERMAN ATTACK IS REPULSED

AFTER depriving him of his rank, the Bordeaux Government announced last night that General de Gaulle, who broadcast from London a "Fight on" appeal to Frenchmen, would be court-martialled.

"He will be charged with refusing to return to his post and addressing an appeal to French soldiers from foreign territory." It was stated General de Gaulle, Under-Secretary for War in M. Reynaud's Government, who is under fifty, came to London when the French military situation became critical to confer with the British Staff. Rapid developments prevented his return before the fall of the Reynaud Government.

General de Gaulle's appeal—Page Seven.

WHILE the Bordeaux Government were discussing handing over their country to Hitler, French troops smashed a German attack on Fort de l'Ecluse, the "Gibraltar of the Rhone."

FIGHTING NAVALLY, THEY ALSO DROVE THE GERMANS OUT OF THE MOUNTAIN ZONE OF BELLEGARDE.

The Germans captured Bellegarde early on Saturday after an attack by artillery, dive-bombers and fighter planes.

French troops dynamited the railway south of Bellegarde to prevent an attack from the north along the Rhone.

The reorganised French Army of the Jura and the Alps, reinforced by Maginot units, held German motorised units south and east of Lyons and drove back advanced columns north-west of Grenoble with heavy losses.

A French radio commentator stated that the French were not only fighting fiercely, but had even launched counter-attacks.

At All Points

The Eastern Army, fighting in square formation, was maintaining close contact with the South-Eastern Army facing the Italians.

This force had completely stopped Italian attempts to advance. Yesterday's French war communiqué stated:—

"Italian attacks in the Alps continue. We repulsed them at all points."

The German High Command claimed that 500,000 crack soldiers had surrendered in... sur-Lorraine.

"Only a few sections of the Maginot Line are still resisting," said the Nazi communique.

BALLOONS GOT TWO BOMBERS

DURING last week's air raids two bombers were brought down by our balloon barrage in addition to enemy losses already reported, says last night's R.A.F. communique.

R.A.F. aircraft delivered a daylight attack on the enemy occupied aerodrome at Merville, to the west of Lille.

Despite heavy anti-aircraft fire a series of shallow dive attacks was made on hangars as well as on aircraft on the landing ground.

Fighters patrolling over France shot down one Messerschmitt 109, and it is considered that six other enemy aircraft were probably destroyed. One of our fighters is missing.

WINDSORS AT MADRID

The Duke and Duchess of Windsor, with their suite, arrived at Madrid from Barcelona last night.

Sir Samuel Hoare, British Ambassador, called on the Duke of Windsor shortly after his arrival in Madrid.

24 POINTS OF DISHONOUR...

THE TERMS

THESE are Germany's armistice terms which have been accepted by the French Government:—

1.—Immediate cessation of hostilities. French troops already surrounded to lay down arms.

2.—For security of German interests, territory north and west of following line to be occupied: Geneva-Dole, Chalon-sur-Saone, Paray le Monial, Moulins, Bourges, Vierzon, thence to twenty kilometres east of Tours, thence south parallel to Angouleme railway to Mont de Marsan and St Jean de Pied de Port. The areas not yet occupied in this territory to be occupied immediately on conclusion of the armistice convention.

(The territory to be occupied is nearly two-thirds of France, including all the north and the industrial areas, all the north-west and all the west coast.)

"After Hostilities"

3.—... ...pied at.... Germany to have all ri..ts of occupying power, excluding local administration. The French Government to afford all necessary facilities. Germany will reduce to a minimum occupation of western coast after cessation of hostilities with Great Britain. French Government to be free to choose for itself the seat of Government in non-occupied territory or even to transfer it to Paris if desired. In the latter event Germany will allow the necessary facilities for administration from Paris of both occupied and unoccupied territory.

4.—French naval, military and air forces to be demobilised and disarmed within a period to be decided with the exception of troops necessary for maintaining order. Size and armament of the latter to be decided by Germans and Italy respectively. French armed forces in occupied territory to be brought back into unoccupied territory and demobilised. These troops will previously have laid down their arms and material in places where they are at the moment of the armistice.

5.—As a guarantee, Germany may demand surrender in good condition of all artillery, tanks, antitank weapons, service aircraft, infantry armament, tractors and munitions in territory not to be occupied. Germany will decide the extent of these deliveries.

6.—All arms and war material remaining in unoccupied territory which are not left for use of French authorised forces to be put in store under German or Italian control. Manufacturers of new war material in non-occupied territory to stop immediately.

7.—Land and coast defences with armaments etc. in occupied territory to be handed over in good condition. All plans of fortifications, particulars of mines, barrages, etc. to be handed over

8.—French Fleet, except that part left free for safeguard of French interests in the French colonies, shall be collected in ports to be specified, demobilised and disarmed under German or Italian control. Germany declares that it has no intention of making for its own purposes during the war the French Fleet stationed in ports under German control, except those units necessary for coast surveillance and minesweeping (except for that part to be determined) of the Fleet destined for...

This was announced in a broadcast last night by General de Gaulle, who was military chief in the Reynaud Cabinet, and who is rallying French resistance. "On the soil of France herself," he declared, "there is no longer an independent Government capable of upholding the interests of France."

Earlier, it was reported in Cairo that the French forces in Syria would not lay down their arms. General Mittelhauser, Commander of this Army, had announced this resolve, and the Governor-General of Syria broadcast his agreement.

There is a spirit of resistance in the French colonies. Britain would give them all the help necessary for continuing the fight.

Base for Attack

The terms accepted by Petain make nearly two-thirds of France, including all the northern provinces and all the west coast, a huge base for attacks on Britain.

They involve the "recall" and internment of the French Navy, the disarming and demobilisation of the Army, and the surrender of all France's armaments, material resources, naval bases and communications for the enemy's use.

These are terms for an armistice only. When France is helpless Hitler could impose much harsher conditions for peace including all territorial demands.

Furthermore, Mussolini has still to take his share.

The German terms do not come into effect until six hours after an armistice agreement with Italy.

Last night the Italian terms were handed to the French representatives given in a villa outside Rome. Mussolini was not present, and Ciano led his representatives.

The Petain Government met for two hours in Bordeaux.

This was the speech broadcast by General de Gaulle from London.

The armistice accepted by the Bordeaux Government is a capitulation.

"We only saw divide France while she suffers, Mr. Churchill must know that our faith to ourselves has not wavered."

At the end of the speech the Marseillaise was played twice.

"This capitulation was signed before all means of resistance had been exhausted. It delivers into the hands of the enemy, who will (says Associated Press).

Contd. on Back Page, Col. 3

K·L·G
Sparking PLUGS

The margin between Governmental demands for K.L.G. plugs and our maximum output is small; delays in fulfilling private orders are sometimes unavoidable, when they occur—we beg your indulgence.

JUST AS GOOD FOR *your* CAR

K.L.G. SPARKING PLUGS LTD., PUTNEY VALE, LONDON, S.W.15.

Hitler's invasion of Belgium and the Netherlands on May 10, 1940 marked the first major offensive since the Western powers had declared war in September 1939. Now referred to as the Battle of France, this invasion meant that the war had started in earnest after months of uncertainty and hesitation.

Ever since the German invasion of Poland, France and Britain had been waiting to see what would happen next. Although the German Army was worn down after the invasion of Poland and resources were low, Hitler decided that an early attack on France might catch the Allied Powers unawares and allow the Germans a swift victory. The German plan was to advance through the Ardennes, the thickly forested region running through Luxembourg and Belgium that was thought to be impassable, making it look as if Belgium were the main target. The real purpose was to draw Allied forces north toward Belgium in order to surround and isolate them. Belgium and the Netherlands had both declared themselves neutral countries, and were unprepared to counter such an attack, so France reacted as expected and sent forces to their aid. Approaching via the Ardennes enabled German forces to bypass the Maginot line, the lengthy defensive line in which the French put all their faith and hope of safety. The plan was successful, and by the end of June, France had surrendered to German occupation.

> 'The invasion of Belgium meant that the war had started in earnest after months of uncertainty and hesitation.'

May 15
New Fashion Item
Nylons go on sale for the first time in New York stores.

June 4
Churchill's Speech
Winston Churchill tells the House of Commons, 'We shall fight on the beaches, we shall fight on the landing grounds, we shall fight in the fields and in the streets, we shall fight in the hills; we shall never surrender.'

June 10
Norway Surrenders
After two months of desperate resistance, Norway surrenders to German forces.

June 14
Auschwitz Opens
A group of 728 Polish political prisoners from Tarnów become the first residents of the Auschwitz concentration camp.

CHURCHILL TAKES OVER

The German invasions of France and the Netherlands had further consequences in Britain. Prime Minister Neville Chamberlain,

'I have nothing to offer you but blood, toil, tears, and sweat.'

having adopted a policy of appeasement with Hitler in an attempt to avoid war at all costs, now came under attack for his inaction and was forced to resign. It was felt that if the British government had acted earlier, instead of holding back and hoping for the best, Hitler might never have got this far. There were two possible candidates waiting in the wings to replace Chamberlain: Lord Halifax, who refused to take office, and Winston Churchill, who accepted. In his first address as prime minister, Churchill told a packed House of Commons, 'I have nothing to offer you but blood, toil, tears, and sweat.'

June 22
France Surrenders
Charles de Gaulle, the French leader, flees to Britain after France surrenders to Germany.

July–October
Battle of Britain
A major campaign between Britain and Germany is fought entirely by their air forces.

August 20
Churchill Praises R.A.F.
Winston Churchill pays tribute in the House of Commons to the Royal Air Force: 'Never in the field of human conflict was so much owed by so many to so few.'

August 21
Trotsky Assassinated
Russian revolutionary Leon Trotsky is assassinated with an ice axe by a Soviet agent in Mexico.

1940

EVACUATION FROM DUNKIRK

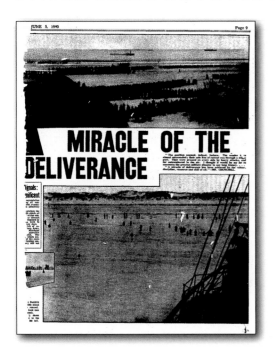

Once German troops had broken through French defensive lines, they cornered British and French troops by forcing them toward the sea at Dunkirk. So it was that in June 1940 an estimated 300,000 men found themselves trapped between the sea and the German Army. In order to prevent their complete annihilation, it was essential to evacuate these troops from the beaches of Dunkirk. However, the water was shallow and no sizeable vessels could get anywhere near the shore. The solution was Operation Dynamo, a mission that involved dispatching around 800 small boats from Britain to rescue soldiers off the beach and deliver them to larger ships waiting farther out at sea. The evacuation operation was completely successful: Winston Churchill called it a 'miracle' that so many had been rescued in such a short time.

Above: British army helmet left on the beach at Dunkirk after the retreat from the Germans.

NAZI ARMY INVADES SOVIET UNION

Despite having signed a non-aggression pact with the U.S.S.R. in 1939, on June 22, 1941, Hitler ordered his troops to invade the country from the south, the west, and the north. The pact had been signed just before Hitler invaded Poland, and for both parties it was a means of securing short-term safety. Nazi Germany and the communist U.S.S.R. could not have been more opposed to each other in terms of ideology, but they both needed security against the Western European powers, so they decided to unite for the time being. The attack, which Hitler boasted on national radio would be the greatest the world had ever seen, took Joseph Stalin completely by surprise. Although Hitler had only 3,000,000 men compared to the Red Army's 9,000,000, German military skill was the more impressive. In Britain, Prime Minister Winston Churchill, who had always been an outspoken opponent of Communism, nevertheless declared: 'The Russian danger is our danger, and the danger of the United States, just as the cause of any Russian fighting for his hearth and home is the cause of free men and free peoples in every quarter of the globe.' Operation Barbarossa, as it was known, lasted for six months, during which time millions were killed on both sides.

September 12
Prehistoric Paintings Discovered
In Lascaux, France, 17,000-year-old cave paintings are discovered by a group of young French hikers. The paintings depict animals and date from the Stone Age.

September 27
Tripartite Pact
Germany, Italy, and Japan sign a pact that forms a military alliance against the Allied Powers.

October 28
Italian Troops Invade Greece
Italy's invasion begins the Balkans Campaign.

November 13
Fantasia Released
The Walt Disney film *Fantasia* is released, but is initially unsuccessful at the box office.

BISMARCK SUNK BY BRITISH

The German ship *Bismarck* had been launched in 1939 and was the pride of the newly rebuilt German fleet. Britain's best hope in the war was her naval superiority, and consequently the Allies were determined to dominate the Atlantic. In May 1941, when the Germans decided to set the *Bismarck* loose in the Atlantic, the German aim was to cause as much damage as possible to the British fleet, and the Allies were determined to catch her.

'All possible resources were targeted at the one aim of capturing the Bismarck.'

All possible resources were targeted at the one aim of capturing the *Bismarck*, and on May 24, two British ships, the *Hood* and the *Prince of Wales*, sighted the *Bismarck* and attacked. There followed a ferocious battle, during which the *Hood* exploded, losing her entire crew of 1,421 men. However, the two British ships had done enough damage between them to cause a fuel leak in the *Bismarck*. She fled toward the coast of France, but, once identified, became a target of Allied guns. The *Bismarck* was eventually sunk under the combined fire of aircraft and warships on May 27, 1941.

January
M&Ms Give Taste of Home
American soldiers are given the candy by the U.S. Army.

February 9
Plea for Arms
Winston Churchill, in a worldwide broadcast, pleads with the U.S. to show its support by sending arms to the British: 'Give us the tools and we will finish the job.'

March 28
Sinatra Makes Film Debut
Frank Sinatra appears in his first film, *Las Vegas Nights*.

April 6
Germany Invades Greece
Nazis occupy Greece. The British forces are evacuated.

1941

JAPANESE ATTACK PEARL HARBOR

On November 17, 1941, the U.S. Ambassador to Japan, radioed a warning to Washington, D.C. He feared that Japan might suddenly and unexpectedly attack the U.S. The aim of such an attack would be to disable the American military presence in the Pacific so that the Japanese could go ahead with their planned invasions of the Malay Peninsula and the Philippines. On November 26, a fleet of six Japanese aircraft carriers headed for Pearl Harbor on the Hawaiian island of Oahu, where the bulk of the U.S. Pacific fleet was stationed. They traveled under strict radio silence and remained completely undetected. Then, on December 2, they received a coded message to carry out the planned attack. Their combined force of 30 ships, 20 submarines, and 360 aircraft hit Pearl Harbor on December 7, 1941. The attack lasted only about three hours, but the Japanese achieved their aim of crippling the U.S. Pacific fleet. They also destroyed most of the aircraft on the Pearl Harbor airfield, making an effective counterattack almost impossible. Around 2,500 American personnel were killed, while the Japanese lost fewer than 100 lives. The day after the attacks, President Franklin D. Roosevelt addressed Congress, which immediately declared that the U.S. was at war with Japan. Two days later, Germany and Italy declared war on the U.S. Thus was America drawn into the Second World War.

U.S. PROMISES TO HELP FEED AND ARM BRITAIN

President Roosevelt persuaded the U.S. government that it should lend aid to Britain. To achieve this he used the comparison of one neighbor lending another a garden hose to put out a fire in his house. The neighbor with the hose, he argued, would not demand the $15 he paid for the hose as payment, but would ask that the hose be returned when the job was finished. With the consent of Congress, F.D.R. signed a 'Lend-Lease' agreement by which the U.S. would loan Britain food and military supplies. Over the next four years, the U.S. lent Britain today's equivalent of $700 billion worth of supplies in food, equipment, and ammunition.

May 1
Citizen Kane
The film *Citizen Kane*, directed by 26-year-old Orson Welles, premieres in New York.

May 9
Secret Code Breakthrough
The German submarine *U-110* is captured by the British Royal Navy. On board is the latest Enigma cryptography machine, which Allied cryptographers later use to break coded German messages.

May 10
Hess Crashes in Scotland
Rudolf Hess, deputy leader of the Nazi Party, crash-lands in Scotland in a Messerschmitt 110, claiming that he wants to meet with King George VI to discuss peace terms.

September 1
Yellow Star Introduced
Jews in Germany are instructed to wear a yellow star with the word *Jude* by the Nazi Party.

1941

SOVIET ARMY HITS BACK AT GERMAN INVASION

Although Stalin received a warning about it from his intelligence services, the German invasion had succeeded in taking the Red Army completely by surprise. The Germans mustered massive numbers of infantry, cavalry, tanks, and aircraft for their three-pronged attack on the U.S.S.R. The Baltic states fell first, and, meeting little resistance, the Germans anticipated a swift victory. Initially, both Stalin and his army were so stunned by the German turnaround that they were paralyzed. But the fact that army officers feared being shot for cowardice if they went on the defensive made them resourceful, and they began to regroup. The Red Army refused to give in, and under Stalin's orders, burned villages to the ground as they retreated, leaving nothing behind for the Germans.

Right: The German military combined tanks, infantry, and aircraft in a tactic known as Blitzkrieg, *or 'lightning war.'*

GERMANS REACH MOSCOW'S OUTER DEFENSES

By the time the Germans approached Moscow, the bitter Russian winter and the torrential rains that turned everything to mud were strongly against them. Tipped off that the Japanese were busy planning an attack on the U.S., Stalin felt free to relocate his most experienced fighters from the Far Eastern borders. When the punishing winter had all but finished off the German Army, the Russians mounted a successful counterattack in December. Although Hitler had at first refused to allow his generals to retreat, on January 15, 1942 he was forced to withdraw. This move marked the first defeat for Hitler since the beginning of his rampage across Europe. However, it was by no means over. By this time, both totalitarian leaders had taken personal command of their armies, and Hitler chose to redirect the attack in the direction of the Caucasus oil fields around Stalingrad. His aim was not only to replenish German supplies, but to use up the last strength of the Red Army, who would rush to defend the oil fields.

October 23
Elephants Might Fly
Walt Disney's *Dumbo* is released and proves to be one of his best cartoons. Its star is a flying elephant with huge ears.

December 4
Women Join War Effort
Churchill calls up women for war service.

December 12
India at War
India declares war on Japan.

Freeze-drying Takes Off
The technique of freeze-drying food is developed commercially during the war years.

1942

BATTLE FOR STALINGRAD RAGES

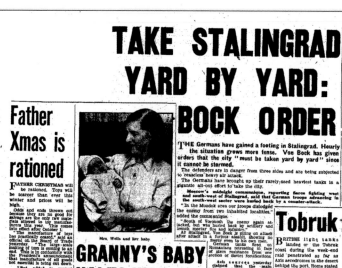

The Battle of Stalingrad, which raged from August 1942 to January 1943, marked the first instance where Hitler's obstinate refusal to give in lost him an entire army. The Sixth Army had been at the forefront of the bid to seize Stalingrad, but the Russians had held firm for three months. By November 19, 1942, the Red Army had succeeded in its plan to encircle the Sixth Army. Hit by this reality just as the harsh Russian winter set in, Commander Friedrich Paulus requested permission to withdraw. Hitler refused and insisted that Paulus should hold firm and fight to the last man. The battle for Stalingrad was fiercely fought

> 'The battle for Stalingrad was fiercely fought on both sides, with hand-to-hand combat in the streets.'

on both sides, with hand-to-hand combat in the streets, but the Russians were determined that the city named after their leader should not be taken. When, on January 31, 1943, Commander Paulus's final 91,000 men were captured by the Russians, he surrendered along with them, a move that infuriated Hitler.

January 1
U.N. Comes into Being
The 'Declaration of United Nations' is signed by 26 Allied Nations in Washington.

January 15
New Leader in India
Mahatma Gandhi appoints Jawaharlal Nehru as his successor.

January 20
Nazis Decide on the 'Final Solution'
Nazis at a conference in Berlin decide that the 'final solution' to the 'Jewish problem' is to move them to camps to die.

JAPAN TAKES SINGAPORE

On February 14, 1942, the island city of Singapore, which had been a British colony since the 19th century, fell into Japanese hands. The battle for the Malay Peninsula had begun in December 1941 – in fact, part of Japan's reason for attacking Pearl Harbor was to handicap U.S. forces and prevent them coming to the aid of Malaya. The battle between the British and the Japanese was fought mainly from the air, and hundreds of civilians were killed in the process. When, on February 8, some 5,000 Japanese soldiers landed in Singapore, the British defenses proved ineffective at withstanding them, and the British general Arthur Percival was forced to surrender. In the process, 62,000 Allied soldiers were taken prisoner, more than half of whom did not survive their captivity. The loss of Singapore meant that Britain no longer held any military position in the east.

Right: British troops surrendering to Japanese soldiers during the fall of Singapore.

ALLIED FORCES WIN VICTORY AT EL ALAMEIN

In 1942, El Alamein, west of Cairo in Egypt, became the focus of the war between the Allies and the German-led 'Axis' powers. The loss of Singapore had done much to weaken British morale, and Prime Minister Winston Churchill was determined that the Allies would win in North Africa. The Afrika Korps, led by German general Erwin Rommel, was aiming for control of the Suez Canal, which would enable them to cut off the major British supply route. Desperate to achieve victory, Churchill sacked his own general, Claude Auchinleck, and replaced him with General Bernard Montgomery ('Monty', as he became known). Helped by the code-breakers at Bletchley Park, Montgomery found out not only Rommel's battle plans, but also his lines of supply, so was able to sabotage them. Despite his consequent shortages, Rommel went ahead and attacked the British at El Alamein, but Montgomery knew that that his rival couldn't hold out long. Monty also had another card to play: Sherman tanks that could wipe out the German Panzer tanks. Partly by outwitting Rommel, and partly by outnumbering the German tanks, the British, Australian, and New Zealand forces under Montgomery managed to crush the Germans and Italians. By November 1942, they were able to declare themselves the victors. The loss of life on both sides was massive: 32,000 Germans and Italians to 13,000 Allies.

June
Gas Chambers
The first mass killing by gas takes place at Auschwitz death camp.

June 7
U.S. Attack on Japan
The U.S. hits Japanese ships poised to attack American carriers at the Pacific island of Midway.

July 14
De Gaulle Renames his Resistance Fighters
General de Gaulle, French leader in exile, states that all the forces resisting his country's occupation will be known as 'Fighting France.'

August 9
Gandhi Arrested
Gandhi and all the other All-India Congress Party leaders are arrested.

1942

BATTLE FOR THE ATLANTIC REACHES CRISIS POINT

Right: An Allied aircraft attacks a German U-boat on the surface of the Atlantic Ocean.

The naval battle for control of the Atlantic lasted for the duration of the war, involving a series of military campaigns rather than a single battle. However, when Winston Churchill coined the phrase 'the Battle of the Atlantic' in 1941, he was referring to the ongoing struggle between German U-boats (submarines) and the British fleet, which reached its height in 1942. German U-boats had been wreaking havoc on the British fleet in the Atlantic since the beginning of the war, seeming to attack any Allied vessel without differentiating between military and non-military. But by 1941, U-boat production had been increased, and they started attacking in 'wolf packs'. Since Britain relied so heavily on imports, the chief aim of the Germans was to cut off supplies and starve Britain out of the war, so their main targets were merchant vessels. Throughout the early part of the war, Britain had focused intelligence efforts on decoding planned German U-boat routes, so British ships were frequently able to evade attack. However, a change in cipher around the time the U.S. entered the war meant that the Allies were failing to anticipate attacks and suffering significant losses as a result. In the winter of 1942–3, the Germans launched a major offensive. When the Americans entered the war, the German U-boats turned their attention to the East Coast of America, causing mayhem within the unprepared U.S. Navy. Even before entering the war, U.S. ships had been escorting Allied convoys carrying supplies, and in early 1942 the German U-boat commander Admiral Karl Dönitz targeted these ships mercilessly, sinking around 88 per month. Now the American ships that had previously been escorting Allied supply vessels were engaged in transporting U.S. troops to Western Europe. Consequently, with a further 480 Allied ships sunk in the second half of 1942, the naval situation had reached crisis point.

> **'German U-boats had been wreaking havoc on the British fleet in the Atlantic asince the beginning of the war.'**

August 22
Brazil at War
Brazil declares war on Germany and Italy.

October 5
Oxfam Founded
Gilbert Murray founds Oxfam, initially named the Oxford Committee for Famine Relief.

October 16
Deadly Cyclone
A cyclone in Bengal (now Bangladesh) kills 40,000 people.

December 2
First Nuclear Chain Reaction
The world's first nuclear reactor is built in Chicago, and Enrico Fermi and a team of scientists achieve the first nuclear chain reaction.

ITALIANS JOIN FORCES WITH THE ALLIES

BIG BATTLE IN ITALY

RAF crew seized Fleet by accident

First to board the Italian fleet after its surrender were the crew of a Wellington reconnaissance plane and they wondered what it was all about!

They knew nothing of the Armistice when they saw the fleet bearing down on their plane, which astonished them as they had landed on the sea. They started to wonder when they noticed that a British plane above the Italian ships was not being fired at.

Picked up by a destroyer and expecting to be treated as prisoners, their astonishment grew when they found the Italian crew lined up in their best uniform and shouting "Bravo, bravo." They were greeted with handshakes and brandy, and only then learned that an Armistice had been signed.

Twin naval bases ours

THE first great battle for Italy is now raging behind the beach-heads which the Allied Fifth Army has established near Naples.

Allied troops are still pouring in, landing from hundred after hundred of invasion barges. Unconfirmed reports say fresh bridgeheads have been made.

A new landing is expected at any moment on the other side of Italy—on both sides of the Northern Adriatic Sea, the backdoor to the German-held cities of North Italy, stated Algiers United Nations radio last night.

The Germans in the Naples area are throwing in everything they have in an all-out effort to hold the Allied thrust, and severe fighting is going on in the hilly country which stretches inland from the coast, reports British United Press.

Stiff Air Resistance

Strong German artillery concentrations have been brought up, as well as formidable air formations, and every Allied advance is stiffly contested.

Allied planes flying hundreds of sorties above the battlefield are doing all they can to keep down the Air attacks on the advancing troops, but ground opposition is still very heavy.

Further down, on the back of Italy's "ankle," Allied troops have taken the great port and naval base of Brindisi after a forty-mile advance overland from its companion port, Taranto.

Both ports are in good working order, making possible an immense and immediate flow of Allied supplies and reinforcements.

All the Italian battle fleet —the largest in Europe after the British Navy—is now in our hands or sunk, except one uncompleted battleship.

Fourteen more Italian submarines and eight destroyers are on their way to Malta, it was officially announced last night.

Four battleships—including

Continued on Back Page

FASCIST CHIEFS FREED BY GERMANS

The Germans in the occupied towns of Italy have freed former Fascist chiefs who were interned after the fall of Mussolini, say reports reaching Chiasso, on the Swiss-Italian frontier.

They are persecuting Socialists, Democrats, Christian Socialists and Liberals who had come to the fore since Badoglio came to power.

ADVERTISER'S ANNOUNCEMENT

Every helping satisfies and sustains!

WELGAR SHREDDED

RUSSIANS IN NOVOROSSISK

RUSSIAN landing parties have battered their way into Novorossisk, vital Black Sea port and German stronghold in the Kuban.

Bitter fighting is still raging in the town.

This was announced in yesterday's German communique, which said:

The enemy who had landed in the western part of the port of Novorossisk were wiped out after bitter fighting.

In the eastern part of the port fighting continues.

In the remainder of the Kuban bridgehead enemy attacks were unsuccessful.

More Soviet advances yesterday were announced in last night's Russian communique, which said:

"West and south-west of Stalino our troops advanced from six to eighteen miles, and occupied over fifty inhabited localities, including the district centre of Stary Kermenchik.

"In the Driluki direction our troops advanced in some sectors from five to twelve miles, and occupied more than seventy inhabited localities, including the town of Gadyach.

"Towards Nezhin we advanced from six to seven miles and occupied more than twenty inhabited localities.

"In the Roslavl direction Soviet forces advanced from four to five miles and occupied more than sixty localities.

"In the Bryansk sector we advanced in some sectors from two and a half to three and three-quarter miles, and occupied more than forty inhabited localities, including several railway stations, one of them twelve miles west of Bryansk.

"South-west of Kharkov advances of from two to two and a half miles were made and several inhabited localities were occupied."

Disorderly Retreat

The Germans are retreating in disorder before the Russian armies pressing them back on to the Dnieper River.

Soviet troops are now within fifteen miles of Nezhin, last rail junction on the road to Kiev.

The gap between Dnepropetrovsk and the Pavlograd area is all that remains to the Germans here for the evacuation of their main forces in the Crimea and the Kuban.

Armoured columns and Cossacks are striking into this gap, and the Germans face another huge disaster.

Infants taught 'give thanks to Hitler'

All German kindergarten schools are teaching infants the following six-line "grace":

"Fold your little hands, bow your little head; think of him who gives us our daily bread. Adolf Hitler is his name. Him we as our saviour claim."

The "grace" was reprinted yesterday in Buenos Aires German language newspapers.

FINNS' TERMS

Finland will never accept unconditional surrender because "no peace is possible without guarantees," said a Finnish Government spokesman yesterday.

Italians offered to fight with us

FULL STORY OF HOW ARMISTICE CAME

So anxious were the Italians for an armistice with the United Nations that Marshal Badoglio promised to go to war against Germany as soon as war broke out in Italy. They sent two envoys with this message. When the first had not returned by the date expected, they sent a second.

This time, to prove their desire for peace was genuine, they released General Carton de Wiart, V.C., from a prison camp to accompany the envoy and take part in the negotiations.

The story of the back-stage moves that led up to the greatest drama of the war was released last night.

Italy's plight was so desperate that the Badoglio Government began making secret overtures almost immediately after the fall of Mussolini on July 25.

It was in the first week in August that British representatives in two neutral countries were approached by Italian diplomats on Badoglio's instructions.

Both explained that the situation in Italy was desperate. The second embassy declared he had been sent to discuss possible armistice negotiations. He was told that the only terms were unconditional surrender. (Details of armistice terms are on page 2.)

In mid-August an Italian general, travelling to Portugal ostensibly on another mission, presented himself, with credentials from Marshal Badoglio, to Sir Samuel Hoare, British Ambassador at Madrid.

The next day he saw Sir Ronald Hugh Campbell, British Ambassador at Lisbon.

"I HAVE COME," THE ITALIAN GENERAL SAID IN EFFECT, "WITH FULL AUTHORITY FROM MARSHAL BADOGLIO TO SAY THAT WHEN THE ALLIES LAND IN ITALY, THE ITALIAN GOVERNMENT ARE PREPARED TO JOIN THEM AGAINST GERMANY."

The British and American Governments considered this serious approach, and at a meeting in Lisbon told the Italian General of the conditions on which they would be prepared to cease hostilities.

These were, first, that Italy must surrender unconditionally, and then accept such

Continued on Back Page

MUSSO. FREED HUNS CLAIM

A special announcement from Hitler's H.Q. last night said:

"GERMAN PARACHUTE TROOPS, MEN OF THE SECURITY FORCES AND WAFFEN S.S. HAVE CARRIED OUT AN ACTION WHICH FREED THE DUCE, WHO HAD BEEN IMPRISONED BY A TRAITOROUS CLIQUE.

"THE DUCE IS AT LIBERTY.

"THE PROPOSED DELIVERY OF THE DUCE BY THE BADOGLIO GOVERNMENT TO THE ANGLO-AMERICANS HAS THUS BEEN PREVENTED."

GERMAN GUN LAW IN ITALY

FIELD-MARSHAL Albert Kesselring, German C-in-C., Southern Italy, has proclaimed martial law in Italian territory under his jurisdiction, according to the German-controlled Italian radio yesterday.

"Organisers of strikes will be shot, and all private correspondence is banned. All crimes against the German armed forces will be dealt with in accordance with German martial law," the decree says.

"The Italian authorities and civil organisations are responsible to me for public order."

The Germans claim they now hold most of the Italian mainland.

"The disarming of the Badoglio army is nearly complete; one of the German...

Two hun...

DANES BLOW UP CITROEN WO...

Saboteurs have blow... big Citroen factory Nyhaven, Denmark, a... stroyed a large crane in N... two goods yard.

Listening to enemy wi... programmes has been bidden by General Hann... who has threatened to ma... illegal to own radio se... his order is obeyed.

The ban on railway tra... was raised yesterday, sta... the German overseas news a... vice.

About 1,200 Danes have be... arrested in Denmark durin... the last fortnight.

Left: The flag of the Italian Navy.

By May 1943, with the German Army halted in North Africa, the balance of power had altered in the Mediterranean and the three-year Italian and German siege of Malta had come to an end. The Axis defeats in the Balkans and North Africa had destroyed Italian confidence in Benito Mussolini as a military leader, and in July 1943 he was successfully ousted by a group of senior military and political figures backed by the king, Victor Emmanuel III. Pietro Badoglio, the new prime minister, then set about extracting Italy from the war and came to a secret agreement with U.S. General Dwight D. Eisenhower, who commanded Allied troops in the Mediterranean. It was announced on September 8, 1943 that the Italians had signed a peace agreement with the Allies, effectively changing sides and therefore committing themselves to the expulsion from Western Europe of their former ally, Germany. Eisenhower went on Algiers radio to announce: 'All Italians who now act to help eject the German aggressor from Italian soil will have the assistance and support of the United Nations.'

> 'Italy signed a peace agreement with the Allies, effectively changing sides and committing to the expulsion of Germany.'

1943

BRITISH INVADE ITALY: GERMANS OCCUPY ROME

Following the British invasion of mainland Italy on September 3, 1943, Germany occupied Rome, allegedly to ensure the safety of the Vatican. Pietro Badoglio, as the new prime minister of Italy, left Rome just before it was occupied by German forces. The Germans acted swiftly as soon as they heard of the Italian surrender, and immediately disarmed the Italian Army. The Germans also sank a fleeing Italian battleship and rescued the deposed Mussolini in order to set him up as leader of a puppet government in Rome. Meanwhile, Badoglio set up temporary government, first in Brindisi and then in Palermo.

Right: Pietro Badoglio

RED ARMY DRIVES THE NAZIS OUT OF SOVIET UNION

Following its surrender at Stalingrad, the German army began to retreat and the Soviets went on the offensive, retaking cities that had been captured by the Nazis. By the time the Germans made their final stand at Kursk, the Red Army had had enough time to prepare, and Stalin's plan to exhaust the German troops by allowing them to do their worst before attacking had been successful. Between them, they had 6,000 tanks, and during the hard-fought battle, each side lost around 2,000 of these tanks. But in the end, the Soviets had superior air forces. Between the summer of 1943 and the spring of 1944, the Red Army fought back with great determination, regaining more cities that had been captured by the Germans. However, progress was slow for both sides, and neither was prepared to give in. As an indication of how closely fought the battle was, the town of Kharkov was taken and retaken four times before the Soviets finally secured it. Eventually, the Red Army succeeded in driving the Nazis out of their country, three years after they had first invaded.

'The town of Kharkov was taken and retaken four times before the Russians finally secured it.'

May 17
R.A.F. Smashes Three Dams
The R.A.F. bombs the Möhne, Sorpe, and Eder dams in the industrial heartland of Germany's Ruhr Valley.

June 1
Passenger Plane Shot Down
A scheduled passenger flight is shot down over the Bay of Biscay by a German Junkers Ju 88. All 17 people on board are killed.

June 1
Frank Sinatra Solo
Frank Sinatra officially starts his solo career when he signs with Columbia Records after leaving Harry James's band. He releases his first hit, *All or Nothing at All*, later that year.

July 25
Mussolini Steps Down
Fascist leader Benito Mussolini resigns as head of the armed forces and the government.

U.S. HALTS JAPANESE ADVANCE IN THE PACIFIC

Between August 1942 and February 1943 the U.S. fought an intense battle for control of the Pacific island of Guadalcanal in a bid to break Japan's naval superiority in the Pacific. It was their first significant campaign since becoming involved in the Second World War. Originally, the agreement between the Allies and the U.S. had been to concentrate first on stopping Germany before addressing the issue of Japanese territorial expansion. However, it was essential for the Allies that they keep supply lines from Australia and New Zealand open, so Japanese domination of the Pacific began to pose a real threat. The island of Guadalcanal was closest to Australia and provided a natural 'camp' from which to conduct Allied offensives in the Pacific. In July 1942, Japanese forces invaded the island, intending to use it as a vantage point in the Pacific. A month later, American forces landed with the intention of recapturing it. During the campaign for control of the island, the Japanese proved weaker on the ground due to the superiority of the U.S. Air Force. However, the Japanese made up for this weakness with their strength at sea, where they showed themselves to be masters of torpedo combat. However, after suffering almost daily bombardment from the air, the Japanese Navy was getting worn down. In the conclusive naval battle in November 1942, the Japanese gave up their attempts to recapture Guadalcanal, and began to evacuate their troops from the island. By February 1943, the Americans were in control of the island.

'It was essential for the Allies to keep supply lines from Australia and New Zealand open.'

Left: The flag of the Japanese Navy.

July 24–August 2
Operation Gomorrah
In a planned joint attack, the British bomb Hamburg by night and the Americans bomb it by day for a full week.

October 13
Italian Reversal
Italy declares war on Germany.

November 28
Big Three Meet
Churchill, Roosevelt, and Stalin meet in Tehran, Iran, to plan the defeat of Germany.

December 3
Radio Audience Along for the Ride
Edward R. Murrow, a newsman for American network C.B.S., tags along with an air crew making a strike on Berlin. The next day he broadcasts his experience on the radio to the American people and the piece becomes known as 'Orchestrated Hell.'

1944

D-DAY: ALLIED FORCES LAND IN NORMANDY

4,000 ships and 11,000 planes take part in attack • German shore guns are quelled—Churchill!

WE HOLD BEACHHEAD

WITHIN a few hours of the mightiest assault in history Allied troops established a beachhead on the Normandy coast yesterday.

Airborne troops are fighting some miles inland. More than 640 naval guns—from 4 to 16 inches—had practically silenced the German coastal batteries. The Allied air force was in absolute control.

All through the day, from the 7 a.m. landings until dusk, Allied fighter-bombers were dive-bombing, glide-bombing and strafing German defences and communications. They flew into the mouths of guns and dived within feet of the bridges.

EISENHOWER HAD 11,000 PLANES FOR THE JOB, AND HIS EXPERTS FORESAW 20,000 SORTIES IN THE DAY.

20,000 SORTIES

CHANNEL ISLAND ATTACK
—German Report

Scaled the Cliffs

Berlin provided the only place-names in the news. They said they were fighting Allied troops on an eighty-mile front between Trouville and Barfleur, on the Cherbourg peninsula.

They spoke of hard fighting around Caen, and of landings in the Seine Bay area.

Tanks, they said, were landed at Aromanches, fifteen miles east of Cherbourg, the start of a great road and rail triangle, leading into a rocky plain.

The Isle of Wight can be seen on a clear day, seventy miles away. In this landing there were 200 boats, and Berlin spoke of:

"THE ENEMY TRYING TO SCALE THE STEEP COAST WITH THE AID OF SPECIAL LADDERS."

Other landings were being made under strong air protection at Ouistreham and Marcouf, and Berlin added: "the landing parties were at once engaged in extremely costly battles."

There is no word at all from the Allied side to support the German statement that we have landed paratroops on Guernsey and Jersey, which lie off the coast.

Hitler's biggest admission was that between Caen and Isigny the Allied tanks had penetrated several miles to the south.

"What a Plan!"

Mr. Churchill gave the House the facts at noon. "This is the first of a series of landings," he emphasised.

BEFORE SUNRISE YESTERDAY AN ARMADA OF 4,000 SHIPS, WITH SEVERAL THOUSAND SMALLER CRAFT, HAD CROSSED THE CHANNEL—WHICH WAS NOT TOO KIND AND SMOOTH.

Mass airborne landings had been successfully effected. The fire of the shore batteries had been largely quelled and landing on the beaches was proceeding.

THE ANGLO-AMERICAN ALLIES ARE (Continued on Back Page)

What the Huns said

The German radio made the first announcement to the world yesterday morning, and throughout the day their military commentators and experts never stopped talking.

"They are coming, they are coming," shouted Captain Sertorius, and Lieutenant-Colonel von Olberg, more dignified, said: "D-Day has dawned—the invasion has begun. There is every indication that the pending Allied invasion must be regarded as of the highest importance which MUST BE TAKEN VERY SERIOUSLY INDEED."

The enemy radio said the invasion began with the landing of airborne troops near the mouth of the Seine and later asserted that the operations extended from Le Havre to Caen and to Cherbourg.

Their early reports said that

"First British prisoner"

Private James Griffith, of Newcastle, was one of the first prisoners to be captured by the Germans, said German radio. He had been fighting in the Caen and Cherbourg region. "The fighting was tough," he said.

German naval forces were in action off the coast and later claimed that a large Allied warship had been set on fire off the northern tip of Normandy. Allied ships were captured.

The Allied fleet was then given an six heavy warships and twenty destroyers.

Le Havre harbour was being bombarded, the Germans announced, and Anglo-American paratroops "baled out on the northern tip of Normandy" to capture several airfield.

As the day went the German submissions increased. Airborne landings were made in great depth and shortly after this was altered to greater depth.

Allied troops, they said, were fighting ten miles inland from the coast.

At least four U.S.A. and British parachute and airborne divisions were in action between Le Havre and Cherbourg.

German air defence forces attacked, it was claimed, and a further statement insisted that many sections of parachute units have been wiped out.

Another report, not quite so certain, said that they were only "partly mauled."

The Germans admitted that the Anglo-American troops fighting at the mouth of the Seine had been reinforced but added hopefully:

"Strong winds and rain showers are hampering the enemy units laden with tanks and troops in particular the smaller ones. They are trying to evade the withering fire of

"FIGHTING ALONG 80 MILES"

Sky troops sweep in

MINEFIELD HAZARDS OVERCOME
(Continued on Back Page)

Right: Beach at St-Laurent-sur-Mer, Normandy, better known as Omaha, one of the five D-Day landing sites.

June 6, 1944, now referred to as D-Day, saw Allied forces land in Normandy in a bid to liberate France from Nazi occupation. These landings marked the start of the Battle of Normandy. Operation Overlord, as it was called, was coordinated by British General Montgomery and U.S. General Eisenhower and involved landing more than 150,000 men on the beaches of northern France while further reinforcements arrived by air. In scale, it was the largest sea-borne assault in history. The sheer numbers involved overwhelmed the German defenses along the coast of France, and as German tanks rolled toward the coast to provide backup, they were attacked by Allied planes. The massive operation also involved a complex web of deception in the run-up to the actual attack. The Allies invented a fake army, complete with rubber and plywood props from a movie studio, to convince German spy planes that the troops would land in Calais. The Allies also used elaborate systems of false information, called misinformation, to deflect the Nazis' attention from the real operation. Even on the day of the attack, the Allies were busy parachuting rubber men into Calais and dropping strips of foil to trick the enemy aircraft radar into picking up a landing in Calais. As a result of all this, when the Germans saw the first Allied ships move toward Normandy, they took this to be diversionary, an attempt to distract their attention away from the real landings in Calais. Within a week, the Allies had succeeded in securing a large section of the French coast and could begin pouring in troops and supplies. Although the overall operation was resoundingly successful, thousands of Allied troops were killed in the process. For example, of the 29 amphibious tanks heading for the beach codenamed Omaha, 27 fell victim to German mines and sank with their crews trapped on board. Thousands more were gunned down as they approached the beaches.

> 'The massive operation also involved a complex web of deception in the run-up to the actual attack.'

January 5
News Travels
The London *Daily Mail* becomes the first transoceanic newspaper.

January 29
Mega-Warship Launched
U.S.S. *Missouri*, the largest warship in the world, is launched.

February 1
D.N.A. Discovered
'Studies on the chemical nature of the substance inducing transformation of pneumococcal types,' a scientific paper written by Oswald Avery, Maclyn McCarty, and Colin MacLeod, is published. In this they explain that genes are made up of D.N.A.

March 10
Female Teachers May Marry
In Britain, the 1944 Education Act lifts the ban on women teachers being married.

1944

GERMAN OCCUPATION OF PARIS ENDS

By mid-August 1944, the French Resistance was closing in on the German occupiers and had begun the battle to liberate Paris from Nazi control. Following a general strike in the city, prompted by the deportation of a further 2,500 French people to Buchenwald concentration camp, the army of the French Resistance called upon the citizens of Paris to mobilize and expel the enemy. Encouraged by rumors that the Allies were close, the Parisians took up arms, constructed barricades, and prepared for a siege. The German occupiers were thrown off-guard and did not have sufficient troops in place. Between August 19 and 24 there was fighting in the streets between the French and Germans, resulting in the death of around 1,000 Resistance members and civilians. On August 25, French troops under General Philippe Leclerc de Hauteclocque entered Paris and delivered an ultimatum to General Dietrich von Choltitz, commander of German occupiers. Leclerc declared: 'I estimate that, from a strictly military point of view, the resistance of German troops in charge of defending Paris cannot be effective anymore. In order to prevent any useless bloodshed, it belongs to you to put an end to all resistance immediately.' Despite Hitler's order not to retreat from Paris before it had been completely destroyed, Choltitz surrendered to the Allies on August 25, 1944. That same day, General Charles de Gaulle, the leader of the Free French who had been living in exile in London since the beginning of the occupation, re-entered his city.

V2 ROCKETS RAIN DOWN ON LONDON

Having failed to destroy Britain from the air and sea, in March 1942 Hitler began to develop plans for long-distance rockets. Thousands of prisoners were set to work building the rockets, and by October 1942 they were ready for mass production. First to be developed was a robot rocket, or pilotless airplane, known as the V1. These weapons, nicknamed 'doodlebugs' and built of plywood and steel, were first launched in June 1944, just before the D-Day landings. However, the long ramps from which they were launched, although hidden in forests, could easily be spotted from the air, making them easy targets for Allied bombs. The Germans therefore switched to mobile ramps and began to fire a steady barrage of V1 rockets at London. Only a small proportion of these hit their target as they were fairly easy to shoot down, so the far more lethal V2 rocket was introduced. This took four minutes to reach its target and carried 2,000 lbs (909 kg) of explosives on board. The V2s could not be detected as the doodlebugs could, so the British counteroffensive tried to make the Germans 'aim' at the wrong place through disinformation. Nonetheless, more than 1,000 V2s were fired on London to devastating effect.

May 30
Monaco Given New Heir
Princess Charlotte of Monaco, with her father's agreement, gives up the throne to her son Rainier on the day before his 21st birthday. She retains the title of Princess of Monaco and goes to live in Paris.

June 1
Colossus II at Work
At Bletchley Park code-breaking facility in England, the Colossus II decryption machine is used for the first time. It is so efficient that the German Navy's Enigma messages can be decoded almost in real time.

July 20
Assassination Attempt on Hitler
Adolf Hitler survives an assassination attempt at the hands of his own officers when a bomb explodes in 'Wolf Lair,' his eastern headquarters.

August 4
Anne Frank Found
A tip from an informer leads the Gestapo to the building in Amsterdam where Anne Frank and her family are in hiding.

1944

U.S. ARMY ENTERS ROME

ROME DEFENCE BASTION IS BREACHED

Rail bombing has 'gummed up' Hun armies in France

THREE months of unparalleled bombing of rail centres to a depth of 100 to 150 miles from the French coast has made it almost impossible for the Germans to switch large quantities of supplies quickly from point to point in France.

An Air Ministry statement last night said that the Germans appear to have abandoned the idea of repairing most of the bombed marshalling yards and have concentrated on repairing only the through lines.

This means that, although the enemy can still bring munitions and weapons straight from Germany to France, it is increasingly difficult for him to switch goods across country.

It has not been possible to repair the locomotive roundhouses, for instance, and even the signalling facilities have often had to be left in their damaged condition.

Since the offensive opened, Bomber Command has attacked thirty-eight key railway points, many of them with such devastating effect that a second attack has not been necessary.

"Our hour of action is at hand"

Mr. Stimson, U.S. Secretary for War, declared yesterday: "The period of decisive action is at hand."

Movement of U.S. troops to the combat areas is rapidly nearing the peak, he told a Press conference.

The U.S. Army has 3,657,000 soldiers deployed throughout the world "strking and preparing to strike victory winning blows by land, sea and air against Germany and Japan."

Declaring that the Royal Navy will have a great part to play in our invasion, Admiral Sir William M. James, Chief of Naval Information at the Admiralty, said in London yesterday:

"We shall have dramatic moments soon. Before long, we shall reach that stage when we begin to launch a great amphibious expedition."

FIFTH Army troops have breached Kesselring's defence zone before Rome. Vital ridges have been captured in the central—Velletri—sector.

A two pronged American assault has now been driven some distance past Velletri itself, and the fall of the town last night appeared imminent.

The battle for the northern hinge of the line, Valmontone, where Allied troops are only a mile from Highway Six, is still raging savagely.

The Germans claimed yesterday the majority of their troops retreating before the Eighth Army along Highway Six toward Rome had now managed to get past the Valmontone bottleneck.

Here the Allied artillery is plastering the road, forcing the enemy to use it only by night.

The German vanguards are now falling back along Highway Six beyond Frosinone, which is in the hands of the Eighth Army.

This retreat is being harried and jammed by air attacks.

One of the most threatening of the Allied thrusts in the centre of the Rome defence line is being made by an armoured spearhead which is seven miles to the west of Velletri.

And Allied infantry got their first sight of Rome, lying twelve miles away, when they captured 2,900ft. Mount Peschio, behind Velletri, and scaled the crest of the long Artemisia Ridge, north of the town.

Mount Peschio was taken by rubber-soled troops in a swift night [...]

U.S. BUILD HUGE "EXPANDING" HOSPITAL FOR D-DAY FIGHTERS

A GREAT U.S. naval base hospital has been set up in England to save the lives of American Bluejackets who may be wounded during the invasion of Europe.

There are over 100 wards, laboratories and operating rooms, and corridors a quarter-mile long.

The normal capacity, 1,000 beds, can be expanded to 1,600 within a few minutes. Forty-five doctors, twelve Hospital Corps officers, 100 naval nurses, 400 hospital orderlies and 185 maintenance men are on duty.

A smooth, simple system, rehearsed many times, provides for meeting wounded men at the doors, diagnosing each case, and sending them to the proper ward within a few minutes.

ADVERTISER'S ANNOUNCEMENT

FRY'S COCOA
and all's well

NATION-WIDE HUNT FOR AERO ENGINES THIEF

COUNTRY-WIDE search is being made for eight new aero-engines, said to be worth £225,000, which were in a six-wheeled lorry stolen outside a garage at Talke, Stoke-on-Trent, Staffs.

Police and Ministry of War Transport officials have searched lanes and minor roads, as well as main trunk routes. Motorists have been questioned.

The lorry had petrol sufficient for a long journey, but it is thought that it was abandoned in some isolated spot, where the thief, instead of finding a sale for the black market, found the aero-engines—not easily disposed of.

Radio 'whoa' stops runaway horse

A runaway horse at Sutterton, near Boston, Lincs, yesterday was stopped—by radio.

The horse, working in a field near the main road, bolted, crashed into a road obstruction, and broke free.

As it galloped down the road, a police car arrived. There was no chance to catch the horse, so the car-driver, Police-Constable Brown, switched on his microphone and shouted, "Whoa!" The horse stopped dead.

Then Police-Constable Brown broadcast soothing words to it, until farm hands took charge.

Blown up, found 22 [...]

A SOLDIER who was blown into the air by the explosion of three boxes of anti-tank grenades during instruction told yesterday how, when he recovered, he found that twenty-two of his comrades—practically all the platoon—had been killed.

Among the dead was the instructing officer, Lieutenant G. B. S. Wilson. Several other men were wounded.

An officer said at the Dymchurch Kent, inquest, yesterday, that there were three possible explanations for the explosion, an Act of God, the heat of the sun, or the head

of a match falling into a box of detonators.

The man who was blown up and survived, Corporal Clarence Oxby, said twenty-five men were on the steps of the sea wall while Lieutenant Wilson was explaining how anti-tank grenades could be ignited by a match.

Lieutenant Wilson struck one match and applied it to a fuse, but the match burned out. He struck a second match and there was a terrific explosion.

Oxby was blown into the air and landed on some concrete.

Three coroners conducting an inquest, returning a verdict of Accidental death.

The killed were: Lieutenant Wilson (28), Hutcherson, near Largs Ayrshire; Herbert Hill (25), Adelphi, Elvington, Dover; Sergeant Robert Kett (25), Sterta-road, Poole; Lance-Corporal John Spring (24), Terrace-street, Islington; Lance-Corporal William Harwood, Gloucester-road, Leicester; Corporal Lansdown (26), Snead Bakery, Walcot, Bath; Private Wilfred Arthur Black [...]

Reminiscent of the final stages of the Tunisian campaign. A column of prisoners, more than 500, being marched to the rear from the Anzio beachhead sector of the Italian front.

The Allies had first landed in Italy in September 1943. After liberating Naples, they had made their way steadily toward Rome, but they had encountered stiff opposition on the journey north. It took them nearly eight months to reach the capital, but by the time they did so, German manpower had been exhausted by fierce battles in the south, and supplies were low. On June 4, 1944, after dropping propaganda leaflets urging Romans to keep off the streets, a division of the U.S. Army marched into Rome. The Germans were already retreating and had left the place largely intact. Thus Rome became the first capital city of the Axis Powers to be liberated by the Allies. As instructed, the citizens of Rome had stayed inside when the changeover took place, but the following day they poured out of their houses to welcome their liberators with open arms.

> **'Rome became the first capital city of the Axis Powers to be liberated by the Allies.'**

Left: Italians take to the streets to celebrate the liberation of Rome.

October 4
Dumbarton Oaks Conference
Allied governments announce plans for a United Nations organization.

November 20
Blackout Ends
London streetlights are back on again as the blackout is lifted.

December 15
Bandleader Missing
Glenn Miller and his plane mysteriously disappear on the way to Paris, giving conspiracy theorists a field day.

December 21
Disney's 'Three Caballeros' Premiered in Mexico City
Commissioned as part of the State Department's 'Good Neighbor Policy', *The Three Caballeros* is Disney's first movie to mix animation and live action.

JAPANESE OCCUPATION OF MANILA IS ENDED

On January 2, 1942, Manila, the capital of the Philippines, had been captured by Japanese forces. American General Douglas MacArthur's decision to withdraw American forces and declare it an 'open city' in the hope that this would keep it safe from Axis bombs had backfired when the Japanese bombed it from the air. During the prolonged Japanese military occupation, the people of Manila had suffered extreme depredation. By the time U.S. forces arrived on January 9, 1945, they were desperate and joined in fighting on the streets. But the Japanese were determined not to lose Manila, and their retreat wrought immense destruction and loss of life. The battle for control of Manila lasted from February 4 to March 3, 1945, and ended in the walled city of Itramuros, where the ruthless fighting in the streets resulted in a horrific number of civilian deaths. Around 100,000 Filipinos are thought to have died during the battle for liberation of the city.

MUSSOLINI EXECUTED

Following the Allied invasion of southern Italy in July 1943 and the subsequent ousting of the Fascist leader Benito Mussolini, the Italians switched sides to join the Allies. However, Mussolini was rescued from captivity by the Germans and made head of the Italian Socialist Republic in Nazi-occupied northern Italy. On April 28, 1945, he was arrested by members of the Italian resistance at Lake Como. The partisans, who were becoming increasingly violent in their underground fight against Nazi occupiers, had spotted him as he attempted to travel to Switzerland. When he realized that they were going to kill him, Mussolini asked to be shot in the chest, but the first two guns failed to fire. Only the third succeeded in killing him, along with his mistress, Clara Petacci. The next day their bodies were hung upside down in a public square in Milan, where they were mutilated by the enraged people.

January 12
Turkey's Channels Open

Turkey opens its straits to Allied shipping, and a month later declares war on Germany.

January 27
Red Army Reaches Auschwitz

Arriving in southern Poland, the Red Army discovers the Nazi concentration camp at Auschwitz, where estimates of the numbers murdered, range from 1 to 3 million.

February 4
Big Three in Conference

The Allied leaders Churchill, Roosevelt, and Stalin meet at Yalta in Ukraine to decide what will happen when the war ends.

February 24
Ahmed Maher Pasha Assassinated

Egypt's Prime Minister Ahmed Maher Pasha is shot dead after reading his country's declaration of war on Germany and Japan.

1945

HITLER COMMITS SUICIDE

By early 1945, it was clear that the Nazis had lost the war. The Russians had entered Berlin, and the German garrison could no longer hold out. Hearing that Mussolini had been executed, Hitler was determined not to suffer the same fate. He retreated to his Führerbunker in central Berlin in January 1945, and there married his mistress, Eva Braun, on April 29. It is believed that on the following day Hitler heard that the Russians had almost reached his bunker, and, after eating lunch, went with his wife into his study – where a shot was heard. When Hitler's valet went in moments later, he found the Führer dead by a single shot through the temple, with the new Frau Hitler also dead by his side, probably from cyanide poisoning. The valet took the bodies outside to burn, but as the Russians had begun to bomb the bunker, he was forced to abandon the hasty cremation. What happened to the bodies thereafter was unknown for a long time, which has caused much speculation as to the truth of Hitler's death. Following the opening of Russian state files, it has now emerged that the charred corpses, along with those of Joseph Goebbels and his family, were buried in a secret unmarked grave. When the whereabouts of the grave became public knowledge in the 1970s, the Russian secret service wanted to avoid the possibility of the site becoming the focus of neo-Nazi attention, so they dug up the bodies, burned them, and scattered the ashes in the Elbe River.

VICTORY IN EUROPE DECLARED AS NAZI GERMANY SURRENDERS

On May 8, 1945, it was announced that Nazi Germany had been defeated, so the Allies declared that date VE-Day to celebrate victory in Europe. Since April 1945, the Allies had been advancing on Germany from the west while the Russians advanced from the east. With their army in tatters and their Führer dead, the new leaders of Germany were forced to offer an unconditional surrender, which was signed by German General Alfred Jodl in the presence of American General Dwight D. Eisenhower at his headquarters in France. In London, King George VI and his wife appeared on the balcony of Buckingham Palace, along with Prime Minister Winston Churchill, to salute the cheering multitude, while their daughters, Princesses Elizabeth and Margaret, mingled with the celebrating crowds in the streets. VE-Day had originally been scheduled for May 9, but news of the German surrender was leaked immediately, and there was no stopping the spontaneous celebration that took to the streets, so it was brought forward a day.

'There was no stopping the spontaneous celebration that took to the streets.'

Above: Winston Churchill joins the Royal Family on the balcony at Buckingham Palace.

March
Anne Frank Dies
At 15 years old, Anne Frank dies of typhus in the Bergen-Belsen concentration camp in Germany.

April 12
President Roosevelt Dies
Following the death of Franklin D. Roosevelt, Harry S. Truman is sworn in as U.S. president.

July 16
The Trinity Test
The first atomic bomb is detonated near Alamogordo, New Mexico.

July 28
Empire State Building Hit by Bomber
The Empire State building, the world's tallest, is accidentally hit at floors 78–79 by a B-25 bomber.

August 14
'Things Go Better with Coke'
'Coke' was not the intended name for this popular fizzy drink as the company was afraid that the nickname would make it a generic product. But people kept asking for 'Coke', so in 1945 'Coke' was registered as a trademark.

ATOMIC BOMB DEVASTATES HIROSHIMA

On August 6, an American B-29 bomber called *Enola Gay* set off for the city of Hiroshima on Honshu Island in Japan. On arrival, at 8.15 a.m., the plane dropped an atomic bomb codenamed 'Little Boy'. The bomb exploded in the air above Hiroshima, causing mass destruction within moments. An estimated 80,000 people were killed immediately, the majority of them civilians. Within six months, injury and radiation had brought the death toll to 90,000–140,000. The survivors, and their children who were exposed to radiation in the womb, suffered an increased incidence of cancer, leukemia, and certain non-cancer diseases throughout their lives. U.S. President Harry Truman had made the decision to drop the bomb as a means of stopping the war in the Pacific by forcing Japan to surrender. Truman had previously urged the Japanese to surrender several times. He felt that his only remaining option was a display of American military power that would convince the Japanese they had lost. After he had dropped the bomb, the copilot of the *Enola Gay* wrote in his log, 'My God, what have we done?'

Left: Part of a preserved building hit by the A-bomb in Hiroshima, Japan.

JAPAN SURRENDERS

In the immediate aftermath of the Hiroshima bomb, there was no Japanese surrender. The Americans therefore decided to bomb a second city – Kokura. On the appointed day, it was hidden by clouds, so the Americans bombed their second choice, Nagasaki, instead. Codenamed 'Fat Man', the bomb was dropped on August 9, 1945. Estimates for immediate civilian deaths range from 40,000 to 75,000. On August 15, Japan surrendered to the Allied Powers. In doing so, Emperor Hirohito imposed one condition – that the monarchy should not be abolished. The Americans agreed to this condition, and Hirohito announced Japan's surrender in a radio address to the nation, acknowledging the new deadly era of atomic warfare embarked on by the Americans: 'The enemy now possesses a new and terrible weapon with the power to destroy many innocent lives and do incalculable damage. Should we continue to fight, not only would it result in an ultimate collapse and obliteration of the Japanese nation, but it would also lead to the total extinction of human civilization.' Days later, U.S. forces occupied Japan.

September 8
Japanese Prime Minister Attempts Suicide
Hideki Tojo, Japan's prime minister during most of the Second World War, attempts suicide before facing a war crimes tribunal.

October
United Nations Established
The United Nations, designed to maintain world peace, is established in New York.

October 21
French Women's Suffrage
Women in France are allowed to vote for the first time.

October
Penicillin Wins Prize
The Nobel Prize for medicine is awarded to Alexander Fleming, Howard Florey, and Ernst Chain for discovering penicillin.

1946

UNITED NATIONS MEETS FOR FIRST TIME

The first session of the United Nations General Assembly was convened on January 10, 1946 at Central Hall in Westminster, London, with representatives from 51 nations in attendance. The Inter-Allied Declaration, signed in London on June 12, 1941, had put the first building blocks in place for the creation of the United Nations by pledging to 'work together, with other free peoples, both in war and in peace'. On January 1, 1942, while the Second World War raged around them, representatives from 26 countries had met in Washington, D.C. to sign the 'Declaration by United Nations', a title suggested by President F.D. Roosevelt. At various conferences that followed during 1944 and 1945, the great powers of the United States, the United Kingdom, the U.S.S.R., and China worked out the structure and organization of the United Nations. On October 24, 1945, the United Nations officially came into existence with the signing of its charter. The elected president of the first session was the Belgian Paul-Henri Spaak, a socialist politician.

> 'The first session of the United Nations General Assembly was convened on January 10, 1946.'

Above: The United Nations building, New York.

January 10
Project Diana a Success
In Project Diana, the U.S. Army Signal Corps aims radar waves at the Moon, which reflect off and bounce back to Earth. This proves that communication is possible between Earth and space, and marks the birth of the U.S. space program.

February 14
Meet ENIAC!
The Electrical Numerical Integrator and Calculator (ENIAC) is the first general-purpose computer. It fills an entire room and weighs around 30 tons.

March 5
Iron Curtain Speech
In a speech at Fulton, Missouri, Winston Churchill talks about the 'Iron Curtain,' warning that the West is now threatened by the Soviet Union.

April 10
Japanese Women Vote
Women in Japan vote for the first time in parliamentary elections.

JUDGMENT AT NUREMBERG

From November 14, 1945 to October 1, 1946, 22 prominent Nazi leaders stood trial as war criminals in Nuremberg, Germany – chosen as a location because its Palace of Justice had been left unscathed by the war and housed a prison on site. It was also considered to be the birthplace of the Nazi Party and therefore a fitting place to dissolve that party once and for all. Those accused of major war crimes were tried by the International Military Tribunal, made up of American, British, Soviet, and French judges and prosecutors. Twelve of the 22 men were sentenced to death, including Hermann Goering, Alfred Rosenberg, and Joachim von Ribbentrop, and were subsequently hanged on October 16, 1946. Goering, however, committed suicide the night before he was due to be executed. The rest of the men were incarcerated in Spandau Prison, Berlin. Aside from bringing individuals to justice, the Nuremberg Trials helped shape future human rights policies in a significant way by defining codes of acceptable behavior and practice in war. Many of those prosecuted expressed repentance at what they had done, some even going so far as to welcome the trials as necessary. For example, Albert Speer, Hitler's personal architect and minister of wartime production, stated that, 'There is a shared responsibility for such horrible crimes, even in an authoritarian state.'

May 7
Start of Great Things
With no machinery and little scientific equipment, engineer Masaru Ibuka and physicist Akio Morita found Tokyo Telecommunications Engineering Corporation, a company set up to repair and build electrical equipment. Now named Sony, it is a global success.

June 2
Women Win Vote in Italy
Italian women are granted the right to vote in elections.

June 4
Juan Perón Elected President
Juan Perón is elected president of Argentina. He and his wife Eva (Evita) are very popular with the Argentinian people.

1946

NATIONAL HEALTH SERVICE FOR U.K.

Prior to the National Health Service Act of 1946, anyone who received medical treatment in the U.K. had to pay for it. Although it had been common practice for doctors to charge wealthy patients more and use the extra profit to subsidize poorer patients, medical care was generally paid for by private health insurance, leaving the poor to resort to charity where they could. British Prime Minister David Lloyd George had been instrumental in setting up a National Insurance scheme in 1911, which required every working person to pay a monetary contribution that was then added to by employers and the government. This National Insurance provided payouts for medical treatment, as well as unemployment and retirement, forming the backbone of the National Health Service. However, the scheme was not applied nationwide, nor was it evenly distributed across various trades and professions. After the Second World War, Clement Attlee's Labour government, acting on the recommendations of the 1942 Beveridge Report entitled 'Social Insurance', formed a National Health Service that was funded by general taxation, offering free medical treatment to all.

Left: British Minister of Health Aneurin Bevan who founded the National Health Service.

CIVIL WAR IN GREECE

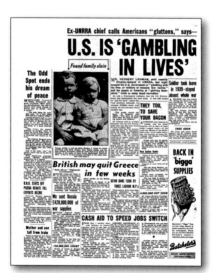

The German occupation of Greece lasted from 1942 to 1944. During this time, the hole created by the absence of the exiled Greek government left room for various resistance groups to gain supporters. The most powerful of these groups was the Communist-led National Liberation Front. Though there were clashes between resistance groups during the occupation, after Greece was liberated in 1944 the groups united against the British-backed Greek government. The National Liberation Front had the backing of Communist states, including Albania, Yugoslavia, Bulgaria, and the U.S.S.R., and formed a united Democratic Army of Greece to oust the Western-backed government. In December 1944, after the Nazis had left, King George II returned to Athens, but elections to reinstate the patriotic party loyal to the king were boycotted by resistance groups. There followed a period of civil war during which the British government helped the Greek government defeat E.L.A.S., the military arm of the National Liberation Front. The Greek Communist Party (K.K.A.) then took over the work of resistance, but the collapse of relations between the U.S.S.R. and Yugoslavia meant they did not have the Communist backing they had been relying on, and by 1948, they too had been defeated.

July 1
U.S. Sends Care Parcels
Parcels of food and supplies are sent to Europe from the U.S.

July 5
Bikini Finds Fame
The bikini, popularized by French car designer Louis Réard, hits the headlines when French dancer Micheline Bernardini models it in Paris.

October 23
Dodgers Sign Jackie Robinson
Jackie Robinson becomes the first African American to sign a contract with a major baseball club, the Dodgers.

December 11
Help for the Children
After the Second World War, the United Nations International Children's Emergency Fund (UNICEF) organization is set up to help children living in countries devastated by war.

INDIA WINS INDEPENDENCE

On August 15, 1947, India finally gained independence from British rule. Although this marked the end of a long struggle for freedom, India's problems were not over. The antagonism had not been exclusively between Indians and their British rulers: it also existed between the Hindus and Muslims within India. In an attempt to resolve the disagreements between Muslims and Hindus at the point of handover, the Asian subcontinent was divided up into Hindu-dominated India and a newly formed Muslim state called Pakistan. This division was to heighten religious tensions between the Muslims and Hindus. At the time of Partition, when lines were drawn between India and Pakistan, much of the tension was focused around the Punjab region, which was divided in two. Thousands of people were dislocated – finding themselves Hindus in Pakistan or Muslims in India – and there was mass migration. Violent unrest over the new arrangements led to severe rioting in the streets, resulting in around 50,000 deaths. After the British departure, Rajendra Prasad became the first President of India, with Jawaharlal Nehru taking office as his Prime Minister. Pakistan became a new member of the United Nations. The union formed from the combination of the Hindu states assumed the name India, which automatically gave it the U.N. seat previously held by British India.

1947

PRINCESS ELIZABETH MARRIES PHILIP MOUNTBATTEN

Millions will hear the Princess say "I will"

"Daily Mirror" Radio Correspondent

WHEN Princess Elizabeth says "I will" at the High Altar of Westminster Abbey this morning she will be heard by hundreds of millions of people.

Four B.B.C. microphones have been installed in the Sanctuary, and they will pick up the voices of the Princess groom and Archbishop of Canterbury.

Fifty engineers will be on duty, and Wynford Vaughan Thomas will give the B.B.C. running commentary during the ceremony. The American networks will share another microphone.

Along the processional route and outside the Abbey commentators will describe the scenes in about twenty languages; their voices will be carried to practically every radio station in the world.

The B.B.C. Home Service will open

its broadcast of the wedding at 11 a.m. with Frank Gillard describing the scenes as the Queen leaves Buckingham Palace. The broadcast will continue until the bridal coach returns to the Palace at about 1 p.m.

As the processions move to the Abbey there will be commentaries from Audrey Russell near the Admiralty Arch, Peter Scott on the roof of St. Margaret's, Westminster, and Richard Dimbleby outside the West Door of the Abbey.

Television cameras will cover the processions, and a special camera will film the bridal procession from the Altar after the ceremony.

Both sound mikes and television cameras outside Buckingham Palace will record the appearances of the Royal Family on the balcony during the afternoon and the departure of the bride and groom for their honeymoon.

For the benefit of people at work this morning recordings will be broadcast in the Light Programme at 8.15 p.m.

The television films will also be sent out from Alexandra Palace at 8.30 p.m.

LT. PHILIP—17 YEARS AGO

This photograph of Prince Philip, wearing Greek national costume, was taken in 1930, when he was nine. It was the treasured possession of Miss Emily Roose, of Plymouth, nurse-governess to the Greek Royal household for twenty-five years, and was signed for her—" Philip, 1930," in schoolboyish writing.

PHILIP IS NOW THE DUKE OF EDINBURGH

THE KING last night gave Lieutenant Philip Mountbatten the titles of Duke of Edinburgh, Earl of Merioneth and Baron Greenwich.

Announcement of the titles, made from Buckingham Palace last night, says the King has also authorised him to use the prefix "His Royal Highness."

21 M.P.s will consider King's offer

A SELECT Committee of twenty-one M.P.s is to be appointed to consider the King's offer to use some of his savings to give Princess Elizabeth an additional income and to give her husband an income.

Sir Stafford Cripps said in the Commons yesterday: "I am sure this House will deeply appreciate his Majesty's recognition of our present economic troubles and the generous and characteristic offer he has made to assist."

The titles were conferred during a private ceremony at the Palace, when he was also made a Knight of the Garter.

It had been anticipated that the Dukedom of Edinburgh would be revived for Lieutenant Philip ever since Princess Elizabeth's speech in Edinburgh last July, when she received the freedom of the city.

Three titles are normally borne by a duke. The second is usually taken as a courtesy title by the duke's first-born son.

The third title, Baron Greenwich of Greenwich, brings London, the heart of the Empire and its first capital city, into the titles of the consort of the Heiress to the Throne.

It is also a tribute to Lieutenant Mountbatten's naval service, for Greenwich has been called the "cradle of the British Navy."

The title Duke of Edinburgh was last revived by Queen Victoria for her second son, Alfred, who died in 1900.

In 1862, Alfred was elected King of Greece, but refused the Crown for political reasons.

The new Duke was present at yesterday's wedding rehearsal.

He watched Princess Elizabeth on her father's arm walk up the aisle, followed by the eight bridesmaids and two page boys.

Royal Wedding

The "Daily Mirror" regrets inability to supply extra copies tomorrow. Newsprint is rationed and the "Daily Mirror" disposes of its full supply every day. A vast public is already disappointed daily, thousands more will be added to this number tomorrow when pictures of this historic event will appear. We are sorry WE HAVE NOT GOT THE PAPER.

The Irish State Coach, in which Princess Elizabeth and the King today drive to the Abbey, will be heated with special hot-water bottles 2ft. long.

Made of aluminium, they will be filled with boiling water and placed under the seat and floorboards.

The famous Glass Coach in which the bride and bridegroom return to the Palace will be similarly heated.

An anti-dim substance will be used to prevent the windows steaming over, which would dis-appoint the vast throng straining to catch a glimpse of the Royal couple and their Majesties.

Yesterday at Buckingham

Continued on Back Page

The Princess's Gown

ABOVE is the royal wedding gown—white satin sparkling with pearls and crystals, embroidered with stars and garlands of roses and wheat.

Its low "sweetheart" neckline is trimmed with pearls. Orange blossom and stars form a deep band round the hem.

The full, swirling skirt—15 yards of satin went to make the frock alone—falls into a slight train. The sleeves are narrow, tight-fitting, ending in embroidery at the wrist.

From the Princess's shoulders will fall a 15ft. fan-shaped train of transparent ivory silk tulle. This, too, is encrusted with

pearls and crystals and embroidered with satin stars.

The veil of white tulle will be caught by a tiara of diamonds and pearls.

The thousands of pearls sewn on to the wedding gown are not real — they were made by a special process in a North London factory.

The Hartnell needle-women who sewed them on and did the rest of the delicate embroidery had to stop every half hour to wash their hands, to make sure the material was not soiled.

Following the Princess will be eight all-white bridesmaids in frocks of ivory silk tulle — full-skirted, the bodices softly gathered, the shoulders swathed in pearl-spotted tulle, bordered with white satin flowers.

The two pages who carry the Princess's train will wear Royal Stuart tartan kilts.

WEDDING WEATHER: RAIN, BUT NO FOG

London's Royal wedding weather, says the Air Ministry, will be dull and misty with occasional rain and drizzle. Thick fog is NOT likely.

Going-away dresses PAGE 2. Wedding details PAGE 5

Whiter teeth, fresher ... that's the ... COLGATE ...

Cleans your breath while it cleans your teeth!

COLGATE RIBBON DENTAL ...

On November 20, 1947, a royal wedding took place between Princess Elizabeth and Lieutenant Philip Mountbatten at Westminster Abbey, London. The couple had announced their engagement in July of that year. Princess Elizabeth and Philip, Prince of Greece and Denmark, had first been introduced to each other in 1939 at the house of the Captain of the Royal Naval College in Dartmouth. They met several times thereafter, as well as keeping up a correspondence. Prince Philip, who was given the title 'Duke of Edinburgh' prior to the wedding, was at the time a naval officer, and he resumed his career after the marriage. His first posting took him to Malta, where his wife joined him when she could. There was some controversy surrounding the union, caused by Philip's Greek Orthodoxy and the fact that his sisters had married German noblemen with Nazi links, but in general the marriage was seen as offering a new future after the deprivations of the Second World War.

Left: The Duke of Edinburgh and other members of the royal family gather for Remembrance Day.

March 1
International Monetary Fund is Founded

An organization is established to set up the rules for commercial and financial relations among the world's major industrial states.

June 24
UFO Spotted

Pilot Kenneth Arnold sees a series of unidentified flying objects near Washington's Mt. Rainier. It is the first widely reported UFO sighting in the United States and – due to Arnold's description of what he saw – leads the press to coin the term 'flying saucer'.

June 25
Anne Frank's Diary Published

The diary of Anne Frank is published after Miep Gies, one of her family's helpers, finds the papers and keeps them safe.

July 8
Was It a UFO?

A 'flying disc' is allegedly discovered in Roswell, New Mexico, U.S.A. There are later suggestions that it was a weather balloon, but some believe that this is a cover-up of the recovery of an alien spacecraft.

U.S. GIVES EUROPE FINANCIAL AID

In the aftermath of the Second World War, the economies of Western Europe were in ruins. In Britain, war debts, a slump in production, and depleted resources that forced the country to rely on expensive imports had all weakened the economy. In addition to this, moves by Prime Minister Clement Attlee to set up a welfare state did not strengthen the situation. On July 15, 1947, in accordance with the Anglo-American Loan Agreement of 1946, Britain declared that the pound sterling could be converted into any currency, but the government was forced to revoke that declaration when a sudden rush on dollar-conversions drained British dollar reserves. Without dollars, the British were unable to import much needed, though expensive, goods. The crisis prompted a British delegation to go to Washington, D.C. to plea for dollar aid to boost their reserves, armed with the threat of total European collapse if Britain was not helped out. Of all the Allied Powers, only the U.S. economy had remained healthy after the war, so it fell to the Americans to rescue Europe from financial meltdown. The Marshall Plan, formulated by U.S. Secretary of State George Marshall, was one resulting European Economic Recovery Program: its aim was to provide grants and loans to Britain and other European countries. However, the plan was not driven purely by generosity. Financially, the U.S. hoped to open European markets to its own excess goods, and politically, the U.S. hoped to prevent socialism taking hold in Europe by making governments financially dependent on the U.S. However, British Foreign Minister Ernest Bevin was all in favor of 'dollar aid' via the Marshall Plan and took it upon himself to organize conferences promoting economic cooperation and free trade across Europe.

> **'Of all the Allied Powers, only the U.S. economy had remained healthy after the war, so it fell to the Americans to rescue Europe from financial meltdown.'**

July 17
Indian Passenger Ship Capsizes
The 406-ton Indian passenger ship *Ramdas* capsizes off the coast of Mumbai. Over 600 passengers perish.

August 7
'Kon-Tiki' Smashed
Norwegian scientist Thor Heyerdahl's raft, the *Kon-Tiki*, smashes into the reef of the Tuamotu Islands after a 4,300-mile (6,900-km) journey across the Pacific, proving that prehistoric peoples could have traveled there from South America.

October 14
First Supersonic Flight
American pilot Chuck Yeager becomes the first man to fly faster than the speed of sound in the Bell X-1, flying at 670 mph (1,072 kph).

December 22
First Practical Transistor Demonstrated
Bell Laboratories in the U.S. develop a device that can control an electric current and amplify it.

1948

GANDHI ASSASSINATED BY HINDU EXTREMISTS

On January 30, 1948, Mohandas Gandhi was murdered by a group of Hindu extremists led by Nathuram Godse. Gandhi, who was 78, was shot three times in the chest at close range by Godse as he was walking to the prayer grounds near his home in Delhi. It was the sixth assassination attempt on the man who had fought tirelessly to gain Indian independence from British rule, and who only months earlier had achieved his aim. The murderers justified the assassination on the grounds that Gandhi favored Muslims and that he had destroyed India by allowing its division into two countries, Pakistan and India. In fact, Gandhi had always promoted respect for all religions, a stance that could not fail to make him unpopular with extremists on all sides. Nathuram Godse, along with another conspirator, was hanged for his part in the murder, while others in the group were imprisoned. Millions of Indians mourned Gandhi's assassination.

'It was the sixth assassination attempt on the man who had fought tirelessly to gain Indian independence from British rule, and haad only months earlier achieved his aim.'

January 12
Supermarket Opens in U.K.
The first British supermarket opens in London.

February 21
First Instant Camera
In New York City, Edwin Land demonstrates the first 'instant camera', the Polaroid Land Camera, to a meeting of the Optical Society of America.

March 27
Aswan Dam Started
The foundation stone is laid of the giant Aswan Dam across the River Nile in Egypt.

April 7
First W.H.O. Assembly
The World Health Organization is founded in Geneva.

1948

APARTHEID INTRODUCED IN SOUTH AFRICA

After 14 years in opposition with his National Party, Daniel Francois Malan (known as D.F. Malan) defeated Jan Smuts on May 28, 1948 to become the new prime minister of South Africa. Malan had originally broken away from the National Party when it merged with Smuts' South African Party because he believed it had lost its purity of vision. This vision, founded on a belief in white supremacy, involved the complete segregation of blacks and whites in South Africa by means of the policy that came to be known as apartheid (meaning 'separateness' in Afrikaans). The ideology behind Malan's National Party was the semireligious idea that Afrikaans-speaking whites were the chosen people, whose destiny it was to rule their fatherland of South Africa. Centered on the Dutch Reformed Church, this ideology grew up around anti-British feeling following the Boer Wars (1880–81 and 1899–1902) and gained strength during prolonged periods of economic and social unrest. With links to Nazism, Afrikaans Nationalism feared black domination and set about disabling the black majority by preventing their economic and political growth. The era of apartheid institutionalized racial discrimination in South Africa until close to the end of the 20th century.

SOVIETS BLOCKADE WEST BERLIN

With Germany defeated, the Western Allies and the U.S.S.R. set about dividing up different areas between themselves. Britain, France, the U.S., and the U.S.S.R. were each assigned their zones, but at the time, the Soviets already held Berlin and the Western Allies occupied various areas outside their agreed boundaries. The Soviets were determined to hold the East of Germany, including the east of Berlin. The Americans were determined that the West of Germany should not fall prey to Communism. When the Soviets eventually retreated from West Berlin, they left it a ruin of its former self, but the Americans stepped in and revived it, while the East continued under Communism. As a result, the two halves of Berlin became vastly different regions. As a reaction to this glaring contrast between East and West, on April 1, 1948, Stalin ordered a blockade on Western supply routes in an attempt to starve the Western Allies out of Berlin. His plan did not work, however, as the Allies began instead to airlift food and supplies into West Berlin, and it continued to thrive. Stalin was forced to abandon his plan in May 1949.

May 4
Hamlet Hits Screens
Laurence Olivier's film version of *Hamlet* makes its world premiere in London.

June 3
Telescope Completed
The Palomar Observatory's Hale telescope, the largest in the world at the time, is completed. The telescope is named in memory of astronomer George Ellery Hale, who had died ten years earlier.

June 21
L.P.s Introduced
Columbia Records holds a press conference to announce the introduction of L.P.s, long playing records replacing previous records which could hold only one song.

August 23
Council of Churches
World Council of Churches is founded in Amsterdam.

1948

BRUSSELS PACT SIGNED

BRITAIN & 4 POWERS SIGN 50-YR. PACT: U.S. CONSCRIPTION CALL

Best yet outlook of food from the Empire

BRITAIN will get more food from the Empire this year than even in pre-war days, Mr. John Strachey, Food Minister, said yesterday.

There will be more eggs, butter and, eventually, more meat from Australia and New Zealand.

Recovery of the Empire and of Europe from drought and war damage has lessened Britain's dependence on the United States and other dollar areas.

We have been able to cut dollar food purchases by one half.

Since the war we have had to buy about half our food from dollar countries and have been getting only half as much food from Europe as before the war.

'In Nick of Time'

This year we shall get nearly half our food from the Empire and Europe instead of only one-third.

From the dollar area—Canada, the U.S.A. and Argentina—we shall get one-quarter.

We're buying roughly three - quarters of our wheat, three-quarters of our bacon, most of our cheese and a little meat from the Canadians.

During the past nine months the Government has completed trade treaties, under which we shall get more food, with Denmark, Poland, Holland, Italy, Hungary, Portugal, France, Spain, Iceland and Eire.

"All this," said Mr. Strachey, "indicates that the non-dollar world is beginning to recover—in the nick of time for us.

"But on no account must this lead to the suggestion that we do not need to grow every ton of food which it is economically possible to grow at home."

Brenda Dorothy Marsh, 25, girl student, gaoled for twelve months at Winchester Assizes yesterday, for trying to blackmail a college lecturer for £300. Story on Page 3.

NO LABOUR 'REVOLT' FROM BAN ON EXTREMISTS

"Daily Mirror" Political Correspondent

THERE will be no "revolt" in the Labour Party over the Government decision to weed out Communists and Fascists from Government posts where they might learn vital secrets.

At yesterday's meeting of the Parliamentary Labour Party, attended by both the Prime Minister and Mr. Herbert Morrison, a number of M.P.s expressed regret that such a step should be found necessary and declared themselves against it in principle.

There was, however, no indication that there was any great opposition and Mr. Attlee's reply appeared to satisfy most of those at the meeting.

EXTRA DUBLIN BOATS FOR EASTER

Holyhead-Kingstown (Eire) boats will run a daylight service as an Easter extra, both ways, from March 24 to April 3 (not Sunday)

TWO major developments in the defence of democracy, personal freedom and political liberty in the West took place yesterday:

1.—Britain, France, Belgium, the Netherlands and Luxemburg signed a fifty-year treaty of economic and military co-operation.

2.—President Truman called on the U.S. Congress to re-impose conscription and to speed Marshall aid to Europe "to curb the growing menace" of Russian expansion.

The five-nation pact, signed in Brussels, provides that if an armed attack in Europe should be made on any one of them the others will give all possible military and other aid.

A permanent council is to be set up which can be immediately called at the request of any of the five countries to deal with "any situation constituting a threat to peace in any area."

It can also be called should there be any danger to economic stability.

Mr. Truman told Congress: "I am here to report to you on the critical nature of the situation in Europe and to recommend action for your consideration."

Then he listed "the most urgent steps towards securing peace and preventing war" as Marshall aid, universal military training and conscription.

"Must be Strong"

These, he said, were the measures "best calculated to give support to the free and democratic nations of Europe, and to improve the solid foundation of our own nation's strength.

"Until the free nations of Europe have regained their strength, and so long as Communism threatens the very existence of democracy, the U.S. must remain strong enough to support those countries of Europe which are threatened with Communist control and police State rule."

He declared that the responsibility for the critical situation was chiefly that of one nation which has "not only refused to co-operate in the establishment of a just and honourable peace but, even worse, has actively sought to prevent it."

TRANSPORT MEN END STRIKE

Cardiff tram and busmen are going back after a 24-hours strike, but they reject the offered 5s. 6d. a week, as an inadequate rise. Manchester has also rejected the 7s. 6d. offer. Liverpool was 100 buses short yesterday when 200 busmen struck.

TO AUSTRALIA FREE—OFFER TO SERVICES

The free passages to Australia scheme will apply to all ex-Service men and women released from the Forces on or before September 30, 1948, the Ministry of Labour and National Service announced last night.

Doctors shout down a plea for statesmanship

"DAILY MIRROR" REPORTER

ALL day yesterday 400 doctor delegates of the British Medical Association roundly refused, in motion after motion, to have anything to do with the National Health Act, due to begin on July 5.

The atmosphere was martial. One speaker after another declared that the time for words was past. Now was the moment for action.

Throughout the day only one voice—the refined Scots voice of Dr. G. Ireland of the Lothians—called for concessions and peacemaking.

Dr. Ireland warned his colleagues that continued conflict, with no attempt to make new offers, would lead to a public reaction against the doctors.

"I don't ask for weakness," he said, "I want statesmanship."

He tried to persuade the meeting to pass a resolution giving representatives power to make concessions on condition that a wholetime salaried service is not introduced.

He spoke in vain.

His quiet attempt to find a way out of the impasse between doctors and Parliament was called "disgusting appeasement" and "scandalous surrender."

His motion was lost.

But Not This . . .

The doctors' general in the fight is Dr. H. Guy Dain, chairman of the Council.

He urged the doctors to restrict their amendments and to concentrate on the main battle which he calls a battle for freedom.

He repeated that the B.M.A. is most anxious to have a health service—but not this health service.

He got the loudest cheer of the day when he declared that the doctors will not serve.

These are his words:

"I should be failing in my duty to the profession and to the public if I did

Continued on Back Page

New Palace strike 'if troops [...]

FORTY-TWO electricians, with twenty-one mates and fitters, working in Buckingham Palace, passed a resolution yesterday that unless troops stoking the Palace boilers are withdrawn they will strike in sympathy with the boilermen already out.

The meeting was held in[side] the Palace g[...] and followed a sev[...] demonstration man[...] 750 strikers.

The marchers were a man in an invalid c[...] Edward Kirkpatrick, liftman, who was par[...] at Dunkirk.

The strikers claim a[...] crease in their £4 17s wage rates.

Advertiser's Announcement

"HIS MASTER'S VOICE"
Push-Button Radio

Above is MODEL 1119 a 5-valve A.C. mains receiver with push-button control for 3 wavebands and 5 stations. Incomparable tone quality. Distinguished walnut finish cabinet.
27 gns. (plus £9 · 4 · 4 tax.)

Also in a similar cabinet MODEL 1467 4-valve, superhet battery receiver with push-button control. Equal in every way—performance, tone, appearance—to a mains set. Complete with batteries.
25 gns. (plus £8 · 10 · 8 tax.)

See the range of "His Master's Voice" Radio, Radiograms and Television on Stand 62, Ideal Home Exhibition.

THE GRAMOPHONE CO., LTD., HAYES, MIDDLESEX

Baronet's daughter falls to her death from train

"Daily Mirror" Reporter

SOCIETY folk, titled and rich, journeyed from London to the country last week-end for a house party.

One of the gayest and most attractive was Mrs. Valerie Josephine Lea, 24, daughter of a baronet and wife of an industrialist.

She was laughing when she left the house on Monday morning, with a peer and her host, to catch a train back to London.

In the train the little

party talked and watched the scenery.

Then, as the train sped through Hampshire, between Liss and Liphook, the carriage door flew open and Mrs. Lea fell to her death.

'LIGHTS OUT' STRIKE

Strike by thirty-four lamp-room attendants yesterday brought five pits of the Monckton (Yorks) collieries to a standstill and made 2,800 men idle.

Someone pulled the communication cord. The train crew sent for help.

But when they got Mrs. Lea to Midhurst Hospital she was dead.

Her mother, Lady Domville, said last night:

"I know what happened, but I may not tell you.

"My daughter had been to a house party for the week-end. She was gay

Continued on Back Page

SWISS VOUCHERS PLAN DROPPED

The system used last year for British visitors to Switzerland, in which part of the travel allowance was drawn in vouchers which could be used to pay hotel, food and travel bills only, has been dropped.

From the monthly quotas of Swiss francs allowed from May to October this year travellers will be allowed a sum based on the length of their visit, and will draw the money in cash, said the Treasury last night.

Mrs. Valerie Lea

On March 17, 1948, the United Kingdom, Belgium, France, Luxemburg, and the Netherlands signed the Brussels Pact, which was largely a security measure to help combat the perceived threat of Communism. The group elected to contribute to a military formation headed by British Field-Marshal Bernard Law Montgomery (known as 'Monty'). The pact formed an early version of what would eventually include America and become N.A.T.O. (the North Atlantic Treaty Organization).

Above: The flag of N.A.T.O.

October 5
Devastating Earthquake
An earthquake in Turkmenistan, U.S.S.R., kills 110,000 people.

December 10
Universal Declaration of Human Rights Adopted
The United Nations General Assembly adopts a Universal Declaration of Human Rights that should be accepted all over the world.

Fast Oven
The microwave oven is invented by American Percy LeBaron Spencer.

Struck Oil
The world's largest oil field, Al-Ghawar, is discovered in Saudi Arabia.

GERMAN DEMOCRATIC REPUBLIC ESTABLISHED

In the years following the Second World War, the wealth gap between the Soviet-held and the Western-held regions of Germany continued to widen. In the Soviet-controlled areas, many Germans had been expelled. Stalin had created a new political party called the Socialist Unity Party. In pursuit of Communist ideals, property and industry were nationalized, a move that brought with it social and economic deprivation. On October 7, 1949, East Germany officially declared itself the German Democratic Republic, a separate socialist state, with Wilhelm Pieck as its president. In anticipation of a decisive break from the Soviets, Britain, France, and America had already united their zones into one Federal Republic of Germany in May 1949, with the city of Bonn as its capital. As a result, a division was created that would cause first the Berlin Wall and then the metaphorical Iron Curtain to be erected. For the next forty years, Germany was to exist as two separate states.

'A division was created that would cause first the Berlin Wall and then the metaphorical Iron Curtain to be erected.'

ALLIES PLAY THEIR ACE IN GERMANY

January 4
Raging Storms Hit Nebraska
A blizzard lasting for almost three days hits western, central, and northern Nebraska in the U.S. High winds drive heavy snow on top of earlier falls. Then the last two weeks of January bring sub-zero temperatures.

January 19
Poe Toaster First Appears
On Edgar Allen Poe's birthday, a dark figure appears at his grave and raises a toast to him. A toaster returns every year on Poe's birthday and has not yet been identified.

February 1
Clothes Rationing Ends
The rationing of clothes enforced during the war, ends in Britain.

March 1
Boxing Champ Retires
Joe Louis retires as heavyweight boxing champion. He was world champion for 11 years and 10 months.

115

1949

ISRAEL'S WAR OF INDEPENDENCE ENDS

Since declaring itself an independent state free from British control on May 14, 1948, Israel had faced a series of armed conflicts with surrounding Arab countries who refused to recognize the State of Israel. The United Nations Partition Plan of November 29, 1947 had agreed to the division of Palestine into two separate states – one Arab and one Jewish – with Jerusalem a multi-racial, multi-ethnic city administered by the U.N. to avoid conflict. Following the declaration of independence, Egypt, Syria, Lebanon, Jordan, and Iraq invaded Israel, launching the War of Independence. At least 726,000 Palestinians become refugees during the conflict. The war continued, with various ceasefires, until the 1949 Armistice Agreements. On February 24, 1949, Israel and Egypt signed an armistice agreement. This was followed by agreements with Lebanon (March 23), Jordan (April 3), and Syria (July 20). The armistice lines stayed in place as Israel's new borders until 1967, with the Gaza Strip and the West Bank being occupied by Egypt and Jordan respectively.

CANDY RATIONING ENDS IN U.K.

In April 1949, the British government announced the end of sweet rationing and allowed each household 5 oz (140 g) of sweets a week. It was also decided that each household should have an extra 7 lbs (3 kg) of sugar. Children and adults alike flocked to sweet shops to celebrate by indulging in their favorite confectionary. Sweets and chocolate were first rationed in 1942, along with many other food items, because of the shortage of supplies. Many, particularly women, took up smoking when sugar became scarce, so the tobacco industry expected a drop in sales once sugar became more widely available. It was soon discovered that the abolition of sweet rationing had been a rash move. The demand for sweets far exceeded the supply of sugar, so the ration had to be put back in place after only four months. It was not lifted again until 1953.

March 2
Flight Around the World
In Fort Worth, Texas, Captain James Gallagher lands the *Lucky Lady II*, a B-50 bomber, after making the first nonstop, round-the-world flight, in 94 hours 1 minute.

April 4
North Atlantic Treaty Signed
In Washington, D.C., 12 countries create the NATO defense alliance, agreeing that an attack on one of them will be considered an attack on them all.

April 18
From Eire to Ireland
Eire leaves the British Commonwealth and becomes the Republic of Ireland.

BRITAIN GAINS FIRST SELF-SERVICE SHOPS

In March 1949, the British government announced that it would license 100 companies to try out self-service shops, which had already been trialed successfully in America. The move marked the birth of the modern supermarket. Instead of queuing to be served, customers would be able to select pre-wrapped items themselves, put them in a basket or trolley, and take their purchases to a checkout near the exit. It was hoped that the altered layout would reduce staffing requirements, thus lowering costs, and make shopping more efficient for everyone.

June 24

Cowboys Hit TV

Hopalong Cassidy becomes the first network television cowboy series, airing on N.B.C. A radio version of *Hopalong Cassidy* is broadcast by the Mutual Broadcasting System in January 1950.

July 27

First Jet-Powered Airliner

The de Havilland Comet, the world's first jet-powered airliner, makes its maiden flight.

December 15

Deadly Typhoon

A typhoon strikes a fishing fleet off the coast of Korea, killing thousands of fishermen.

December 28

No UFOs

After an official inquiry, the U.S. Air Force reports that 'flying saucers' do not exist.

HAPPY

*This was the
happiest
picture of all*

—AND GLORIOUS

1950-1959

As people across the world began to press for greater liberty and equality, in the U.S. the Civil Rights movement championed the cause of African Americans. The Alabama bus boycott saw Martin Luther King Jr. emerge as a charismatic leader of the movement, advocating non-violent resistance to discrimination. A yearning for freedom, too, was at the heart of the ever-increasing desire to reach outer space. In the decade that saw the first satellites launched into orbit, this sense of urgency began to develop into rivalry between the Soviet Union and America.

By the 1950s, post-war scarcity in Britain had begun to ease, and rationing finally ended. A sense of fun and frivolity was returning. The Festival of Britain showcased national talent, and the coronation of Queen Elizabeth II gave everyone a chance to let off steam and celebrate in style. But the loss of most of its empire left Britain's power on the world stage diminished.

At the same time as consumerism was rising, the Communist movement was gaining momentum as it spread across the globe. In Korea, the Communist North invaded the South, who appealed to the U.S. for help. In Cuba, the military dictator Batista was overthrown by the young revolutionary socialist Fidel Castro. But as one socialist era was beginning, another was ending when Stalin's death brought his reign of terror to a close in the Soviet Union.

1950

NORTH KOREAN TROOPS ENTER SOUTH KOREA

S. KOREA PLEADS FOR QUICK AID AS REDS THREATEN CAPITAL

REPORTS from Japan last night said that North Korean Communist troops had reached the outskirts of Seoul, South Korea's capital.

South Korea's troops were earlier reported to be falling back rapidly on the capital in face of hammer blows from 70,000 invaders with seventy tanks.

Behind a spearhead of tanks, the Communists were pushing on from the South Korean town of Uijungbo, twelve miles to the north, where resistance collapsed before powerful thrusts from the Russian-trained forces.

As this news was flashed to Tokio, the South Korean National Assembly appealed to President Truman for "rapid and effective" aid to beat off the invader.

The appeal referred to the invasion as "an act of destruction against the peace of the world."

In a Washington statement last night President Truman said the United States would vigorously support the efforts of the Security Council to end the "serious breach of the peace" in Korea.

Steps were being taken to speed and increase assistance "of the type being furnished under the Mutual Defence Assistance Programme."

"Those responsible for this act of aggression must realise how seriously the government of the U.S. views such threats to the peace of the world."

General MacArthur's headquarters in Japan had already announced that ten Mustang fighter aircraft were being sent to Korea.

Mr. Attlee and Mr. Ken-

Continued on Back Page

IN GERMANY THEY ARE ASKING: CAN IT HAPPEN HERE?

Millions of West Germans are asking themselves: Can it happen here? The parallel between Germany and Korea is too close to be comfortable for them, cables David Walker from Berlin.

Except for the vital fact that occupation troops are still in this country, Korea's position before the Red invasion was not very different from that of Germany today.

The newspaper "Die Welt" after stating that there is no need to weaken...

They put their food into the ice bank

FOOD banks where people can store fruit, vegetables, fish and other produce are now open in some English towns. For as little as 3d. a pound they can rent ice-cold larders for a year to keep food, bought cheaply in times of plenty, for use when it is scarce.

Leading the way in this experiment in cutting the cost and raising the standard of living is the bank in Tinkers Drove, Wisbech, Cambs.

It is run on the same lines as a cash bank. Clients are issued with passbooks, in which all deposits and withdrawals of food are recorded.

The 4,000 "depositors" include some who come forty miles from seven counties to put perishable food into their "strong boxes." And there is a long waiting list to join.

Two weeks ago a branch office was opened in Peterborough. Already there are almost 200 members.

Lockers and bins—long white tiers of them—in hundreds of yards of frozen corridors contain almost everything that the small farmer and allotment holder can produce. There are fish, hams, bacon, pheasants, cauliflowers, cabbages, sprouts, beans, peas—even flowers.

Some have been stored for two months, some for two years. With the temperature 2 deg. below zero, these products, carefully packed, come out as fresh and appetising as they went in.

The hares and pheasants that were shot in winter are taken out in summer, when they are as rare on the market as they are expensive. The fruits of summer are eaten in winter.

Christmas in Wisbech is one of fresh plums, apricots and strawberries.

Mrs. Albert Hussey, a young mother who grows her own vegetables, has no doubts about the Food Bank. "We have the best of everything any time we want it," she said, "and sometimes at half the price in the stores. It's a housewife's dream."

'Look! There's the Princess'

Children from the village school at Mersham, near Ashford, Kent, sit on the church wall to watch Princess Elizabeth and Countess Mountbatten as they leave after yesterday's christening of Michael, the month-old son of Lord and Lady Braborne. Princess Elizabeth was a godmother to the baby, a grandson of Lady Mountbatten. The ceremony was conducted by the Archbishop of Canterbury in the 600-year-old parish church.

REJECT S-PLAN AND SOVIET DREAM COMES TRUE—EDEN

MR. Anthony Eden, deputy Leader of the Opposition, opening the two-day debate on the Schuman Plan in the House of Commons yesterday, said: "I say deliberately that in all its dreams Russia could hope for nothing better than the reduction of Britain to the status of an observer in Franco-German relations.

"We ought to have been better prepared for the French initiative. We ought to have had proposals of our own. But, best of all, we should have taken the initiative ourselves some time since."

The Opposition motion suggests that the Government should accept the French invitation, but that—like the Dutch—they should receive freedom of action if the Paris discussions "show the Plan not to be practicable."

Mr. Churchill and Mr. Attlee will wind up the debate today.

Mr. Eden said the news from Korea shows the need for all free countries, East and West, to agree.

No event could give more confidence than to eliminate the possibility of future war between France and Germany.

France's peace initiative...

SMUTS: POOR NIGHT

General Smuts spent a poor night, stated a bulletin issued yesterday. "There has been no real setback, however," the bulletin added.

TEST SHOCKS FOR ENGLAND

ENGLAND are struggling in the second Test match with the West Indies at Lord's. They scored only 151 in their first innings in reply to the West Indies' total of 326.

A burst of defiance by the last - wicket pair, Wardle and Berry, produced 29 runs—second best

stand of the innings. The men who had England's batsmen scratching for runs and scrambling to preserve their wickets were the young spin bowlers Sonny Ramadhin and Alfred Valentine.

They succeeded on the "easy" wicket where England's spinners had failed on Saturday. Hutton and

Washbrook figured in an opening partnership of 62 but the next six wickets realised only 60 runs. Then Wardle hit a gallant 33 not out.

Wicketkeeper Clyde Walcott shared in the dismissal of four men.

Peter Lake's match report—See Page Ten.

On June 25, 1950, several units of the Communist North Korean People's Army crossed the north–south divide and invaded the Republic of Korea in the south. The attack came without warning, and the Republic of Korea was unprepared for war; their minimal troops were forced to retreat toward their capital, Seoul. Two days later, after North Korea had failed to abide by a United Nations Security Council resolution to withdraw, American President Truman took the decision to involve the United States in the war. He offered significant military support to assist the Republic of Korea in fighting back against the Communist onslaught, and by August, the United States Congress approved a budget of $12 billion to be spent on military involvement in Korea.

January 21
Israel Has Capital City
The Israeli Knesset passes a resolution making Jerusalem the capital of the new state.

January 26
Indian Republic is Formed
Rajendra Prasad is sworn in as the first president of the Republic of India.

February 12
Einstein Warns the World
Physicist Albert Einstein warns that nuclear war could end in mutual destruction.

March 8
Soviets Develop Bomb
The Soviet Union announces that it has developed a nuclear bomb.

U.S. WARNS SOVIET UNION TO STAY OUT OF YUGOSLAVIA

For some time, U.S. foreign policy toward Central Europe was uncertain. Although the anti-Communist stance of the U.S. was clear, its relationship with Communist Yugoslavia under Marshall Josip Broz Tito, who had shown a great deal of independence from the Soviet Union, was an ambivalent one. However, in January 1950, George Allen, the new U.S. ambassador to Yugoslavia, issued a clear warning to the Soviet Union when he announced that America would not stand by idly if the Soviets attacked Yugoslavia. Stopping in London on his way to the Yugoslav capital, Belgrade, Allen told a press conference that U.S. foreign policy had always been to resist aggression, wherever it came from and whomever it was directed against.

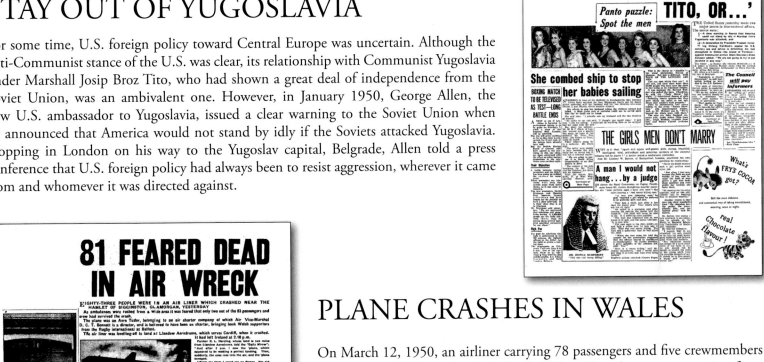

PLANE CRASHES IN WALES

On March 12, 1950, an airliner carrying 78 passengers and five crewmembers crashed in a field in Llandow, South Wales. The plane was returning from Dublin, Ireland, where the passengers had all been supporting their country at an international Rugby Union match between Wales and Ireland. Only three people on the plane survived. The survivors had all positioned themselves at the tail end of the plane before the crash. The dead included nine players from Welsh rugby clubs. According to eyewitnesses, the airliner was flying too low as it approached the runway in Llandow, and when the pilot tried to correct its position, the nose lifted too high, bringing the plane into a vertical position before the engine stalled and the plane plummeted to earth. An investigation into the crash eventually ruled accidental death, although the possibility of pilot error was investigated. There was speculation that unbalanced luggage had altered the plane's center of gravity, and Fairflight, the company that owned the plane, was ordered to pay a fine and damages. The tragedy was the worst air disaster of its time.

April 27
Apartheid Laws in South Africa
South Africa passes the Group Areas Act, formally segregating people by race.

May 13
Formula 1 Begins
The first Formula 1 race is held at Silverstone race track, England.

August 15
Earthquake Shakes India
An earthquake in Assam, India, causes flooding that leaves 5 million homeless.

October 2
Peanuts First Published
Charles M. Schultz's comic strip *Peanuts* appears in seven U.S. newspapers.

1950

U.N. SUPPORTS SOUTH KOREA

On June 27, 1950, the United Nations Security Council passed a resolution urging all of its 52 member states to give military support to South Korea following the North's invasion. In the early days of the Korean War, U.N. member states stalled. Britain and Australia, for example, both held back and claimed that they would not be committing troops. As a result, U.S. and South Korean troops suffered heavy losses initially, and were pushed south toward Japan. Eventually, however, swayed by the prospect of friendship with the U.S., and in the face of further pleas from the U.N., other countries began to commit troops to the cause. The Korean War was to last three years and involve more than 20 countries, resulting in around 2 million civilian deaths in addition to the military losses. U.N. and South Korean forces together suffered around 500,000 casualties; North Korea and China's losses were in the region of 1,500,000 million.

SACRED STONE STOLEN BY SCOTTISH NATIONALISTS

Below: Westminster Abbey

In the early hours of Christmas Day 1950, the Coronation Stone was stolen from beneath the Coronation Chair behind the High Altar at Westminster Abbey in London. During the robbery, the Coronation Chair, which had seen the coronation of 27 British monarchs, was also damaged. The stone, variously known as the 'Stone of Scone' and the 'Stone of Destiny', had long been a point of contention between the English and the Scots. In the 13th century, when Edward I of England first defeated the Scots and annexed Scotland, he took the sacred stone, regarded by Scots as a talisman, from the castle of Stone, the ancient crowning place of Scottish kings. As soon as police were alerted to the missing stone, they sealed the border with Scotland. Despite this unprecedented measure, the stone did cross the border into Scotland, where it found. Once the stone was returned to Westminster Abbey, the whole episode was viewed as a prank, although when the thieves were apprehended, they insisted that it had been a political act. In the end, they were never prosecuted because it was too difficult to prove that the British Crown actually 'owned' the stone.

November 1
Attempt on Truman's Life
Puerto Rican nationalists attempt to kill U.S. President Harry Truman.

December 11
Muslim Riots in Singapore
Eighteen people are killed in riots in Singapore as Muslim protestors demonstrate against the British colonial government. The unrest lasts for two days.

December 12
America's First Female Rabbi
Paula Ackerman is the first woman to perform rabbinical duties in the U.S.A.

December 28
Britain's First National Park
The Peak District in England is designated Britain's first national park.

1951

BRITAIN CELEBRATES NATIONWIDE FESTIVAL

The Festival of Britain, an event first conceived during the difficult post-war years when Prime Minister Clement Attlee presided over 'austerity Britain', was intended to complement the newly formed welfare state. Although officially a celebration of past and current achievements, the festival was also the left-wing government's declaration that Britain would move into a future of social equality. As a celebration of Britain's history and culture, it was intended to boost morale after the war, but as a political manifesto, it was also meant to shape a new British identity based on equality. The nationwide exhibition covered industry, science, and the arts, as well as everyday life, showcasing the best in design. The Royal Festival Hall, which still stands on London's South Bank, was the only building erected during the festival and intended as a permanent structure.

'As a popular celebration of Britain's history and culture, it was intended to boost morale after the trauma of the war.'

Right: The South Bank, London, which today is a thriving center for the arts.

January 9
U.N. Opens Headquarters
The United Nations' new headquarters opens in New York.

February 6
85 Die in Train Crash
A passenger train derails in New Jersey, killing 85 people..

March 29
Spies Receive Death Sentence
In the U.S., Ethel and Julius Rosenberg are sentenced to death for spying.

April 18
Treaty of Paris is Signed
Six European nations sign the Treaty of Paris to form the European Coal and Steel Community.

3,000,000 TEEN-AGE BRITONS AWAIT FESTIVAL 'GO'

By PAUL CAVE

A THOUSAND BONFIRES WILL BE THEIR SIGNAL
+
They'll show the world THEIR work and play
+
PAGEANTS, PROCESSIONS, FETES AND SERVICES

BRITAIN'S teen-agers are rolling up their sleeves to show fathers and mothers and overseas' visitors just what THEY can do for the Festival of Britain.

NO ENGLISH WIFE COULD STAND THIS, SAYS JUDGE

Stokes gets new job as raw-materials chief

By BILL GREIG

CHAMPION NEAL BROWN
Going to To succeed The new
Ministry of Robens at Minister of
Agriculture. Fuel Ministry Works.

Trapped Britons fight way out

BUTTER UP 6d. A POUND

Pleased as PUNCH
FRY'S MILK CHOCOLATE
RICH MILK CHOCOLATE CARAMEL FUDGE
and what value 4½d

123

1951

BURGESS AND MACLEAN SPY SCANDAL

Guy Burgess and Donald Maclean were members of a Soviet spy ring in Britain known as the Cambridge Five (although they were also commonly referred to as the Cambridge Four, since the suspected fifth man was not formally identified for some time). All members of the ring went to Cambridge University, and had at some point belonged to a secret debating society known as the Apostles, although they were recruited at different times and not while at Cambridge. During the Second World War and for some time afterwards, various members of the group passed sensitive information to the U.S.S.R. As committed Communists, they worked their way up through the British Civil Service and the British Secret Service, all the while passing information to the K.G.B. By 1951, British intelligence had long known that there was a mole within the British Embassy in Washington, D.C., and they commissioned Kim Philby to investigate Donald Maclean, not knowing that Philby was himself a member of the Cambridge Five. Philby instructed Guy Burgess, who worked with Maclean in the embassy, to warn Maclean that he was a chief suspect. On hearing this information, Burgess and Maclean both suddenly and publicly defected to the U.S.S.R. It had never been part of the plan that Burgess would defect, too, and this action cast immediate suspicion on Kim Philby, with whom he was known to be close. Although Philby called a press conference to declare his innocence, he also defected to the U.S.S.R. in 1961 as suspicion about him increased.

WEST GIVES MORE FREEDOM TO FEDERAL REPUBLIC OF GERMANY

Toward the end of the 1940s, the British, French, and American zones of West Germany had begun to merge politically and economically in preparation for the handover of power back to the Germans. The Allies had formed an economic council that united their zones and paved the way for reunification of the separate parts, as well as setting measures in place for self-government. By 1949, a constitution had been established for a new self-governing Federal Republic of Germany, and following elections, that government was formed in August 1949 with its provisional capital in Bonn. The former capital of Berlin was still a separately administered zone, divided into four zones, three of which were controlled by the Allied powers. It was surrounded by Soviet-occupied territory. In 1951, Britain, France, and the U.S. gave up their control of West Germany's foreign affairs, and the Republic began to re-establish links with its European neighbors in its own right. West Germany quickly joined the European Coal and Steel Community, an alliance between France, Italy, Belgium, Luxembourg, and the Netherlands. When the outbreak of the Korean War in 1950 prompted the U.N. to call for German rearmament to guard against Communist invasion, it was proposed that rearmament take place under the umbrella of a European Defense Community, an expansion of the European Coal and Steel Community. However, France pulled out, fearing a loss of autonomy, and a wider Western European Union was established instead, with regulatory powers over the armies of its member states. Although the Western Allies still occupied parts of Berlin and British troops remained in Germany, by the mid-1950s, the Federal Republic of Germany was a sovereign state in charge of its own military.

May 3
Royal Festival Hall Opens
The London concert hall is opened by King George VI, marking the start of the Festival of Britain.

July 20
Jordan's King Assassinated
King Abdullah I of Jordan is killed while at Friday prayers in Jerusalem.

August 12
The Catcher in the Rye Published
J.D. Salinger's novel is published and becomes a bestseller.

September 8
Peace Treaty Signed with Japan
Forty-eight nations sign a treaty with Japan to formally end the Pacific War.

CHURCHILL WINS GENERAL ELECTION

On October 26, 1951, the Conservative Party won the general election in Britain by a small margin, bringing Winston Churchill, the leader of the party, into the office of Prime Minister for a second time. At 76, he was the second-oldest prime minister in history to take office, second only to the Victorian politician William Gladstone, who was 83 when he formed his final government. Churchill succeeded Labor Prime Minister Clement Attlee. The

'At 76, he was the second-oldest prime minister in history to take office.'

Conservatives had campaigned on the promise of a 'strong and free' Britain and warded off Labour's depiction of Churchill as a warmonger. At the time, Britain was facing a rapid increase in the cost of living, a severe housing shortage, and an indebted economy burdened by the costs of rearming after the Second World War. In his victory speech, Churchill stressed the need for solidarity and an end to party rivalry so that everyone could pull together to work out the best way to restore the nation.

Right: When he died in 1965, Winston Churchill was given a full state funeral.

Election race drama

TORIES IN —OVERALL LEAD MAY BE 17

But most votes go to Labour Party

THE Conservatives will form the next Government, with an overall lead expected to be under twenty. This was the result of the Election as it emerged last night after a day of drama in which the issue—stalemate or a sizeable majority—was always in doubt.

'...have all much in common'

A kiss for Mr. Attlee

Mrs. Attlee kisses her husband, tired after his arduous election campaign, but pleased with his personal success in the polls at West Walthamstow, London. The Attlee family spent part of the day at Transport House, Labour Party H.Q., studying the election results.

The new House —and the old

	With 7 results to come	Today	Old House
Tory and Allied Parties		318	298
Labour -		294	315
Liberal -		5	9
Others - -		1	3

GAINS AND LOSSES

	Gains	Losses
Labour - - - -	3	22
Tory - - - - -	23	1
Liberal - - - -	1	4

HOW THE VOTES WENT

	AFTER 613 RESULTS	TOTAL VOTE IN 1950
LAB.	13,865,019	13,295,736
TORY	13,614,730	12,526,686
LIB.	707,635	2,621,489
COMM.	21,640	91,815
OTHERS	143,792	233,751

OTHER WOMEN'S LIVES

She delights in dancing!

hard work doesn't catch her on the wrong foot!

sleep sweeter—Bourn-vita
Made by Cadburys

October 16
Pakistan Prime Minister Killed
Prime Minister Liaquat Ali Khan is assassinated in Rawalpindi.

November 1
War Games
The U.S. military holds exercises to prepare for nuclear war in the Nevada Desert.

November 11
Perón Reelected
Juan Perón is reelected president of Argentina.

December 20
Nuclear Power Plant Opens
The world's first nuclear power plant, an experimental site in Idaho, opens.

December 24
Libya Gains Independence
Libya, in North Africa, wins independence from Italy.

1952

ELIZABETH BECOMES BRITAIN'S NEW QUEEN

HISTORIC PICTURES

Tomorrow's 'Daily Mirror' will be a specially enlarged issue portraying

THE MOST MEMORABLE SCENES

of the London procession and burial at Windsor of King George VI

Angry miners say 'No more Italians'

By HAROLD HUTCHINSON

THIRTY angry men met in the Miners' Union office in London yesterday and hotly decided they would no longer give their approval to the introduction of Italian miners.

That is as good as saying that no more Italians will be able to enter British mines until the miners' leaders change their minds.

Cause of their anger was Mr. Victor Raikes, Conservative M.P. for Garston, Liverpool. Three weeks ago he said publicly that "the real objection by British miners to Italian workers is not so much the danger of unemployment but that the Italians have a certain sex appeal towards miners' wives and daughters."

Poured in

Denunciations of the speech poured in to the miners' leaders. For their part they had never been keen on Italians but had given grudging approval. Mr. Raikes provided them with the excuse they needed to withdraw that approval.

They were angry too. But the miners would never allow the public touch of an obscure Tory M.P. to disturb them unless they were also ready to use it to suit their own purpose.

So when the union leaders met they unanimously decided to ask the Coal Board to suspend any further recruitment of Italians. Any pits where the men might have been willing to accept Italians will now refuse.

Sir William Lawther, president of the Union, let fly at Mr. Raikes in a stinging statement for his "base and vulgar insinuations."

Whether a humble apology by Mr. Raikes would mollify the miners is doubtful since it is at least doubtful if they want to be mollified.

What it amounts to is that if the Coal Board wants more men, it will have to recruit them in Britain.

The Duchess of Kent (left) driving to Buckingham Palace yesterday with her sister, Princess Olga of Yugoslavia, who is here for the King's funeral.

King Frederik of Denmark, in naval uniform, arrives at Liverpool-street Station London, with Queen Ingrid. They travelled from Denmark by ship.

General Eisenhower, Supreme Allied Commander, with his wife next to him, arriving at Westminster with a friend to see the King lying in state last night.

ALL NIGHT THE GREAT CROWDS PAY HOMAGE

GREAT crowds paying homage to their dead King passed through Westminster Hall yesterday at between 5,000 and 9,000 an hour. It was decided to keep the doors open until 6 a.m. today—three and a half hours before the funeral procession is due to start.

When the hall was opened at 8 a.m. yesterday 25,000 people were already waiting in the snow and cold wind, with tens of thousands more on their way to join the great queue.

As ambulance men gave aid to fainting and frozen people in the waiting thousands the flow of mourners through the Hall was at one time speeded-up to allow the people to pass the catafalque ten deep.

For twenty minutes in the afternoon the Duchess of Kent watched the scene from an alcove of the Hall.

With her she had her three children, the Duke of Kent 16, who had flown from his school in Switzerland to attend the funeral; Princess Alexandra, 15, Prince Michael, 9, and the Duchess's sister Princess Olga.

Not Wearing Veil

Most of the people looking towards the coffin did not see the Royal mourners.

The Duchess, who wore a short, black seal coat over a black dress, and a black velvet hat was unveiled.

Before the Royal party left Princess Alexandra, who was wearing a short, black coat and skirt and a black beret, curtsied to the King's coffin, The Duchess's sons bowed low.

Earlier in the day the Archbishop of Canterbury (Dr. Fisher), who has been

Continued on Back Page

TODAY'S WEATHER

Air Ministry weather forecast for the funeral:
LONDON: Sleet showers, with sunny intervals.
WINDSOR: Dry and windy.

FREE 14 PIECES 2 PUZZLES IN 1

NOVELTY PUZZLE

from FRY'S COCO

Get one NOW before they all go!

Please send me a FREE NOVELTY PUZZLE from J-lb. tin (or two 1-lb. cartons) of Fry's. I enclose 3d. stamp for postage and packing, to Somerdale, Bristol.

NAME

ADDRESS

TODAY'S GUIDE to the funeral for spectators, television viewers and listeners is on Pages 2 and 11

Princess Elizabeth and Prince Philip were in Kenya at the start of a tour of the British Commonwealth when, on February 6, 1952, they were sent news of her father King George VI's sudden death. The news meant that, at the age of 25, Princess Elizabeth had become Queen Elizabeth II. She immediately flew back to Britain and was met by Prime Minister Winston Churchill. There followed a 16-week period of official mourning, after which it was deemed acceptable to celebrate the accession of the new monarch. In her address to the nation, Queen Elizabeth declared: 'I shall always work, as my father did throughout his reign, to uphold constitutional government and to advance the happiness and prosperity of my peoples, spread as they are all the world over.' The coronation did not take place until the following year, but the Queen embarked on her official duties immediately, including the annual State Opening of Parliament and a weekly meeting with the Prime Minister.

She also undertook a series of regional tours, taking her to every part of Britain, as well as a wide-ranging tour of the Commonwealth, which took her to countries never before visited by a British monarch.

Left: Queen Elizabeth II at the State Opening of Parliament.

February 6
First Open Heart Surgery a Success
A mechanical heart is used during surgery for the first time in the United States. The operation is a success.

March 22
Hundreds Die in Tornados
Tornados in the Mississippi River Valley leave 208 people dead.

March 27
Letter Bomb in Munich
A letter bomb addressed to West German Chancellor Konrad Adenauer, explodes at Munich police station.

April 9
Revolution in Bolivia
The government of Hugo Ballivián falls in Bolivia. The new revolutionary government promises widespread reforms to help the poor.

DIARY OF ANNE FRANK PUBLISHED IN ENGLISH

On April 30, 1952, the diary of Anne Frank was first published in Britain under the title *The Diary of a Young Girl*. Originally published in Dutch by her father in 1947, it recounts the experiences of a Jewish family hiding from the Gestapo in Nazi-occupied Amsterdam, from the point of view of 13-year-old Anne. The Franks had moved from Nazi Germany to the Netherlands in 1933. They were forced into hiding in July 1942 when the Nazis occupied the Netherlands.

The Franks occupied a small apartment with another family, and in Anne's diary she details the difficulties of their shared life, as well as the joys that the world around her continues to reveal, despite living in fear. The apartment was raided in August 1944, and the families were sent to Auschwitz and Bergen-Belsen concentration camps. Anne died at Bergen-Belsen aged 15, together with her sister. Her mother died in Auschwitz-Birkenau. Her father, Otto Frank, survived, and when he returned to Amsterdam, he discovered Anne's diary among salvaged family papers. The commentary of the aspiring writer is by turns petty and sublime: she expresses her daily irritations and criticisms, the feelings of awakening sexuality typical of a girl her age, as well as comments that reveal a wisdom beyond her years. On a particular day weeks before her capture, she wrote: 'I hear the approaching thunder that, one day, will destroy us ... and yet when I look up into the sky, I somehow feel that everything will change for the better ... that peace and tranquility will return once more.'

KENYANS REBEL AGAINST BRITISH RULE

In November 1952, a revolutionary movement dedicated to the violent overthrow of colonial rule in Kenya began to attack European settlers in a bid for independence. Resentment of the British was felt most keenly by the Kikuyu in the Highlands who, by the 1950s, had become badly treated, poorly paid tenant farmers on their own land. After peaceful attempts to win reform failed, the independence fight became concentrated on the Kikuyu Central Association, which took responsibility for the uprising and began to raise funds and weapons. Rebels began to prepare for military action and pressured the moderate Kenya African Union into supporting the cause of independence. On October 20, 1952, the Colonial Office in London declared a state of emergency in Kenya. The war was to last eight years, with atrocities committed on both sides, but with a huge imbalance in casualties: 32 Europeans were killed, while the Kenyan death toll was in excess of 20,000. The rebels were referred to as Mau Mau in the British press, a term of unknown origin. Although Britain won the war in military terms, they eventually made the political and social concessions originally demanded by the Kenyans, and Kenya won its independence in 1963.

May 3
Plane Lands at North Pole
Two U.S. airmen land a plane on the geographical North Pole.

May 18
Woman Sails Atlantic Solo
Ann Davison leaves Plymouth, England, to sail the Atlantic solo. She arrives in Dominica in December.

July 13
East Germany Forms an Army
East Germany announces that it will form a National People's Army.

July 19
Olympic Games Begin
The 15th Olympiad begins in Helsinki, Finland.

1952

BRITAIN TESTS ITS FIRST NUCLEAR BOMB

In the years immediately following the end of the Second World War, the British Labour government, under Prime Minister Clement Attlee, had secretly begun to develop atomic weapons. Although a committee met regularly on this development, its existence was not known about for many years. The aim was to ensure that Britain could match the U.S.A. and the U.S.S.R. The team assembled to build an atomic bomb was led by the British physicist William G. Penney, who had been instrumental in the development of the American bomb. The first plutonium production reactor was built in Windscale (now called Sellafield) in the North of England, in October 1950, but it did not go into operation until February 25, 1952, producing its first plutonium metal five weeks later. The small size and high population density of Britain meant that it was impossible to find a suitable site to test such

'The explosion left a crater in the seabed 20 ft (6 m) deep and 1,000 ft (326 m) across that is still there today.'

weapons. So instead the team set about sourcing a site in other Commonwealth countries, eventually settling on the Montebello Islands in Australia. On September 15, 1952, the first British nuclear device, code-named 'Hurricane', left Windscale for Australia. It was a plutonium-implosion bomb, similar to the type dropped on Nagasaki, and although most of the plutonium had been manufactured at Windscale, some of it came from Canada. On October 3, 1952, 'Hurricane' was placed inside the shell of the 1,450-ton frigate HMS *Plym*, which was anchored in 40 ft (12 m) of water 1,300 ft (400 m) from the shore of Trimouille Island. The explosion left a crater in the seabed 20 ft (6 m) deep and 1,000 ft (326 m) across that is still there today.

November 4
Eisenhower Wins U.S. Election
Republican Dwight D. Eisenhower is elected president of the United States.

November 25
The Moustrap Opens
The Agatha Christie play *The Mousetrap* opens in London. It is still playing today, more than 20,000 performances later.

December 5
London Chokes on Smog
The Great Smog, a cold fog filled with coal fumes, covers London for five days. Thousands die.

STALIN DIES

IS STALIN DEAD?

Mystery of bulletin from the Kremlin

By JAMES CAMERON

'I couldn't stop kissing her'
—ALLEGED STATEMENT BY MAN ACCUSED OF MURDER

NOW RUSSIA FACES THREE BIG QUESTIONS

Who will be the new master?

FILM STAR IS 'VERY ILL'

MALENKOV
Stalin's 'favourite'.

CROCODILE TEARS

Bulletin No. 3 from the Kremlin

by Cassandra

Star finds 'the way to the stars'

IKE PASSES ON HIS OFFER

NEW even better! PUNCH
MILK CHOCOLATE CARAMEL FUDGE
and still only 4d

Right: St. Basil's Cathedral on Red Square, Moscow, Russia.

On March 5, 1953, Soviet dictator Joseph Stalin was declared dead, apparently of a brain hemorrhage, at his country home outside Moscow. The official announcement of his death was made by his closest political allies, including Lavrentiy Beria, Nikita Kruschchev, and Georgi Malenkov, and came after days of uncertainty following the announcement that he was seriously ill. His body was laid out in the Hall of Columns near the Red Square, Moscow, and millions of Russians crammed the streets to see it. Although Stalin had ruled ruthlessly and inflicted terrible deprivation on his people, many were hypnotized into such reverence for the leader they called 'Father' or 'God' that they wept openly on seeing his body. The fervor surrounding his death was so intense that hundreds of people were crushed to death in the crowds gathering to see the body. There was widespread speculation as to who would succeed him as leader, as well as speculation as to whether he had really died of natural causes.

'The fervor surrounding his death was so intense that hundreds of people were crushed to death in the crowds gathering to see the body.'

January 31
North Sea Floods
A tidal surge floods large parts of the Netherlands, killing 2,000 people.

February 28
D.N.A. Discovered
Scientists James Watson and Francis Crick announce that they have discovered the D.N.A. molecule.

March 26
New Polio Vaccine
Jonas Salk develops a vaccine for polio, which is made available two years later after testing for safety.

May 29
Mt. Everest Conquered
Edmund Hillary and Tensing Norgay reach the summit of Mount Everest.

1953

ELIZABETH II CROWNED

CORONATION SOUVENIR
HAPPY
This was the happiest picture of all
—AND

Right: Buckingham Palace, where the Queen appeared after her coronation.

On June 2, 1953, more than a year after the death of her father King George VI, Queen Elizabeth II was crowned at a ceremony in Westminster Abbey in London. Her coronation was witnessed by more than 8,000 guests who filled the Abbey, including heads of state from all over the Commonwealth. The Archbishop of Canterbury, Dr. Geoffrey Fisher, presided over the ceremony, which involved the Queen's acceptance of the four symbols of authority: the orb, the scepter, the rod of mercy, and the royal ring of sapphires and rubies. The Archbishop placed the St. Edward's Crown on her head, and a shout of 'God Save the Queen!' was heard, followed by gun salutes. In a radio broadcast the Queen declared to the nation: 'Throughout all my life and with all my heart I shall strive to be worthy of your trust.' The streets between Buckingham Palace and Westminster Abbey were lined with crowds of well-wishers, 3 million strong, hoping to catch a glimpse of the golden state coach. The B.B.C. broadcast the ceremony live on radio and television across the world. It was the first coronation to be televised, and there had been debate as to the properness of televising such a solemn event, but the sales of television sets had rocketed in the months leading up to the coronation, and everyone crowded around the black-and-white 14-inch (35-cm) screens to see the event. It had been the Queen's own decision to televise the coronation, so that as many people as possible around the world could participate in the momentous occasion. The crowds in London, some of whom had camped out overnight to ensure a good position, were rewarded when the Queen appeared on the balcony of Buckingham Palace. In the evening, there was a display of fireworks in London and street parties spread across the country.

> **'The Archbishop placed the St. Edward's Crown on her head, and a shout of "God Save the Queen!" was heard, followed by gun salutes.'**

June 7
Italian Election
The Christian Democrats win a majority in the Italian general election.

June 17
Berlin Uprising
The Soviet Union sends troops into East Berlin to put down an uprising of workers.

July 4
Miners Strike
There are riots in Poland as coal miners strike.

July 26
Castro Attacks Cuban Barracks
Fidel Castro leads a failed attack on Moncada Barracks in Santiago de Cuba.

ROSENBERGS EXECUTED

Julius and Ethel Rosenberg, both from Jewish immigrant families in New York, had met when they were just 18 and 21 at the Young Communists' League. Julius Rosenberg later qualified as an electrical engineer and worked in the Army Signal Corps. As a member of the Communist Party U.S.A., and one with access to military material, Rosenberg was recruited by the K.G.B. and began to provide design information about U.S. defense systems. Julius also recruited his wife's brother, David Greenglass, who worked at the Los Alamos National Laboratory on the development of the hydrogen bomb. Although the U.S. and U.S.S.R. had briefly been allies during the Second World War, there was great hostility and distrust between the two nations. The U.S. was particularly concerned that the Soviets might get hold of information about U.S. atomic weapons. Suspicious of how quickly the Soviets had managed to develop their own atomic bomb, the U.S. government soon tracked down insiders who they believed had passed information to the Soviets, and David Greenglass was questioned. He confessed to having passed drawings of the implosion atomic bomb to his brother-in-law, Julius Rosenberg, via his sister Ethel. Greenglass later retracted his accusation, claiming he had acted to save his wife and children and had never realized that the death penalty would be involved. The Rosenbergs were both arrested, and although Ethel's personal involvement was difficult to pin down, she was charged with conspiracy to commit espionage. Their trial was widely and unsympathetically publicized. Julius and Ethel Rosenberg were convicted of espionage on March 29, 1951 and sentenced to death – the first and last American citizens to receive such treatment during the entire Cold War period. Judge Irving Kaufman, the man who sentenced the Rosenbergs, accused them of being responsible for the deaths in the Korean War. He said, 'By your betrayal, you undoubtedly have altered the course of history to the disadvantage of our country.' Though many prominent figures, including the Pope, appealed for the couple to be spared, the Rosenbergs were executed by electric chair on June 19, 1953. Their two sons were adopted by teacher and songwriter Abel Meeropol. The Rosenbergs' execution is now widely viewed as a miscarriage of justice prompted by a heightened level of fear and hysteria during the Cold War.

> 'Rosenberg was recruited by the KGB and began to provide design information about U.S. defense systems.'

August 8
Soviets Get the Bomb
The Soviet Union announces that it has developed a hydrogen bomb.

August 18
Sex Report
The Kinsey Report is published in the U.S. It is the most extensive report on sexual habits ever written.

November 9
Cambodia Wins Independence from France
Cambodia becomes an independent constitutional monarchy.

December 23
Beria Executed
Former head of Stalin's secret police, Lavrentiy Beria, is executed for treason in Moscow.

FRENCH FORCED OUT OF VIETNAM

France had first begun to colonize Indochina in the late 1800s, setting up protectorates in Vietnam, Laos, and Cambodia. The Democratic Republic of Vietnam, led by Ho Chi Minh, was created after the Second World War. With British assistance, Viet Minh forces expelled the Japanese forces that had infiltrated Vietnam after France surrendered to Nazi Germany during the war. However, from 1946 to 1953, there were various outbreaks of violence between the French colonists and the Communist Viet Minh. By 1954, the French were desperate to win a decisive victory against the Viet Minh. General Navarre, in charge of the French troops, decided to provoke an all-out battle in order to give the French the best chance of securing a major victory. Convinced that if he blocked the Viet Minh's route to Laos he would force them to attack, he set up a French fortress in Dien

'The French, trapped, cut off from supplies and coming under increasing mortar fire, appealed for American assistance.'

Bien Phu. However, Navarre had wrongly assumed that the Viet Minh, under General Giap, would stage a frontal attack. Instead, they surrounded French forces in Dien Bien Phu and began digging trenches. They then moved inward, digging more trenches, while simultaneously bringing in massive reinforcements. By the time they had encircled the French, the Viet Minh outnumbered them five to one. The French, trapped, cut off from supplies, and coming under increasing mortar fire, appealed for American assistance. But President Eisenhower stalled, waiting to see what British Prime Minister Churchill would do, while Churchill was keen to await the outcome of the Geneva peace talks. Eventually, after suffering massive losses, the French were forced to withdraw from Vietnam. Between November 1953 and May 1954, the French had lost 7,000 lives and a further 11,000 soldiers had been taken prisoner. The French defeat led to the Geneva Accords, which divided Vietnam into the Communist North and the pro-West South.

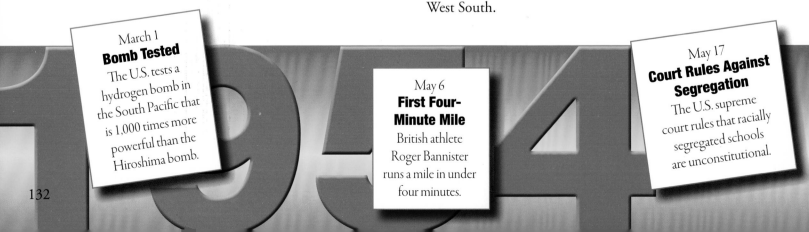

March 1
Bomb Tested
The U.S. tests a hydrogen bomb in the South Pacific that is 1,000 times more powerful than the Hiroshima bomb.

May 6
First Four-Minute Mile
British athlete Roger Bannister runs a mile in under four minutes.

May 17
Court Rules Against Segregation
The U.S. supreme court rules that racially segregated schools are unconstitutional.

NASSER TAKES CONTROL OF EGYPT

Following the 1952 nationalist revolution in Egypt, the Egyptian monarchy was overthrow by an army faction known as the 'Free Officers', with Colonel Gamal Abdul Nasser at its head. Setting themselves up as the Revolutionary Command Council (R.C.C.), they nominated a president and a prime minister, abolished civil titles, and ordered all political groups to rid their parties of corruption. The Egyptian monarchy had long been seen as under British control, and it was the common aim of the Free Officers to free Egypt from British interference. The revolution prompted King Farouk to abdicate in favor of his son and flee the country, but even though the monarchy remained in name, its days were numbered. Muhammed Naguib, a respected army officer and hero of the 1948 Arab–Israeli War, was nominated as President and Ali Mahir as Prime Minister – but it was Nasser who pulled the strings. He set about creating an independent republic and righting the imbalance of wealth and power in the country. The R.C.C. dealt harshly with opposition to its regime and eventually banned all political parties in 1953. In the same year, Egypt was declared a republic and the monarchy was officially abolished. A struggle followed between President Naguib and Nasser for control of the government – a struggle eventually won by Nasser. Nasser's chief aim was to evacuate the British from the base that they held at the Suez Canal. However, the British would only consider entering negotiations if the Egyptians signed the Baghdad Pact, a defense agreement designed to ward off a Soviet invasion. But Nasser, who was more wary of Western imperialism than Soviet Communism, would not agree to this. Instead, he managed to negotiate a British evacuation, with certain conditions attached, that allowed the British to return to their Suez Canal base if Egypt or Turkey were attacked. The Anglo-British agreement did not earn Nasser much popularity among his people, and there was an attempt on his life by the Muslim Brotherhood, but his nationalist reforms in Egypt steadily increased his popularity and consolidated his position.

Left: Sunset in the Egyptian capital, Cairo.

June 17
Coup in Guatemala
The reformist government of Jacobo Arbenz is overthrown in a C.I.A.-backed coup.

July 4
Rationing Ends in U.K.
The last form of food rationing in the U.K., meat rationing, ends.

August 24
President Vargas Kills Himself
Facing charges of conspiracy to murder, the president of Brazil, Getulio Vargas, kills himself.

July 7
Elvis Debut
Elvis Presley performs on the radio for the first time, singing 'That's All Right.'

1954

MCCARTHY KICKED OUT OF SENATE

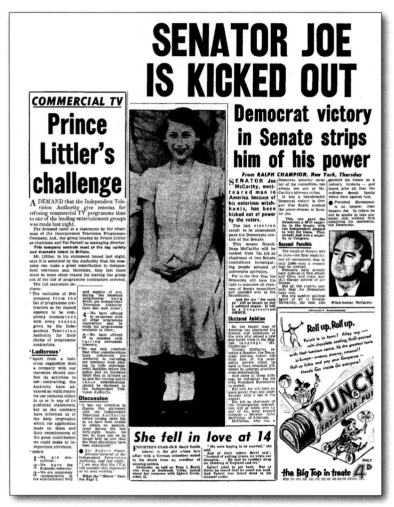

Joseph McCarthy was a self-made man who worked his way up from uneducated farm boy to Republican senator. His first election to office was as a Republican circuit court judge, and it was achieved by means of a campaign that hinted at the senility and financial corruption of his Democrat opponent. After the war, when he ran for the Senate office as a Republican candidate, he tarnished the name of his Republican rival Robert La Follette by deriding his lack of military service (when in fact he had been too old to join) and falsely accusing him of war profiteering. In the Senate, McCarthy made a name for himself as a harsh dealer, in one instance suggesting that striking miners should be enlisted in the army and then shot for insubordination. He was not popular, and some of his past deceptions began to surface. When it came time for his re-election in 1950, McCarthy searched for a way to keep hold of his position of power and decided to launch a brutal attack on American

> **'McCarthy searched for a way to keep hold of his position, launching a brutal attack on American Communists.'**

Communists within the government. He teamed up with the journalist Jack Anderson and feared F.B.I. boss J. Edgar Hoover, and together they created a list of Communist subversives within the Democrat ranks. McCarthy devoted all his energy to exposing politicians who were so-called 'loyalty risks'. In this climate of Red hysteria, Republican Dwight D. Eisenhower was elected President in 1952. McCarthy continued to pursue his campaign, now targeting writers, artists, actors, and academics and prompting many to leave the country for Europe in disgust. Gradually, more and more journalists and broadcasters gained the confidence to speak out, and McCarthy's reputation was steadily eroded. One newspaper article said: 'In this long, degrading travesty of the democratic process, McCarthy has shown himself to be evil and unmatched in malice.' He was finally fired from the Senate in 1954. McCarthy died three years later from cirrhosis of the liver caused by severe alcoholism.

October 18
First Transistor Radio
Texas Instruments makes the first transistor radio in the U.S.

October 31
Algeria Revolts
The Algerian National Liberation Front begins armed campaign against French rule.

November 14
Nasser Made President
Prime Minister Gamal Abdel Nasser is made President of Egypt.

December 2
McCarthy Condemned
The U.S. Senate votes 67–22 to condemn Senator Joseph McCarthy.

Deember 24
Laos Wins Independence
Laos becomes a constitutional monarchy independent from France.

PRINCESS CHOOSES ROYAL POSITION OVER LOVE

Queen Elizabeth II's sister Princess Margaret first met Group Captain Peter Townsend when she was still a teenager. He was equerry to her father King George VI and at the time was married, with two children. Townsend later separated from his wife and became romantically involved with Margaret. The affair was kept out of the press for many years, but at the Queen's coronation, when Princess Margaret was still only 22, she let slip a gesture of familiar affection when she brushed some fluff from his jacket, and the news of their relationship broke at last. Queen Elizabeth, who already knew of their plans to marry, had asked them to wait until after her coronation to announce the news. Marrying a divorcé was still viewed with considerable disapproval, especially in light of the Church's stance that Christian marriage could never be dissolved. According to the British constitution, however, Princess Margaret needed only the permission of her sister to marry up until the age of 25. Once she was older than 25, she needed the permission of Parliament. Group Captain Townsend was still working in the royal household at the time, and soon after the coronation he was sent to Brussels to work for the British Embassy. He was away for two years, and in that time Princess Margaret turned 25. She was already well aware that Parliament would not consent to the marriage, so if she wanted to go ahead with it, her only choice was to renounce her title, including any financial income that went with it, as well as her succession to the throne. She chose instead to renounce Group Captain Townsend, and, on October 31, 1955, issued a statement through the press that she would not marry him. She said: 'I have reached this decision entirely alone, and in doing so I have been strengthened by the unfailing support and devotion of Group Captain Townsend.' Princess Margaret later married the photographer Antony Armstrong-Jones in 1960.

MARGARET DECIDES:

DUTY BEFORE LOVE

PRINCESS MARGARET, in this dramatic announcement from Clarence House last night, told the world that she had renounced the love of Peter Townsend:

"I would like it to be known that I have decided not to marry Group Captain Peter Townsend. I have been aware that, subject to my renouncing my rights of succession, it might have been possible for me to contract a civil marriage. But, mindful of the Church's teaching that Christian marriage is indissoluble, and conscious of my duty to the Commonwealth, I have resolved to put these considerations before any others. I have reached this decision entirely alone, and in doing so I have been strengthened by the unfailing support and devotion of Group Captain Townsend. I am deeply grateful for the concern of all those who have constantly prayed for my happiness.
(Signed) Margaret."

...nsend leaves—alone SEE BACK PAGE

Left: Princess Margaret meets The Beatles in November 1963.

January 25
Atomic Clock
Scientists at Columbia University develop an atomic clock that is accurate to within one second every 300 years.

February 28
Israelis Enter Gaza
Israeli troops enter Egyptian-controlled Gaza in pursuit of attackers. Tensions between Israel and Egpyt rise.

March 20
Rock'n'Roll Movie
American teenagers dance in the aisles to the music of Bill Haley in the film *Blackboard Jungle*.

April 5
Churchill Resigns
Eighty-year-old Winston Churchill resigns as Prime Minister of the U.K.

April 18
Einstein Dies
Physicist Albert Einstein dies in Princeton, New Jersey, at the age of 76.

1955

CIVIL UNREST IN CYPRUS ESCALATES

By the 1950s, around 80% of the residents of Cyprus were Greek. The Greek government claimed a right of ownership over the island, and Greek Cypriots longed for *enosis* – or union with Greece. But Turkish Cypriots made up about 18% of the population, and looked to Turkey as their homeland. Turkey had been the legal owner of the island until 1923, when it was colonized by Britain. In 1951, an organization of Greek Cypriots seeking *enosis* formed a military wing known as E.O.K.A. ('National Organization of Cypriot Fighters' in the Greek language). The decision to take arms was prompted by the refusal of the British to consider loosening their hold on Cyprus. In 1955, British troops were posted to Cyprus after being evacuated from Egypt. Anti-British riots broke out, and on April 1, 1955, E.O.K.A. launched a campaign of violence against British rule in a series of planned attacks on police and military institutions. After a few months of attacks and counterattacks, a tripartite conference was convened in August 1955 in London, with representatives from the Greek, Turkish, and British governments. All sides were dissatisfied by the conference, which achieved nothing concrete. Shortly afterwards, Cyprus was offered a limited form of self-government. The offer was rejected, and E.O.K.A. continued its campaign of violence, using explosives and weapons smuggled in from Greece. Talks between British Governor Harding and Cypriot representative Archbishop Makarios were unsuccessful, and Makarios was eventually exiled. However, the level of violence on Cyprus only increased. It was not until 1960 that an agreement was reached. Rather than union with Greece, Cyprus was granted full independence.

MALENKOV FORCED OUT IN U.S.S.R.

Following the death of Joseph Stalin in 1953, Georgy Malenkov was the sole leader of the U.S.S.R. for six months, until Nikita Khrushchev was made First Secretary, creating a power share. It was a time of increasing treachery within the U.S.S.R., making it impossible to judge whether associates were allies or enemies. During the two years of Malenkov's premiership, from 1953 to 1955, he tried to move the U.S.S.R. toward the production of consumer goods, rather than relying solely on heavy industry. He also spoke out against the nuclear armament program. However, he soon fell out of favor, just as he had watched others fall. His previous association with Lavrentiy Beria, who had been executed as a traitor in 1953, tarnished his reputation, and Khrushchev seemed to offer more rapid reform. Malenkov was fired from the government in February 1955. He would try once more to seize power from Khrushchev in 1961, a move that got him thrown out of the Communist Party and exiled from the U.S.S.R.

May 9
West Germany Joins N.A.T.O.
The newly formed Federal Republic of Germany joins N.A.T.O.

May 14
Warsaw Pact Signed
The Soviet Union and Communist regimes in Eastern Europe sign a defense treaty as a response to N.A.T.O.

July 13
Ellis Hanged
Ruth Ellis is hanged for the murder of her lover, the last woman to be executed in the U.K.

August 20
Riots in North Africa
Hundreds are killed in anti-French riots in Morocco and Algeria.

August 27
New Book of Records
The *Guinness Book of World Records* is published for the first time.

ACT PASSED TO END KILLER SMOG

The winter of 1952 to 1953 was a particularly cold one in the U.K. As a result, more coal than usual was burned in household fires, and more people used their cars. The combined effect of increased soot, tar, and exhaust fumes created thick smog that hung in the air over London for four days. It became known as the Great Smog. The smog was so thick that it infiltrated buildings – cinemas and theaters were forced to close – and made transportation almost impossible.

'In the course of a few months, death rates multiplied by almost ten.'

Substances in the smoke combined with sulfur dioxide to form a lethal acid rain, and hospitals were swamped with the sick. In the course of a few months, death rates multiplied by almost ten: most victims were the vulnerable, both young and old, and most fatalities involved respiratory problems. In all, thousands of deaths were attributed to the smog. In the following year, the smog reappeared – though less critically – and hospitals went on red alert. The increasing gravity of the situation forced the government to seriously address the issue of air pollution, and officials from the Ministry of Housing worked on new proposals throughout 1955. The result of this work was the Clean Air Act of 1956.

KILLER SMOG
London gasps again
HOSPITALS READY FOR VICTIMS

David saved his mother's life

DAILY MIRROR REPORTER

IT'S that killer smog again— the worst this winter.

Down it came over London as dusk fell. As it grew thicker and dirtier last night, hospitals prepared for casualties.

One hospital doctor told me: "Unless conditions improve, we expect the first unfortunate victims in the morning."

It was the *smoke* and not the *fog* in last night's smog that made it the deadliest this winter—and one of the worst since the four-day smog of December, 1952, that was blamed for nearly 4,000 deaths.

How It Happened

The Air Ministry explained it like this: Early frost left a layer of cold air over London, undisturbed by wind. Chimneys poured out smoke that was trapped under this "umbrella." That cold bell didn't budge. So the smog imprisoned below—almost 100 per cent. smoke"—grew thicker and thicker. The damp-rot brought the usual traffic difficulties.

From many parts of the Home Counties came reports: Visibility down to 150 yards ... 50 yards ... 15 yards.

The last three races at West Ham greyhound stadium were abandoned. London Airport had to close down.

But that was not the worst.

Thousands of Londoners coughed and gasped in the swirling, yellow-grey murk.

Clear Patches

Here and there there were clear patches, while a few streets away people spluttered and wheezed with handkerchiefs pressed over their mouths.

Will the smog last? Early-morning forecast from the Air Ministry was: Winds later today may blow it away.

Jets streak to the aid of Snowland.—See Back Page.

In Piccadilly-circus last night.

DAVID BALL, 14, hugs his mother with burned hands in hospital last night.

Those hands, and the calling to mind of a few words spoken by his father, saved the life of David's mother yesterday. David was almost ready to go to school in the morning ... then he found a hole in one of his socks.

David's mother, Mrs. Jane Ball, got out her needle and thread. She stood in her nightdress by the roaring fire of her home in Glencoe-road, Coventry.

Suddenly a spark flew from the fire. It landed on Mrs. Ball's nightdress, which immediately burst into flames.

David stopped her running out of the room and tried to beat out the flames with his hands. Then the words of his father, a fireman for twenty years, came back to him: "When people are on fire, wrap them in a rug."

David did just that—and put the flames out. He telephoned for an ambulance.

Mrs. Ball, who is forty-nine, said in hospital: "I panicked. If I hadn't been for David I wouldn't be here now."

A fireman said: "If more people acted like David there would be fewer tragedies."

IKE WANTS CHINA TRUCE

A DRAMATIC move by President Eisenhower is reported in World News Spotlight on the Back Page.

September 19
Perón Ousted
Argentinian President Juan Perón is overthrown in a military coup.

September 30
James Dean Dies
Actor James Dean dies when his car crashes at high speed in California.

November 12
End for Ellis Island
The immigration center on Ellis Island in New York Harbor closes.

December 1
Parks Makes a Stand
African American Rosa Parks is arrested in Alabama for refusing to give up her seat on a bus.

December 14
United Nations Expands
Sixteen nations join the U.N., the biggest single expansion since it was formed.

1956

BOYCOTT ON BUSES ENDS SEGREGATION

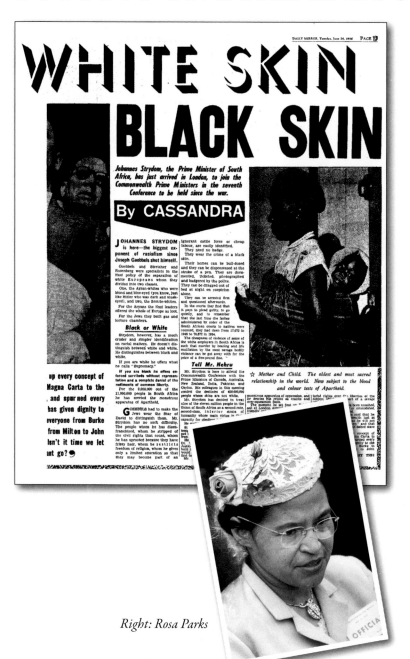

Right: Rosa Parks

Although the American Civil War had brought about the abolition of slavery in America, a massive divide remained between North and South in terms of their policies toward African Americans. In the South, a strict enforcement of black and white segregation remained in place despite a federal ruling banning segregation in public education. A movement to desegregate, or integrate, buses in Montgomery, Alabama was instigated in 1949 by a black academic, Jo Ann Robinson, after she was abused by a bus driver for refusing to move to the back of a bus. Over the next few years, there were a few well-publicized incidents involving blacks who refused to give up their bus seats to whites. The most famous was the case of the seamstress Rosa Parks, who was arrested for her refusal to give up her seat. In 1954, Jo Ann Robinson wrote to the Mayor of Montgomery, warning him of the planned boycott. When, on December 1, 1955, Rosa Parks was arrested, the bus boycott was launched. The boycott had the backing of a group of ministers, including Martin Luther King Jr., who formed the Montgomery Improvement Association (M.I.A.) to manage the boycott. It took a great deal of organization, since most black people relied on the bus service to get them to work, and the white city officials did everything in their power to make it difficult, including prosecuting the black cab services that had begun to charge a 10-cent fare (the same as the bus fare). There were several acts of violence, including the bombing of Martin Luther King's home, but still the boycott continued, and various attempts at negotiating an end came to nothing. Next, it was decided that the ringleaders should be arrested using an old law prohibiting boycotts, and Dr. King was the first defendant to be tried, receiving a $1,000 fine and 386 days in jail. The original aim of the movement had been to make the segregation policy fairer, but now complete desegregation on the buses was the goal. The M.I.A. took the issue to the federal court, and segregation on public buses was ruled to be unconstitutional. On December 21, 1956, with the federal ruling that buses could no longer be segregated, the boycott ended. The Civil Rights movement had won its first major victory.

February 25
Stalin Denounced
Soviet leader Nikita Khrushchev attacks the cult of personality surrounding Stalin.

March 23
Pakistan Celebrates
A national holiday is held in Pakistan to celebrate its becoming an Islamic Republic.

April 19
Princess Grace
Actress Grace Kelly marries Prince Rainier III of Monaco to become Princess Grace.

April 22
Morocco Joins the U.N.
Newly independent Morocco joins the United Nations.

May 8
Groundbreaking Play Opens
John Osborne's *Look Back in Anger* marks a new era of political theatre in the U.K.

SUEZ CRISIS DEEPENS

On October 29, 1956, Britain, France, and Israel launched an attack on Egypt following Egypt's decision, three months earlier, to nationalize the Suez Canal. The British had taken control of the canal when they occupied Egypt in 1882. In the 1950s, the canal played a vital role in the passage of oil from the Middle East to Europe, and Britain presided over a massive garrison of some 80,000 military personnel at their Suez Canal base. In July 1952, the military coup of the Free Officers movement in Egypt ousted the British-backed monarchy, eventually leading to the staged evacuation of the British from their Suez base in October 1954. The new Egyptian republic under General Nasser was angered by Britain's role in the creation of Israel and had begun a policy of refusing access through the canal to ships bound to or from Israel. The United States had previously offered to fund the building of the Aswan Dam. But in July 1956, their offer was withdrawn after Nasser officially recognized the People's Republic of China. Nasser responded by ordering the immediate nationalization of the Suez Canal. The nationalization dealt a severe blow to Britain, in both economic and military terms. In August 1956, crisis talks were held in London between the British, French, and Americans. The French and British agreed to work together, and three months after the nationalization, they enlisted Israeli support in a bid to regain control of the Suez Canal. The plan was that Israel would invade Egypt, and Britain and France would intervene and insist on the need for Anglo-French protection of such an important area. Although the military operation was successful, U.S. President Eisenhower was concerned that the Soviet Union would become involved, and U.S. opposition eventually forced the British and French to abandon their hard-won position. The U.N. General Council demanded that Britain and France withdraw from Egypt immediately, which they did. British Prime Minister Anthony Eden announced a ceasefire on November 6, 1956, without consulting France or Israel, and then resigned as Prime Minister, having lost political authority over his handling of the crisis. U.N. peacekeepers were stationed in the region to restore stability, marking the first use of U.N. personnel in this way.

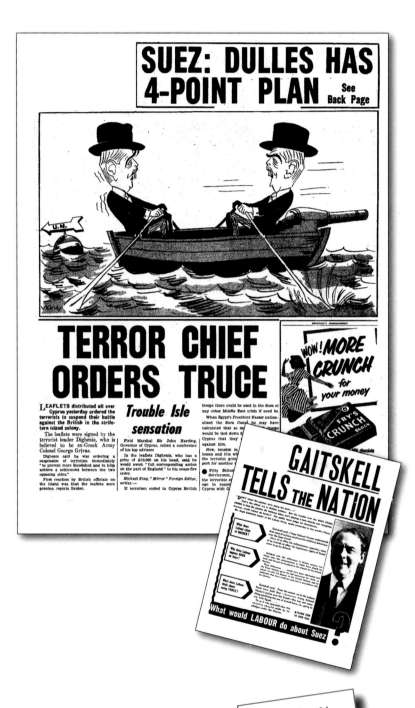

May 24
First Eurovision Song Contest
Lys Assia wins the inaugural Eurovision Song Contest for Switzerland.

June 10
Revolt in Argentina
A Peronist revolt in Argentina is crushed. Twenty-six revolt leaders are executed.

June 28
U.K. Votes to End Hanging
The House of Commons votes to end capital punishment but is overruled by the House of Lords.

August 11
Artist Killed in Car Crash
American artist Jackson Pollock dies aged 44 after crashing his car.

September 21
Dictator Assassinated
Anastasio Somoza, the dictator of Nicaragua, is shot dead.

1956

NEW DRUG TO FIGHT POLIO USED IN BRITAIN

Polio, the common term for *anterior poliomyelitis*, is a viral disease of the nervous system that can cause complete paralysis and death. Until the 1950s, there were outbreaks of polio every summer, affecting between 15,000 to 30,000 each year. In 1949, Professor John Enders made the Nobel Prize-winning discovery that the polio virus could be grown in large quantities, and for the first time, the possibility of a vaccine became real. However, turning a living virus into a 'killed' vaccine requires an additional substance to destroy the sickness-producing effect without preventing the production of antibodies. In 1952, Jonas Salk, head of the Virus Research Laboratory at the University of Pittsburgh, used formaldehyde to 'inactivate' the viral matter so that it would cause antibody production without causing the disease. In April 1954, the first polio immunization campaign was launched in the U.S., focusing on schoolchildren. That same year, hundreds of people contracted polio from Salk's vaccine, and many died. Apparently, the virus had not been completely inactivated. However, the vaccine was redeveloped, despite intense controversy, and in the summer of 1955, over 4 million doses were administered in the United States. By 1956, the vaccine was being used in the U.K., and by 1959, it was available in nearly 100 other countries. In 1958, a new form of the vaccine, developed by American physician Albert Sabin, would become available in oral form. This was a live virus, but it was a rare type that had been isolated specifically because it did not penetrate the central nervous system.

NEW WATER SPEED RECORD

Englishman Donald Campbell was as obsessed with speed as his father Malcolm Campbell had been. Sir Malcolm Campbell had set 13 speed records on land and water, and his son Donald began his own attempts in his father's boat *Bluebird K4*. However, Donald soon realized that he would need a new craft to set new records, and so the *Bluebird K7* was built for him. The boat was made entirely of metal and had a jet engine. It was a time of exciting technological advances, and the British nation was thrilled. In 1955, Donald Campbell reached 202 mph (324 kph) on Coniston Water in the Lake District of England, breaking the world water-speed record. In 1956, he reached 225 mph (362 kph).

Above: Donald Campbell in Bluebird.

October 24
Soviets Invade Hungary
The Red Army crosses into Hungary to put down an anti-Soviet revolution.

November 6
Ike Wins Second Term
President Dwight D. Eisenhower wins the U.S. presidential elections.

December 2
Castro Enters Cuba
Fidel Castro lands in Cuba to start a guerrilla war against the Batista regime.

December 5
Britain's First Female Judge
Defense barrister Rose Heilbron is appointed the U.K.'s first female judge.

STRAY DOG BECOMES FIRST CREATURE IN SPACE

On October 4, 1957, the U.S.S.R. launched a satellite called *Sputnik 1* into space. The satellite was a 183-lb (83-kg) metal sphere, outstripping anything the Americans had been preparing to launch, and it became the first artificial satellite to successfully orbit the earth. The day after the launch, it was reported in the Russian newspaper *Pravda*: 'As the result of a large, dedicated effort by scientific-research institutes, the world's first artificial satellite of the Earth has been created. On October 4, 1957 in the U.S.S.R. the first successful satellite launch has been achieved. According to preliminary data, the rocket launcher carried the satellite to the necessary orbital speed of about 8,000 meters per second. At the present time the satellite is moving in an elliptical trajectory around the Earth, and its flight can be observed in the rays of the eastern and western Sun with the help of simple optical instruments.' Although the Americans were beaten in the space race, they did not hold back congratulating the Russians for this major achievement. Only a month later, the Russians launched a second artificial satellite, *Sputnik 2*, weighing 250 lbs (114 kg); this time with a living passenger on board in the form of a stray dog named Laika. At the time, there was a good deal of controversy over the cruelty inflicted on Laika, and though the Soviets acknowledged that she would not return alive, they claimed that she would die painlessly during the journey. At the time, it was reported that Laika had survived for several days in orbit, but it was revealed in 2002 that she died of overheating and panic not long after takeoff. But she had by then served her purpose in proving that a living being could survive takeoff, and opened up the possibility of humans undertaking space travel.

'Sputnik 1 became the first artificial satellite to successfully orbit the earth.'

Above: Laika installed in the tiny cabin of Sputnik 2.

January 10
Britain Has New Prime Minister
Harold Macmillan becomes the Prime Minister of the U.K. following Anthony Eden's resignation.

March 6
Ghana Wins Independence
Ghana is the first African country to win independence from Britain.

March 25
E.E.C. Formed
Six European nations sign the Treaty of Rome to establish the European Economic Community.

April 12
Poem Seized for Obscenity
U.S. customs seize a copy of Allen Ginsberg's poem *Howl* for obscenity.

1957

FIGHT TO DESEGREGATE SOUTH CONTINUES

The Civil Rights Act of 1957, which had been squeezed through the U.S. Congress after Senator Lyndon B. Johnson watered it down, outlined measures for desegregation, including permitting black students into previously white-only schools. The Governor of Arkansas, Orval Faubus, was determined to oppose the federal law of desegregating schools. In September 1957, on the day that Little Rock High School was due to accept its first African-American students, Governor Faubus stationed 270 National Guards at the school, ostensibly to prevent any outbreak of violence. In truth, the Guards were there to prevent the nine black students from entering the school. The students stayed away for the first day of term, but on the second day, they were accompanied to school by two white ministers and two black ministers. The National Guards barred their entry, and white students and adults alike hurled verbal abuse. The whole episode was televised, drawing attention to the ugly reality of segregation in the South. A state governor had been seen the world over disobeying federal law, and President Eisenhower was forced to act. When the nine students made a second attempt to enter the school some weeks later, the President sent 1,000 paratroopers to keep order. Although the nine students eventually made it through the school year, it was a year filled with hatred, abuse, and resentment. In the school year of 1958 to 1959, Faubus closed all schools rather than allow blacks into white schools. The first attempts to end segregation had failed.

QUEEN VISITS NEW YORK

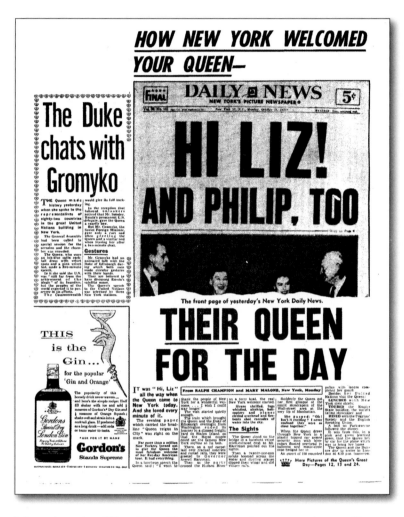

More than 1 million New Yorkers turned out to welcome Queen Elizabeth II at the end of her five-day American tour to promote the U.N. in October 1957. Overhead planes performed victory rolls to the sound of a 21-gun salute.

April 24
Sky at Night Begins
Patrick Moore presents the first episode in the long-running astronomy show *The Sky at Night* on the B.B.C.

May 2
McCarthy Dies
Senator Joe McCarthy dies of cirrhosis of the liver brought on by years of alcoholism.

May 15
Matthews Retires
Footballer Stanley Matthews plays his last game for England in a 23-year-long international career.

June 27
Hurricane Destroys Town
The town of Cameron, Louisiana, is flattened by Hurricane Audrey, killing 400 people.

July 25
Tunisia Becomes Republic
Habib Bourguiba is elected President of Tunisia and abolishes the monarchy.

IKE'S PROUD SPACE ROCKET BOAST

In the ongoing space race between the U.S. and the U.S.S.R., President Eisenhower was proud to announce in November 1957 that the Americans could bring a rocket *back* from space; a feat that he was sure the Russians had not yet achieved. As proof, at a press conference he held up the very cone-shaped rocket head that he said had been to space and back. The cone was intended to hold an H-bomb warhead in the experimental X-17 rocket, and Eisenhower's announcement signaled to the American people that they were ahead of the Soviets in the space race. To drive the point home, Eisenhower told the nation: 'Although the Soviets are obviously ahead of us in satellite development, the overall military strength of the free world today is greater than that of the Communist countries.' He added, 'We are well ahead of the Soviets in the nuclear field, both in quantity and in quality, and we intend to stay ahead.'

> **'President Eisenhower was proud to announce in November 1957 that the Americans could bring a rocket back from space; a feat that he was sure the Russians had not yet achieved.'**

Left: A Jupiter-A rocket launched by the Army Ballistic Missile Agency in 1957.

August 28
Senator's Epic Speech
U.S. Senator Strom Thurmond makes a 24-hour-long speech in a failed attempt to block a civil rights bill.

November 1
Mackinac Bridge Opened
The Mackinac Bridge in Michigan opens to traffic, and becomes the world's longest suspension bridge.

November 25
Ike Suffers Stroke
U.S. President Eisenhower suffers a stroke that leaves his speech impaired.

December 4
Train Crashes in London
Ninety-two people die when a train crashes in Lewisham in London.

December 6
U.S. Rocket Blows Up
The rocket blows up on the launch pad in the U.S.'s first attempt to launch a satellite into space.

1958

FRANCE VOTES FOR NEW REPUBLIC

Above: Charles de Gaulle

French statesman Charles de Gaulle was a military man who had distinguished himself in both world wars, and led the Resistance group, the Free French, after France fell to the Nazis. As president and military commander of the Free French, he had successfully led them to liberate Paris from the Nazis in August 1944. After the liberation of France, de Gaulle became the provisional president of the new France, but over the following years he was both in and out of power. By May 1958, France was on the brink of civil war over the issue of Algeria's independence. De Gaulle was called back to office to deal with the crisis, and he drafted the constitution of a Fifth Republic of France. The new constitution granted more power to the president and was designed to put an end to a series of weak governments. De Gaulle himself became the first president of the new republic on January 8, 1959.

February 1
New Arab State
Egypt and Syria unite to form the United Arab Republic. Nasser is nominated as president.

February 23
Fangio Kidnapped
Argentinian racing driver Juan Manuel Fangio is kidnapped by Cuban rebels. He is released the next day.

February 25
C.N.D. Launched
In Britain, the Campaign for Nuclear Disarmament is launched by philosopher Bertrand Russell.

March 27
New Soviet Premiere
Nikita Khrushchev becomes the new leader of the Soviet Union.

May 13
Protesters Storm Offices
French Algerians, fearing a French withdrawal from Algeria, seize government offices in Algiers.

SOCCER AIR TRAGEDY

On February 6, 1958, a plane carrying Manchester United Football team and their entourage back from a European Cup match in Belgrade crashed while taking off from Munich Airport. Seven Manchester United players died in the accident, depriving the country of some of its most promising football talent. The team was known as the 'Busby Babes' after their manager Matt Busby and the nation mourned the loss of such youthful promise. Their star striker, Bobby Charlton, was one of the survivors. In total, 21 people died in the crash, including sports journalists and team managers. The British European Airways plane had stopped to refuel in Munich, Germany, where there was a heavy snowstorm. Twice the pilot tried to take off, and on his third attempt, he overshot the runway, crashing into a house, and the plane burst into flames. The runway had been swamped in slush, leaving the plane unable to take off. The pilot was later cleared of any blame.

Above: A clock at Manchester United's ground, Old Trafford, showing the time of the crash.

PROTESTORS MARCH AGAINST THE BOMB

In 1950s Britain, mainstream protest against the development of nuclear weapons came under the wing of the Campaign for Nuclear Disarmament (C.N.D.). However, a more radical group also existed. This group was known as the Direct Action Committee Against Nuclear War (D.A.C.), and its aim was to halt nuclear armament via marches, vigils, industrial action, and civil disobedience. D.A.C. leaders were prepared to go to jail for their actions and had systems in place to enable protest to continue while their leaders were jailed. The D.A.C. was headed by Harold Steele, and their first major action was a march on the Atomic Weapons Research Establishment at Aldermaston in 1958. From that point on, the C.N.D. took over and made the march from Aldermaston to London an annual event over the Easter weekend.

'DAC leaders were prepared to go to jail for their actions.'

June 16
Nagy Hanged
The anti-Soviet former Prime Minister of Hungary, Imre Nagy, is hanged for treason.

June 29
Brazil Win World Cup
Brazil beat Sweden 5–2 in the final to win their first World Cup.

July 29
N.A.S.A. Created
The National Aeronautics and Space Administration is formed to further the U.S.'s space program.

September 1
Cod War
A conflict over fishing rights breaks out between Iceland and the U.K. It is popularly known as the Cod War.

October 21
Women in Lords
Female peers are allowed to sit in the British second chamber, the House of Lords.

1958

KING KILLED IN IRAQI COUP

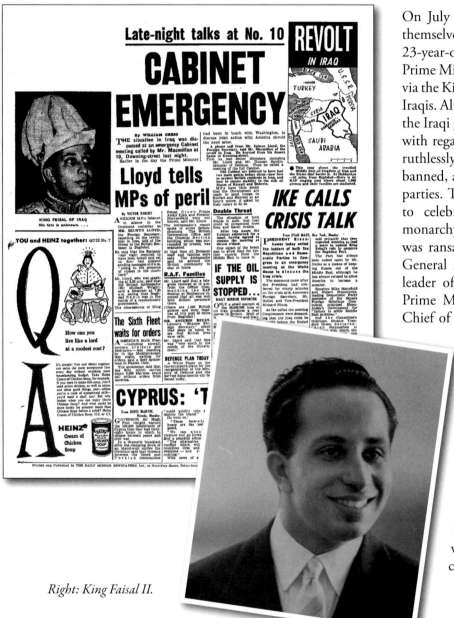

Right: King Faisal II.

On July 14, 1958, an army group of Arab nationalists calling themselves the Free Officers seized power in Iraq, assassinating 23-year-old King Faisal II, as well as members of his family and the Prime Minister of the Iraqi-Jordan Alliance. British control in Iraq via the King had long been a source of violent resentment for many Iraqis. Although this control had officially come to an end in 1932, the Iraqi government upheld British interests to the last, especially with regards to oil. Under the monarchy, all resistance had been ruthlessly stamped out, with any form of protest or demonstration banned, as well as opposition political parties. The people took to the streets to celebrate the overthrow of the monarchy, and the British Embassy was ransacked and set alight. Major-General Abdul Karim el Qasim, the leader of the coup, declared himself Prime Minister and Commander-in-Chief of the new Iraqi regime, which would be a 'people's republic' closely allied to its Arab neighbors. He immediately set about making a defense pact with the United Arab Republic (U.A.R.), a recently formed alliance of Egypt and Syria. Western powers were concerned not only about their own oil interests in the region but about the stability of the Baghdad Pact, the defense pact between Turkey, Persia, and Pakistan that was aimed at protecting the Middle East from the threat of Soviet Communism. Following emergency meetings, British and U.S. troops were sent to Jordan and Lebanon to guard against possible copycat Arab nationalist revolts.

> **'British control in Iraq via the King had long been a source of violent resentment for many Iraqis.'**

October 28
New Pope Elected
Angelo Giuseppe Roncalli is elected the new Pope. He takes the name Pope John XXIII.

November 10
First Bossa Nova Record
Joao Gilberto makes the first Bossa Nova record in Rio de Janeiro.

November 30
French Elections
Supporters of Charles de Gaulle win a parliamentary majority in France.

December 5
Britain's First Motorway
The Preston Bypass, the first stretch of motorway in Britain, is opened.

NIXON SPEAKS ON SOVIET TELEVISION

On July 24, 1959, during Richard Nixon's 11-day tour of the U.S.S.R., the American Vice-President and Soviet leader Nikita Khrushchev engaged in a heated public debate about the relative merits of capitalism and Communism. While walking together around an American trade fair in Moscow, they stopped at a mock-up of an American kitchen boasting all the latest gadgets, including a refrigerator, toaster, and juicer. Khrushchev waved it off dismissively, claiming that although the Americans thought to impress the Soviets with their technological advancement, the Soviets themselves already had all these gadgets in their own kitchens. Nixon replied: 'We do not claim to astonish the Soviet people. We hope to show our right to choose. We do not wish to have decisions made at the top by government officials who say that all homes should be built in the same way.' From there, the argument escalated, with Khrushchev threatening Nixon over foreign military bases and Nixon declaring that the Americans would not be dictated to. Khrushchev then boasted that the Soviets built better rockets, a claim that Nixon tried to counter by implying that the U.S. could equal them. Eventually, the two men laughed off their argument and apologized, but what made this exchange into international news was that it was filmed on the first video tape recorder. Unexpectedly, Khrushchev allowed Nixon to make a televised address to the Soviet people, and Nixon used the occasion to once again denounce Communism, warning of dire consequences if it was forcibly spread beyond Soviet borders. Nixon's popularity on returning home was considerably increased.

Right: An American cooker from the 1950s.

January 3
Alaska Made a State
Alaska becomes the 49th state of the U.S.A.

February 1
Swiss Men Vote Against Female Suffrage
In a referendum, men in Switzerland decide to deny women the vote.

February 3
The Day the Music Died
Musicians Buddy Holly, Ritchie Valens, and the Big Bopper are killed in a plane crash.

April 17
Kind of Blue
Jazz trumpeter Miles Davis releases his seminal album *Kind of Blue*.

1959

BATISTA FLEES CUBA

On January 1, 1959, the Cuban dictator Fulgencio Batista fled his country in the face of a revolutionary coup led by Fidel Castro. While declaring that government forces had been victorious in the Battle of Santa Clara against Castro's guerrilla forces, Batista simultaneously evacuated his family, his cabinet, and his military aides to the Dominican Republic, Florida, and New Orleans on various planes. He left behind a military junta to rule in his absence, but it was swiftly toppled by rebel forces. A former soldier, General Batista had twice held absolute power in Cuba, first from 1933 to 1942 and then again from 1952. His regime had enjoyed the support of the United States for a number of years, but his loss of popularity forced the U.S. to consider alternatives. Faced with the prospect of Castro's 'leftist' revolutionary group, the U.S. continued to support Batista, albeit halfheartedly. However, Batista's own people had become increasingly disillusioned with his government. On the other hand, Fidel Castro offered hope and change with his fiery nationalistic talk and personal charisma. On January 7, 1959, he and his followers – including his brother Raúl Castro and Ernesto 'Che' Guevara – entered Havana in triumph. Cubans everywhere celebrated the departure of Batista and welcomed Castro with open arms. The U.S. was increasingly concerned about the safety of their interests in Cuba. It was not long before the new leader Castro nationalized American properties and made strong ties with Communist Russia. The U.S. reacted by cutting all ties with Cuba and bringing a trade and travel embargo into force.

May 28
Monkeys in Space
Two rhesus monkeys on board a U.S. spaceship return to Earth alive.

July 17
Early Human Skull Found
A skull of an early hominid, named *Australopithecus*, is discovered in Tanzania.

July 27
Holliday Dies
U.S. singer Billie Holliday dies of liver failure aged 44.

August 21
Hawaii Becomes U.S. State
Hawaii is made the 50th state of the United States.

September 15
Khrushchev in America
Soviet premier Nikita Khrushchev begins a 13-day visit to the U.S.A.

SOVIET ROCKET LANDS ON THE MOON

On September 12, 1959, the U.S.S.R. launched a second rocket aimed at the Moon, and this time the target was reached. The first attempt, launched on January 2, 1958, had successfully launched, but it missed the Moon and continued out into space. It was necessary for the Moon rocket, *Luna 2*, to reach a speed of 7 mps (11 kps) in order for it to counter the pull of Earth's gravitational force and break away from the Earth. *Luna 2* reached the Moon, 236,875 miles (382,056 km) away, 36 hours after its launch – 1 minute and 24 seconds later than estimated. On board were various scientific instruments intended for measuring the magnetic fields of the Earth and Moon, among other things. The instruments were sealed in a container to prevent any contamination of the Moon. The container also held the Communist 'sickle and star' flag, although the U.S.S.R. denied that it would be making any territorial claims on the Moon. The successful landing took place just days before Soviet leader Nikita Khrushchev was due to visit Washington, D.C. The timing was extremely opportune given the competitive nature of the space race between the U.S. and the U.S.S.R.

Right: The Soviet 'sickle and star' flag.

RED FLAGS LANDED BY MOON ROCKET

By RONALD BEDFORD

BULL'S-EYE! Russia's Moon Rocket thudded into its target at two minutes and twenty-three seconds past ten last night — just eighty-three seconds behind schedule.

And jubilantly, Moscow radio announced: "For the first time, man has succeeded in reaching another body in space."

The impact could not be seen from earth but it was tracked on Britain's giant radio-telescope at Jodrell Bank, Cheshire.

JODRELL BANK RADIO DRAMA

MOSCOW KEEPS RADIO WATCH

IT'S NEW! IT'S SENSATIONAL!
It's the wonderful "Triumph"
LUXURY ELECTRIC WASHING MACHINE
£22

September 26
Typhoon Hits Japan
Over 5,000 people are killed when Typhoon Vera hits the Japanese island of Honshu.

October 21
New York Museum Opens
The Guggenheim Museum in New York opens its doors to the public.

December 1
Antarctic Agreement
Twelve countries, including the United States and the Soviet Union, sign a pact to preserve Antarctica.

December 2
Dam Collapses
The Malpasset Dam in southern France collapses, flooding the town of Frejus and killing over 400 people.

December 9
Ike in India
U.S. President Eisenhower visits India and addresses the country's parliaments.

149

1960-1969

The 1960s were witness to some of the world's most memorable and momentous events. At the beginning of the decade, John F. Kennedy became America's youngest president. His idealism promised to place America center-stage in a modern civilization that championed equal rights and world peace, but his assassination three years later cut short that promise. Civil rights activist Martin Luther King, Jr. was also assassinated, in 1968, but had already done much in his battle against racial segregation. Meanwhile, another freedom-fighter, Nelson Mandela, was imprisoned for sabotage during his campaigns on behalf of the oppressed black population of South Africa.

Although the Soviets beat the Americans in the space race by getting the first man into orbit around the Earth in 1961, the Americans won the race to the Moon when the Apollo mission successfully landed Neil Armstrong and Buzz Aldrin on the lunar surface. In 1969, the entire world watched the Moon landings, marveling at the potential for the future contained in that magical moment.

But at a time when the spirit of adventure was courageously breaching new frontiers, the world also came close to nuclear war when the Soviet Union shipped nuclear missiles to a base in Cuba in 1962.

J.F.K. WINS U.S. PRESIDENTIAL ELECTION

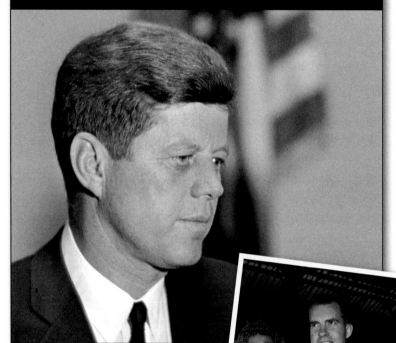

GIANT U.S. RUSH TO VOTE

'In his inauguration speech, he made the famous declaration: "Ask not what your country can do for you – ask what you can do for your country"'

Above: Richard and Pat Nixon.

On November 8, 1960, at the age of 43, John F. Kennedy made history by becoming the youngest ever and first Roman Catholic President of the United States. In a presidential campaign that featured televised public debates for the first time, Kennedy narrowly defeated the Republican candidate, Richard Nixon, winning over the nation with confidence and charisma that perfectly suited the medium of television. One of the major issues that divided the two candidates was American foreign policy, particularly the Cold War with the Soviet Union. Nixon claimed that the Republican administration had successfully contained the spread of Soviet power over the previous eight years and that the young Kennedy lacked the necessary experience to handle such dangerous matters. Kennedy, on the other hand, claimed that the Republicans, under 'Ike' Eisenhower, had allowed the U.S.A. to fall behind in the arms race, to the point where it was in danger of being outstripped by Soviet technological advances. He also accused the Republicans of needlessly losing Cuba to the Soviets through a lack of proactive intervention. Kennedy won the election, but foreign policy failures dogged his administration. In his first two years in office, the Cold War grew colder: the Bay of Pigs invasion, when a U.S. force of expatriate Cubans tried to invade Cuba and oust Fidel Castro, ended in defeat and led directly to the Cuban Missile Crisis the following year, and the erection of the Berlin Wall to separate the democratic and Communist halves of Germany. However, Kennedy's brief administration was also characterized by his special brand of idealism. He vigorously supported equal rights and world peace, while also tackling poverty and encouraging cultural and artistic development. In his inauguration speech he made the famous declaration, 'Ask not what your country can do for you – ask what you can do for your country,' and it was this spirit of personal responsibility and sacrifice in a common cause that lived on after his death.

'Kennedy's brief administration was also characterized by his special brand of idealism.'

February 3
Apartheid Under Attack
U.K. Prime Minister Harold Macmillan condemns South Africa's apartheid policy in a speech given in Cape Town.

February 9
Walk of Fame Inaugurated
Actress Joanne Woodward is the first person to be commemorated with a star set into the pavement on Hollywood Boulevard.

March 8
Elvis Leaves the Army
'The King' finishes nearly two years of military service.

April 21
Brazil Inaugurates New Capital City
After four years of construction, the inauguration of Brasília is celebrated across the country.

PROTESTERS KILLED IN APARTHEID SOUTH AFRICA

The apartheid laws that underpinned the regime of Hendrik Verwoerd, Prime Minister of South Africa, were designed to separate the privileged white citizens from the black masses. One such law required black South Africans to carry passbooks, which, beyond identification details, noted if they had paid taxes or been arrested. These books had to be stamped every month by employers, and if a black man stepped outside his front door without carrying his pass, he could be arrested, imprisoned, and fined. The African National Congress (A.N.C.), the most significant of the anti-apartheid groups, had been campaigning peacefully for many years against the institutionalized oppression of black people. But when, in April 1960, it organized a demonstration against the discriminatory passbook laws, a more militant group, the Pan African Congress (P.A.C.), joined in, calling for mass civil disobedience. The leader of the P.A.C., Robert Mangaliso Sobukwe, pleaded for all black males to

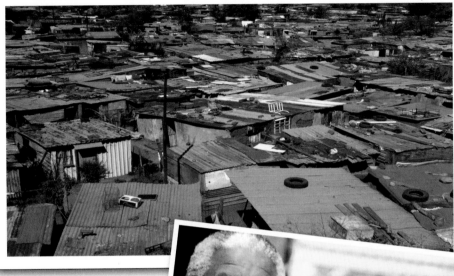

FURY IN SOUTH AFRICA

'In the mayhem that followed ... 69 people were shot dead ... including innocent bystanders and children.'

descend on police stations without their passbooks and demand to be arrested. His aim was to create a mass demonstration against the ruling white oppressors that could be witnessed the world over. In most locations there were some arrests and one or two casualties. However, in Sharpeville, near Johannesburg, the situation erupted into an outbreak of brutality that would never be forgotten. Initially, there were 20 policemen to 20,000 black protestors. Although the crowd was unarmed, there was some stone-throwing, and the police called in reinforcements. As

scuffles continued and the crowd advanced on the police station, the police chief panicked and gave the order to load and fire. In the mayhem that followed, the unarmed crowd scattered in terror, and 69 people were shot dead within a couple of minutes, including innocent bystanders and children. The incident prompted international outrage, and for the first time worldwide attention was drawn to the situation that apartheid policies were creating in South Africa.

Above: In 1996, Nelson Mandela, the first president of a democratic South Africa, signed the country's new constitution at Sharpeville, the scene of the 1960 massacre.

May 16
First Laser Tested
U.S. scientist Theodore Maiman builds the first working prototype of a laser using synthetic ruby.

June 16
Psycho Premiere
Alfred Hitchcock's stylish suspense movie thrills audiences around the world despite lukewarm reviews.

June 30
Belgian Congo Crisis
Belgium's grant of independence to the Congo triggers a four-year crisis in a struggle to gain control of the country's mineral resources.

July 20
World's First Woman Prime Minister
Sirimavo Bandaranaike becomes the Prime Minister of Sri Lanka (or Ceylon as it was then known).

1960

U.S. PILOT SHOT DOWN OVER SOVIET AIRSPACE

On August 19, 1960, American pilot Francis Gary Powers was sentenced to ten years in a Soviet prison after pleading guilty to spying for the C.I.A. Captured after his U-2 plane entered Soviet airspace and was shot down on May 1, Powers admitted to spying for the American government, but the evidence found in the plane's wreckage, including tape recordings of signals from Soviet radar stations, incriminated him anyway. He was also in possession of a poisoned pin with which he was meant to commit suicide under torture. Powers had been recruited by the C.I.A. after leaving the U.S. Air Force, and had been told that his espionage work would involve flying along the Soviet border in an attempt to pick up radio and radar signals. The incident created bad press for the government of President Eisenhower (right), particularly when America was publicly denounced by the Soviet prosecutor for deliberately sabotaging world peace. The prosecutor further claimed that it had been America's deliberate intention to jeopardize the international summit due to be held in Paris. The aim of the summit was to discuss a relaxation of Soviet–U.S. relations and the possibility of arms control, and it was indeed canceled when Soviet leader Nikita Khrushchev pulled out over the Powers incident. Powers himself spent two years in a Soviet jail before being swapped with Soviet spy Colonel Rudolph Abel in a mutual and highly publicized handover.

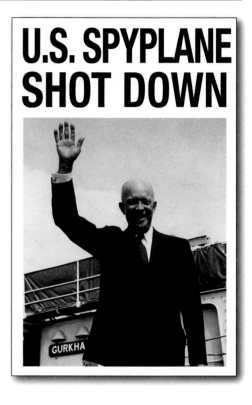

U.S. SPYPLANE SHOT DOWN

PRIME MINISTER OF CONGO EXECUTED

EXECUTED

In September 1960, Patrice Lumumba, African anti-colonialist and first prime minister of independent Congo, was deposed from power only two months after being instated. He had long fought for independence from the Belgian rulers, and when it was granted, the first elections were set for May 1960. Lumumba was duly elected, but his fiercely anti-colonialist inauguration speech provoked various authorities present. His first mistake as prime minister was to increase the pay of all government employees, except those in the army. This sparked an immediate army revolt, which quickly erupted into full-blown civil war, with the Katanga province declaring its own independence with Belgian backing. President Kasa-Vubu fired Lumumba from his government, and chaos ensued. The U.S.S.R. intervened on behalf of Lumumba, while the U.S. backed the Belgians and set up its own candidate, Joseph Mobutu, to oppose both Lumumba and Kasa-Vubu. Initially, Lumumba was under U.N. protection, but when he escaped and attempted to set up his own government, he was on his own. He was arrested in December and executed by firing squad on January 17, 1961.

September 5
Cassius Clay Takes Boxing Gold
Cassius Clay (later Muhammad Ali) wins the Light Heavyweight gold medal at the Rome Olympics.

September 10
O.P.E.C. Established
The Organization of the Petroleum Exporting Countries (O.P.E.C.) is formed at a meeting in Baghdad with the aim of securing stable oil prices.

October 1
Nigeria Becomes Independent
Britain grants Nigeria independence, although the Queen remains Head of State until 1963.

October 27
Lady Chatterley's Lover Trial
After a six-day trial, D.H. Lawrence's novel is ruled not obscene, after publisher Penguin mounts a defense to prove that the book has 'redeeming social merit'.

1961

SOVIETS LAUNCH MAN INTO SPACE

FIRST MAN IN SPACE

On April 12, 1961, the Soviet spacecraft *Vostok 1* was launched into space with a man on board: thus did Russian cosmonaut Yuri Gagarin became the first man to go where no man had gone before. After completing one orbit of the Earth, which took 108 minutes, Gargarin ejected himself from the craft and parachuted safely to the ground (although it was claimed at the time that he landed *with* the spacecraft, as required by official rules). The spacecraft was controlled automatically, so Gagarin had no power over its course. This was done to protect him, as it was not yet known how a human being would react to the weightlessness of space. However, he was in possession of an envelope containing a set of codes that would unlock the controls system and enable him to pilot the spacecraft in case of an emergency.

'After completing one orbit of the Earth, which took 108 minutes, Gargarin ejected himself from Vostok 1 and parachuted safely to the ground'

Above: A rocket similar to the type used to blast Gagarin into space, and a stamp issued to celebrate the event.

January 24
Nuclear Bombs Dropped on U.S. Soil
A B52 bomber flying over North Carolina breaks up in mid-air, dropping two nuclear bombs. Safety devices prevent disaster.

January 31
First Chimp in Space
Ham, a male chimp, is the sole passenger on a sub-orbital test flight. Ham survives the flight and landing and lives until 1983.

February 5
War Breaks Out in Angola
The emergence of three independence groups in the Portuguese colony leads to a wave of violence.

February 9
Beatles' First Performance
A lunchtime session at the Cavern Club, Liverpool, sees the debut of new local band The Beatles.

April 11
Bob Dylan's Debut
Dylan plays his first paying gig, supporting John Lee Hooker at a New York club.

1961

CASTRO'S ARMY DEFEATS U.S. INVADERS IN CUBA

The 1959 Cuban Revolutionary War that had toppled dictator Fulgencio Batista and placed Communist revolutionary Fidel Castro in power had drastically altered relations between the U.S. and Cuba. In March 1960, President Eisenhower had approved a C.I.A. plan to train a group of U.S.-based Cuban exiles to invade Cuba. If successful, anti-Castro exile José Miró Cardona would take over the government of Cuba. By the time the invasion came about, John F. Kennedy was President, and he gave the go-ahead even though the secret mission was so widely publicized that Castro himself knew of it. The invasion began on April 15, 1961 with the aerial bombing of Cuban airports. For this, U.S. Second World War planes were painted to look like Cuban Air Force planes. Not only were they unsuccessful, but their poor disguise made American involvement clear for all to see. This caused Kennedy to cancel the second planned air strike. On April 17, some 1,400 Cuban exiles landed at the Bay of Pigs, an area chosen for its obscurity but that proved to be unhelpful territory from which to launch an invasion. The mission was a complete failure: within three days of the landings, 1,189 of the paramilitaries had been captured by Castro's 20,000-strong force, and more than 100 were killed. The incident caused embarrassment for the new President, and Kennedy sacked the C.I.A. director promptly.

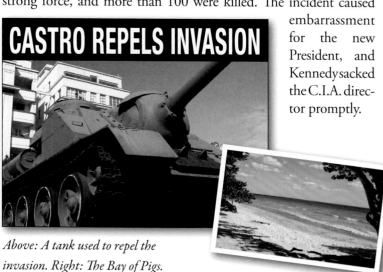

Above: A tank used to repel the invasion. Right: The Bay of Pigs.

BARBED WIRE DIVIDES BERLIN

On August 13, 1961, the people of Berlin awoke to discover that a wall of barbed wire had been constructed along the border between East and West Germany, and no one was allowed to cross it. The barbed wire was soon replaced with a permanent concrete structure 12 ft (4 m) high and over 66 miles (106 km) long. The wall was in complete violation of the post-war agreement that placed Berlin under the control of four powers – Britain, France, the U.S.S.R., and the United States – and it provoked international outrage. However, both Britain and the U.S.A. were reluctant to intervene, despite pleas from West Germany, and in fact saw the wall as a positive signal that the East Germans and Soviets would leave the rest of Berlin alone. Meanwhile, the East German government, with Soviet support, was planning to separate from the rest of Germany. The wall divided families and cut off East Berliners from their jobs in West Berlin. Although the official justification for the wall was that it would protect East Germany from Western aggression and spies, the reality was that it acted as a one-way block to prevent East Germans from fleeing to the West. The Berlin Wall stayed in place for 28 years, during which time around 200 people were killed trying to cross it because border guards had been instructed to shoot potential defectors. It did not come down until the Communist government resigned in 1989.

BERLIN IS DIVIDED

'The wall divided families and cut off East Berliners from their jobs in West Berlin.'

May 17
South Africa Leaves Commonwealth
South Africa officially leaves the Commonwealth of Nations.

June 16
Nureyev Defects
After a run of performances in Paris, the brightest young star of Soviet ballet, Rudolf Nureyev, defects to the West.

July 2
Ernest Hemingway Commits Suicide
The American author shoots himself after a bout of depression.

September 10
Crash at Italian Grand Prix
German driver Wolfgang von Trips is killed along with 14 spectators when he crashes at Monza.

October 30
Nuclear Test
The Soviet Union detonates a 58-megaton-yield hydrogen bomb known as Tsar Bomba over Novaya Zemlya.

U.N. SECRETARY GENERAL DIES

On September 18, 1961, a plane carrying the U.N. Secretary General Dag Hammarskjöld between two Congolese provinces exploded and crashed, instantly killing 14 of its 15 passengers. The only survivor, who died of his injuries days later, explained that the plane was about to land in Ndola, where Mr. Hammarskjöld was due to hold face-to-face talks with the leader of the breakaway Katanga province in the Congo. But at the last minute Mr. Hammarskjöld ordered the pilot to divert elsewhere. Soon after, there were three explosions on board, and the plane went down. The Swedish statesman, who had been U.N. Secretary General for the previous eight years, had done much to promote peacekeeping in troubled regions, including China and the Middle East, and was posthumously awarded the Nobel Peace Prize. In the six weeks before his death, Hammarskjöld had visited 21 countries and territories in Africa, and entered troubled waters by providing U.N. military intervention in the Congo after it descended into civil war following independence. The move had angered the Soviets, who thought he was supporting colonial rule in Africa, and they called for his resignation. While tributes for the deceased statesman poured in from foreign leaders all over the world, the Soviets were silent.

U.N. LEADER KILLED IN AIR CRASH

Right: The headquarters of the United Nations in New York.

November 11
Catch-22 Published
Joseph Heller's satirical novel was written in the late 50s but does not appear in print until 1961. The title of the novel has passed into common usage to mean a no-win situation.

December 11
U.S. Troops Arrive in Vietnam
U.S. aircraft carrier *Core* arrives in Saigon with a cargo of over 30 helicopters and 400 servicemen to support the South Vietnamese in their struggle against the Communist North. The event marks the start of America's military build-up in the area.

December 15
Eichmann Sentenced to Death
Adolf Eichmann, who organized the deportation of Jews to the Nazis' extermination camps, is sentenced to death by an Israeli court. He was captured by Israeli agents in Argentina.

1962

SATELLITE COMMUNICATIONS ARRIVE

WONDERFUL TELSTAR

Above: The original Telstar.
Right: A modern telecommunications satellite and dish receiver.

In 1960, the company AT&T, which enjoyed a monopoly in terrestrial communications in the U.S. at the time, teamed up with N.A.S.A. to design and create the first satellite communications system. Called Telstar, the system involved having 55 satellites in orbit at the same time, and 25 ground stations spaced across the globe to receive signals. The Telstar spacecraft was designed and built by Bell Telephone Laboratories, and N.A.S.A. provided and operated the launch vehicles.

Although it was not, in fact, the first ever communications satellite, Telstar is the best known, and is generally considered to have launched the era of satellite communications. N.A.S.A.'s chief of communications has explained why so many people mistakenly think Telstar was the first of its kind: 'This impression was a result of the tremendous impact upon the public by the first transmission of live television across the Atlantic Ocean. Telstar 1 was launched on July 10, 1962, and on that same day live television pictures originating in the United States were received in France.' Receiving stations had been set up in the U.S. state of Maine, as well as in France and Britain. The day after its first transmission, President Kennedy made the following statement: 'The successful firing and subsequent operation of the Telstar communications satellite is an outstanding example of the way in which government and business can cooperate in a most important field of human endeavor. There is no more important field at the present time than communications, and we must grasp the advantages presented to us by the communications satellite to use this medium wisely and effectively to ensure greater understanding among the peoples of the world.'

'The system involved having 55 satellites in orbit at the same time, and 25 ground stations spaced across the globe to receive signals.'

January 15
Yves Saint-Lauren Launches Own Label
At the age of 25, the Algerian-born French fashion designer founds his own label.

March 1
New York Plane Crash
A Boeing 707 crashes soon after takeoff from New York's Idlewild Airport, plummeting into Jamaica Bay, and causing the death of all 95 passengers and crew on board.

April 8
Bay of Pigs Trial
The largest mass trial in Cuba's history ends with the conviction of over 1,000 Cuban exiles who had attempted to invade the country in 1961.

April 23
Stirling Moss in Coma After Crash
The racing driver is almost killed in a crash at Britain's Goodwood circuit.

U.S. AND SOVIET UNION CLASH OVER CUBA

The Cuban Missile Crisis is so far the closest the world has ever come to nuclear war. In the ongoing arms race between the U.S.S.R. and the U.S.A., the Soviets were behind and desperate to improve their position. Aware that America already possessed missiles powerful enough to wipe out the entire Soviet Union, while Soviet missiles could reach only Europe, the U.S.S.R. decided to create a nuclear base closer to the U.S. from which they would be able to pose a genuine threat. In April 1962, Soviet premier Nikita Khrushchev approached Fidel Castro, his Communist ally in Cuba, with the idea of setting up a Soviet nuclear missile on his island. Castro was delighted with the plan, which would solve his concerns over a second American invasion of Cuba. On October 15, 1962, U.S. spy-planes garnered information that Soviet missile bases were being built in Cuba and that the missiles were already being shipped over. After several days of intense talks, President Kennedy made the information public and openly declared that, if Soviet missiles were not removed from Cuba, the move would be viewed as an offensive on the United States. On October 22, Kennedy set up a naval quarantine around the island. Four days later, Khrushchev, realizing that he could not contend with the combined might of the U.S. Navy's artillery pointing directly at him, responded by letter, stating that the Soviets would remove their missiles if America would promise not to invade Cuba. To the entire watching world, it seemed that nuclear war was on the point of breaking out in earnest. International tension reached a peak on October 27, when an American U-2 spy-plane was shot down over Cuba. In a second letter, Khrushchev also demanded that the Americans deactivate their missile bases in Turkey, but Attorney General Robert Kennedy chose to ignore this and instead agreed to guarantee that the U.S. would not attack Cuba. Tensions finally eased on October 28, when Khrushchev began to remove Soviet missiles from Cuba and dismantle the stations.

'The Cuban Missile Crisis is so far the closest the world has ever come to nuclear war.'

KHRUSHCHEV SENDS MISSILES TO CUBA

Right: A ballistic missile.

May 3
Tokyo Train Disaster
A train crashes north of Tokyo. Over 160 people are killed.

June 22
Plane Crash in Guadeloupe
An Air France Boeing 707 jet crashes at Guadeloupe's Le Raizet airport, killing all 113 passengers and crew on board.

July 20
Hovercraft Service Launched
The world's first hovercraft passenger service opens between Moreton in England and Rhyl in Wales.

July 21
Rolling Stones' Debut Gig
The Rolling Stones make their first ever live appearance, at London's Marquee Club.

1962

MARILYN MONROE DIES OF OVERDOSE

On August 5, 1962, the actress Marilyn Monroe was found dead in the bedroom of her Los Angeles home. She had died from an overdose of sleeping pills, and the coroner ruled it a 'probable suicide'. The world-famous film star was only 36 at the time of her death, and it was rumored that she had been due to remarry her second husband, baseball star Joe DiMaggio. Born Norma Jeane Mortenson to an impoverished mother with mental health problems, Marilyn Monroe spent her childhood between foster homes and orphanages. She then shot to fame after being spotted by a fashion photographer. At the age of 20, Monroe signed a contract with the film studio 20th Century Fox, and starred in several box-office hits, including *The Seven Year Itch*, *Gentlemen Prefer Blondes*, and *Some Like It Hot*. She became a sex icon across the globe, but in her professional life she was considered difficult to work with and had been typecast as a dumb blonde. After three failed marriages, the last to playwright Arthur Miller, Monroe was romantically linked with various public figures, including President Kennedy. Only months before her death, she famously sang the President a breathy version of 'Happy Birthday', her last public performance.

FIRST AMERICAN IN SPACE

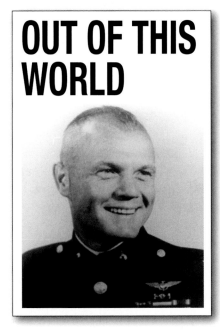

OUT OF THIS WORLD

'After successfully orbiting the Earth, John Glenn became an instant national hero.'

On February 20, 1962, the Americans finally achieved what the Soviets had already achieved less than a year earlier – they sent a man into space to orbit the Earth. American astronaut John Glenn, in the Mercury capsule *Friendship 7*, circled the globe three times in 4 hours and 56 minutes, covering 80,000 miles (130,000 km) and reaching speeds of 17,000 mph (27,000 kph). There were 24 American ships on standby at various points across the globe, each one ready to recover the spacecraft when it landed. Eventually it executed a successful splashdown in the Atlantic Ocean between Bermuda and Puerto Rico, and was picked up by a U.S. destroyer. Glenn had originally been selected as one of seven test pilots for N.A.S.A. in 1959 because he met all the necessary criteria: apart from being one of the best test pilots in the country, he was in excellent physical shape, less than 40 years old, shorter than 5 ft 11 in (182 cm), a qualified jet pilot, and had a degree in engineering. After successfully orbiting the Earth, John Glenn became an instant national hero.

October 5
Beatles Release First Single
'Love Me Do' is the first release from new Liverpool beat combo The Beatles.

October 5
First James Bond Film
The first big-screen appearance of 007 takes place at the London Pavilion, and features Sean Connery as the MI6 agent.

December 21
U.S. Offers Nuclear Bombs to U.K. and France
President Kennedy offers to sell Polaris nuclear missiles to Britain and France. France declines the offer, but Britain accepts.

CIVIL RIGHTS MARCH ON WASHINGTON D.C.

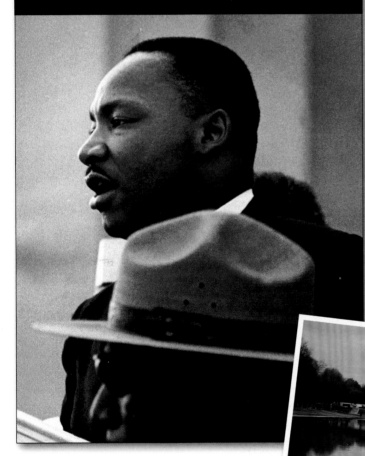

MARCH ON WASHINGTON

Throughout 1963 there was racial unrest in Birmingham, Alabama, and international sympathy for the civil rights movement was heightened by media coverage of the police using attack dogs and fire hoses against protestors, some of them children. Demonstrations frequently turned into riots, and Martin Luther King Jr. was arrested during one such riot for not carrying an identity card, but he continued to advocate civil disobedience against unjust laws. There were further demonstrations throughout the United States, culminating on August 28, 1963 in a march on Washington, D.C., which was attended by six different civil rights organizations. The march attracted around 250,000 supporters and was given wide broadcast coverage. The aim of the march was to achieve meaningful civil rights legislation, an end to racial segregation and public acts of discrimination, increased job opportunities for African Americans, and an end to police brutality. In short, it was for 'jobs and freedom'. President Kennedy supported the march, although originally he had been against it, purely on the grounds that it might stall the progress through Congress of a civil rights bill. On the day, the marchers, a quarter of them white, marched from the Washington Monument to the Lincoln Memorial. It was a calm, nonviolent protest from beginning to end. All of the leading civil rights leaders spoke, and Martin Luther King Jr.'s rousing speech became one of the most famous in history. He began by urging the crowd not to collapse into violence, saying, 'Again and again, we must rise to the majestic heights of meeting physical force with soul force.' He then moved on to his now landmark 'I have a dream' theme, looking forward to an America in which his children would 'not be judged by the color of their skin but by the content of their character'. The phrase has been repeated ever since and has come to represent the heart of Dr. King's teachings.

'Martin Luther King Jr.'s rousing speech became one of the most famous in history.'

Right: The Lincoln Memorial, where Dr. King delivered his 'dream' speech.

January 2
North Vietnamese Down U.S. Choppers
Five U.S. helicopters are shot down during a botched operation over the rice marshes southwest of Saigon.

March 22
Beatles Release First Album
Recorded in a single day, *Please Please Me* is rushed out to capitalize on the success of the single of the same name.

May 18
Riots in Alabama
In the U.S., civil rights protestors are attacked and Martin Luther King is arrested. President Kennedy sends in troops to quell the subsequent riots.

May 25
Organization of African Unity Established
At a meeting in Addis Ababa, Ethiopia, 32 countries form the Organization of African Unity.

1963

MONEY STOLEN FROM BRITISH MAIL TRAIN

THE GREAT TRAIN ROBBERY

On August 8, 1963, a gang of 15 robbers held up the Glasgow-to-London mail train and fled with £2.6 million. The train, which had run without event every night for 125 years, was forced to stop in the early hours of the morning by signals the gang had tampered with. The driver was stunned with a blow, and in a 20-minute operation, the thieves uncoupled the engine and front two

Above: Ronnie Biggs celebrates 25 years since the Great Train Robbery.

carriages, drove them up the line, and transferred 120 sacks of money into a waiting truck. Most of the used banknotes were due to be destroyed, but they had not been marked and were all untraceable. The meticulously planned heist, which was to go down in history as the 'Great Train Robbery', was the master plan of Bruce Reynolds, who evaded capture until 1969. Two others, Ronnie Biggs and Charlie Wilson, escaped abroad, while the remaining 12 were convicted after a large-scale, six-month police operation and given significant jail terms. Ronnie Biggs was discovered in Brazil, but not brought to justice because Brazil has no extradition treaty with England. However, in 2001 he finally returned to the U.K. of his own accord and was sent to prison.

FRENCH BLOCK U.K.'S ENTRY INTO E.E.C.

The Second World War had made European countries strongly aware of their relative weakness when acting alone, and post-war reliance on American aid made the need for greater European integration – both economically and politically – all the more pressing. European states realized that to contend with the U.S. and U.S.S.R. superpowers, they would need to form a homogenous unit. In 1946, Winston Churchill recognized the need to 're-create the European family … to provide it with a structure under which it can dwell in peace, in safety, and in

DE GAULLE BLOCKS U.K. FROM EUROPE

freedom'. He foresaw the creation of what he called a united states of Europe. The first stage of this allowed free trade between European states and the pooling of natural resources, with the Treaty of Paris creating the European Coal and Steel Community, consisting of France, Germany, Italy, Belgium, the Netherlands, and Luxembourg. Next, the European Economic Community (E.E.C.) was enshrined in the 1957 Treaty of Rome. Reluctant to give up its sovereignty, Britain kept away from the E.E.C. However, realizing its growing economic strength, British Prime Minister Harold Wilson decided to apply for entry in 1962. In January 1963, French President Charles de Gaulle rejected the application on the grounds that Britain did not have a European mindset and was too attached to its Commonwealth. De Gaulle was known to be anti-British in his stance on Europe, and was particularly wary of American intervention in European affairs, which he felt would be a side-effect of British membership of the E.E.C.

June 16
First Woman in Space
Lieutenant Valentina Tereshkova is carried into orbit aboard the Soviet rocket *Vostok 6*.

June 26
Kennedy Visits Berlin
President Kennedy offers U.S. support for the residents of West Germany.

August 5
Nuclear Test Ban Treaty
The U.S., U.K., and Soviet Union sign a treaty banning the testing of nuclear weapons in the atmosphere, under water, or in space.

August 18
Civil Rights Landmark
James Meredith becomes the first black person to graduate from the University of Mississippi, U.S.A, with a degree in political science.

U.S. PRESIDENT SHOT DEAD

On November 22, 1963, the world was stunned by the assassination of U.S. President John F. Kennedy. He was 46 and had been in office for only three years when a gunman fired on the presidential car as it traveled from the airport to downtown Dallas, Texas. The Governor of Texas, John Connally, who was riding alongside him, was also seriously wounded. Although the two men's wives were also in the presidential car, they were unhurt. Bullets had struck President Kennedy's head and throat, and he died 35 minutes later in hospital. The shots were believed to have been fired from a School Book Depository building, and the rifle found at the scene was thought to be the assassin's weapon. One hour after the shooting, a policeman approached Lee Harvey Oswald, whom he believed matched the description of an employee reported missing from the School Book Depository in Dallas. The policeman was shot dead by Oswald, who was arrested immediately. Oswald was himself shot dead by a nightclub owner, Jack Ruby, two days later, before he was able to be tried for the assassination. After his arrest, Oswald denied shooting the President and claimed he had been made a scapegoat. John F. Kennedy had represented vibrant hope and progress to a new generation of Americans, so his death struck terrible grief in the nation. Vice-President Lyndon B. Johnson was sworn into office as President the same day. According to a recent opinion poll, 70% of Americans believe there was a wider assassination plot behind the shooting, which has been covered up. There is still no agreement as to who was responsible, with speculation ranging from Fidel Castro to Lyndon Johnson, via the F.B.I. and the C.I.A.

KENNEDY ASSASSINATED

Right: The School Book Depository.

Right: J.F.K.'s simple grave with its eternal flame in Arlington Cemetery.

August 30
Cold War 'Hotline' Established
Following the Cuban missile crisis of 1962, the U.S. and Soviets set up a new communication system between them, for use in emergencies.

November 1
World's Largest Telescope Opened
The Arecibo Observatory is the world's largest radio telescope, with a reflector of nearly 1,000 ft (330 m).

November 18
Push Button Telephone Launched
Pennsylvania, U.S.A., sees the introduction of the world's first touch-tone telephone service, featuring telephones with push buttons instead of a dial.

1964

CAPITAL OF ALASKA REDUCED TO RUBBLE

Although March 27, 1964 seemed like any other Good Friday to Alaskans preparing for the holiday weekend, it was to become the day the fault line under the mountains surrounding Prince William Sound finally gave in to the years of pressure from shifting tectonic plates, giving rise to the worst earthquake Alaska had ever experienced. Earthquakes were a part of life in Alaska, but the people of Anchorage, the capital of the state, soon realized that this one was in a different league: the ground rolled in waves, cracks 30 ft (9 m) wide opened and closed, houses collapsed, lampposts toppled, and trees were torn from the ground. Within the space of five minutes, the capital lay in ruins. But Anchorage was not the only Alaskan city to be devastated by this earthquake. In the city of Valdez, the ground rose in waves 3 ft (1 m) high, and the area was hit by tsunamis throughout the night. In the city of Seward a chunk of the waterfront slipped into the ocean, and an oil tank farm caught fire. Other towns lost parts of their waterfront, and in Kodiak, tsunamis destroyed half of the fishing fleet and carried off two fish canneries. In addition, the U.S. states of Oregon, California, and Hawaii, and as far

'Earthquakes were a part of life in Alaska, but the people of Anchorage soon realized that this one was in a different league'

afield as Japan, were also struck by tsunamis resulting from the earthquake, while seismic waves were felt in Seattle, Washington state, as well as Texas and Florida. With a magnitude of 9.2 on the Richter scale, the earthquake was the second most powerful in recorded history, claiming 128 lives, most of them caused by the resulting tsunamis. Fortunately, the death toll was relatively low compared to other major earthquakes around the world, largely because Alaska is so sparsely populated.

Right: The placid appearance of modern-day Anchorage belies the upheavals of the past.

January 11
Health Risks of Smoking Highlighted
A report by the U.S. Surgeon General identifies a causal link between smoking and cancer (as well as other diseases).

February 6
Plans for Channel Tunnel Announced
The British and French governments announce a plan to build a tunnel between the two countries. However, it is not until 1984 that a company is selected to build the tunnel.

February 7
Beatlemania Hits America
The Fab Four's arrival in the U.S. is marked by a crowd of several thousand screaming fans.

February 25
Muhammad Ali Is Heavyweight Champion
Cassius Clay beats heavyweight champion Sonny Liston in seven rounds. Shortly afterwards he changes his name to Muhammad Ali.

NELSON MANDELA CONVICTED OF SABOTAGE

When the African National Congress (A.N.C.) was banned in South Africa following the Sharpeville Massacre, its leaders felt they had no alternative but to resort to illegal and sometimes violent means to achieve their goals. Their aim was an end to the oppression of the black population in South Africa, which meant an end to the state that had been built on the system of apartheid. The underground A.N.C. now began to plan for an armed struggle. When Nelson Mandela, a lawyer and leading figure in the A.N.C., was arrested on charges of sabotage, he pleaded guilty. Mandela famously told the court: 'I do not deny that I planned sabotage. I did not plan it in a spirit of recklessness nor because I have any love of violence. I planned it as a result of a calm and sober assessment of the political situation that had arisen after many years of tyranny, exploitation, and oppression of my people by the whites.' Mandela was arrested in Rivonia, Johannesburg, along with seven other A.N.C. members. On June 12, 1964, all eight men were found guilty and sentenced to life imprisonment. In sentencing them, Judge Quartus de Wet said he was not convinced that they were acting to alleviate the suffering of black Africans, but instead detected personal ambition for power in their actions. Mandela had already been tried for high treason in 1956, but after a four-year trial, he had not been convicted. Despite international disapproval and a world petition given to the United Nations, Nelson Mandela remained in prison for 27 years.

'Despite international disapproval and a world petition given to the United Nations, Nelson Mandela remained in prison for 27 years.'

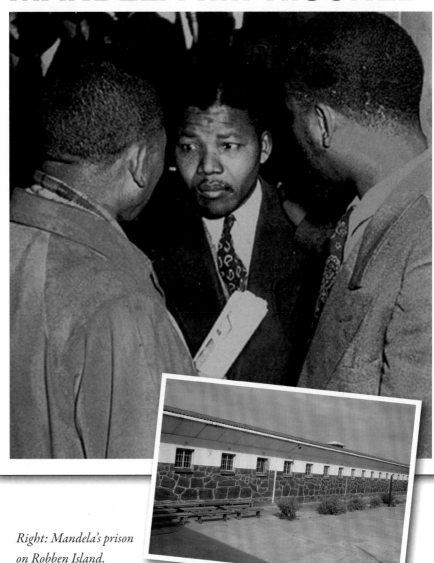

MANDELA IMPRISONED

Right: Mandela's prison on Robben Island.

March 15
Richard Burton Marries Liz Taylor
The two actors met on the set of Cleopatra. Burton is Taylor's fifth husband, and she is his second wife.

April 4
Beatles Claim Top Five Chart Positions
With Beatlemania in full swing, the band occupy all five of the top slots in the U.S.A.'s Top 40.

April 17
Ford Mustang Launched
The Ford Motor Company introduces this iconic car at the New York World's Fair.

April 25
Little Mermaid Statue Decapitated
The famous statue sits in Copenhagen Harbor as a tribute to the ballet of the same name.

1965

U.S. INVOLVEMENT IN VIETNAM INCREASED

Following independence from France, Vietnam had been divided into the Communist North and French-backed South. The North wanted Vietnam united under Communist rule, and in 1959, with the support of the southern National Liberation Front, or Viet Cong, attacked the South. When Lyndon B. Johnson (right) took his oath as U.S. President, he declared: 'We can never again stand aside, prideful in isolation. Terrific dangers and troubles that we once called "foreign" now constantly live among us.' Perceived as chief among these dangers was Communism. Days later, Johnson was told by his advisors that America's limited involvement to date in the Vietnam War was doing no good and that America would either have to withdraw altogether or significantly escalate its military commitment. When Viet Cong guerrillas attacked an American base in February, President Johnson responded by approving the bombing of a North Vietnamese army camp. Thereafter, without any official announcement, the U.S. began to commit greater numbers of troops to the cause of the South Vietnamese. Operation Rolling Thunder was launched on March 2, 1965, with 100 American fighter-bombers heading for targets in North Vietnam. The campaign was meant to take just eight weeks, but ended up lasting three years. The first U.S. combat troops to arrive in Vietnam were marines, 3,500 of them, and they landed at China Beach to defend an American air base. Even when a further two marine battalions were sent to Vietnam on April 1, 1965, President Johnson still did not inform the American people that the United States was involved in offensive operations. During this time, North Vietnam rejected several attempts by Johnson to negotiate a peace settlement, with the result that America committed more and more troops to crushing the Communist North.

MORE TROOPS FOR VIETNAM

Left: Entrance to the Viet Cong tunnels at Chu Chi. These warrens were vital to guerrilla warfare.

January 30
Churchill Buried
Former British Prime Minister Winston Churchill is given a full state funeral in London.

February 6
Soccer Legend's Last Game
Stanley Matthews plays his final match in England's First Division, as he turns out for Stoke City at the ripe old age of 50.

March 7
Bloody Sunday
Civil rights protestors are attacked by State Troopers in Selma, Alabama, on a day that becomes known as Bloody Sunday.

April 23
Pennine Way Opened
The walking trail in the North of England is completed.

April 28
U.S. Troops Enter Dominican Republic
President Johnson sends the U.S. army into the Dominican Republic in defense of the country's military government after an uprising by supporters of former President Juan Bosch.

MALCOLM X SHOT DEAD AS WIFE LOOKS ON

The man who began life as Malcolm Little and, after a youth of crime, converted in prison to the Nation of Islam, was assassinated in New York City on February 21, 1965 by members of the group he had once championed. Renamed Malcolm X by the Nation of Islam leader Elijah Muhammad, he was released from prison in 1952, and subsequently devoted his life to the cause of black rights. However, he was opposed to the civil rights movement headed by Martin Luther King Jr., rejecting integration and endorsing the Nation of Islam view that all whites were evil. His oratory impressed many people, but by 1963 his bluntness was beginning to alienate him from the Nation of Islam. When he described the assassination of President Kennedy as 'chickens coming home to roost', adding that it made him glad rather than sad, Elijah Muhammad banned him from public speaking for 90 days. On March 8, 1964, Malcolm X broke from the Nation of Islam and

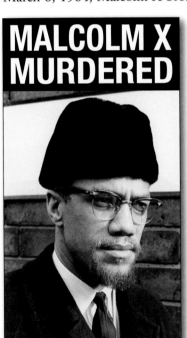

announced his intention of forming the Organization of Afro-American Unity. His popularity increased, but the Nation of Islam began making death threats against him. On February 14, 1965, his house was burned to the ground, but his family survived. Seven days later, while addressing an audience in Manhattan's Audubon Ballroom, Malcolm X was shot by three men, the first with a sawn-off shotgun, the others with pistols. In all, he was shot 16 times. Three members of the Nation of Islam were arrested and imprisoned for his murder.

FIRST EVER SPACEWALK

Right: An Australian stamp marking the first U.S. spacewalk.

Ever since the U.S.S.R. had won the race to send the first man into space, the Americans had wanted their own 'first'. N.A.S.A.'s *Gemini 4* program aimed to deliver this, its goal being that an American would be the first to walk in space. By early 1965, astronauts were in training, and Ed White looked set to be the first man to exit a spacecraft and engage in extra-vehicular activity. Once again, though, the Soviets got there first, and on March 18, 1965, Aleski Leonov became the first man to walk in space. When *Gemini 4* launched in June 1965, Ed White got his walk, but with more advanced technology. He carried a handheld gas jet, which he could use to 'fire' himself back to the spaceship if he came loose from his tether. White walked in space for around half an hour, and the pictures appeared in newspapers across the globe. On his return, he was awarded the N.A.S.A. Space Flight Medal, and posthumously received the Congressional Space Medal of Honor.

April 28
Australian Troops Sent to Vietnam

Australian Prime Minister Robert Menzies announces his intention to increase his country's involvement in the Vietnam War. The first Australian combat troops arrive a month later.

May 29
Hundreds Die in Mining Disaster

Nearly 300 workers are killed in an accident at a coal mine in Dhanbad, India.

July 25
Dylan Goes Electric

Folk singer Bob Dylan causes uproar among folk music fans by playing an electric guitar at the Newport Folk Festival in Newport, Rhode Island.

August 9
A New Island State

Singapore leaves the Federation of Malaysia to become an independent nation. Lee Kuan Yew is the new country's first prime minister.

1965

MASSIVE POWER CUT IN NORTH AMERICA

On November 9, 1965, there was a serious disruption to the power supply in the northeastern provinces of America and Canada. The major incident occurred when a maintenance worker set a protective relay to trip at too low a value. As a result, an area covering 80,000 sq miles (207,000 sq km), including Ontario in Canada, and Connecticut, Massachusetts, New Hampshire, Rhode Island, Vermont, New York, and New Jersey in the United States, was plunged into darkness and did not regain power for 12 hours. The power cut affected 25 million people, and only those areas with independent old-fashioned generators were able to maintain any power. Sparks from the affected power stations were widely reported as 'fireballs' in the sky, and these in turn became inflated into sightings of U.F.O.s (Unidentified Flying Objects). The official explanation of the 'fireballs' was made known the following day.

RHODESIA BREAKS TIES WITH BRITAIN

On November 11, 1965, Ian Smith, Prime Minister of Rhodesia (now Zimbabwe), made a Unilateral Declaration of Independence from Britain. The move was deemed illegal by the British, and economic sanctions were immediately imposed. Britain's aim had been to help Rhodesia toward black-majority rule. But although blacks outnumbered whites in Rhodesia by 16 to one, Smith had declared that they would never rule the country. To this end, he suppressed black political parties and detained their leaders. British Prime Minister Harold Wilson made it clear that Britain would support Rhodesia's independence only if Smith's regime allowed for majority rule. Meanwhile, the declaration of independence isolated the country economically and increased violence between blacks and whites. Although Smith declared Rhodesia a republic in 1969, it was still not internationally recognized. Eventually, he was forced to hand over power to the elected black leader Robert Mugabe in 1980.

Below: Robert Mugabe, who became leader when Ian Smith stepped down.

October 3
Che Leaves Cuba
Cuban President Fidel Castro announces that Che Guevara has resigned from the Cuban government and left the country.

November 8
Britain Abolishes the Death Penalty
The Murder Act 1965 is given Royal Assent, thus formally ending the death penalty in the U.K.

November 24
Mobutu Seizes Power in Congo
Lieutenant-Colonel Mobutu Sese Seko overthrows President Joseph Kasavubu to take power in Congo.

June 26
Soviet Scientist Denounced
Agronomist Trofim Lysenko, whose false ideas regarding heredity have guided official Soviet agricultural policy for two decades, is officially denounced.

BRADY AND HINDLEY JAILED FOR LIFE

On May 6, 1966, 28-year-old Ian Brady and his lover Myra Hindley were jailed for life for the murders of three children. The pair was convicted of torturing and murdering Edward Evans (17), Lesley-Ann Downey (10), and John Kilbride (12) in what became known as the 'Moors Murders'. In each case the children had been lured to the couple's Manchester home, subjected to sexual abuse and torture, and then brutally murdered. Their remains were buried on remote moorland in Lancashire and Yorkshire. Brady and Hindley were arrested for the murders after Hindley's brother-in-law, David Smith, witnessed the murder of Edward Evans as an intended 'initiation ceremony' into the killings. Smith, terrified by what he saw, later called the police. Brady confessed to the crimes, and he and Hindley were each given three life sentences. The pair also murdered two other children, Pauline Reade and Keith Bennett. When they were taken back to the moors in the 1980s to identify the burial sites, the remains of Pauline Reade were uncovered, but Keith Bennett's body has never been found. Hindley died in prison at the age of 60, even though she had completed her 30-year sentence. Brady remains in a psychiatric hospital, where he has been on hunger strike for several years.

THE MOORS MURDERS

Left: Ian Brady (third from left) leads police officers back to Saddleworth Moor, searching for the remains of the victims whose bodies were not found in the initial investigation.

'The children were sexually abused and tortured, and then brutally murdered.'

January 1
Coup in Central Africa
Jean-Bédel Bokassa takes power in a military coup in the Central African Republic.

January 19
Indira for India
Indira Ghandi is elected Prime Minister of India. She is the daughter of Jawaharlal Nehru, who was independent India's first Prime Minister.

March 1
Soviet Space Probe Reaches Venus
Soviet space probe *Venera 3* crashes into Venus. It is the first spacecraft to land on another planet.

March 4
'More Popular than Jesus'
In an interview with the London newspaper the *Eveneing Standard*, John Lennon claims that The Beatles are now more popular than Jesus.

1966

LONE GUNMAN BRINGS TERROR TO CAMPUS

On August 1, 1966, Charles Whitman, a student at the University of Texas in Austin, shattered a peaceful summer's day on campus. Whitman killed 14 people and wounded 32 others during a shooting rampage on and around campus after murdering his wife and his mother in their homes. Whitman seemed destined for the American Dream – he was good-looking, came from a prominent and wealthy family, and did well in school and sports. However, under the seemingly idyllic facade, Whitman's family was troubled, mainly due to physical and emotional abuse from his father. In a bid to please his father, as well as remove himself from his father's abusive behavior, Whitman joined the U.S. Marines in 1959. He won several performance medals, exceled at rapid fire shooting, and earned a scholarship to study engineering in Austin. But Whitman immediately floundered in his studies and he took up gambling. Although his marriage to Kathy Leissner in 1962 steadied him for a while, his life continued to unravel and he acknowledged, via journal entries, that he was on the verge of doing something terrible. Although he was seeing a psychiatrist and taking medication, Whitman's self-control snapped on July 31. After killing his wife and mother, he climbed to the observation deck of the white granite tower of the University of Texas administration building and started shooting. After he held police at bay for a while, assault teams got close enough to gun him down.

> **'His life continued to unravel and he acknowledged, via journal entries, that he was on the verge of doing something terrible.'**

UNIVERSITY KILLINGS

March 20
World Cup Stolen
The World Cup trophy, popularly known as the Jules Rimet trophy, is stolen from an exhibition in London. It is found in a hedge a week later by a dog named Pickles.

March 31
Labour Win
Harold Wilson's Labour government wins the general election in the U.K.

April 21
Ethiopian Emperor Visits Jamaica
The emperor of Ethiopia, Haile Selassie, visits Jamaica. He meets with leaders of the Rastafarian movement, who revere him as an incarnation of God.

May 26
Guyana Becomes Independent
The South American state wins independence from the United Kingdom.

SCHOOL CRUSHED BY COAL SLURRY IN SOUTH WALES

MINING DISASTER

On the morning of Friday, October 21, 1966, Tip No. 7, a heap of colliery waste that lay 500 ft (153 m) high above the village of Aberfan in Wales, began to slide. Below it were the Panglas Schools, which were just about to break for half-term. There was low cloud on that day, so no one could see the heap of waste beginning to slide, but they could hear it. The coal slurry had been liquefied by springs beneath the heap, and it flowed as fast as molten lava. No one had time to get out of the way before the liquid waste destroyed a farm, killing its inhabitants, and engulfed Panglas Junior School, killing 109 children and five teachers. A subsequent inquiry found the National Coal Board (N.C.B.) negligent and entirely responsible for the disaster. The tip should never have been placed on top of known springs, had already slid twice in the past, and had never been inspected, though it was known to be a hazard. The N.C.B. tried to deny responsibility, and avoided paying compensation to the bereaved families until some years later. Scandalously, the chairman of the N.C.B., Lord Robens, staged a false resignation, and he himself wrote his M.P.'s letter of refusal to accept the resignation. The Aberfan disaster was one of the worst ever cases of negligence and cover-up, the shameful facts of which only emerged 30 years later when related documents became public.

Left: Aerial view of Aberfan after the disaster.
Right: Memorials to the children killed in the deluged school.

September 6
'Architect of Apartheid' Killed
The Prime Minister of South Africa, Hendrik Frensch Verwoerd, the primary architect of the country's policy of apartheid, is stabbed to death during a parliamentary session.

September 30
Speer Released
Architect and former Nazi government minister Albert Speer is released from Spandau Prison after serving a 20-year sentence.

November 30
Barbados Wins Independence
The Caribbean island wins its independence from Britain.

December 31
Art Theft in London
Thieves steal millions of pounds' worth of artwork from Dulwich Picture Gallery.

1967

OIL TANKER SPILLS ITS LOAD

On March 18, 1967, the supertanker *Torrey Canyon*, carrying 120,000 tons of oil, struck a rock between the Isles of Scilly and Land's End in Cornwall, England. Instantly, its 31 million gallons (141 million litres) of oil began to leak out into the sea between England and France, destroying the majority of the marine life along the coasts of both countries and contaminating miles of beaches. Because such a major environmental disaster had never occurred before and had not been anticipated, there were no emergency plans in place, and some knee-jerk reactions, such as spraying the slick with gallons of chemical dispersants, caused even greater harm. It was estimated that these chemicals had killed more marine life than the oil itself. The crew was lifted to safety by helicopter, and the tanker was bombed for two days in an attempt to sink it and burn up the rest of its oil. The *Torrey Canyon* eventually sank 12 days later, but the effects were felt for years afterwards. An inquiry in Liberia, where the ship was registered, found that the captain was to blame for the disaster, as he had taken a short cut in order to reach his destination in Wales earlier.

'The tanker was bombed for two days in an attempt to sink it and burn up the rest of its oil.'

SHATTERED TANKER BREAKS UP IN GALE

Above: Burning off the oil and cleaning up the beaches.

DYING MAN GETS NEW HEART

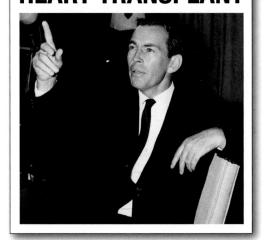

WORLD'S FIRST HEART TRANSPLANT

The world's first human heart transplant was performed by Professor Christiaan Barnard (left) in South Africa on December 3, 1967. The patient was Mr. Louis Washkansky, whose heart was about to fail, and the donor was a young woman who had been killed in a car accident. Professor Barnard had devoted his professional life to the development of heart surgery, and had the opportunity to work in Minneapolis, Minnesota, with Professor Owen Wagensteen, a pioneer of experimental surgery. When the heart-lung machine was perfected in the United States, Professor Barnard was given one as a gift to take back to his native South Africa. He returned to Groote Shuur Hospital in the Western Cape in 1958 and assembled a cardiac team ready to perform a cardiac bypass operation. He also practiced performing kidney transplants until eventually, in 1967, he felt that his team was ready to perform the first heart transplant. The operation took nine hours and was deemed to be successful. However, Mr. Washkansky died 18 days later from pneumonia, though his new heart was apparently still beating strongly to the end.

January 14
Human Be-In
The 'Human Be-In' is held in Golden Gate Park, San Francisco, a prelude to the Summer of Love.

March 7
Union Leader Sent to Jail
Jimmy Hoffa, president of the Teamsters union in the U.S., begins an eight-year sentence for attempting to bribe a jury.

April 21
Coup in Greece
The military seize power in Greece. Ex-Prime Minister Andreas Papandreou is imprisoned.

April 24
Cosmonaut Dies
Vladimir Komarov is the first Soviet cosmonaut to die when the parachute of his space capsule fails during re-entry into the Earth's atmosphere.

ISRAEL AND ARAB STATES FIGHT SIX DAY WAR

WAR IN THE MIDDLE EAST

The combined Anglo-French-Israeli invasion of Egypt during the crisis over the Suez Canal in 1956 had left many lasting effects on the region. Although Egypt succeeded in recapturing the canal, the U.N. ordered the invaders to leave and installed a peacekeeping force to maintain order. While Israel withdrew its troops from the Sinai Peninsula, and Egypt agreed to reopen the canal to Israeli shipping, Israel declared the borders agreed in the 1949 armistice no longer valid, and the Arab states still refused to recognize the existence of Israel, so major issues remained unresolved. When, in 1965, a dispute arose between Israel, Jordan, and Syria over access to water, the Israel Defense Forces (I.D.F.) carried out a series of air strikes designed to stop water diversions set up in Syria. In November 1966, when a border mine exploded and killed Israeli soldiers, Israel attacked a Jordanian region of the West Bank, which Israel claimed harbored Palestinian terrorists. King Hussein of Jordan, who had good relations with the U.S. and was generally a peaceable influence in the region, was forced to retaliate, and mobilized his army on November 20, 1966. A further dispute between Israel and Syria over land being farmed by Arabs in the demilitarized zones prompted an exchange of fire. In 1966, Egypt and Syria signed a mutual defense pact, agreeing to help each other if attacked. Over the ensuing months, Syrian-Israeli disputes continued, escalating into almost constant bombing and shelling on both sides, but without a formal declaration of war. In May 1967, the commander of Egypt's Army informed the peacekeeping United Nations Emergency Force (U.N.E.F.) that Egypt was prepared to go to war with Israel as soon as Israel attacked any Arab state, and he asked U.N. troops to withdraw for their own safety. The commander of U.N.E.F. tried to negotiate, but in the end was forced to withdraw, and Egypt began to remilitarize the Sinai Peninsula. While U.N. troops were preparing to depart, hostilities broke out in earnest on June 5, 1967, when Israel initiated an air strike on Egyptian airfields. Jordan and Syria promptly joined forces with Egypt, and over the next six days Iraq, Saudi Arabia, Sudan, Algeria, Morocco, and Tunisia also sent troops. By June 10, though, Israel had captured the Gaza Strip, the Sinai Peninsula, the West Bank, and the Golan Heights, and the Arab states were forced to sign a ceasefire.

'Disputes continued, escalating into almost constant bombing and shelling on both sides.'

Right: The Sinai Peninsula, where Egypt mustered its troops for the Six Day War against Israel.

April 27
Expo 67 Opens
A World's Fair in Montreal, Quebec, is opened by Canadian Prime Minister Lester Pearson.

May 2
U.K. Applies to Join E.E.C.
Prime Minister Harold Wilson announces his intention to apply for membership of the E.E.C.

June 28
Israel Annexes East Jerusalem
Israel takes control of the whole of the city of Jerusalem.

July 1
Color T.V. Reaches the U.K.
The first ever color broadcast is made from the Wimbledon tennis championship.

1967

BIAFRANS DECLARE INDEPENDENCE

On May 30, 1967, the people of Biafra in Nigeria proclaimed their independence only a few years after Nigeria itself had gained independence from Britain. Occupying the eastern region of Nigeria, the people were mainly Igbo and had fled massacre by another tribe. The people of Biafra numbered some 30 million, but their numbers were no advantage when faced with food blockades. General Yakubu Gowon (below), leader of Federal Nigeria, immediately cut off all supply lines to the breakaway state. Coming under international pressure, the Nigerian military government eventually allowed the Red Cross to deliver medical aid, but it is estimated that millions of Biafrans died of starvation. British involvement on

behalf of the starving Biafrans was tainted by the fact that the British government was selling arms to Nigeria. For three years the Biafrans held out in appalling conditions, but they were eventually beaten by federal troops and their republic ceased to exist in January 1970.

CIVIL WAR IN NIGERIA

Left: Colonel Ojukwu, leader of the Biafran separatists.

RIOTS IN THE U.S.A.

RIOTS SWAMP DETROIT

In the 1960s, the U.S. city of Detroit, in Michigan, had serious economic and social problems. The roots of these lay in the 1940s and 1950s, when white inhabitants, who resented the influx of black migrants, built physical barriers between neighborhoods and tried to bar black residents from social housing. Urban regeneration projects in the 1950s, which involved building new freeways from city to suburbs, invariably resulted in the complete destruction of predominantly black neighborhoods. Lack of housing became a major problem and caused forced integration, which increased hostility between blacks and whites. By the 1960s, several predominantly white neighborhoods had become predominantly black. Added to this, the Detroit police, who were notoriously racist and brutal, made frequent raids on bars in black neighborhoods. One such raid, on the night of July 23, 1967, intended to round up a few drunks from an after-hours drinking establishment. Instead police found a bar full of people celebrating the return of two men from the Vietnam War. The police called in reinforcements and arrested all 82 of those present, but rioting and vandalism broke out. Over the next five days the situation grew worse and spread across the city. By the time the police and military regained control, 43 people were dead, 1,189 injured, and 7,000 had been arrested.

August 5
The Piper at the Gates of Dawn Released
British band Pink Floyd release their debut album.

September 3
Swedish Drivers Cross the Road
At 5 a.m. local time, all the traffic in Sweden switches from left-hand drive to right-hand drive to fall in line with the rest of Scandinavia.

November 8
Local Radio Station Launched in the U.K.
B.B.C. Radio Leicester, the B.B.C.'s first local radio station, goes on air. Within a few years, the B.B.C. dominates local radio.

November 30
Pakistan People's Party Founded
Zulfiqar Ali Bhutto is the first chairman of the new political party.

MARTIN LUTHER KING SHOT DEAD

On the evening of April 4, 1968, Martin Luther King Jr., the inspirational leader of the civil rights movement in America, was shot dead on the balcony of his motel in Memphis, Tennessee. Dr. King was a deeply religious man, a gifted preacher who advocated peaceful protest and fought with bravery and dignity for equal rights and social integration for African Americans. The F.B.I. arrested a white man named James Earl Ray for the fatal shooting. However, many, including King's own family, believed Ray to be innocent, and the involvement of the F.B.I. itself was strongly suspected. Ray was sentenced to 99 years and died in prison, despite claiming that he had been part of a larger conspiracy. Dr. King had gone to Memphis in March 1968 to support a strike among black sanitation workers over unfair treatment, but, to his dismay, the protest march turned violent. Not wanting the movement to be tainted by violence, he returned in April to counsel the people against violence, before leading another peaceful march. Dr. King knew on April 3, when he addressed the audience in Memphis, that his life was in danger. There had been a bomb threat the day before, and he had recently been stabbed, but he said in his speech: 'Like anybody, I would like to live a long life; longevity has its place. But I'm not concerned about that now. I just want to do God's will. And he's allowed me to go to the mountaintop. And I've looked over, and I've seen the Promised Land. I may not get there with you. But I want you to know tonight that we as a people will get to the Promised Land. And so I'm happy tonight; I'm not worried about anything; I'm not fearing any man. Mine eyes have seen the glory of the coming of the Lord.' After his assassination, rioting broke out in cities across America.

'Dr. King knew on April 3, when he addressed the audience in Memphis, that his life was in danger.'

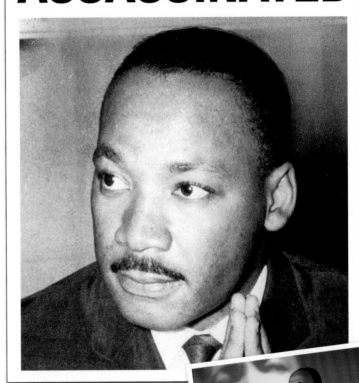

MARTIN LUTHER KING ASSASSINATED

Right: Coretta Scott King, widow of the assassinated civil rights leader, became a campaigner herself after his death.

Above: The great man's son, Martin Luther King III, campaigns widely against poverty.

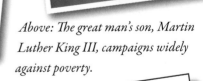

January 30
Viet Cong Offensive
The Viet Cong launches a series of attacks across South Vietnam in an attempt to spark an uprising against the Saigon government.

March 16
Mai Lai Massacre
U.S. troops kill hundreds of unarmed civilians in Vietnam. The massacre is revealed a year later to worldwide condemnation.

March 16
Kennedy Enters Race
Senator Robert F. Kennedy enters the race for the Democratic Party presidential nomination.

March 22
French Students Occupy University
Eight students occupy offices in the University of Nanterre, the first in a series of protests across France.

March 31
Johnson Steps Down
Lyndon Johnson announces that he will not seek re-election as U.S. president.

'CURSE OF THE KENNEDYS' STRIKES AGAIN

On June 5, 1968, Robert Kennedy, a younger brother of John F. Kennedy, was fatally shot in the head while delivering a victory speech in the ballroom of a Los Angeles hotel. At the time, U.S. Senator Robert Kennedy was the favorite for the Democrat presidential candidacy in the forthcoming election, and he had just won the California primaries. The gunman was a 24-year-old Palestinian man named Sirhan Bishara Sirhan, and it was assumed that Senator Kennedy's well-known support for Israel was behind the assassination. Robert Kennedy died the following day in the hospital, after emergency brain surgery failed to save him. Sirhan Sirhan was sentenced to life in prison, but, as ever, theories emerged about more complex conspiracies behind the shooting – the second Kennedy assassination in a decade.

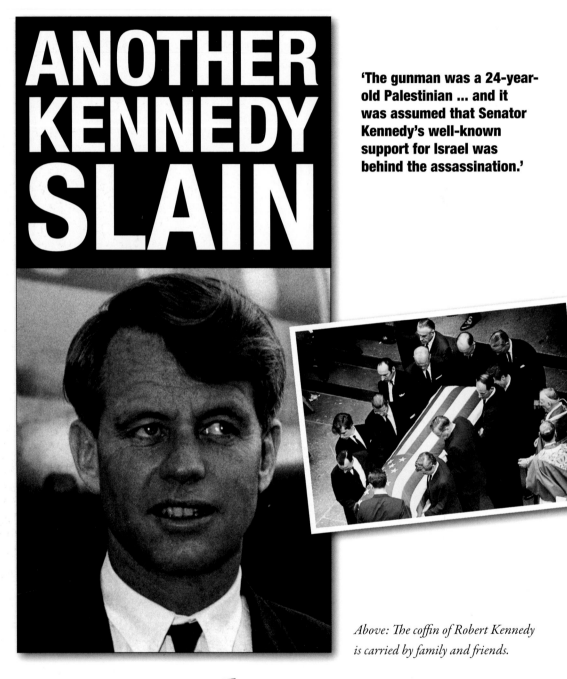

ANOTHER KENNEDY SLAIN

'The gunman was a 24-year-old Palestinian ... and it was assumed that Senator Kennedy's well-known support for Israel was behind the assassination.'

Above: The coffin of Robert Kennedy is carried by family and friends.

April 2
Bombs Exploded in German Shop
Bombs placed by German terror group the Red Army Faction explode at a department store in Frankfurt.

April 7
Racing Driver Clark Killed
Former Formula 1 champion, Scotland's Jim Clark, is killed in a crash in a race in Germany.

May 14
Apple Records Founded
The Beatles found their own record label.

1968

SOVIET TANKS ROLL INTO PRAGUE

SOVIETS INVADE CZECHOSLOVAKIA

After the Second World War, Czechoslovakia was tightly controlled by the U.S.S.R. For more than a decade, the country was subject to externally enforced restrictions on every aspect of life – social, economic, and political. Then gradually, during the 1960s, cultural changes began to emerge, and there was new freedom in the fields of music, literature, fashion, and the media. The Soviets disapproved of this Westernization, but Czechoslovakia's new leader, Alexander Dubček, who came to power in January 1968, brought about official reforms aimed at increasing political freedom. His aim was to establish basic human rights in the legal system and to bring an end to political persecution. The reforms were an attempt to create, in Dubček's own words, 'socialism with a human face', but his decentralization of the economy and democratization of the political system were met with increasing hostility from the U.S.S.R. The period that subsequently became known as the 'Prague Spring', for its reawakening of artistic and political freedom, came to an end in August 1968 when the U.S.S.R. led Warsaw Pact forces in an invasion of Czechoslovakia, with the declared intention of 'normalizing' what they saw as revolutionary forces. Alexander Dubček and other leaders of the reform were taken away to Moscow. The Soviet occupation of the country lasted for 20 years. The only reform to survive the Soviet counter-revolution was the division of Czechoslovakia into two separate republics, one Czech and one Slovak, but state administration remained strictly centralized.

Left: Prague is the capital of the Czech Republic, now a member of the E.U.

May 29
Manchester United Win European Cup
They beat Portuguese champions Benfica 4–1 in the final at Wembley Stadium, London. They are the first English club to win the trophy.

June 3
Warhol Shot
Artist Andy Warhol is shot and wounded by radical feminist Valerie Solanas.

October 2
Massacre in Mexico
Ten days before the start of the Olympic Games in the city, hundreds of student demonstrators are shot dead by police in Mexico City.

October 16
Black Power Salute
American sprinters Tommie Smith and John Carlos raise their arms in a black power salute during a medals ceremony at the Olympics.

1969

MEN LAND ON THE MOON

ONE SMALL STEP...

Right: Crowds in Trafalgar Square in central London watched the Moon landings on a giant T.V. screen.

Apollo 11 was the fifth mission of the Apollo Project and the third to take humans to the Moon. The space flight was launched on July 16, 1969, and it culminated in Commander Neil Armstrong and lunar module pilot Edwin 'Buzz' Aldrin walking on the Moon. The resounding success of the mission was heightened by its fulfillment of President Kennedy's statement of hope in 1961: 'I believe that this nation should commit itself to the goal, before this decade is out, of landing a man on the Moon and returning him safely to Earth.' The *Apollo 11* launch from the Kennedy Space Center in Florida was watched by thousands of people who had gathered around the site, as well as by millions more across the globe on television screens. On July 19 the spacecraft reached the Moon and orbited 30 times. The lunar module, named *Eagle* after the national bird of the United States, then separated from the command module and, on July 20, landed on the Moon, with Neil Armstrong and Buzz Aldrin inside. The module had just 25 seconds' worth of fuel remaining after a longer-than-expected descent, and when Neil Armstrong spoke the words, 'The *Eagle* has landed,' there was all-around relief at NASA's command base in Houston, Texas. Six hours later, in the early morning of July 21, Neil Armstrong descended from the lunar module and stepped onto the surface of the Moon. It was then that he uttered the now famous words: 'That's one small step for [a] man, one giant leap for mankind.' The moment was broadcast on T.V. to around 600 million people across the globe. It was filmed in 'slow-scan' mode, and then

> **'The lunar module had just 25 seconds' worth of fuel remaining after a longer-than-expected descent'**

January 12
Led Zeppelin 1
Seminal British rock band Led Zeppelin release their eponymous debut album.

January 20
Nixon Becomes President
Republican Richard Nixon becomes the 37th president of the U.S.A.

February 4
Arafat Becomes Leader of P.L.O.
Yasser Arafat is elected leader of the Palestine Liberation Organization.

April 22
Round-the-World Sailor Returns
British sailor Robin Knox-Johnston arrives back in Falmouth, England, 10 months after he had left to complete the first ever non-stop solo round-the-world voyage.

a conventional T.V. camera filmed the slow-scan monitor. Although this meant that the images lost their quality and definition, few people cared: it was clear enough that men had landed on the Moon. While they were up there, Armstrong and Aldrin had various tasks to complete, such as depositing the Early Apollo Scientific Experiment Package, planting the American flag, collecting rock samples, and photographing the lunar module so that N.A.S.A. engineers could examine its condition. They also briefly spoke to President Nixon in the White House. Armstrong reported that moving around was easy, except for a tendency to slip on the fine Moon dust. The men had initially been allowed 34 minutes on the Moon's surface, but their tasks took longer than expected, so Houston decided to allow them a further 15 minutes. The astronauts then re-entered the lunar module and blasted off to be reunited with the command module *Columbia*, which pilot Michael Collins had maintained in orbit during their activities. On July 23, the three astronauts made a T.V. broadcast to the world, during which they thanked all those working behind the scenes, and Buzz Aldrin commented: 'We feel that this stands as a symbol of the insatiable curiosity of all mankind to explore the unknown ... Personally, in reflecting on the events of the past several days, a verse from Psalms comes to mind: "When I consider the heavens, the work of Thy fingers, the Moon and the stars, which Thou hast ordained, What is man, that Thou art mindful of him?"' *Apollo 11* splashed down to Earth on July 24, 1969. The astronauts had to endure three weeks in quarantine, but they were then paraded before the American people in a series of ecstatic celebrations.

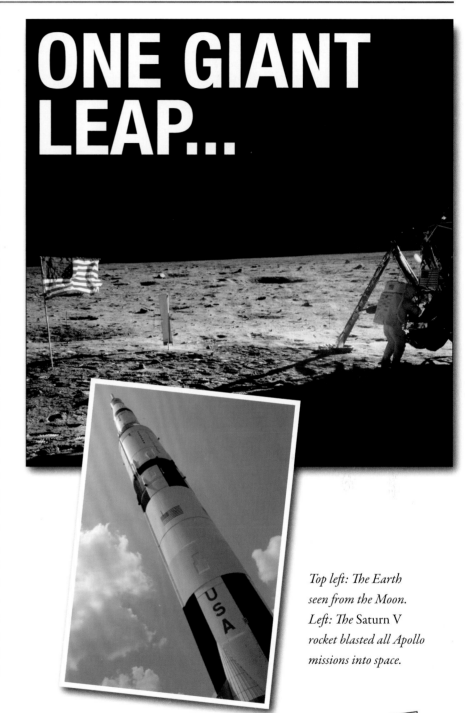

ONE GIANT LEAP...

Top left: The Earth seen from the Moon.
Left: The Saturn V rocket blasted all Apollo missions into space.

May 26
Lennon and Ono's Bed-In
John Lennon and Yoko Ono begin a week-long Bed-In in Montreal to protest against the Vietnam War.

June 28
Stonewall Riots
A series of demonstrations are held in New York City after police raid the Stonewall Inn in what is perceived as an attack on gay people.

July 1
Prince of Wales Invested
Prince Charles is invested as the Prince of Wales at Caernarfon Castle.

July 14
Football War
Following a soccer match in which El Salvador beat Honduras, riots break out in Honduras protesting against the 300,000 Salvadorean workers in the country. El Savaldoran troops invade in response. A ceasefire comes into effect six days later.

1969

CONCORDE UP!

On March 2, 1969, the supersonic airliner Concorde made its maiden flight. The Anglo-French project, in which the British had initially invested £155 million, produced a plane that could reach speeds of up to 1,300 mph (2,097 kph) – faster than the speed of sound. During the first flight, however, Concorde's French pilot maintained a moderate 300 mph (484 kph) and was airborne for only 27 minutes. The flight was considered a great success, however, and a British pilot completed his own test flight seven days later. Concorde made its first supersonic flight on October 1, 1969. Commercial flights were not launched until 1976, and these included a London–New York flight that took just three and a half hours. However, there had always been doubts about the commercial viability of Concorde, and it was estimated that it would end up costing Britain £900 million. Despite early excitement, the aircraft soon hit problems: heavy fuel consumption at a time when fuel prices were rising made it hugely expensive, and small fuel tanks prevented it from entering the trans-Pacific market. In 2003, Air France and British Airways announced that Concorde was no longer financially viable, and it made its final flight on October 23, 2003.

> **'The Anglo-French project ... produced a plane that could reach speeds of up to 1,300 mph (2,097 kph) – faster than the speed of sound.'**

THE SUPERSONIC AGE

Left: Concorde's prototype went into construction in 1969.
Right: The in-service aircraft made a farewell tour of its routes in 2003.

August 9
Sharon Tate Murdered
A heavily pregnant Sharon Tate, wife of director Roman Polanski, and three of her friends, are murdered in Los Angeles by members of a cult led by Charles Manson.

August 15
Woodstock Begins
The Woodstock Festival in upstate New York begins.

September 1
Coup in Libya
King Idris is ousted in a military coup in Libya. Colonel Muammar al-Gaddafi takes power.

October 29
First Message Sent Over ARPANET
The forerunner of the internet is used for the first time.

October 31
Wal-Mart Founded
U.S. retail giant Wal-Mart is incorporated as Wal-Mart Stores, Inc.

BATTLE OF THE BOGSIDE IN NORTHERN IRELAND

TROOPS SENT TO NORTHERN IRELAND

Left: The Bogside area of Derry is still predominantly Catholic. Life is much more peaceful since the 1998 Good Friday Agreement.

Throughout 1969 there had been clashes between the Royal Ulster Constabulary (R.U.C.) and the nationalist residents of the Bogside area in Derry, who continued to oppose the government of Northern Ireland. The local population (predominantly Catholic) made every effort to resist the intrusion of the R.U.C., and there were several forced 'invasions' into the district, resulting in casualties on both sides. In July 1969, the Derry Citizens Defence Association (D.C.D.A.) was established to prepare for anticipated trouble on the occasion of the loyalist Apprentice Boys March in August. Nationalist leaders of the D.C.D.A. made it clear that the people of the Bogside would do everything within their power to keep out the R.U.C. On the eve of the march, women and children were evacuated and barricades were erected. The march went ahead as planned, on August 12, 1969, and there were clashes between the R.U.C. and nationalists in the Bogside, which soon escalated from stone throwing to full-scale rioting. For some time the people of Bogside stood firm and warded off the R.U.C., but by the evening the R.U.C. had breached the barricades. In an attempt to end the battle the Minister for Home Affairs at Stormont authorized the use of tear gas. Over the next two days, the debilitating gas was fired into the Bogside, and residents used homemade petrol bombs in retaliation. The residents took control of a block of flats and, from that position, rained down bombs on the R.U.C. Amid rumors that the Irish Army was coming to their aid, the residents held out, even when the R.U.C. began to use live ammunition. In the end, it was the British Army who stepped in to rescue the R.U.C., and the Battle of the Bogside promptly ended at 4 p.m. on August 14, 1969.

'On the eve of the Apprentice Boys March, women and children were evacuated and barricades were erected.'

'The march ... soon escalated from stone throwing to full-scale rioting.'

November 9
Alcatraz Seized
A Native American group, led by Richard Oakes, occupies Alcatraz Island in San Francisco Bay. They hold the island until 1971.

November 14
Apollo 12 Launched
N.A.S.A. sends its second manned mission to the Moon.

November 21
U.S. Agree to Return Japanese Island
The U.S. and Japanese governments agree that Okinawa, a Japanese island controlled by the U.S. since the end of the Second World War, should return to Japanese sovereignty.

December 2
Jumbo Jet's First Flight
The first Boeing 747 flies from Seattle to New York City.

1970-1979

The 1970s saw a sharp rise in global terrorism. It was the era of the Palestine Liberation Organization (P.L.O.), who in the cause of a Palestinian homeland made hijacking airliners and taking hostages the trademark of terrorists, and the Provisional Irish Republican Army (I.R.A.), who embarked on a series of bombing campaigns designed to intimidate the British government into relinquishing Northern Ireland.

In Britain, where pounds, shillings, and pence had given way to the decimal currency, there were troubled economic times ahead. The oil crisis in the Middle East and miners' strikes at home combined to bring the energy industry to its knees, and prompted a three-day week to conserve resources. However, the mood was lightened and morale boosted by the Queen's Silver Jubilee, celebrating 25 years of her reign. Meanwhile, in the United States, President Nixon was found guilty of underhand political dealings and colluding in illegal activities. The Watergate scandal that was to force his resignation dragged on for more than a year.

In the age of sexual liberation, with the contraceptive pill widely available to help prevent unplanned pregnancies, there was also a crucial scientific advance in the area of fertility when the first 'test tube baby', Louise Brown, was born.

HAPPY ENDING FOR APOLLO 13 MISSION

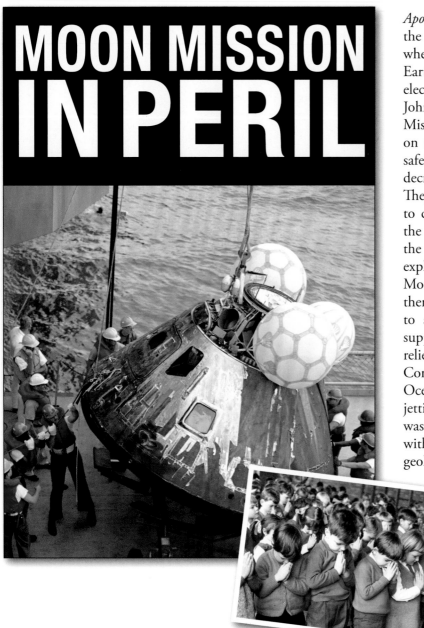

MOON MISSION IN PERIL

Apollo 13 was due to be the third space mission to land men on the Moon. But on April 14, 1970, 56 hours into the mission, when the spacecraft was about 200,000 miles (320,000 km) from Earth, an onboard oxygen tank blew up. The explosion cut the electricity and water supply, and the astronauts – James Lovell, Jr., John Swigert, Jr., and Fred Haise, Jr. – could hear gas escaping. Mission control abandoned all thought of landing the astronauts on the Moon and instead concentrated on getting them home safely. The crew was forced to abandon the Service Module, where decreasing air pressure was making the atmosphere intolerable. They took refuge in the Lunar Module, *Aquarius*, and prepared to curve around the Moon and head back to Earth. However, the explosion had also disabled the navigation system, so instead the men had to rely on the Sun to guide them home. Had the explosion occurred after the lunar landing, when the Lunar Module would have already detached from the Service Module, there would have been no hope. As it was, the three men managed to survive on the Lunar Module's emergency battery power supply. Four days later, on Friday April 17, 1970, to the immense relief of the crew, mission control, and the watching world, the Command Module, *Odyssey*, splashed down safely in the Pacific Ocean. The Lunar Module and the Service Module had both been jettisoned before re-entry to the Earth's atmosphere. The crew was unharmed and was flown to American Samoa to be reunited with their families. The aim of the mission had been to conduct geological experiments to help establish the age of the Moon. Sadly, this was not accomplished, but the survival of the astronauts was of paramount concern.

Left: School children pray for the safe return of Apollo 13.

January
The Big Freeze
The coldest weather in years closes schools, shops, and airports across Europe, causing an influenza outbreak and a rise in the cost of heating oil.

January 15
End of War in Nigeria
Biafran rebels surrender, ending the war for independence in Nigeria.

March 1
Vietnam War Escalates
American war planes bomb the Ho Chi Minh trail in Vietnam, the main route between North and South Vietnam, made up of many intricate jungle paths.

HOSTAGE CRISIS IN MIDDLE EAST

On September 6, 1970, the first major act of Middle Eastern terrorism occurred when members of the Palestine Liberation Organization (P.L.O.) hijacked four commercial airliners. They flew three of the planes, with their hostages, to the Jordanian desert near Amman, and, after negotiations had secured the evacuation of all passengers in return for the release of P.L.O. terrorists in prison, they blew up the planes. The passengers were subsequently kept hostage for some weeks during negotiations. King Hussein of Jordan prepared to use military force against the P.L.O., but before he did so, he sought assurance from U.S. President Nixon that if Syria or Iraq came to the defense of the P.L.O. and attacked Jordan, America would lend military support. Henry Kissinger, U.S. Secretary of State, came up with an alternative plan: he suggested that King Hussein ask Israel for help in defeating the P.L.O. By joint agreement between King Hussein, President Nixon, and Israeli Prime Minister Golda Meir, the Israelis launched air strikes on Palestinian strongholds in Jordan. Around 2,000 P.L.O. fighters, as well as several thousand Palestinian civilians, were killed in the military action. Although Syria attempted to intervene on behalf of the Palestinians, they withdrew when faced with a joint U.S.-Israeli threat. King Hussein lost the support of his Arab neighbors. Although the P.L.O. had been ejected from Jordan, the group moved to Lebanon and grew stronger, thanks to Soviet support.

FOUR JETS HIJACKED

'The first major act of Middle Eastern terrorism occurred when members of the P.L.O. hijacked four commercial airliners.'

Left: Golda Meir was Prime Minister of Israel from 1969 to 1974.

April 10
Beatles Break Up
The world's most famous rock group holds a press conference to announce that they have disbanded, upsetting millions of fans around the world.

May 4
Students Shot
The U.S. National Guard fires on students demonstrating against the Vietnam War at Kent State University in Ohio, killing four.

May 8
Beatles' Last Album
The Beatles release their last album, *Let It Be.*

June 10
Younger Voters
President Nixon lowers the voting age in the U.S. from 21 to 18.

1970

WAR IN JORDAN

Following the Six-Day War with Israel in 1967, Jordan lost the West Bank of the Jordan River to Israel, displacing thousands of Palestinians who fled into Jordan. Yasser Arafat regrouped his militant Palestine Liberation Organization (P.L.O.) in Jordan and carried out military attacks on Israel, often prompting retaliations that, in turn, killed Jordanians. In response to the P.L.O.'s guerrilla tactics within his country, King Hussein of Jordan, who remained unpopular with Arab militants for his involvement in peace talks with Israel, authorized the shelling of Palestinian refugee camps in an attempt to flush the P.L.O. out of Jordan. In June 1970, this situation escalated into a state of civil war between Jordanian troops and Palestinian guerrillas, with the P.L.O. seizing control of the city of Amman. On June 9, several shots were fired at King Hussein's car, but he managed to escape unharmed, although his driver was wounded.

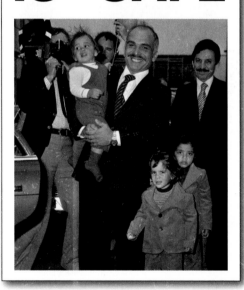

'The situation escalated into a state of civil war between Jordanian troops and Palestinian guerrillas'

U.S. IN CAMBODIA

At the beginning of 1970, U.S. President Nixon told the American people that the U.S. Army would withdraw from Vietnam as soon as possible. The North Vietnamese had long ago entered Cambodia despite the country's neutrality, and by March 1970, they had overthrown the Cambodian King, Norodom Sihanouk, and General Lon Nol was in power. Realizing that taking control of Cambodia would enable the North Vietnamese to carry out attacks on South Vietnam far more easily, President Nixon was forced to commit further U.S. troops to aid the Cambodians in repelling their invaders. His justification to the American people was that, if he did not commit troops to Cambodia, the lives of 150,000 American troops would be seriously endangered. Over the course of a 60-day action involving 30,000 U.S. troops, more than 10,000 North Vietnamese were killed and supply depots were seized. In June 1970, President Nixon announced that the mission in Cambodia had been successful, despite the fact that it had sparked further protests throughout the United States against the war.

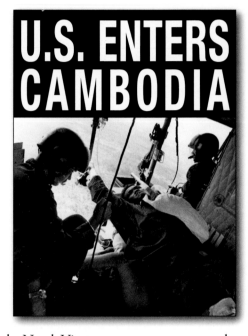

'President Nixon was forced to commit further U.S. troops to aid the Cambodians'

August 26–30
Music Festival
About 600,000 people enjoy the largest-ever rock festival on the Isle of Wight, featuring Jimi Hendrix; The Who; The Doors; Chicago; Richie Havens; Joan Baez; Ten Years After; Emerson, Lake & Palmer; and Jethro Tull.

September 18
Jimi Hendrix Dies
Jimi Hendrix dies in London from a drug overdose. Born Johnny Allen Hendrix on November 27, 1942, one of the many songs he is remembered for is his electric guitar version of the 'Star Spangled Banner'.

October 15
New President of Egypt
Anwar Sadat becomes the third President of Egypt upon the death of Nassar. Sadat re-institutes the multi-party system in Egypt, and shares the 1978 Nobel Prize for Peace with Israeli Prime Minister Menachim Begin.

November 9
Charles de Gaulle Dies
Born November 22, 1890, de Gaulle led the Free French Forces during the Second World War and was the first President of the French Fifth Republic, from 1959 to 1969.

BANGLADESH FIGHTS FOR INDEPENDENCE

Since the 1947 partition of India created Pakistan as a separate state, there had been increasing differences between the people of West Pakistan and the people of the East. The two regions were at odds culturally, economically, and politically. West Pakistan dominated the new country politically and exploited the more populous East by diverting state funds to its own ends. West Pakistan also kept East Pakistan out of government by rigging the voting system so that the greater population in the East could not alter the balance of power. In the 1970 national elections, the Awami League, the East Pakistan political party led by Sheikh Mujibur Rahman, won a majority of seats in the National Assembly. However, the Pakistan People's Party of Western Pakistan refused to allow him to form a government. Instead they suggested creating roles for two prime ministers, one for the East and one for the West. In response, Rahman called a general strike in March 1971 and rallied his people to fight for independence from West Pakistan. On March 25, 1971, the Pakistan Army launched Operation Searchlight, a military crackdown on rebellion and nationalism in the East, which has in subsequent years been described as a genocide. The operation consisted of the systematic murder of thousands, or even millions, of Bengali civilians. Sheikh Mujibur Rahman declared Bangladesh (formerly East Pakistan) as an independent country, and on April 17, 1971, he formed a government-in-exile in Mujib Nagar, India, where masses of Bengali refugees had fled. In the civil war that followed, the collection of Bangladeshi guerrilla forces, known as Mukti Bahini, received support and training from India. By the end of 1971, Pakistan was increasingly afraid of Indian involvement in their civil war and tried to ward it off with a pre-emptive strike on Indian airfields. India promptly invaded Pakistan and, together with the Mukti Bahini, defeated them. In the 1972 Simla Agreement with India, Pakistan recognized Bangladesh as an independent country in exchange for the release of Pakistani prisoners of war.

WAR IN BANGLADESH

Left: Mukti Bahini fighters threaten Razakars, who fought alongside the Pakistani Army.

January 25
Idi Amin Seizes Power
Idi Amin takes over as ruler of Uganda in a bloodless coup.

February 15
Concorde Flies
Supersonic Concorde's maiden flight takes place in France.

April 5
Mount Etna
In Sicily, a violent eruption of Mount Etna threatens villages and destroys an observatory.

April 24
March Against the War
Approximately 500,000 people march against the Vietnam War in Washington, D.C., along with about 125,000 protesters in San Francisco.

June 14
North Sea Oil
Norway starts production.

1971

BELFAST BAR BOMBED

On December 4, 1971, a bomb exploded in a crowded bar in Belfast, killing 15 people, including two children. It was one of the first major atrocities that launched the era often referred to as 'The Troubles'. Tramore Bar, more commonly known as McGurk's, was in a Catholic area, which baffled those who assumed that the Provisional Irish Republican Army (I.R.A.) had planted the bomb. The I.R.A., however, denied involvement, accusing a loyalist paramilitary group. The owner of the bar, Patrick McGurk, whose wife and daughter were killed in the blast, appeared on television with a public plea against retaliation: 'What's done can't be undone,' he said. After the bomb went off, fights between Catholics and Protestants broke out across the city. Despite the strange choice of target, for many years the belief continued that the explosion was caused by an I.R.A. bomb – the explanation given that it had gone off by mistake. It was not until 1977 that the driver of the getaway car confessed that the bomb had been planted by the loyalist paramilitary group the Ulster Volunteer Force. The driver was given 15 life sentences for his part in the crime, but no one else has since been arrested in connection with the bombing, despite calls by the victims' families to reopen the case.

VIOLENCE FLARES IN NORTHERN IRELAND

DECIMALIZATION FOR U.K.

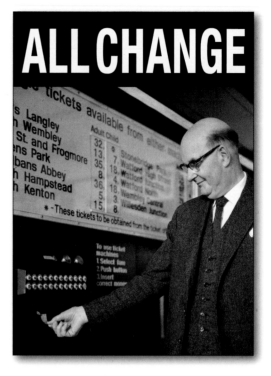

ALL CHANGE

'The United Kingdom and Ireland switched from the units of pounds, shillings, and pence to the decimal system.'

On February 15, 1971, the United Kingdom and Ireland switched from the units of pounds, shillings, and pence to the decimal system. Previously, £1 was made up of 20 shillings, and 1 shilling was made up of 12 pence. This system stretched back to Roman times, when a pound of silver was worth 240 silver pieces. Following decimalization, a pound consisted of 100 'new pennies'. The Americans pioneered the decimal system of money in 1786 when they established that $1 was worth 100 cents. The U.K. decision to go decimal had been delayed by discussions about scrapping the pound in favor of a smaller unit. However, in March 1966, James Callaghan, Chancellor of the Exchequer, announced the decision to make the change to decimal in 1971 and to retain the pound as the unit of currency. His announcement was greeted with cheers in the House of Commons. After Britain had made this change, several Commonwealth countries followed suit.

June 22–26
First Glastonbury
The first Glastonbury Festival, held on Worthy Farm in southwest England, was attended by only 1,500 people. Organized by Michael Eavis over the years, the first event was not a business success, although its headline act was T. Rex. The festival is now a tradition, famous for its mud and big acts.

July 3
Jim Morrison Dies
Jim Morrison, a legend in rock and roll, dies in Paris. Born in Florida on December 8, 1943, he is the charismatic lead singer and lyricist for The Doors.

August 16
Bombs in Britain
The I.R.A. starts its campaign of mainland bombing in Britain.

September
First Commercial V.C.R.
Although there were many variations preceding the V.C.R., Sony is credited with the world's first commercial videocassette recorder, using the Betamax format.

FIGHTING ON STREETS OF NORTHERN IRELAND

In July 1970, political parades and marches were banned in Northern Ireland for a period of six months in an attempt to stamp out growing violence. But the fighting continued in the streets, and the presence of the British Army did nothing to calm the situation. By the summer of 1971, the government at Stormont, under the last Northern Irish Prime Minister, Brian Faulkner, introduced a policy of internment without trial as an emergency measure. In total, 342 Republicans and Nationalists were arrested in dawn raids, and more than 200 of them were imprisoned without trial. Fighting in Belfast and Derry escalated, with gun battles in the streets claiming 12 lives. Following the 1971 bombing in the Tramore Bar (McGurk's) and the killings of 1972's Bloody Sunday, the British government announced that it would adopt an emergency measure of direct rule, dealing with security itself. This emergency measure was meant to last for a 12-month period but ended up lasting 25 years.

'The fighting continued in the streets, and the presence of the British Army did nothing to calm the situation.'

Above: The Parliament of Northern Ireland at Stormont was suspended in 1972.

October 1
Disney World
Walt Disney World opens in Florida.

November 15
World's First Microprocessor
The 4004, the world's first single-chip microprocessor, is released by Intel. This breakthrough allows the future embedding of intelligence in inanimate objects and, eventually, the personal computer.

November 24
Skyjack!
The world's only unsolved skyjacking takes place in a severe thunderstorm over Washington State. D.B. Cooper parachutes from a Northwest Orient Airlines plane with $200,000 ransom. Neither he nor the money is ever seen again.

December 19
A Clockwork Orange
Based on the novel by Anthony Burgess, Stanley Kubrick's influential and controversial film, portraying a decaying and violent society, is released. Kubrick withdraws the film from U.K. cinemas in 1973.

UGANDAN ASIANS ARRIVE IN GREAT BRITAIN

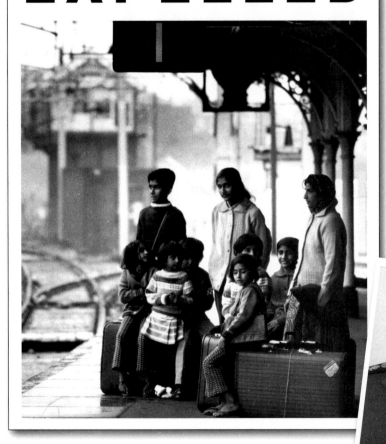

UGANDAN ASIANS EXPELLED

In 1971, General Idi Amin seized power in Uganda by military coup, declaring himself President. In August 1972, he made the decision to expel the country's Asian population. At the time, around 80,000 Asians resided in Uganda. Resentment against Asians was growing because, through hard work and good business sense, they had made themselves the most commercially successful citizens. General Amin subsequently amended his expulsion order to include only those Asians who were not Ugandan citizens, which reduced the number to around 60,000. Since Uganda was a former British colony, the majority of the expelled Asians held British passports, and when they were forced from Uganda, the obvious choice was Great Britain. The situation was viewed with some alarm in Britain, particularly by its right-wing politicians, who argued against the need to accept the expelled Asians into Britain. However, in the end, around 30,000 Ugandan Asians did arrive in Britain, for the most part penniless, since they had been expelled without any compensation for the homes or businesses they were leaving behind. The expulsion made General Amin popular among many of the black majority, and members of the army, whom he valued highly, were rewarded with Asian property and businesses. The economy, however, went into drastic decline, with cement and sugar factories grinding to a halt.

> **'Resentment against Asians was growing because, through hard work and good business sense, they had made themselves ... commercially successful'**

Left: Idi Amin claimed God had told him to expel Ugandan Asians.

March 4
An Offer You Can't Refuse
The film *The Godfather*, starring Marlon Brando and Al Pacino, is released. The film wins three Academy Awards and is later ranked second in American cinema history, behind *Citizen Kane*. Based on the book by Mario Puzo, the film is directed by Francis Ford Coppola.

March 24
Northern Ireland
British direct rule over Northern Ireland begins.

May 4
Greenpeace Emerges
The world's most well-known environmental activist group is renamed, having been known previously as the Don't Make a Wave Committee.

May 22
Nixon in Russia
Richard Nixon becomes the first American president to visit the U.S.S.R. He is not very warmly welcomed by President Nikolai Podgomy, Prime Minister Alexei Kosygin, and Foreign Minister Andrei Gromyko.

TERROR AT MUNICH OLYMPICS

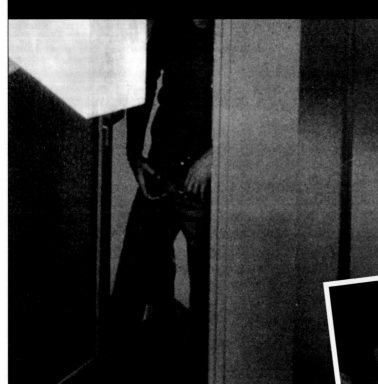

MASSACRE AT OLYMPICS

On September 5, 1972, eight Arab terrorists with ties to Fatah, Yasser Arafat's branch of the Palestine Liberation Organization (P.L.O.), infiltrated the Olympic Village at the Munich Games and took nine Israeli athletes hostage. The terrorists had called themselves the Black September Organization after the 1970 Israeli airstrikes that killed thousands of Palestinians. After taking their hostages, the terrorists declared themselves Palestinians and demanded the release of 234 Arab terrorists held in Israeli jails, as well as the release of two held in a German prison and a guarantee of their own safe passage out of Germany. After hours of negotiations, the German authorities made it look like they agreed to fulfill the terrorists' request and arranged for helicopters to take them to an airfield. However, the German authorities had secretly positioned gunmen to kill the terrorists when they arrived at the airfield, while sparing the hostages. The rescue plan failed, leading instead to a shoot-out between the terrorists and the German authorities. One terrorist managed to set off a grenade in his helicopter, killing everyone onboard, while another shot dead the rest of the Israeli hostages. In all, 11 Israeli athletes and coaches, five terrorists, and one German policeman were killed. Three of the terrorists were captured alive and held in German jails, but they were later released following the hijacking of a German plane.

Right: Israeli swimmer Shlomit Nir at a memorial service for the murdered athletes.

Above: The Olympic Stadium in Munich, Germany.

May 22
Sri Lanka
Ceylon becomes the republic of Sri Lanka, with a new constitution.

May 26
Treaties Signed
Nixon and Brezhnev sign the SALT 1 Treaty in Moscow, as well as the Anti-Ballistic Missile Treaty.

June 8
Kim Phúc
The iconic image of nine-year-old Kim Phúc, running from her Vietnamese village Trang Bang, where a napalm bomb had just been dropped, makes a serious impact on efforts to stop the war.

June 17
Watergate Break-In
The Democratic National Committee headquarters in the Watergate Building, in Washington, D.C., is broken into by five White House operatives who are arrested, starting a chain of events that will lead to U.S. President Richard Nixon's resignation.

1972

MASS MURDER AT LOD AIRPORT

TERRORIST AIRPORT OUTRAGE

'The three men opened fire at random, killing 24 bystanders, including 16 Christian pilgrims from Puerto Rico.'

On May 30, 1972, three members of the Japanese Red Army carried out a terrorist attack on behalf of the Popular Front for the Liberation of Palestine at Lod Airport in Tel Aviv. Airport security forces were on the alert for a Palestinian attack and allowed the smartly dressed Japanese men with violin cases to pass them by. Once inside the airport, the three men opened fire at random, killing 24 bystanders, including 16 Christian pilgrims from Puerto Rico. One of the terrorists was shot by an Israeli security guard, another committed suicide by letting off a grenade, and the last was arrested.

BLOODY SUNDAY

In 1969, the Provisional Irish Republican Army (I.R.A.) began its campaign of violence against Unionists in Northern Ireland. Regiments from the British Army were sent to Northern Ireland to keep the peace, but their presence provoked further violence. Inspired by the Civil Rights movement in America, the Northern Ireland Civil Rights Association was formed and began to stage demonstrations. During one such demonstration in the Bogside area of Derry on Sunday January 30, 1972, 28 Civil Rights members were shot by soldiers of the British Parachute Regiment. Fourteen of the protestors died, six of them teenagers, and eyewitnesses claimed that all were unarmed and most were running away from

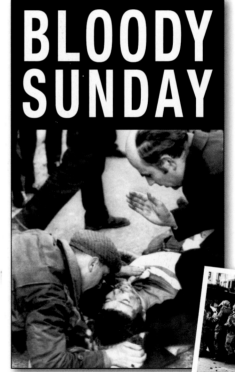

the soldiers when they were shot. The incident became known as 'Bloody Sunday'. It bolstered the popularity of the I.R.A., and many Catholics in Northern Ireland who had previously supported the British government now shifted their loyalty to the Republic of Ireland. Two highly controversial inquiries failed to lay the blame squarely on the British government.

Right: British soldiers shelter from stones on Bloody Sunday 1972.

August
Going for Gold
U.S. swimmer Mark Spitz wins seven gold medals at the Munich Olympics.

August 11
Leaving South Vietnam
American ground troops withdraw from South Vietnam.

September
First Pocket Calculators
The world's first really pocket-sized electronic calculator is the Bowmar 901B, based on Texas Instruments Company components. It is the first with an L.E.D. display; the first hand-held to use a single integrated circuit; and the first electronic calculator to run on replaceable batteries. Hewlett Packard also have a pocket calculator in 1972, so-called because it is the exact size to fit into William Hewlett's shirt pocket. It is the first scientific calculator, with trigonometric and exponential functions.

December 23
Survivors Eat to Live
The 16 survivors of a plane crash in the Andes Mountains in Argentina are forced to eat the remains of the crash victims in order to stay alive in the freezing temperatures, without food or medical supplies, until rescued 10 weeks later.

U.S. LAUNCHES FIRST SPACE STATION

SKYLAB IN ORBIT

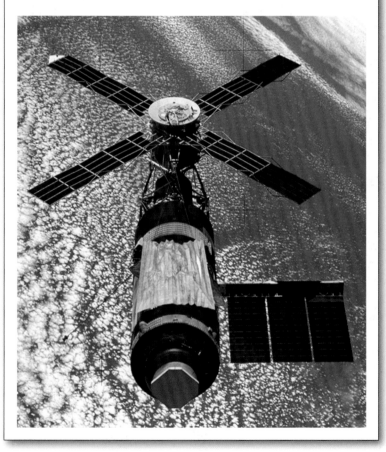

On May 14, 1973, the U.S. launched *Skylab*, its first space station, into space. It was to act as a space laboratory for only one year, but instead it remained in orbit around Earth for six years. During that time there were three manned missions to the *Skylab* space station, which enabled astronauts to conduct scientific research and undertake space walks. Around 2,000 hours of scientific and medical experiments took place on *Skylab*. It was during some of these experiments that the Sun's coronal holes were discovered. Other experiments investigated the astronauts' adaptation to long periods of microgravity.

'Around 2,000 hours of scientific and medical experiments took place on Skylab.'

Right: A re-creation of the inside of Sklylab.

Above: Skylab *was the second space station to be visited by a human crew.*

January 1
New Members for E.E.C.
The U.K., the Republic of Ireland, and Denmark join the European Economic Community (E.E.C.), later to become the European Union.

January 14
Aloha
Elvis Presley's television special, *Aloha from Hawaii*, is transmitted. It has over 1 billion viewers worldwide.

April 3
Can You Hear Me?
The first cellular telephone call is made by Martin Cooper, who conceived the original idea of the phone, in New York City.

April 4
Twin Towers
The World Trade Center is officially opened in New York City.

TRUCE IN VIETNAM

PEACE PROTESTERS

As soon as he was elected in 1969, U.S. President Nixon made clear his intention to bring to an end the Vietnam War. However, it was not until October 1972 that he managed to persuade Communist North Vietnam to the negotiating table. The North had up to that point resisted negotiations, but a prolonged campaign of American air strikes had begun to have an effect. Although President Nixon was quick to agree terms with the North, the South Vietnamese President Nguyên Văn Thiêu was unhappy with the situation, which left the South vulnerable to attacks from the thousands of North Vietnamese soldiers still in occupation after the Americans pulled out. Peace negotiations broke down, and President Nixon launched one final military push in order to crush the North. On December 18, 1972, a massive bombing campaign began, targeting Hanoi. It succeeded in driving the North Vietnamese back to the negotiating table. This time an agreement was reached, and in Paris, on January 27, 1973, it was signed by all parties. However, once the American troops withdrew, North and South Vietnam continued to fight. Each country was determined to defeat the other. It was another two years before hostilities would end, with the North finally conquered the South. The American commitment to defending South Vietnam had failed.

> 'As soon as he was elected in 1969, U.S. President Nixon made clear his intention to bring to an end the Vietnam War.'

WATERGATE HITS NIXON

On June 17, 1972, a group of men broke into the Watergate Hotel, the site of the Democratic National Headquarters. Their aim was to uncover incriminating evidence against the Democratic Party and to bug their offices. The men were members of a security group known as the 'Plumbers', made up of former C.I.A. and F.B.I. men who worked for the Republican government of Richard Nixon and got their name because they 'fixed leaks' in the Republican administration. They had performed similar jobs before, but on this occasion they were careless, and a security guard alerted the police. All of the men were arrested, and it was then that their connections to the government began to emerge. Although President Nixon was elected to a second term, the scandal that would discredit him began to unfold. In May 1973, the Senate started to investigate, and when it was discovered that President Nixon taped all conversations that occurred in his office, Special Prosecutor Archibald Cox Jr. demanded that he hand over the tapes. Nixon stalled. By October, he still had not handed over the tapes, and when Cox continued to insist, Nixon had him fired. But he faced even tougher treatment from the next Special Prosecutor, Leon Jaworski. Nixon finally handed over some of the tapes, but two crucial ones were missing and some of them had erasures. By July 1974, Nixon was still refusing to cooperate, and Jaworski named him as a co-conspirator in the

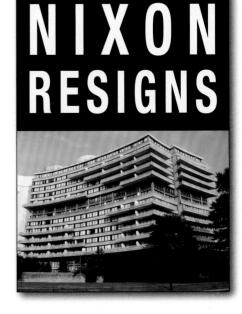

Watergate trial. The House of Representatives voted to impeach the President, and on August 8, 1974, Nixon resigned.

April 8
Picasso Dies
Pablo Picasso is one of the most recognized of the 20th-century artists, as a painter and sculptor, as well as for his lifestyle. Born on October 25, 1881, he was, among other achievements, the co-founder of the Cubist movement.

May 25
Tubular Bells
Mike Oldfield's successful album *Tubular Bells* is released.

September 11
Pinochet Takes Power
General Augusto Pinochet leads an American-backed junta after a military coup in Chile, during which President Salvador Allende commits suicide.

October 6
Yom Kippur War
Egypt and Syria attack Israel on Yom Kippur, the Jewish Day of Atonement. The war ends on October 26, when Israel wins, just as a U.N. ceasefire comes into effect.

WEST HIT BY CRIPPLING ENERGY CRISIS

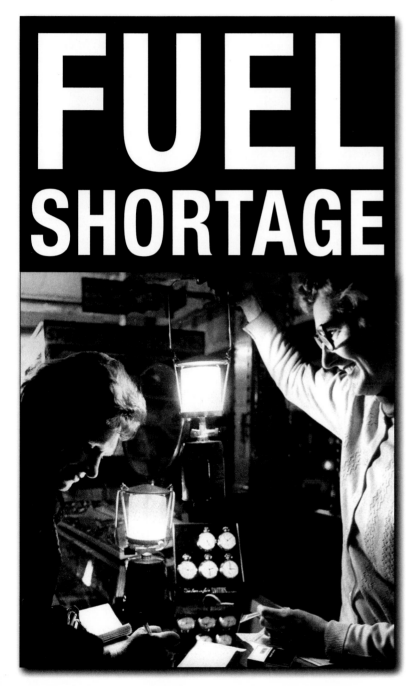

On October 17, 1973, the members of the Organization of Arab Petroleum Exporting Countries (O.A.P.E.C.) proclaimed an oil embargo against the United States and other countries if they continued to support Israel in the Yom Kippur War. Countries affected included the U.S., U.K., Canada, Japan, and the Netherlands. The embargo coincided with a decision by O.A.P.E.C. to raise the price of oil as a way of stabilizing the exporters' incomes. This also came after considerable stress and rapid inflation in the world economy after the U.S. had pulled out of the Bretton Woods system, whereby only the dollar had been tied to the gold standard and other currencies had been tied to the dollar. The most hard-hit countries responded with a wide variety of initiatives to reduce their dependency on Arab oil. In order to immediately deal with depleted fuel supplies, in the U.K., Prime Minister Edward Heath introduced tough measures, including gasoline rationing. In the long term, the oil embargo changed Western policy towards energy use and conservation and led to more restrictive monetary policy to better fight inflation.

'The most hard-hit countries responded with a wide variety of measures to reduce their dependency on Arab oil.'

Right: Conservative Edward Heath was Prime Minister of the U.K. from 1970 to 1974.

October 12
Supplies to Israel
The U.S. begins Operation Nickel Grass, airlifting weapons and supplies to Israel.

October 20
Sydney Opera House
Queen Elizabeth II opens the Sydney Opera House, after 14 years' construction.

December 15
Jean Paul Getty III Found
After being kidnapped, Jean Paul Getty III is found alive in Italy after his grandfather pays about $2.8 million. The kidnappers had cut off one ear and sent it to the family, to prove they would kill their captive unless money was paid.

December 31
U.K. in Trouble
The U.K. is declared a State of Emergency as fuel supplies dwindle.

1974

THREE-DAY WEEK FOR THE U.K.

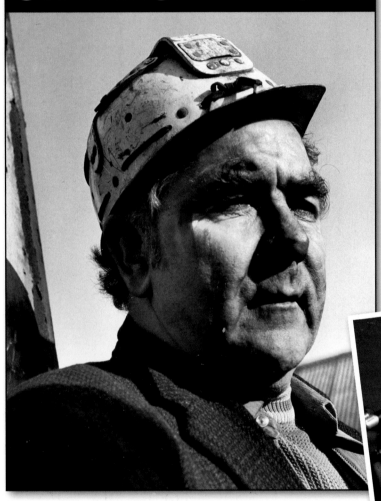

MINERS' STRIKE SHAKES THE U.K.

From January 1 to March 7, 1974, a three-day working week was declared by Conservative Prime Minister of the U.K. Edward Heath as an emergency measure to conserve electricity. Great Britain's electricity supply had been seriously reduced as a result of miners' strikes that followed the government's decisions in 1972 and 1973 to cap pay raises in an effort to halt rising inflation. Industrial action followed across the country, most notably among coal miners, whose unions claimed their pay was not keeping up with inflated prices. This industrial action had a disastrous effect on the country. Coal supplies rapidly declined, and in order to conserve what remained, the Prime Minister put into action a policy designed to keep the country running. The three-day week meant that commercial businesses could only operate on three consecutive days in a week. The ruling did not apply to essential services, and radio and T.V. broadcasting companies were also allowed to continue as normal, probably in order to keep up morale. However, even these industries had to close down at 10.30 p.m. Heath lost the 1974 election, and Labour's Harold Wilson became the next prime minister. Wilson followed through with the recommendation of a pay board appointed by Heath that the miners receive an exceptional 29% pay raise.

'Coal supplies rapidly declined, and in order to conserve what remained, the Prime Minister put into action a policy designed to keep the country running.'

Left: Harold Wilson was Prime Minister of the U.K. from 1964 to 1970 and 1974 to 1976.

February 4
Bankrobbing Heiress
Heiress Patty Hearst is kidnapped by the Symbionese Liberation Army, and goes on to rob a bank with them on April 15, declaring herself an urban guerrilla. Arrested in September 1975, her jail sentence is commuted by President Carter and she is later pardoned by President Clinton.

March 31
B.E.A. + B.O.A.C. = B.A.
The airline British European Airways (B.E.A.), founded in 1946, merges with the airline British Overseas Airways Corporation (B.O.A.C.), founded in 1939, to create British Airways (B.A.).

April 6
ABBA Wins
The Swedish group ABBA, an acronym formed from the first letters of the band's first names, wins the Eurovision Song Contest with the song 'Waterloo.'

June 26
Barcodes In
The universal product code, now called a barcode, is first scanned on a pack of Wrigley's chewing gum, at a supermarket in Troy, Ohio, U.S.A.

CYPRUS INVADED

The population of the Mediterranean island of Cyprus has long been mixed, with around 78% Greek-Cypriots, 18% Turkish-Cypriots, and the remainder Armenians, Maronites, and Latin-Cypriots. A former British colony, Cyprus had become an independent republic in 1960. For centuries, Greeks and Turks lived side by side in apparent harmony despite their religious differences. In fact, churches and mosques stand next to each other all over the island. However, during the 20th century, divisions and resentments began to surface. Then, on July 20, 1974, Turkey invaded Cyprus, declaring that the minority Turks on the island needed their protection. Turkey also claimed that the constitution of Cyprus as a republic was under threat. The Turkish military operation was in response to a Greek military-backed coup in Cyprus that deposed the Cypriot president with the apparent intention of annexing the island to Greece. Turkey launched a second attack in August 1974, this time seizing more than one third of the territory of Cyprus. In total, 200,000 Cypriots fled their homes in fear of the approaching Turkish Army, and over 2,000 are still unaccounted for, both Greek-Cypriot and Turkish-Cypriot. The Turks claimed the northern section of Cyprus as a federated Turkish state. Although this state has never been internationally recognized, over 100,000 new Turkish immigrants have settled in the region. The last major effort to settle the dispute was the U.N. Annan Plan of 2004. It gained the support of Turkish-Cypriots but was rejected by Greek-Cypriots.

'The Turkish military invasion was in response to a Greek military-backed coup in Cyprus that deposed the Cypriot president'

Left: A mosque in the Turkish portion of the island's capital, Nicosia.

July 1
Female Head of State
Isabel Perón becomes the interim President of Argentina until March 24, 1976, after the death of her husband Juan Perón, who died while in office. She is the first non-royal female head of state in the western hemisphere.

July 17
I.R.A. Bomb
A bomb explodes at the Tower of London, killing one and injuring 41.

August 9
Nixon in Disgrace
Richard Nixon resigns from the office of the President of the United States in order to avoid being impeached by Congress over his role in the Watergate scandal. Gerald Ford becomes President.

September 12
Haile Salasie Out
The Emperor of Ethiopia, Haile Salassie, is deposed and his son, Crown Prince Asfaw Wossen, is given the throne, reigning until 1975.

1974

PUBS BOMBED BY I.R.A.

The minority Catholics in Northern Ireland held a long-standing resentment toward the Protestants and the British authorities, who appeared to favor Protestants over Catholics. During the 1960s, there was growing support for the Provisional Irish Republican Army (I.R.A.), which opposed British rule in Ireland. After the British introduction in August 1971 of internment without trial for suspected terrorists, the I.R.A. campaign of violence increased and spread from Ireland to the mainland of Britain. Initially, attacks were aimed at military targets in Great Britain, but gradually they became more haphazard. Frequently, bombs were planted in public places to kill or injure civilians. The I.R.A. began to lose the sympathy of its less militant supporters. Following the Birmingham pub bombings of November 21, 1974, in which 21 people died, the British government brought in a Prevention of Terrorism Act that allowed for terrorist suspects to be held for extended periods before trial.

Right: An I.R.A. bomb exploded at the Earl's Court Boat Show in London in January 1974.

LUCAN MURDER

'Lady Lucan ran into the pub nearest her house with blood pouring from wounds on her head.'

On November 8, 1974, Richard John Bingham, 7th Earl of Lucan, disappeared after his children's nanny was found murdered in their home. The Lucans had separated, and Lord Lucan did not live at the house with his children and their mother. The police were alerted to the murder after Lady Lucan ran into the pub nearest her house with blood pouring from wounds on her head. Her version of events was that the nanny, Sandra Rivett, went down to the basement kitchen just before 9 p.m. to make a cup of tea and did not return. When Lady Lucan went to investigate, she found the basement in darkness and was attacked by a man. She managed to distract him and escaped. It has generally been assumed that Lucan murdered Sandra Rivett by mistake, believing that she was his wife. Her body was found in a sack in the basement. She had been beaten with a piece of lead pipe. Lucan's car was later discovered on the south coast of England. There were bloodstains on the seats and a length of lead pipe that matched the murder weapon. Lord Lucan has never been found, although various unconfirmed sightings have been reported. He was officially declared dead in 1999.

October 1
Golden Arches
The first McDonald's opens in London.

October 30
I Am the Greatest
Muhammad Ali regains his world heavyweight boxing crown, from the boxer George Foreman, in Zaire.

November 13
Amityville Horror
Ronald DeFeo Jr. murders his parents and his four younger siblings in Amityville, Long Island, U.S.A. The case is the inspiration for the book and film entitled *The Amityville Horror*.

November 24
Lucy
A skeleton of the hominid *Australopithecus aferensis* that lived between 3.9 and 2.9 million years ago is discovered in Ethiopia and named Lucy.

November 30
McCartney Soars
Paul McCartney and Wings release the album *Band on the Run*.

SOUTH VIETNAM SURRENDERS

After the U.S. withdrew from the Vietnam War, the battle continued to rage between North and South Vietnam for a further two years. However, when the U.S. also withdrew aid from South Vietnam in 1975, they could no longer cope alone. On April 21, 1975, Xuân Loc fell to the North Vietnamese. It was the last city protecting the capital, Saigon, and when it fell, the South Vietnamese President Nguyên Văn Thiêu fled the capital, eventually setting in Great Britain. By April 27, the North Vietnamese had surrounded Saigon. By April 30, the South Vietnamese had surrendered – the Vietnam War was over. Saigon became Ho Chi Minh City, and Vietnam became one country, ruled by the Communist North.

NORTH VIETNAM WINS WAR

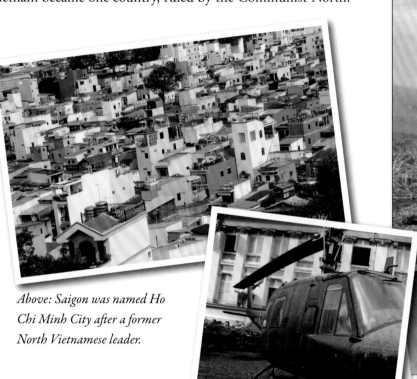

Above: Saigon was named Ho Chi Minh City after a former North Vietnamese leader.

Right: A U.S. helicopter displayed in Vietnam.

Left: In 1975, Saigon's town hall was renamed the People's Committee Building.

March 1
Color T.V.
Color television transmissions begin in Australia.

April 4
Microsoft to Go
Bill Gates founds Microsoft in Albuquerque, New Mexico.

April 17
Cambodia Taken
The Communist Khmer Rouge forces take Cambodia.

June 12
Gandhi Guilty
Indira Gandhi, India's Prime Minister, is found guilty of electoral corruption.

June 20
Just When You Thought it Was Safe
The film *Jaws* is released, starring Roy Scheider and Richard Dreyfuss.

1975

THE JACKAL TAKES O.P.E.C. MINISTERS HOSTAGE

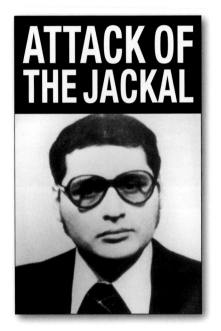

ATTACK OF THE JACKAL

The notorious terrorist Ilich Ramírez Sánchez, better known as 'Carlos the Jackal', committed his most infamous act of terror when, in 1975 in Vienna, he organized the kidnapping of 42 members of the Organization of Petroleum Exporting Countries (O.P.E.C.). A Venezuelan by birth, he had converted to Islam, joined the Popular Front for the Liberation of Palestine in 1970, and committed himself to bringing down Western democracies. After attending terrorist training camp in Amman, Jordan, he was given the pseudonym Carlos and carried out a number of bombings in London and Paris. In December 1975, he was put in charge of a terrorist mission to kidnap O.P.E.C. ministers at their conference in Vienna, Austria. Part of the plan was that he and his team would execute Saudi Arabia's Oil Minister, Sheikh Ahmed Zaki Yamani, and Iran's Minister of the Interior, Jamshid Amouzegar, while keeping the others hostage. The group carried out the operation as planned, killing several police officers, security guards, and anyone else who tried to disarm them. However, they did not succeed in executing the Saudi and Iranian ministers, instead taking 42 hostages on a plane to Algiers. Carlos was eventually paid off by an unknown Arab ruler, and he released the hostages, escaping unhurt with the vast sum of money (rumored to be in the region of $20 million). He was finally extradited to France in 1994, and in 1997, he was sentenced to life imprisonment.

AUSTRALIA'S PRIME MINISTER DISMISSED

When Edward Gough Whitlam was elected Prime Minister of Australia in 1972, he immediately put into action a program of social and cultural reforms. He abolished conscription and withdrew troops from the Vietnam War. He was determined that Australia should develop a more independent foreign policy, instead of simply following the U.S. Domestically, he dramatically improved and expanded social services, put measures in place to ensure greater equality, particularly for women, and reformed the education system. He also introduced universal health insurance. Whitlam took a tough stance on racial discrimination and ended the race criterion in immigration applications. Whitlam achieved an incredible amount in a short space of time, but it all cost vast amounts of money, and Australia's economy suffered as a result: both inflation and unemployment increased. Though the Labour Party held the House of Representatives, the Senate remained hostile. In October 1975, the Senate refused to pass the Whitlam government's budget until an election was held in the House of Representatives. Whitlam refused to call an election, and when the Governor-General John Kerr heard of the deadlock, he dismissed Whitlam on November 11, 1975.

AUSTRALIAN PM SACKED

July 11
Terracotta Army Found
China's Terracotta Army is discovered by local farmers in Xi'an, Shaanxi province. Dating from the time of the first Chinese Emperor in 210 B.C.E., there are estimated to be more than 8,000 soldiers, 130 chariots, and 700 horses, most of which are still buried for their safekeeping.

July 17
Greetings in Space
The American and Soviet spacecraft dock in space, and the two commanders in charge of their vessels shake hands.

August 1
Helsinki Accord
The agreement officially recognizing Europe's national borders and respect for human rights is signed in Finland.

THATCHER LEADS CONSERVATIVES IN U.K.

Margaret Thatcher, who was to become Great Britain's first female Prime Minister, took over the leadership of the Conservative Party from Edward Heath in 1975 after the Conservatives lost the general election. After leaving Oxford University, she had become a research chemist and then a lawyer before going into politics. She had been a member of Parliament for Finchley in North London since 1959 and Secretary for Education in Heath's government. At the next general election, the Conservatives came to power, and Margaret Thatcher became Prime Minister in 1979. Her policies were famous for dividing the nation, and people either loved or loathed her. Her steely determination earned her the nickname of the 'Iron Lady' – a term that was first coined by the Soviets. Her domestic policies included privatization of state-owned companies, reduced taxes, and decreased spending on social services. She began to reform the system of welfare and reduced the power of the labour unions. Thatcher had a close political friendship with U.S. President Ronald Reagan, who shared her advocacy of a free-market economy.

Above: Margaret Thatcher with Prime Minister Ted Heath in 1974.

Though victory in the 1982 Falklands War against Argentina boosted her popularity, her introduction of the poll tax, which was regarded as penalizing the poor, and her anti-Europe stance lost her support during the late 1980s. She was forced to resign as Prime Minister in 1990 after a challenge to her leadership of the Conservative Party.

THATCHER WINS

Left: Thatcher's husband Denis was a loyal supporter and a self-confessed 'right-winger'.

September 16
Lebanon Conflict
Civil war breaks out in Lebanon.

October 29
Yorkshire Ripper
Peter Sutcliffe, later known as the Yorkshire Ripper, commits his first murder, in Leeds, England.

November 22
The Reign in Spain
The monarchy returns to Spain after the death of General Franco on November 20, with Juan Carlos declared King.

December
Step to Equality
The Sex Discrimination and Equal Pay Acts come into force in the U.K.

350 DIE IN SOWETO RIOTS

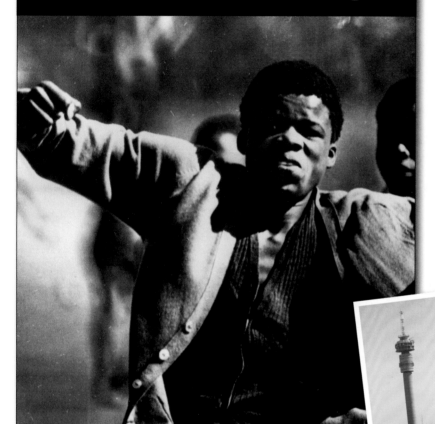

VIOLENCE ERUPTS IN SOUTH AFRICA

One of the ways in which the white government of South Africa hoped to limit the power of black South Africans was to rule that only the Afrikaans language should be taught in black schools. The black population recognized this for what it was – an attempt to bar them from mainstream society and to prevent any escape from poverty through education. In Soweto, a township of Johannesburg where the majority of the black population lived in basic accommodation, protests broke out against the education ruling in June 1976. On June 16, 10,000 students marched through the streets, shouting, 'Down with Afrikaans!' When the police surrounded them, the protestors threw stones, and the police responded by firing into the crowds. The violence spread to the suburbs of Johannesburg, journalists were kept from the area, and Prime Minister Vorster declared, 'This government will not be intimidated, and instructions have been given to maintain law and order at all costs.' It is estimated that around 350 people died in the Soweto riots, which prompted a chain reaction of violence in the country, leading to more deaths. But the campaign against apartheid was strengthened by these public clashes, which aroused international sympathy for the plight of black South Africans.

'When the police surrounded them, the protesters threw stones, and the police responded by firing into the crowds.'

Right: Johannesburg is the largest city in South Africa and the center of a wealthy gold and diamond trade.

January 21
Elegance in the Sky
Concorde begins commercial flights – and the age of supersonic travel has begun. Two flights take off from London and Paris at the same time, bound for Bahrain and Rio de Janeiro. Permission to fly in the U.S. is not granted until May 24, when the plane starts flights to Washington, D.C. and, in 1977, to New York City, its most successful route.

March 24
Perón Deposed
The Argentine military deposes President Isabel Perón.

April 1
New Prime Minister
James Callaghan becomes Prime Minister of the U.K., after Harold Wilson resigns in a live, unexpected television announcement.

WESTERNERS FLEE LEBANON

After the kidnap and killing of the incoming American ambassador, Francis E. Meloy Jr., along with the U.S. Economic Counselor Robert O. Waring, in Beirut on June 16, the American government called for Americans to leave the war-torn city. The men had been on their way to meet the new Lebanese President, and had just crossed what was called the Green Line, between Beirut's Christian and Muslim sectors, when they were taken by the Popular Front for the Liberation of Palestine. Their bodies were found a few hours later in Muslim west Beirut; they had been shot – casualties of Beirut's 14-month civil war. The British embassy in Beirut organized a road convoy to take Westerners to Damascus, but the route was considered unsafe and, after two attempts, the journey had to be called off. Instead of leaving from the British embassy, the refugees, consisting of about 270 Americans, 97 British, and other Westerners, gathered on the beach along with the 40-hour supply of food and water they had been advised to take, where an American navy ship rescued them on June 20.

BEIRUT EVACUATED

Left: U.S. president Gerald Ford oversaw the planning of the evacuation by the American military.

April 1
The Big Apple
Apple Computer Company is officially formed by Steve Jobs and Steve Wozniak.

May 25
May the Force be with You
The first *Star Wars* film, called *Star Wars* at the time, starring Harrison Ford, Carrie Fisher, and Mark Hamill, is released.

July 4
Born on the 4th of July
The U.S. celebrates its bicentennial, the 200th anniversary of the Declaration of Independence.

August 1
Lauda Critical
Racing champion Niki Lauda suffers extensive burns in the German Grand Prix in Nürburgring.

1976

OPERATION ENTEBBE

On June 27, 1976, as an Air France flight from Israel made a stopover in Athens, a group of armed hijackers, members of the Popular Front for the Liberation of Palestine, boarded the plane and ordered it to fly to Entebbe, Uganda. Ugandan dictator Idi Amin was a conspirator in the hijacking, and he provided armed guards for the plane while it was at the airport. The hijackers announced that, if 54 convicted terrorists were not released from jail, they would blow up the plane. From the 246 passengers, all non-Israelis and non-Jews were released, leaving 105 hostages. While the French and Israeli authorities bought time by negotiating, the Israel Defense Forces (I.D.F.) was planning a rescue operation. On July 3, the I.D.F. set off in five planes for Entebbe Airport. In addition to 200 paratroopers, the planes also carried a black Mercedes and some Land Rovers, which were to be used as a decoy by posing as a V.I.P. visit to the airport. The operation was almost perfectly executed. Just after midnight on July 4, the I.D.F. planes were heading home. Four hostages had been killed in the process, as well as one Israeli commander, eight hijackers, and many Ugandan soldiers.

Above: Ugandan dictator Idi Amin.

LIFE ON MARS?

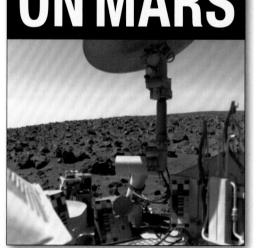

In 1975, N.A.S.A. launched its space program to Mars. The Viking program consisted of two space probes, *Viking 1* and *Viking 2*, each made up of an orbiter, which would photograph the surface of Mars, and a lander, which would conduct scientific tests on the planet's surface. The purpose of the mission was to discover as much as possible about the composition of the atmosphere and surface of Mars. The *Viking 1* lander touched down on Mars on July 20, 1976, while *Viking 2* landed on September 3. One of the main questions it was hoped the Viking mission could answer was whether there was life on Mars. The majority of the experiments indicated that the organic matter necessary for life was not present, but there was enough doubt cast by the limitations of equipment and conditions on the planet to leave the question unanswered.

Above: A full-scale model of the lander.

October 19
Chimps Threatened
The chimpanzee is placed on the endangered species list.

November 21
Rocky
The film *Rocky*, the first in the series of the same name, starring Sylvester Stallone, is released.

November 25
When the Band Stops Singing
Popular American-Canadian rock group The Band holds its farewell concert, *The Last Waltz*, in San Francisco.

December 8
Eagles Hit
The American rock band The Eagles release their album *Hotel California*, one of the top-ten bestselling albums.

HAPPY ANNIVERSARY

The celebrations for Queen Elizabeth II's Silver Jubilee commemorated the 25 years since she ascended the throne on February 6, 1952. The Queen marked her jubilee year by touring the Commonwealth, visiting 36 countries including Western Samoa, Tonga, Fiji, New Zealand, Australia, Tasmania, Papua New Guinea, Canada, and the West Indies. A week of celebrations in June opened with a beacon lit in Windsor, England, on June 6, launching a chain of lit beacons across the country. The next day, the Queen traveled in the Gold Stage Coach to St. Paul's Cathedral, London, for a service of thanksgiving, and later she appeared on the balcony of Buckingham Palace to greet the crowds. More than 1 million people lined the streets to watch the procession, and a further 50 million watched it on television. At a celebratory lunch, the Queen declared, 'I want to thank all those in Britain and the Commonwealth who, through their loyalty and friendship, have given me strength and encouragement during these last 25 years.' There were street parties all across the country. On Thursday June 9, the Queen took a ceremonial boat trip down the River Thames from Greenwich to Lambeth.

QUEEN CELEBRATES JUBILEE

Above: An estimated 100,000 street parties were held in the U.K. in June 1977.

Above: The Queen in New Guinea in February 1977.

January 20
Carter Is President
Jimmy Carter is sworn in as President of the U.S.

January 31
Pompidou Centre
The Centre Georges Pompidou in Paris is officially opened by French President Valéry Giscard d'Estaing.

May
Baby Mammoth Found
A reindeer herder finds a young mammoth preserved in ice in northwest Siberia. The mammoth, with trunk and eyes intact and with some fur still on its body, is believed to have died about 10,000 years ago, at the time of the last Ice Age.

March 10
Planet Ringed
Three astronomers, James L. Elliot, Edward W. Dunham, and Douglas J. Mink, discover rings around the planet Uranus.

JUMBO JETS COLLIDE

AIRPORT DISASTER

On March 27, 1977, two Boeing 747s – one K.L.M. and one Pan Am – collided just above the runway at Los Rodeos Airport in the Canary Islands. A series of unfortunate circumstances had come together to cause the world's worst aviation disaster, with 583 lives lost. The K.L.M. flight was taking mostly Dutch tourists to a vacation in the Canary Islands and was due to land at Las Palmas, the islands' main airport. The Pan Am flight was taking American tourists to the Canary Islands to begin a 12-day Mediterranean cruise. Both planes, along with various others, were diverted from Las Palmas Airport because of a terrorist bomb explosion in the airport and the threat of another to follow. At Los Rodeos Airport, to which both planes were diverted, the passengers left the plane but had returned by evening when the all-clear was given. By then, it was getting foggy, and the crews were eager to be on their way. The captain of the K.L.M. flight was especially determined that his crew should not exceed their maximum allowed flight time, as employment laws were very strict in Holland. Both planes were lined up and ready to depart. Due to poor communication between the two planes and air traffic control, with messages misunderstood or not heard, the K.L.M. plane took off before it was meant to and crashed head-on into the Pan Am plane, which was taxiing along the runway. Although the captain of the K.L.M. plane desperately tried to pull up, it still tore off the top of the other plane and both burst into flames. Most of the passengers were killed by the impact or fire. Only 90 people survived.

> 'A series of unfortunate circumstances had come together to cause the world's worst aviation disaster, with 583 lives lost.'

April 2
The Winner
Red Rum wins his third Grand National race at Aintree in England. The famous Grand National is held each year on a Saturday afternoon in April. Run over a distance of 4.5 miles (7.5 km), there are 30 fences to jump, and there are many injuries to the horses. Many British people who do not normally watch or bet on horse racing at other times of the year bet on this race. The winner is almost impossible to predict.

June 15
Spanish Elections
Democratic elections are held in Spain for the first time in 41 years.

July 5
Bhutto Out
Pakistani Prime Minister Zulfikar Ali Bhutto is ousted by the Chief of the Army Staff, General Zia ul-Haq, who imposes martial law.

July 13
The Lights Went Out on Broadway
New York City suffers a total blackout when the electric grids fails, leaving the city and its workers and inhabitants without power for 25 hours.

'THE KING' IS DEAD

On August 16, 1977, Elvis Aaron Presley was found dead on the bathroom floor of his Graceland home in Memphis, Tennessee. He was 42 years old. The official cause of death was given as 'cardiac arrhythmia', or irregularity of heartbeat. What was not made public was that the irregular heartbeat had been caused by an overdose of several prescription drugs. When this information leaked, Elvis Presley's father sealed the autopsy report, which will not be reopened until the year 2027, 50 years after the death. Elvis shot to fame during the 1950s with his good looks, sexy moves, and catchy rock-and-roll songs, which combined gospel, rhythm and blues, and country, thereby crossing racial divides. He received the nickname 'The King', and in 1950s America he was as much disapproved of as he was worshiped. He was often told to tone down his hip swinging at live concerts because of the effect on young girls, who fainted en masse. After his death, fans flocked to Graceland, which immediately became a pilgrimage site and remains a hugely popular tourist attraction to this day. At the same time, conspiracy theories began to emerge that Elvis had faked his own death, and the idea that he is still alive continues to surface today.

'He was often told to tone down his hip swinging at live concerts because of the effect on young girls, who fainted en masse.'

ELVIS DIES

Above: Elvis's grave is located in the grounds of his Graceland home, where he used to watch three T.V.s at once (left).

September 12
Steve Biko Dies
Civil rights leader and great anti-apartheid campaigner Steve Biko dies of head wounds while in police custody in South Africa. He coined the phrase, 'Black is beautiful'.

September 26
Laker's Skytrain
Freddie Laker, yet to be knighted, launches his inexpensive airline, Skytrain, in the U.K.

December 1
More Children's Television
Nickelodeon, the children's cartoon television channel, launches as the Pinwheel Network in Ohio, U.S.A.

December 25
Charlie Chaplin Dies
Charlie Chaplin, one of the world's great silent comics, as well as actor, director, producer, and musician, dies. He was born on April 16, 1889, in England.

1978

914 DIE AT JONESTOWN

![MASSACRE AT JONESTOWN]

Right: Bodies litter the ground at Jonestown following the mass suicide.

The People's Temple, a 'Christian' doomsday cult, was established in Indiana in the 1950s by James Warren Jones. At the time it was highly unusual for its multiracial congregation, and 'Jim' Jones preached a gospel of freedom, love, and equality that impressed upon its members the need to help the sick and the poor. This later developed into 'apocryphal socialism', which preached the imminent end of the world in a nuclear attack. After investigations began into Jones' claimed cures for cancer and heart disease, the Temple moved to California and then, amid further investigations of illegal activities, to Jonestown, Guyana, in South America. There, the Temple group leased 4,000 acres of jungle and formed the 'People's Temple Agricultural Project' to cultivate the land. It was there that Jones developed his theory of 'translation', whereby he and his followers would all die together and be transported to another planet where they would live in bliss. When Tim Stoen, a senior member of the Temple, left, he revealed that people were being held against their will in appalling conditions, and he started a group called Concerned Relatives. This group convinced Californian Congressman Leo Ryan to visit Jonestown to inspect conditions and practices. Congressman Ryan visited Jonestown on November 18, 1978, and when 16 members of the group decided to fly back to the States with him, they were all followed to the airport by Temple security guards who opened fire. Five people were killed, including Congressman Ryan. Jim Jones now knew that he was trapped. He managed to convince the majority of his followers to engage in a mass suicide by drinking poison. Most of them did, but some, who were clearly unwilling, were evidently murdered either with poison injection or by being shot. Only a few managed to escape into the jungle. The dead were numbered at 914: 638 adults and 276 children.

> **'Jones managed to convince the majority of his followers to engage in a mass suicide by drinking poison.'**

January 23
No More Sprays
Sweden becomes the first country to ban aerosol sprays because of fears about damaging the Earth's ozone layer.

February 15
Ali vs Spinks
Leon Spinks makes history when he defeats Muhammad Ali in 15 rounds in Las Vegas, to take the World Heavyweight Champion title. Ali regains the title from Spinks in New Orleans on September 15.

February 15
Majority Rule
White Prime Minister Ian Smith of Rhodesia (now Zimbabwe), along with three black leaders, agrees to black majority rule in the country.

March 3
Rhodesia Attacks
Rhodesia attacks Zambia.

FIRST TEST-TUBE BABY BORN

WORLD'S FIRST TEST-TUBE BABY

On July 25, 1978, Louise Brown, the world's first 'test-tube baby', was born in the U.K. Her mother, Lesley Brown, had been unable to conceive because of blocked fallopian tubes and had undergone experimental fertility treatment to become pregnant. The treatment was pioneered by Dr. Patrick Steptoe, a gynecologist, and Dr. Robert Edwards, a physiologist, who had begun experimenting with artificial conception in 1966. Their method involved removing eggs from a woman's ovary, fertilizing them with sperm in a glass (*in vitro*), and replanting them in the womb. However, until Lesley Brown's success, none of the 80 women who had trialed the method had been able to stay pregnant beyond a few weeks. On November 10, 1977, Lesley Brown underwent the treatment. She became the first woman to undergo a healthy pregnancy, and nine days before her due date, her daughter was delivered by caesarian section. Louise Brown was perfectly healthy and went on to have a child of her own. The success of the process gave new hope to millions of couples unable to conceive. For some, it also raised ethical issues. The main concern was whether the disposal of fertilized eggs, which is common practice in the process of in vitro fertilization (I.V.F.), is in effect disposing of human lives, if life can be counted as having started at the point of fertilization. There were also concerns at the time as to how this power to create life might be used in the future, by pre-selecting the gender or features of a child and disposing of fertilized eggs that do not meet these criteria.

Above: The pioneering team of Steptoe and Edwards.

STATESMAN MURDERED

ITALIAN MINISTER KILLED

As leader of the Christian Democracy Party in Italy, Aldo Moro had twice served as Prime Minister between 1963 and 1976. He had been out of office for two years when he was kidnapped on March 16, 1978; five bodyguards and a chauffeur were shot dead in the process. The left-wing Red Brigades gunmen who had kidnapped him demanded the release of 15 Red Brigades members, including their leader on trial in Turin, but Italian Prime Minister Giulio Andreotti refused to negotiate with them. Moro was held hostage for two months, during which time he made frequent appeals to the Italian government to negotiate with his kidnappers, as did his family and the Pope, but Andreotti remained firm. Aldo Moro's body was later found in the trunk of a Renault car in Rome, riddled with bullets, eight weeks after he had been kidnapped. The Red Brigades was a left-wing terrorist group formed in 1970 with the aim of overthrowing the capitalist government of Italy.

June
Charon Discovered
Pluto's largest moon, Charon, is discovered by astronomer James Christy.

July 8
Borg Again
Björn Borg wins the Wimbledon men's tennis singles for the third successive time, beating Jimmy Connors, who then goes on to beat Borg in the U.S. Open.

Walking Tall
Discovered accidentally in 1976, an archeological site in Laetoli, Tanzania, is excavated, revealing three different sets of footprints made by human ancestors that walked upright more than 3.6 million years ago.

August 6
Pope Dies
Pope Paul VI dies.

TANKER SPILLS CARGO OF CRUDE OIL

OIL SLICK HITS FRANCE

On March 16, 1978, the tanker *Amoco Cadiz* was en route from the Persian Gulf to Rotterdam, Holland, when it crashed against rocks off the coast of Brittany, France, spilling its cargo of 227,000 tons of crude oil. The tanker's steering system had failed, and although a German tug boat attempted to tow it, its massive weight could not be controlled. Despite the best efforts of the crew, the tanker ran aground on Portsall Rocks. It then gradually split in two as it crashed repeatedly against the rocks for two weeks, and its entire cargo emptied into the sea. The oil contaminated over 200 miles (320 km) of French coastline, and France sued the American company Amoco for compensation. After a lengthy legal battle, France was eventually awarded the equivalent of 190 million euros, less than half of the amount they had sued for. The oil slick destroyed vast amounts of marine life and had a long-term effect on local economies along the coast that relied on shellfish and oyster fishing. Although it was claimed that lessons had been learned, this was not the last oil slick to occur in the 20th century.

'Although it was claimed that lessons had been learned, this was not the last oil slick to occur in the 20th century.'

Left: The coast of Brittany, France, suffered long-term environmental damage from the spill.

August
Turin Shroud
The Turin Shroud goes on display for the first time in 45 years. The cloth is a very old, linen fabric marked with the image of a man's face. It is believed by some people to be the burial cloth that covered Jesus Christ.

September 17
Camp David Accord
Prime Minister Anwar Sadat of Egypt and Prime Minister Menachem Begin of Israel sign 'A Framework for Peace', witnessed by President Jimmy Carter.

September 28
Pope Dies
Pope John Paul I dies, after only 38 days as Pope.

October
Pope Chosen
Pope John Paul II takes office. Polish-born, he is the first non-Italian Pope in over 400 years.

I.R.A. BOMB KILLS MOUNTBATTEN

Admiral of the Fleet, the Earl Mountbatten of Burma, who was also Prince Philip's uncle, was murdered by the Provisional Irish Republican Army (I.R.A.) while on a fishing trip in Ireland on August 27, 1979. Lord Mountbatten had spent his life serving in the Royal Navy, and his funeral upheld British Naval traditions. His coffin, bearing an admiral's hat, his sword of honor, and his gold stick, was carried on a naval gun carriage through the streets, and his horse Dolly led the parade with her master's boots turned backward in the stirrups. The Earl's funeral procession through London, from Wellington Barracks to Westminster Abbey, to the sound of brass from the Royal Marine bands, was watched by thousands along the route. The manner of his death had shocked and greatly saddened the nation. Mountbatten had been on vacation with his family when a bomb placed in his fishing boat was detonated from the shore by members of the I.R.A. His 14-year-old grandson Nicholas died with him, as did his daughter's mother-in-law and Paul Maxwell, a 15-year-old local boy who was working as crew. Mountbatten's daughter, Lady Patricia, and her husband and another son, Timothy, were also in the boat and were seriously injured – so much so that Lady Patricia could not attend the funeral of her father or son. The great-grandson of Queen Victoria, Lord Mountbatten was christened Louis Francis Arthur Victor Nicholas Battenberg, but when George V created the House of Windsor, the name Battenberg was changed to Mountbatten.

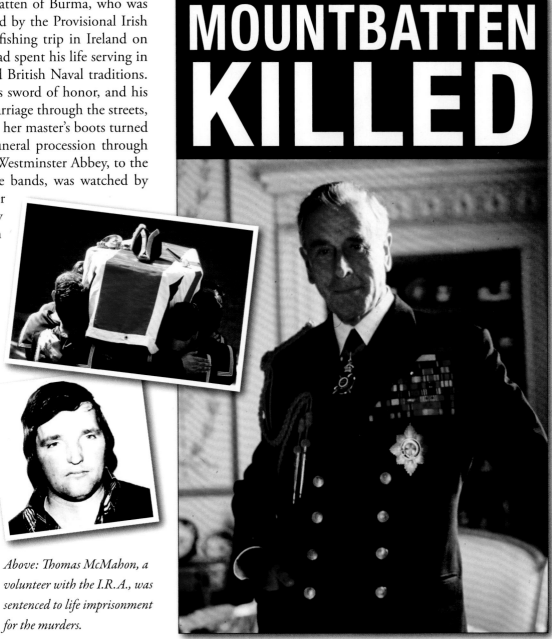

MOUNTBATTEN KILLED

Above: Thomas McMahon, a volunteer with the I.R.A., was sentenced to life imprisonment for the murders.

January 8
Vietnam vs Khmer Rouge
The Vietnamese defeat the Khmer Rouge ruling party in Cambodia.

February 1
Khomeini Is Back
The exiled religious leader and politician Ayatollah Khomeini returns to Iran.

March 28
Three Mile Island
The most serious nuclear civilian accident in the U.S. takes place, with the partial meltdown of a reactor at Midtown, a suburb of Harrisburg, Pennsylvania.

April 1
Republic of Iran
Iran is declared a republic.

May 4
Iron Lady Takes Power
Margaret Thatcher becomes the first female Prime Minister of the U.K., after the Labour government loses a general election.

DEATH OF A NATION

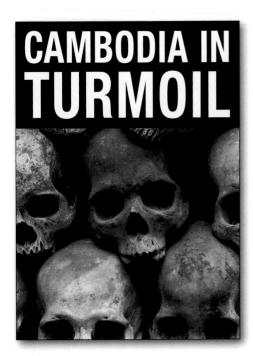

During the 1970s, Cambodia, known at the time as Democratic Kampuchea, was ruled over by a Communist government led by a former school teacher, Saloth Sar, who called himself 'Pol Pot'. The brutal regime ruled by terror, keeping themselves hidden away but constantly 'watching', letting the Cambodian people know that they were now their parents and must be obeyed. Pol Pot was the Secretary General of the Cambodian Communist Party, known as the Khmer Rouge, and under his dictatorship, millions of Cambodians died. Mentally unstable and paranoid, Pol Pot tried to carry out idealistic policies that involved evacuating the population out of the cities and into the countryside and abolishing money markets, private property, religion, and schools. Everyone was forced to wear a uniform and work in the fields for over 12 hours a day. Pol Pot was trying to follow the Soviet model of increasing agricultural output to generate funds for industrialization, but Cambodia had just come out of five years of civil war and the country was weak. A rejection of Western medicine, paired with widespread crop failure, led to millions of deaths as the workers in the countryside shipped their harvests to the city in order to fulfill their quota and ended up starving themselves. In January 1979, when Vietnamese forces invaded Cambodia, they uncovered fields full of the skeletons of the dead: millions of men, women, and children who had been brutally executed as enemies of the state.

SPY UNMASKED

Sir Anthony Blunt, an art historian, professor at the University of London, director of the Courtauld Institute of Art, and surveyor of the Queen's Pictures, was revealed in 1979 as a member of the Cambridge Spy Ring. While studying at Cambridge University, Blunt had joined the Cambridge Apostles, a secret society of Marxists. Blunt was recruited as a spy by the U.S.S.R. in 1934, joined the British Army in 1939, and in 1940 became a member of the U.K.'s security agency, MI5. He was knighted in 1956 for his work as surveyor of the British royal family's art collection. He had also carried out a secret mission for the royal family when he went to Germany after the war to recover incriminating letters sent by the Duke of Windsor to Adolf Hitler. When his fellow spies Guy Burgess and Donald Maclean defected to the U.S.S.R. in 1951, Blunt was questioned, but no concrete evidence against him was found. However, when, in 1979, another former Cambridge student claimed that Blunt had tried to recruit him as a spy, Blunt finally confessed. The Queen was informed, and she stripped him of his knighthood. After Prime Minister Margaret Thatcher publicly named Blunt, he fled to Europe, where he lived for some time. When he returned to London, he found that he had underestimated the strength of public feeling against him. On one occasion, he was booed out of a movie theater. Life in the public eye became intolerable, and his long-time partner tried to kill himself by jumping from a window. Blunt died in London in 1983.

SPY SCANDAL

June 1
Zimbabwe Born
Rhodesia is re-named Zimbabwe.

June 18
SALT-2
U.S. President Jimmy Carter and Soviet President Leonid Brezhnev sign the SALT-2 arms limitation treaty.

June 22
Sony Walkman to Go
Sony launch the Portable Walkman in Tokyo, and change the way people listen to music forever.

July 11
Skylab Down
The U.S. space station *Skylab* re-enters the Earth's atmosphere, scattering debris in the Indian Ocean and over Western Australia.

July 16
Saddam Gains Power
Saddam Hussein becomes President of Iraq.

212

18 DIE IN I.R.A. BLASTS

'The deaths of the 18 British soldiers by two bombs in a carefully planned attack, was the largest single loss of life for the British Army since the Second World War.'

1979 was a year of Provisional Irish Republican Army (I.R.A.) terror. In addition to over 90 civilian murders carried out by the I.R.A. that year, the most infamous acts of terror were the killing of Lord Louis Mountbatten, on August 27, followed just hours later by the massacre of 18 British soldiers near Warrenpoint, South Down, close to Northern Ireland's border with the Irish Republic. The deaths of 18 British soldiers by two bombs in a carefully planned attack, was the largest single loss of life for the British Army since the Second World War. It was the first time in Northern Ireland that the I.R.A. used remote-controled bombs. There were no command wires: the bombs were detonated by radio waves from the top of a mountain, in a beautiful, rural, unpopulated area called the 'Narrow Water.' The first was an 800-lb (360-kg) bomb, hidden by bales of hay in a trailer by the side of the road, detonated as a three-vehicle convoy passed by. This killed six soldiers of the Second Battalion Parachute Regiment. The surviving troops immediately cordoned off the area and called for reinforcements. Members of the Queen's Own Highlanders flew in by helicopter from their base in County Armagh. Twenty minutes later, as their helicopter was leaving the scene with some of the injured men on board, the second bomb was detonated. The I.R.A. had known that the British Army would set up a command point, and had hidden a second bomb in milk pails against a gate lodge, the likeliest point for the command. Another 10 soldiers from the Parachute Regiment were killed, along with two from the Queen's Own Highlanders. The perpetrators escaped into the safety of the Irish Republic.

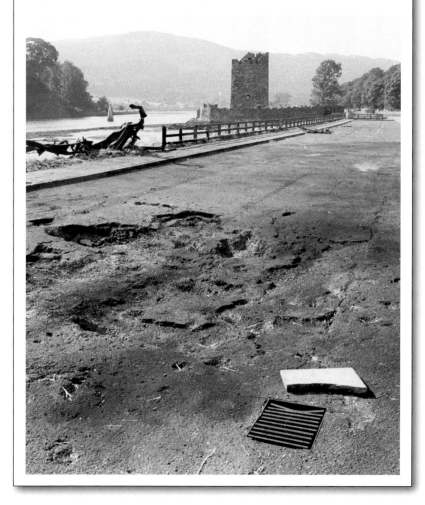

SOLDIERS MASSACRED

July 20
Sandinistas Win
The Sandinista rebels win the civil war in Nicaragua.

September 1
Jupiter Pictures Home
The space probe *Pioneer* sends back pictures of Jupiter.

November 30
Another Brick
Pink Floyd release their famous album *The Wall* in the U.K.

December 11
Mother Theresa
Mother Theresa is awarded the Nobel Prize for Peace for her work with the poor, in India and abroad.

December 27
The Red Army
The Soviet Union invades Afghanistan and seizes control.

1980-1989

The 1980s opened in an upbeat mood, with business and economies booming, a global community opening up, and in England the elation of a royal wedding like no other, with the nuptials of Prince Charles and Lady Diana Spencer. However, the decade was also beset by military disputes. In the midst of a prolonged war between Iran and Iraq, the assassination of the peace-keeping Egyptian premier upset relations in the troubled region even further. Argentina invaded the Falkland Islands, drawing the British military to their defense, and America invaded Grenada, demonstrating its growing global power.

In the middle of the decade, the Live Aid Concert, organized by Bob Geldof in response to the famine in Ethiopia, raised an unprecedented £150 million to help feed the starving in Africa. The simultaneous concerts in London and Philadelphia struck a chord with the people and donations poured in, astounding even the organizers in their generosity.

By the close of the decade, relations between the United States and the Soviets had significantly improved, so much so that Presidents Reagan and Gorbachev would sign a treaty genuinely limiting arms production and pledging to destroy stockpiles. The treaty marked the start of a new era, characterized by openness and trust. In Germany, the Berlin Wall was bulldozed, signaling the gradual integration of once Communist regimes into the capitalist West.

1980

POLAND SEES LAUNCH OF SOLIDARITY UNION

STRUGGLE FOR DEMOCRACY

'The Gdansk Shipyard Strike sparked 20 further strikes, and the deputy prime minister was forced to negotiate with Walesa'

On August 14, 1980, unemployed Polish electrician Lech Walesa led a strike involving thousands of workers at the Lenin Shipyard in Gdansk. Although the secret police had tried to arrest him that same morning, Walesa managed to avoid them, and climbed over the shipyard wall to lead the strike. The strikers were protesting against low wages and a rise in food prices, but the most important change to come out of the strike was the creation of an independent trade union that was actually allowed to strike. It was the first time that such a union had existed in a Communist country. In fact, some years earlier in Poland, people had been killed by police for daring to strike. The Gdansk Shipyard Strike sparked 20 further strikes, and the deputy prime minister was forced to negotiate with Walesa, who emerged from the talks and announced to the cheering crowds of workers, 'We have an independent, self-governing trade union. We have the right to strike!' The right to strike was granted under the International Labor Organization, but had never before been exercised in a Communist country. Walesa's historic announcement marked the establishment of the Solidarity trade union in September 1980. A year later, when it was outlawed, a quarter of Poland's population belonged to the union. The Communist government, under pressure from their Soviet masters to crack down, declared martial law and arrested the movement's leaders, including Walesa. However, Solidarity continued to operate underground, with support from American trade unions and from Pope John Paul II. It was not until 1989, responding to Western encouragement and in the midst of economic depression, that Solidarity formed a government under Walesa in the first free elections to be held in the Communist bloc.

Left: The Gdansk shipyard, site of the strike that led to the formation of the Solidarity union.

March 4
Mugabe to Power
Robert Mugabe is elected Prime Minister of Zimbabwe.

April 10
Border Opens
The border between Spain and Gibraltar is opened again, having been closed since 1969.

April 18
Independence in Zimbabwe
Zimbabwe, following the troubled years after its declaration of independence, becomes truly independent.

April 29
Hitchcock Dies
Sir Alfred Hitchcock, eminent movie director, particularly noted for his suspenseful psychological thrillers, dies at the age of 81.

HUGE VOLCANIC ERUPTION

Mount St. Helens in the Cascade Mountains of Washington State is one of the most active volcanoes in North America. It is estimated that the Cascade Range has been volcanically active for 40,000 years, while Mount St. Helens itself has been active only for the past 2,500 years. It had not erupted for 123 years when, in March 1980, a series of small earthquakes in the region alerted volcanologists to impending trouble. They issued a warning to local authorities, who in turn evacuated the area. Scientists were able to set up equipment to monitor the volcano eruption in a way that had never before been possible, but even so it was impossible to gauge exactly when the volcano would erupt. On May 18, 1980, a research scientist named David Johnston was about 5 miles (8 km) from the main crater when he radioed to the Vancouver base, 'This is it!' Moments later he was killed under a heap of molten lava. An earthquake had triggered a volcanic eruption with about 500 times the force of an atomic bomb. Around 150 square miles (400 sq km) of forest were flattened by the flow of lava before it moved on to houses and cars. A cloud of ash darkened the sky and hung over several cities across northwestern America. In all, 57 people and 7,000 big-game animals died as a result of the eruption, although it could have been far worse if early evacuation had not been put into effect.

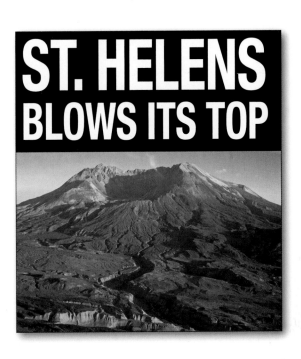

START OF IRAN–IRAQ WAR

Throughout the 20th century, border disputes between Iran and Iraq were commonplace, but since 1975 there had been relative peace. This came to an end with the 1979 Islamic Revolution in Iran, which brought Ayatollah Khomeini into power. Saddam Hussein's invasion of Iran in 1980 was prompted partly by fear of Khomeini's extreme religious regime, but also by his probable support of the oppressed Shia Muslims in Iraq. However, the official reason for the invasion was a dispute over the oil-producing regions along the border. In early 1980, Saddam executed the leaders of an Iranian-supported Shia group and deported other Shias of Iranian extraction to Iran. He then canceled the 1975 treaty between the two countries and announced that the Shatt al Arab region now belonged to Iraq. This launched full-scale hostilities between Iran and Iraq, but neither side was apparently able to clinch the swift victory it had expected. The war was to last for almost eight years, causing huge loss of life and permanent damage to both countries.

May 8
Tito Dies
Yugoslavia's long-serving president, Josip Tito, dies after 27 years in power.

May 21
The Empire Continues
The latest Star Wars movie, *The Empire Strikes Back*, is released.

May 22
Pac-Man
The world's best-selling arcade game, Pac-Man, is launched.

June 1
C.N.N. Takes to the Airwaves
Ted Turner's Cable News Network, commonly known as C.N.N., goes live in the United States.

1980

THE SIEGE BUSTERS

S.A.S. STORM EMBASSY

On April 30, 1980, six gunmen stormed the Iranian Embassy in Kensington, London. They were members of an Iranian rebel group that opposed the strict religious regime of Ayatollah Khomeini, and their demands included the release of 91 political prisoners held in Iran. The gunmen took a number of people hostage, including a policeman, members of the British media, and tourists, as well as Iranian Embassy officials. Four days into the siege, the terrorists dumped the body of an Iranian press officer outside the embassy and threatened to kill the rest of the hostages before blowing up the building. At this point, the British government decided it was time to act and sent 30 members of the anti-terrorist branch of the Special Air Service (S.A.S.) to carry out Operation Nimrod. The rescue mission, on May 5, was televised live and showed the masked rescuers entering the building, throwing grenades, and emerging 15 minutes later with 19 hostages. One hostage was killed and two were injured in what was otherwise seen as a successful mission. Five of the terrorists were killed, and the sixth was sentenced to life imprisonment. The S.A.S., whose motto is 'Who Dares Wins', had previously been an institution under threat, but the well-publicized mission catapulted them to fame as international heroes.

BEATLE SHOT DEAD

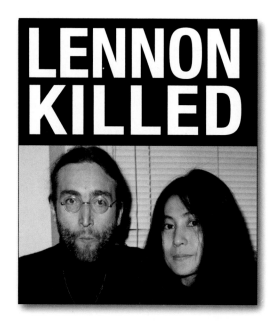

LENNON KILLED

By 1980, John Lennon was living in New York with his second wife, Yoko Ono, and their five-year-old son Sean. They had recently moved to the Dakota apartment buildings and were under F.B.I. surveillance because of their pacifist activities, but they came and went freely without any security. On December 8, 1980, a mentally unstable man named Mark David Chapman asked John to autograph his latest album, *Double Fantasy*. Hours later, Chapman approached the Lennons outside their apartment building and called out John's name. John turned to face him and Chapman shot him five times. Lennon was rushed to a nearby hospital, but was pronounced dead on arrival. Chapman did not attempt to flee. When arrested by police he was holding a copy of J.D. Salinger's book *The Catcher in the Rye*. On December 10, John Lennon was cremated in New York. Thousands of fans gathered in Central Park, and a ten-minute silent vigil was held all over the world.

Right: The Dakota building in New York.

July
U.S. Boycotts Olympics
The U.S. Olympic team boycotts the summer Olympic Games in Moscow in protest at the Soviet war in Afghanistan.

July
Borg Wins ... Again
Tennis ace Björn Borg defeats John McEnroe in what is later described as the greatest men's singles final at Wimbledon. It is Borg's fifth successive Wimbledon singles title.

August 2
Bologna Bomb
A bomb planted by terrorists kills 85 people and wounds more than 200 at the train station in Bologna, Italy.

November
Who Shot J.R.?
More than 100 million people watch the season finale of the television show *Dallas* to learn who shot the famous character J.R.

PRINCE CHARLES MARRIES LADY DIANA SPENCER

On July 29, 1981, the 'fairy-tale' wedding of Prince Charles and Lady Diana Spencer took place at St. Paul's Cathedral in London. Hundreds of thousands of people flooded the streets, trying to catch a glimpse of the new princess, while an estimated 750 million watched on T.V.

Twenty-year-old Lady Diana was taken to the cathedral in a glass coach. She wore a dress of ivory taffeta and antique lace, with a 25-ft (7.5-m) train, designed by David and Elizabeth Emmanuel. Lady Diana's walk down the aisle took three and a half minutes. After the Church of England ceremony, conducted by Archbishop of Canterbury Dr. Robert Runcie, the Prince and Princess of Wales traveled in an open-topped carriage through the streets to Buckingham Palace, where they appeared on the balcony and shared a kiss, to the delight of the crowds below. They then withdrew to a private wedding breakfast attended by 120 guests. Less than a year later, the princess gave birth to a son, William. A second son, Harry, was born two years later. By that time, the couple's marriage was already showing signs of strain. The couple officially separated in 1993.

> '**Hundreds of thousands of people flooded the streets ... to catch a glimpse of the new princess, while an estimated 750 million watched on T.V.**'

ROYAL WEDDING

Left: St. Paul's Cathedral, the 17th-century church where Charles and Diana married amid huge public interest.

January 4
Yorkshire Ripper
The serial killer Peter Sutcliffe, known as the Yorkshire Ripper, is arrested at last, having killed 13 women and attacked another seven.

January 20
Movie-Star President
Former Hollywood actor Ronald Reagan is inaugurated as President of the United States.

February 9
Rock 'n' Roller Dies
Bill Haley, considered by many to be the first ever rock and roll musician, dies.

March 29
Run London Run
The first London Marathon, with 7,500 runners, takes place between Greenwich and Westminster.

1981

REAGAN SHOT IN ASSASSINATION ATTEMPT

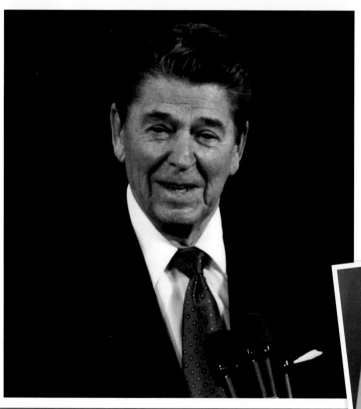

SHOTS FIRED AT PRESIDENT

On March 30, 1981, the 70-year-old U.S. President Ronald Reagan, who had been in office only 69 days, was shot after leaving the Hilton Hotel in Washington, D.C. The president had been addressing an audience of union representatives, and as he turned to respond to waiting press upon leaving the building, he was shot by 25-year-old John Hinckley Jr. The White House Press Secretary, a policeman, and a Secret Service agent were also seriously injured by the gunman. President Reagan underwent an operation and recovered fully, going on to win a second four-year term in office. John Hinckley Jr., who had a history of stalking famous people, was diagnosed as mentally ill at his trial and was committed to a psychiatric hospital. His declared motivation had been a desire to impress the actress Jodie Foster, with whom he had a psychotic obsession.

'Ronald Reagan ... was shot after leaving the Hilton Hotel in Washington, D.C. ... The White House Press Secretary, a policeman, and a Secret Service agent were also seriously injured by the gunman.'

Left: Jodie Foster, the actress with whom Ronald Reagan's attempted assassin was infatuated.

May
New French Premier
François Mitterrand is elected President of France.

May 11
Bob Marley Dies
The musician and singer-songwriter Bob Marley, famous for the reggae music he made with his band The Wailers, dies of brain cancer in Jamaica at the age of 36.

June 5
New Disease
The first cases of A.I.D.S. are announced.

June 12
Great Adventure
The movie *Raiders of the Lost Ark*, starring Harrison Ford, is released to great acclaim.

UNSUCCESSFUL ASSASSINATION ATTEMPT ON POPE JOHN PAUL II

On May 13, 1981, a professional assassin named Mehmet Ali Ağca shot Pope John Paul II several times as he walked through St. Peter's Square in Rome. The Pope was hit by four bullets, two lodging in his lower intestine, one in his left hand, and one in his right arm, before the assassin was wrestled to the ground and disarmed. The Pope was rushed to hospital, where he was operated on and eventually recovered, despite having lost almost three-quarters of his blood. The real origins of the assassination attempt have never been discovered. Ağca, who received life imprisonment in an Italian court, gave so many different versions of events that investigators have never been able to pin down the real motive. Pope John Paul II forgave his would-be assassin and even visited the man in prison. In 2000, Ağca was extradited to Turkey, where he was also found guilty of other crimes, and his sentences are now running concurrently.

Right: St. Peter's Square in Rome, where Pope John Paul II was shot.

ANWAR SADAT MURDERED

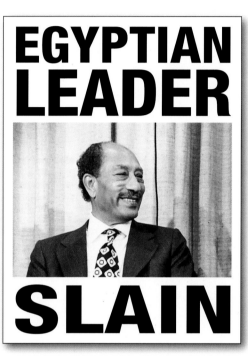

When Egyptian President Anwar Al Sadat signed a peace treaty with Israel in 1979, he effectively signed his own death warrant. Although the move had won him a Nobel Peace Prize, it also implied that the Palestinian issue would not be resolved. Thus, he alienated himself from his Arab neighbors, as no Arab nation but Egypt had the military capacity to take on Israel. Meanwhile, Sadat cracked down on criticism in his own country by increasing censorship and jailing opponents. He also regularly falsified the result of political referendums to imply that he had his people's support. When, in June 1981, violence erupted between Muslims and Coptic Christians, culminating in mass slaughter in a Cairo slum, Sadat treated both sides with equal brutality. It was the final insult to his people. On October 6, 1981, while attending a military parade, Sadat was assassinated by a group of Muslim fundamentalists, with the aim of imposing Islamic rule in Egypt.

August 1 M.T.V. The music channel M.T.V. is launched in the U.S.A.

August 24 Beatle Killer Sentenced Mark David Chapman is sentenced to 20 years to life for killing John Lennon in Manhattan in 1980.

September 19 No Sounds of Silence Simon and Garfunkel give a free concert in Central Park, New York, which is attended by half a million people.

December Golan Heights Annexed Israel announces that it will annex Syria's Golan Heights, captured in 1973.

1982

FALKLANDS WAR BREAKS OUT

TASK FORCE SENT TO FALKLANDS

Left: Captured Argentine troops were bewildered by the hostility of the Falkland Islanders, and by their own defeat.
Right: Many men were lost in naval battles during the Falklands War.

On April 2, 1982, Argentine forces invaded the British-controlled Falkland Islands in the South Atlantic. Ever since they had been claimed by Britain in 1833, the islands had been a source of dispute between Argentina and Great Britain. The Falklands, known as Las Malvinas to the Argentines, lie off the coast of Argentina but are English-speaking. The Argentine troops were surprised to find that the islanders did not view them as liberators. Although the British government had warned Rex Hunt, the Governor of the Falklands, some days earlier that the Argentines planned to invade, he could muster only 80 Royal Marines to defend the islands. Hunt initially rejected calls to surrender, but when 3,000 Argentine troops landed at Port Stanley, the handful of Marines were unable to withstand them. By the afternoon, Governor Hunt ordered British troops to surrender. Immediately, the British government under Prime Minister Margaret Thatcher prepared a naval force to retake the islands. During the war that followed, 655 Argentines and 255 British servicemen lost their lives before the Argentine troops finally surrendered on June 14, 1982. Margaret Thatcher then announced, 'We went to recapture the islands, to restore British sovereignty, to restore British administration. I do not intend to negotiate on the sovereignty of the islands in any way except with the people who live there.' The Falklands remain in British hands, and Argentine resentment still simmers.

> **'We went to recapture the islands, to restore British sovereignty, to restore British administration. I do not intend to negotiate ... in any way except with the people who live there.'**

February 5
Laker Collapse
Sir Freddie Laker's budget airline Laker Airways collapses, leaving approximately 6,000 people stranded in holiday destinations.

March 26
Vietnam Memorial
The groundbreaking ceremony for the Vietnam Veterans Memorial is held in Washington, D.C.

April 25
Israel Out of Sinai
Israel withdraws from the Sinai Peninsula in line with the Egyptian–Israeli Peace Treaty.

May 8
Villenueve Dies
French-Canadian racing driver Gilles Villenueve is killed in a qualifying race for the Belgian Grand Prix.

HOLLYWOOD PRINCESS DIES

On September 14, 1982, Her Serene Highness Princess Grace of Monaco died of fatal injuries after losing control of the car she was driving and plunging off the road into a ravine. The princess had been returning from her family's country house in France with her youngest daughter, Stéphanie, who also was injured. Princess Grace died of a brain hemorrhage the next day in hospital: it is believed that she may have suffered a minor stroke while driving, which is what caused her to lose control of the car. Before marrying Prince Rainier III of Monaco, Princess Grace had been the Hollywood movie star Grace Kelly, starring in two of Alfred Hitchcock's most successful movies, *Rear Window* and *Dial M for Murder*. Her husband and her three children, Caroline, Albert, and Stéphanie, were at her hospital bedside when she died. Princess Grace was buried in the royal family's vault after a service in St. Nicholas Cathedral in Monaco.

Above: The principality of Monaco.

PRINCESS KILLED IN CAR CRASH

SLAUGHTER IN BEIRUT CAMPS

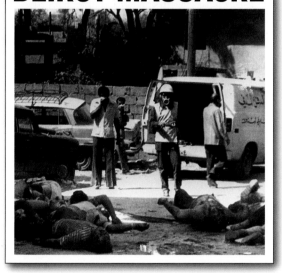

BEIRUT MASSACRE

On September 16, 1982, hundreds – or possibly even thousands – of Palestinian civilians in two refugee camps in Beirut were slaughtered. The massacre occurred when the Israel Defense Forces (I.D.F.) allowed members of a Lebanese Christian group called the 'Phalangists' to enter the camps. Israel had invaded Lebanon three months earlier. Ariel Sharon, the head of Israel's Defense Ministry, was later found to be partially responsible for the slaughter because he was perfectly aware of the hostility that existed between the Palestinians and Lebanese Christians, especially following the assassination of the Phalangist leader only days earlier. For some time, the Phalangist militia had been supplied with arms by Israel in support of their fight against the Palestine Liberation Organization (P.L.O.). The I.D.F. had let the Phalangist militiamen into the Sabra and Shatila camps under the pretense of flushing out any P.L.O. terrorists hiding there. The final death toll is still a matter of dispute, and estimates range between 300 and 3,000, including many women and children. The United Nations condemned the slaughter as an act of genocide.

June 10
Call Home
The much anticipated movie *E.T.*, directed by Steven Spielberg, is released and becomes a box office smash hit.

June 21
Son and Heir
Prince William Arthur Philip Louis Windsor, first son of Prince Charles, is born, becoming second in line to the British throne after his father.

August 17
Compact Discs
The first commercial C.D.s are released to the public.

October 1
First C.D. Player
Sony launches the first compact disc player, the CDP101.

1982

LONG-TERM PROTEST AGAINST NUCLEAR WEAPONS

HUMAN CHAIN FOR PEACE

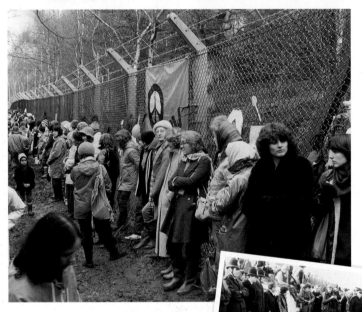

Right: Greenham Common protestors attempted to prevent the delivery of cruise missiles by sitting in the road.

In 1981, a group of women organized a march from Cardiff in Wales to the U.S. Air Force base at Greenham Common in England, to protest against the proposed storage there of cruise missiles. When they arrived at Greenham Common, four women chained themselves to the airbase gate in order to attract media attention. After the planned march came to an end, several of the women decided to set up a permanent peace camp there, which soon attracted increased support, and numbers grew. By January 1982 it was a fully fledged, women-only peace camp, and the seven gates of the base were named for the colors of the rainbow. The protestors were threatened with eviction but, encouraged by the Labour Party's moves toward disarmament, were determined to stay. The evictions began in May 1982, but those arrested were quickly replaced by others. Following a national call for support, many more women arrived, and on December 12, 1982, over 30,000 of them formed a human ring around the airbase. Approximately 2,000 women were arrested for their blockading action, but the encirclement and its consequences simply inspired further support. Despite these protests, the cruise missiles were still housed within the airbase, so the Greenham Common women decided to file a lawsuit against President Ronald Reagan. The protestors were denied a hearing, but they still gained massive publicity and support in the United States. British Prime Minister Margaret Thatcher continued to do everything in her power to evict the camp members, with considerable success, but their popular support continued to grow.

> '**Following a national call for support, many more women arrived, and on December 12, 1982, over 30,000 of them formed a human ring around the airbase.**'

October 29
'Dingo' Mother Jailed
Lindy Chamberlain, the Australian woman who claimed that her baby was taken by dingos, is jailed for murder. She is later exonerated of all charges.

November 10
Brezhnev Dead
Leonid Brezhnev, Premier of the Soviet Union, dies.

December 1
What a Thrill
Michael Jackson's album *Thriller* is released and eventually becomes the biggest-selling album of all time.

December 2
First Artificial Heart
Dr. Barney Clark, a dentist, becomes the first person to receive the Jarvik-7, an artificial heart, in an operation performed by surgeon William DeVries.

COMMUNIST COUP PUT DOWN BY U.S. TROOPS

U.S. INVADES GRENADA

On October 13, 1983, there was a violent military coup on the Caribbean island of Grenada, in which the former deputy prime minister, Bernard Coard, mobilized the army in order to seize power and form a Marxist government. The coup was a matter of concern to neighboring Caribbean islands, but also to the U.S. government, largely because it was perceived as a Communist threat that had strong support from Cuba. U.S. President Ronald Reagan used the presence of around 1,000 American medical students in Grenada as a front for invading the island on October 25, 1983.

Reagan also claimed that neighboring Caribbean islands had appealed for American intervention. U.S. troops stormed in full force, and it took only two months to conquer Coard's military government. The Marxist regime was replaced with a U.S.-friendly government. The invading troops then departed, satisfied that they had demonstrated to the Communist leaders, both in the U.S.S.R. and in Cuba, that revolutionary politics could not be spread too close to American soil without inviting repercussions.

America's allies in Europe made clear their disapproval of the unilateral U.S. invasion, but by that time the mission had already been accomplished. Although the United Nations tried to pass a motion denouncing the American invasion, U.S. representatives at the U.N. managed to block it.

> 'The coup was a matter of concern to neighboring Caribbean islands, but also to the U.S. government, largely because it was perceived as a Communist threat that had strong support from Cuba.'

Left: Grenada looks like a tropical paradise, but it was the scene of violent upheaval when U.S. troops invaded to put down a Marxist coup.

January 3
Volcanic Eruption
Kilauea, a volcano on the island of Hawaii, starts erupting and is still erupting today.

March 5
Hawke Elected
Labour candidate Bob Hawke is elected Prime Minister of Australia.

March 23
Another Star Wars
U.S. President Ronald Reagan announces his first plans for an enemy missile intercept system, commonly known as Star Wars.

March 25
Moonwalking
Michael Jackson first performs his 'moonwalk'.

1983

SOVIETS DOWN PLANE

![SOVIETS SHOOT DOWN JUMBO]

On September 1, 1983, Korean Air flight 007 was shot down by the U.S.S.R. after it strayed into Soviet airspace on its way from the United States to Seoul, South Korea. All 269 passengers were killed.

'The Soviets did admit that they had shot down the aircraft, but they argued in their defense that it had not contacted their air traffic controlers or responded to radio communications'

Due to a failed navigational system, the pilot of the Boeing 747 jetliner did not realize that he had strayed off course and was too close to a Soviet military complex and naval base. The following day, the Soviets did admit that they had shot down the aircraft, but they argued in their defense that it had not contacted their air traffic controllers or responded to radio communications, so they had reason for alarm. It had been too dark for the Soviet fighter pilots to see that the plane was a civilian passenger jet.

AMERICA'S FIRST FEMALE ASTRONAUT

Dr. Sally Ride was born in Los Angeles, California in 1951. After abandoning an early ambition to make a career in professional tennis, she enrolled at Stanford University, where she completed a bachelor's degree in English and physics, a master's degree in physics, and then a doctorate in astrophysics. In 1977, she was one of 8,900 people to answer a N.A.S.A. ad looking

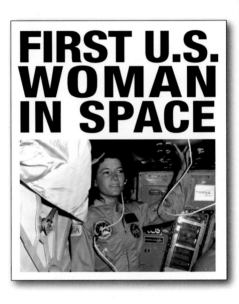

for potential astronauts, and was one of six women among the 35 people chosen. After completing her space flight training in August 1979, Dr. Ride acted as the on-orbit capsule coordinator on two space shuttle missions, but then, in 1983, she became the first American woman in space when she went on the *Challenger* mission that launched on June 18. The mission lasted for 147 hours and achieved several 'firsts', including the first use of a robotic arm in space to retrieve a satellite, a procedure that Dr. Ride had worked to develop. She took part in several other missions before retiring as a N.A.S.A. astronaut in 1987. Since that time, Sally Ride has been a professor of physics at the University of California, San Diego, and director of the California Space Institute.

Left: The launch of a space shuttle.

April 11
Gandhi the Oscar-Winner
Richard Attenborough's movie *Gandhi* wins eight Oscars.

May 14
Diaries Faked
The 'Hitler Diaries' are exposed as fakes, but are later published by *Stern* magazine.

July 15
New Computer Game
The innovative Nintendo Entertainment System is launched in Japan.

July 21
Cold in July
The lowest temperature on Earth is recorded at Vostok Station, Antarctica, when the mercury sinks to -128.6°F (-89.2°C).

ATTACK ON U.N. TROOPS IN LEBANON

During the 1980s, U.S. Marines were stationed in Beirut, Lebanon, as part of a U.N. peacekeeping force. Their aim was to stabilize the civil war-torn country, which was also suffering at the hands of the Palestine Liberation Organization and the Israeli Army. In the aftermath of the 1982 Israeli invasion of Lebanon, the U.N. stationed U.S., British, Italian, and French troops there in exchange for an Israeli withdrawal. On October 23, 1983, a suicide bomber drove a truck packed with explosives into the U.S. Marine barracks. As a result, 241 of the 300 U.S. troops sleeping inside were killed. Minutes later, there was a second blast at the compound that housed the French troops, and a further 58 military personnel were killed. The terrorists were part of a splinter group of Shi'a Islamist organization Hezbollah, which was a relatively small guerrilla operation at the time of the attacks. Three months later, President Ronald Reagan pulled the U.S. troops out of Lebanon, but the civil war continued to rage for another seven years. Joe Ciokon, a navy journalist who survived the blast, neatly summed up the attack: 'We walked into the middle of a family feud, and they all turned their guns on us.'

'241 of the 300 U.S. troops sleeping [inside the barracks] were killed. Minutes later there was a second blast ... and a further 58 military personnel were killed.'

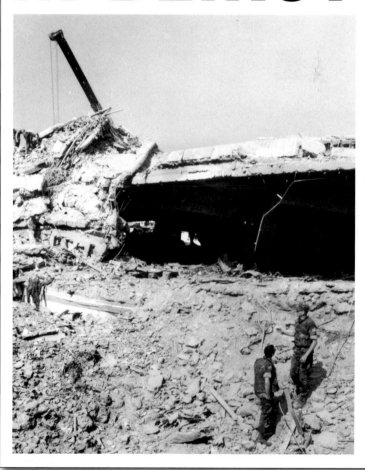

BOMBINGS IN BEIRUT

October
Walesa Peace Prize
Lech Walesa, the popular leader of the Solidarity Party in Poland, is awarded the Nobel Peace Prize.

October 13
Cellular Phone Network
The first U.S. mobile cellular telephone network is launched in Chicago by Ameritech Mobile Communications, now known as Cingular.

October 25
My Word
The software program Microsoft Word is released.

December 17
Harrods Bomb
I.R.A. terrorists bomb the world-famous Harrods department store, killing six people and injuring 90.

1984

GRAIN STORES FULL BUT THOUSANDS LEFT TO DIE

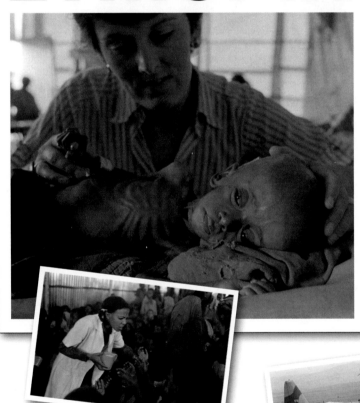

FAMINE IN ETHIOPIA

Above and right: Aid workers struggled to cope with the famine, even after food was flown in.

The famine that devastated Ethiopia between 1984 and 1985 had been building up for several years. The drought of 1981 had destroyed an entire harvest, which meant that supplies were already nonexistent when the lack of rain in 1984 threatened another bad harvest, with grain especially hard hit. There were early warnings of the potential famine, but Western aid was slow in coming and remained insufficient to deal with it. The Marxist military government in Ethiopia, under the leadership of Mengistu Haile Mariam, was spending vast amount on weapons, and Western governments feared that aid would only be diverted to pay for the ongoing civil war in Eritrea and Tigre. This made them reluctant to provide aid in early 1984 when aid agencies warned that thousands had already died of starvation and thousands more would do so if something was not done. Ironically, while Ethiopians were dying from lack of food, Europe was enjoying a grain surplus, but still food was not diverted, largely because the West did not trust the socialist government to distribute it properly. Eventually, aid agencies were forced to buy European grain on the open market. In an attempt to shame Western governments into action, the international charity Oxfam donated $800,000 (£500,000) to Ethiopia, the largest single donation the charity had ever made. Meanwhile, widespread television coverage of people dying of starvation in Ethiopia was prompting an exceptional outpouring of private donations. In three days, the British public alone donated $8 million (£5 million), and within two months, the Western public had donated a total of $160 million (£100 million). In music, the Band Aid single 'Do They Know It's Christmas?', as well as two Live Aid concerts, raised millions more.

> '**While Ethiopians were dying from lack of food, Europe was enjoying a grain surplus, but ... the West did not trust the socialist government to distribute it properly.**'

January 24
First Mac
Apple introduces its Macintosh computer.

February 7
Look, No Rope
Two astronauts on the tenth space shuttle make the first untethered space walk.

February 14
Olympic Ice Champions
British ice dancers Jayne Torvill and Christopher Dean score 12 perfect sixes for their interpretation of Ravel's *Bolero* in the 1984 Winter Olympics.

April 23
A.I.D.S. Identified
U.S. and French scientists identify the virus known as A.I.D.S.

1984

BHOPAL DISASTER

POISON CLOUD KILLS THOUSANDS

On December 3, 1984, a leak in Union Carbide's pesticide plant in the city of Bhopal, India, caused toxic gas to escape, killing and disabling thousands of people. It was one of the worst industrial accidents in history. The toxic gas methyl isocyanate (M.I.C.) spread out across the city, burning eyes, lungs, and other organs on contact. Around 3,000 people died in the days immediately following the disaster. Tens of thousands more were permanently disabled, and it is estimated that another 20,000 people have since died as a direct result of the leak. After an investigation, Union Carbide (an American company) claimed that the leak had been caused by employee sabotage. Campaigners, though, claimed that cost-cutting measures had lowered safety standards. In 1989, Union Carbide paid $800 million (£470 million) in compensation to the Indian government. Victim support groups are seeking far more than this, and are pursuing a lawsuit against Union Carbide's boss, Warren Andersen, on charges of culpable homicide.

Right: Birth defects are very common among Bhopali children, even those born years after the disaster.

GANDHI SHOT BY HER OWN GUARDS

INDIRA GANDHI KILLED

'In the days following the assassination, riots broke out in the streets ... and more than 1,000 Sikhs were thought to have been killed.'

On October 31, 1984, the Indian Prime Minister, Indira Gandhi, was shot dead while walking in her own private gardens in New Delhi. The assassins were two Sikh bodyguards, motivated by their anger over the storming of the Golden Temple in Amritsar earlier that year in which 2,000 Sikhs had been killed. Prime Minister Gandhi had received death threats following the massacre at the Golden Temple, and only the day before the killing had said in a political rally, 'I don't mind if my life goes in the service of the nation. If I die today, every drop of my blood will invigorate the nation.' In the days following the assassination, anti-Sikh riots broke out in the streets of New Delhi. The police turned a blind eye, and 1,000 more Sikhs were thought to have been killed. Gandhi's son Rajiv succeeded her as Prime Minister. In 1989, Satwant Singh and Kehar Singh were hanged for her murder.

June 6 — Temple Stormed
Indian government troops storm the Golden Temple at Amritsar, the Sikhs' holiest shrine, killing about 2,000 people.

June 22 — Virgin Takes to the Air
Virgin Atlantic Airways' inaugural flight takes place.

July 28 — Summer Olympics Boycott
The Soviet Union, along with 13 other countries, boycotts the Los Angeles Olympics on the grounds that the U.S. is using them for political purposes.

August 5 — Burton Dies
Sir Richard Burton, renowned actor, dies at the age of 58.

1984

FIRST LINE-FREE SPACE WALK

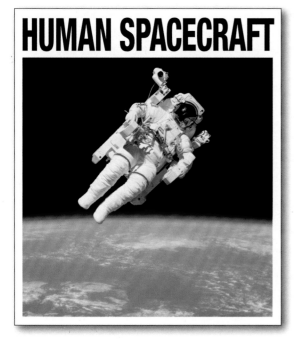

The *Challenger* flight in February 1984 was to be the American space shuttle's tenth mission. Captain Bruce McCandless had waited 18 years to make his first space flight, and on February 7, five days into the mission, he became the first human to walk freely in space. McCandless stepped out of the shuttle without being secured by a safety line, as had always been common practice, using instead a manned maneuvering unit (M.M.U.). This groundbreaking step opened up new possibilities for the future of human activity in space.

Right: Bruce McCandless after his historic space walk.

I.R.A. HITS CONFERENCE

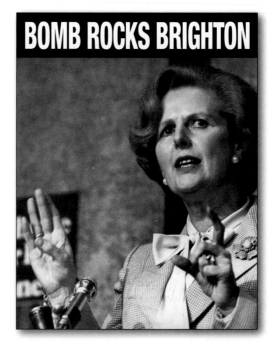

'Five people were killed by the blast, including one member of parliament, and 34 others were injured.'

In the early hours of October 12, 1985, a bomb went off at the Grand Hotel in Brighton, England, where the Conservative Party was holding its annual conference. The force of the explosion ripped off the front of the hotel and tore through eight floors. Five people were killed by the blast, including one member of parliament, and 34 others were injured. Prime Minister Margaret Thatcher and her husband escaped harm, but two members of her political cabinet were seriously injured. The Provisional Irish Republican Army (I.R.A.) immediately claimed responsibility, declaring, 'Today we were unlucky, but remember we only have to be lucky once; you will have to be lucky always.' Patrick Magee, thereafter known as the 'Brighton bomber', had planted the bomb in the hotel weeks earlier. He was sentenced to 35 years in prison, but was released in 1999 under the terms of the Good Friday Agreement. Failing to be swayed by the explosion, Margaret Thatcher insisted that the conference would proceed as planned the next morning. She began her opening address by declaring, 'This attack has failed. All attempts to destroy democracy by terrorism will fail.'

September 15
Another Son for Charles
Prince Henry Charles Albert David is born and becomes third in line to the throne, after his father Prince Charles and older brother Prince William.

September 26
Hong Kong
The U.K. and China sign an initial agreement that will give Hong Kong back to China in 1997.

October 16
Greenhouse Effect
Scientists warn that carbon monoxide pollution is causing the Greenhouse Effect.

November
Band Aid
Thirty-six of the best-known British and Irish musicians gather in a recording studio in Notting Hill, London, to record 'Do They Know It's Christmas?'

ROCKED WITH LOVE

The Live Aid Concerts, held in London and Philadelphia on July 13, 1985 to raise money for famine-stricken Africa, were the brainchild of musicians Bob Geldof and Midge Ure. Their original aim was to raise $1.6 million (£1 million), but in the end they raised a breathtaking $250 million (£150 million) to be donated to the starving multitudes in Africa. Around 90,000 people attended the events, and a further 1.5 billion people watched live television coverage that was broadcast to 100 countries. The idea for the concerts came from the success of the 1984 Band Aid single 'Do They Know It's Christmas?', another Geldof-Ure project, which itself raised $12 million (£8 million). The concerts ran for 16 hours across the two locations and brought together a record number of world-famous performers from both sides of the Atlantic, including Mick Jagger and Tina Turner, who performed a duet, David Bowie, Queen, Paul McCartney, Bob Dylan, Sting, Bryan Ferry, U2, Eric Clapton, Madonna, Elton John, and Dire Straits. The largest single donation came from the royal family of Dubai, who pledged $1.6 million (£1 million) in a phone conversation with Bob Geldof.

Left: The Live Aid concerts had an amazing array of stars from the music industry.

January 17
No More Red Phone Boxes
British Telecom announces that its iconic red telephone boxes will be phased out.

February 10
Mandela Rejects Freedom
Despite having been in prison for 21 years, Nelson Mandela rejects an offer of freedom from the South African government, saying he will not leave until apartheid has been abolished.

April 15
Black and White Can Marry
South Africa ends its ban on interracial marriage.

May 25
Deadly Cyclone
A tropical cyclone kills 10,000 people in Bangladesh.

1985

HELP FOR PEOPLE IN WAD KHOLI CAMP IN SUDAN

REFUGEES FLOOD INTO SUDAN

In January 1985, around 35,000 Ethiopians poured over the border into Sudan, fleeing the fighting and famine in their own country. After months of traveling, those who had survived ended up in the Wad Kholi camp, where a solitary doctor was suddenly faced with thousands of starving men, women, and children. At first, around 70 people died every day, half of them children, but once the charity Save the Children moved in with aid and medical staff, that number began to decrease. Thousands more Ethiopian refugees continued to pour into the camp, but their chance of survival increased thanks to massive private donations that succeeded in reaching their intended target.

> 'Around 70 people died every day, half of them children, but once the charity Save the Children moved in with aid and medical staff, that number began to decrease.'

R.A.F. COACH HITS PETROL TANKER

On February 11, 1985, a Royal Air Force coach carrying R.A.F. bandsmen on a tour of Germany was involved in a crash with a petrol tanker, killing 19 of its passengers. Although 24 of the bandsmen managed to scramble to safety, they were unable to help the 17 others who were trapped inside and overcome by the flames. It is thought that the rear emergency exit door was jammed.

BAND MEMBERS KILLED IN COACH CRASH

June 17
Discovery Channel
John Hendricks launches the Discovery Channel in the U.S.A.

July 10
Rainbow Warrior Sunk
French agents sink the Greenpeace ship *Rainbow Warrior* in Auckland Harbour, New Zealand.

August 31
Titanic Found
Oceanographer Robert Ballard and his team find the wreck of R.M.S. *Titanic* on the ocean floor.

September 19
Mexico City Quake
An earthquake in Mexico City kills 9,000 people and destroys 95,000 homes.

DAM BURSTS IN ITALY

An earthen dam in northern Italy burst on July 20, 1985, taking the lives of hundreds of people. Onlookers described how a wall of mud and water 150 ft (45 m) high swept through the mountain village of Stava in the Dolomites, leaving destruction in its wake. It was the peak of the tourist season in the popular mountain resort when the dam gave way and the wave of muddy water crashed through crowded hotels and houses. Three hotels were completely wiped out; the guests were mainly Italian and Austrian, alongside other Europeans and Americans. The floodwaters flattened houses, uprooted trees, and buried cars over a 3-mile (5-km) stretch of land. The dam had been constructed 20 years earlier to hold back an artificial pond that was used to purify minerals excavated from a fluoride mine. It had just been examined for possible damage before it burst.

'It was the peak of the tourist season in the popular mountain resort when the dam gave way and the wave of muddy water crashed through crowded hotels and houses.'

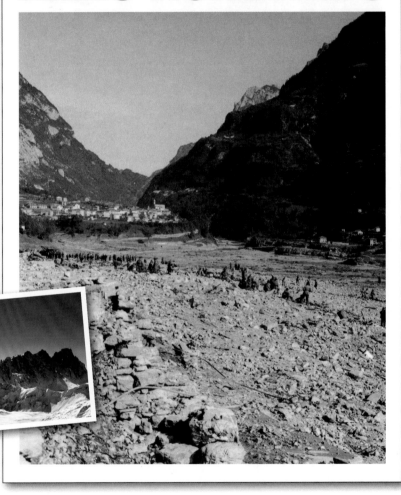

BURST DAM KILLS HUNDREDS

Above: The Dolomite mountains of northern Italy, where the dam burst occurred.

October 2
Rock Hudson Dies
American film and television actor Rock Hudson, the first celebrity to admit publicly to having A.I.D.S., dies of the disease.

October 11
Orson Welles Dies
Famous film director and producer Orson Welles dies at the age of 70.

November 19
Reagan and Gorbachev
U.S. President Ronald Reagan and Soviet Premier Mikhail Gorbachev meet for the first time in Geneva.

November
Windows for the World
The Microsoft Corporation releases Windows 1.0, its first version of the program.

1986

MAJOR ACCIDENT AT CHERNOBYL POWER STATION

NUCLEAR DISASTER

Right: The town of Chernobyl was evacuated after the nuclear disaster.

On April 26, 1986, an accident occurred at the Chernobyl nuclear plant in Ukraine (then part of the U.S.S.R.) that killed 28 people immediately and had massive repercussions in the surrounding area for many years to come. Much of the panic at the time was due to unknown quantities: it was the first nuclear accident, so no one was sure what effect the leaked radiation would have or how far it would spread. The faulty design of the nuclear reactor caused an unexpected power surge during a routine test, and this led to an explosion that lifted off the reactor cover and released fission by-products into the atmosphere. A second explosion followed, causing 1,200 tons of graphite to burst into flames, releasing far more radioactivity into the atmosphere. An investigation found that, in addition to the design error, staff training was poor, and this was directly linked to the isolationist policies of the U.S.S.R. On the day of the disaster, 28 people, mainly firefighters, died as a result of their direct exposure to radiation, and 19 more died later, with many more suffering lasting damage. On May 2, around 45,000 local residents were evacuated from homes within a 6-mile (10-km) radius of the nuclear power plant. This zone was extended to 18 miles (30 km) within days. Initial rumors were exaggerated and did a lot to spread a culture of fear, mistrust, and fatalism. There have been long-term effects for the local population, such as an increased likelihood of contracting leukemia, but many of these effects have been found to be less drastic than originally anticipated. On the positive side, the Chernobyl incident was thought to be a contributing factor to the lifting of the 'Iron Curtain' around the U.S.S.R.

> **'The faulty design of the nuclear reactor caused an unexpected power surge ... and this led to an explosion that lifted off the reactor cover and released fission by-products into the atmosphere.'**

January 9
Kodak Out of the Picture

After losing a patent battle with Polaroid, Kodak quits the instant camera business.

January 20
Channel Tunnel Announced

The U.K. and France announce their intention of building a tunnel under the Channel.

January 23
Hall of Fame

The first inductions into the Rock 'n' Roll Hall of Fame are held, and include Chuck Berry, Elvis Presley, and Buddy Holly.

February 7
Duvalier Flees Haiti

Haitian President Jean-Claude Duvalier, known as Baby Doc, flees to France, causing widespread joy in Haiti and ending a dynastic rule that lasted 28 years.

SPACE SHUTTLE *CHALLENGER* EXPLODES OVER CAPE CANAVERAL

On January 28, 1986, the American space shuttle *Challenger* exploded one minute after liftoff, killing all seven astronauts on board. In Cape Canaveral, Florida, their family and friends watched in horror from the ground, while millions more watched live televised coverage, as the space shuttle burst into flames, showering the surrounding area with debris. An investigation found the cause of the explosion to be a leak through a faulty seal in one of the rocket boosters. On board were five men and two women, including a teacher, Christa McAuliffe, who had won a competition to join the crew. President Reagan led the nation in mourning for its national heroes. In a televised address the same evening he said, 'We will never forget them, nor the last time we saw them this morning as they prepared for their journey and waved goodbye and slipped the surly bonds of Earth to touch the face of God.' The tragedy dealt a massive blow to human space travel: although the *Challenger* had previously flown nine successful missions before the 1986 disaster, it was two years before N.A.S.A. resumed manned missions into space.

> 'We will never forget them, nor the last time we saw them ... as they prepared for their journey ... and slipped the surly bonds of Earth to touch the face of God.'

Left: The seven-member team pose with a model of the shuttle.

February 19
Mir Launched
The Soviet Union launches the Mir space station.

February 25
Marcos Defeated
President Ferdinand Marcos of the Philippines is overthrown.

March 11
Comet Back
Haley's Comet, visible once every 75 years, can be seen in the northern hemisphere.

April
Help to Quit Smoking
Nicorette chewing gum, designed to help smokers quit by providing nicotine in decreasing amounts, is put on the market.

1986

PREMIER SHOT DEAD IN STREET

The Swedish Prime Minister Olof Palme was shot dead as he left a movie theater in Stockholm, Sweden, with his wife Lisbeth on the night of February 28, 1986. Lisbeth was also shot, but her wounds were not fatal; Prime Minister Palme, however, was pronounced dead on arrival at hospital. A Social Democrat opposed to the political stance of what he called 'the Reagans and the Thatchers', Palme conducted his government informally and did not use bodyguards. He often walked unaccompanied around the streets of Stockholm, and the Swedish people were proud that theirs was a country where the Prime Minister was free to do so. Olof Palme was a firm supporter of the working classes, and a peace campaigner who took a strong interest in developing countries. At a time when the right wing dominated Western politics, Palme believed that the left wing was about to have its day, and often received criticism at home for his apparent Soviet sympathies. Christer Pettersson, a drug addict and petty criminal, was found guilty of his murder and sentenced to life imprisonment in 1989. However, the verdict was contested, and Pettersson was eventually released due to lack of evidence and motive. The crime remains unsolved.

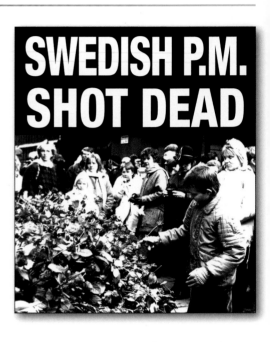

SLAUGHTER ON FLIGHT 073

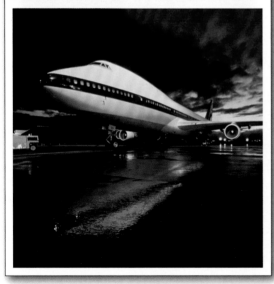

On September 5, 1986, four hijackers disguised as airport security staff and armed with guns and grenades managed to board a Pan Am flight that was due to take off from Karachi Airport on its way to New York. They immediately fired shots to seize control of the plane, but the cabin crew had just enough time to warn the pilots, who escaped through a cockpit hatch, thereby grounding the plane at the airport. After seizing the passengers' passports, one hijacker, Zayd Safarini, grabbed Rajesh Kumar, a 29-year-old resident of California who had just gained U.S. citizenship, and made him kneel with his hands on his head. When Safarini's demands for a new flight crew were not met, he shot Rajesh Kumar in the head and threw him out of the plane. The hijackers then lost control and began shooting randomly at passengers. In the chaos that followed, Pakistani authorities entered the plane, also shooting. Although passengers tried to escape through emergency exits, 22 people were killed, most of them Indian or Pakistani, and a further 150 were injured. All of the hijackers were sentenced to life imprisonment. Their plan had been to fill the plane with explosives and fly it into the Israeli Defense Ministry.

April 15
U.S. Against Libya
The United States launches an airstrike against Libya.

May 16
Top Gun
The film *Top Gun*, starring Tom Cruise and Kelly McGillis, is released.

June 29
Branson Fastest
Entrepreneur Richard Branson breaks the transatlantic speed record in his powerboat.

August 19
Woman Found
Picasso's famous painting *Weeping Woman* is found in a locker in Melbourne, Australia, two weeks after being stolen.

STOCKMARKET TAKES WORLDWIDE DIVE

On October 19, 1987, the world's financial markets suffered a sudden drop in value. It began with a crash on Wall Street that saw the Dow Jones lose 22.6% of its value (an equivalent loss of $500 billion/£300 billion). This led to a fall of 300 points on the F.T.S.E. Index, which is equivalent to an instant loss of $40 billion (£25 billion). In the U.S.A. the chairman of the New York Stock Exchange said, 'This is the nearest thing to a financial meltdown I've ever come across,' while President Reagan announced he was confident that the U.S. economy would survive. The crash came after a couple of years of fast growth in a 'bull' market – one characterized by hostile takeovers and relentless company mergers. The idea behind this type of market was that financial growth was limitless, and the way to keep it going was to keep buying companies. In order to raise the money to do this, many companies sold 'junk bonds', which are bonds that return high interest but also have a high risk attached. The investing public kept buying and buying these bonds with increasing greed, effectively buying nothing. As ever, when the bubble burst, panic set in: stocks were sold wholesale and values were wiped out. In this case, the fall was exacerbated by rising interest rates, a falling dollar, and fears of a looming war with Iran. Although it was the most drastic drop in the market's history, 'Black Monday', as it was called, did not lead to a depression, and it was not long before interest rates began to fall and investors began to buy again.

Right: Stockmarket traders worked at high speed – here on two phones at once – to offload stocks that had plummeted in value.

SHARES CRASH

January
Woman in Hall of Fame
Aretha Franklin is inducted into the Rock 'n' Roll Hall of Fame, the first woman to be so honored.

January 29
Reforms in Soviet Union
President Gorbachev begins reforms in the Soviet Union based on *perestroika* (restructuring) and *glasnost* (openness).

February 22
Andy Warhol Dies
Artist and filmmaker Andy Warhol, born August 6, 1928 in Russia and known for his involvement in the pop art movement, dies.

April
New Cartoon
The Simpsons cartoon appears for the first time on *The Tracey Ullman Show* in the U.S.A.

1987

U.S. AND U.S.S.R. AGREE TO CUT NUCLEAR ARSENALS

NUCLEAR WARHEADS CUT

'It was not until Ronald Reagan and Mikhail Gorbachev entered into negotiations that the arms race finally came to a real halt.'

At the height of the Cold War, the U.S. and the U.S.S.R. held between them 30,000 nuclear warheads. In the 1970s, negotiations had opened up between U.S. President Richard Nixon and Soviet leader Leonid Brezhnev; these negotiations were known as the Strategic Arms Limitation Talks. These were aimed at limiting future weapons growth rather than reducing stockpiles, but they failed to achieve anything concrete. It was not until Ronald Reagan and Mikhail Gorbachev entered into negotiations that the arms race finally came to a real halt. After a 1986 summit between Reagan and Gorbachev, the Intermediate-Range Nuclear Forces Treaty was established, whereby both countries agreed to eliminate their ground-launched ballistic missiles, both nuclear and conventional, with a firing range of between 300 and 3,400 miles (480–5,440 km). Similar agreements had been discussed before, but the difference this time was that both countries agreed to let the other side carry out inspections to verify that the terms of the treaty had been met. As a result, by 1991 more than 2,500 weapons had been destroyed and subsequent leaders of both countries continued to agree to joint limitations.

Above: A mobile Russian missile launcher.

June 19
Creationism vs Evolution
In a landmark ruling regarding a Louisiana state law, the U.S. Supreme Court rules that creationism does not have to be taught in public schools whenever evolution is taught.

June 22
Fred Astaire Dies
Fred Astaire, born May 10, 1899, film and stage dancer, known for partnering dancer Ginger Rogers, dies.

July
Barbie Convicted
Former Gestapo boss Klaus Barbie is convicted of crimes against humanity during the Second World War in Lyons, France, and jailed for life.

August 17
Rudolph Hess Dies
Rudolph Hess, Hitler's deputy at the start of the Second World War, is found dead in his cell, a suspected suicide, in Spandau Prison.

BRITISH NEGOTIATOR TAKEN HOSTAGE

KIDNAPPED

Terry Waite had been an envoy of peace, negotiating for the release of hostages in Beirut, when he was taken hostage himself on January 20, 1987. As an envoy of the Archbishop of Canterbury, Terry Waite represented the Church of England on peace missions and had already successfully negotiated the release of several hostages held in Iran and Libya. In 1985, he became involved in negotiations to release four British hostages held in Lebanon by the extremist Islamic Jihad Organization. In January 1987, he went against advice and took the dangerous step of going alone with his contact, without guards or weapons, to meet the hostages. Blindfolded, he was taken on a four-day journey, supposedly to meet the hostages. It was only when he stepped down through a trapdoor and the door closed behind him that he realized he too had become a hostage. Terry Waite was held in Lebanon for a total of five years, four of which were spent in solitary confinement.

FERRY DISASTER

On March 6, 1987, a car ferry owned by the company Townsend-Thoresen (now part of P&O) capsized near Zeebrugge off the coast of Belgium, killing 190 people. The accident happened as a result of human error: the bow doors had been left open, and water began to pour into the car decks as soon as the ferry set sail. An inquiry discovered what it called a 'disease of sloppiness' at every level of the company's hierarchy. In 1989, a charge of corporate manslaughter was brought against P&O and, although the trial collapsed, it succeeded in establishing 'corporate manslaughter' as a possible criminal charge. Three individuals within the company were found guilty of manslaughter.

DISASTER IN THE CHANNEL

September 16
Climate Change
An international agreement to protect the ozone layer is signed.

October 15
Storms in Britain
Britain experiences its worst storms of the century, unforecast by meteorologists, killing 23 people.

December 18
Perl Created
Larry Wall creates the programming language Perl.

December 20
Disaster at Sea
The worst peacetime sea disaster takes place when a ferry sinks in the Tablas Straits in the Philippines, killing about 4,000 people.

1988

LOCKERBIE PLANE DISASTER

DISASTER AT LOCKERBIE

On December 21, 1988, Pan Am flight 103 exploded in mid-air and landed on the town of Lockerbie in Scotland. The flight was traveling from London to New York with 243 passengers onboard. All passengers onboard were killed, as well as 16 crewmembers and 11 people on the ground, bringing the total fatalities to 270. Onlookers described a massive fireball 300 ft (90 m) high, and the huge impact as the plane hit the ground caused debris to scatter for hundreds of miles. The plane landed in a residential area, crushing houses and cars. The investigation that followed revealed that a bomb had exploded onboard, and a murder inquiry began. Eventually, after a three-year joint investigation by the Scottish policing agency, the Dumfries and Galloway Constabulary, and the F.B.I., two Libyan intelligence agents were charged with the bombing. Abdel Basset Ali al Megrahi was jailed for life in 2001, but Lamin Khalifah Fhimah was found not guilty. Megrahi is currently serving his sentence in Greenock Prison in Scotland, despite frequent appeals for a retrial, and he continues to declare his innocence. Although Libya has never officially admitted carrying out the bombing, the government has accepted responsibility for the actions of its officials, and in 2002, Libya offered $2.7 billion (£1.7 billion) in compensation to the victims' families.

'Onlookers described a massive fireball 300 ft (90 m) high, and the huge impact as the plane hit the ground caused debris to scatter for hundreds of miles.'

Right: The ditch made by the plane.

Left: A firefighter looks on as cars blaze, set alight by the crash.

January 26
Australia's Birthday
Australia celebrates its bicentennial.

February 5
Comic Relief
In the U.K., the first Comic Relief Red Nose Day raises millions of pounds for charity.

March 24
Vanunu Sentenced
Mordechai Vanunu is sentenced to 18 years in prison for advising *The Sunday Times* in London about Israel's nuclear program.

April
The Great Seto Bridge
The Great Seto Bridge, at 8.2 miles (13.1 km) the world's longest two-tiered bridge system, opens in Japan.

U.S. DOWNS IRANIAN AIRLINER

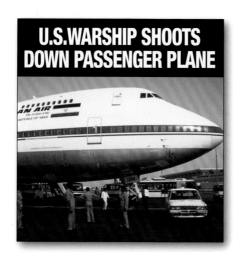

U.S. WARSHIP SHOOTS DOWN PASSENGER PLANE

The U.S. and Iran were unofficially waging war at sea in 1988. As the U.S. escorted Kuwaiti tankers in and out of the Persian Gulf, they shot down an Iranian civilian airliner, mistaking it for a fighter plane. The passenger jet, en route to Dubai, had veered 4 miles (6 km) off course, bringing it close to the battleground. A U.S. ship picked it up on radar and, after warning it several times by radio to change course and stay away, shot down the plane using a heat-seeking missile. The sky was hazy and the U.S. afterwards claimed that the military personnel involved had not seen the plane before they shot, and they believed it to be a hostile Iranian fighter jet. There were 290 people onboard, and all were killed. It was the first time the U.S. military had shot at a civilian plane. U.S. President Reagan called the incident a 'terrible human tragedy' and apologized to the bereaved families, but he maintained that the U.S. Navy had acted 'in a proper defensive action'. The Iranians referred to it as a 'barbaric massacre' and vowed to avenge their innocent dead.

EARTHQUAKE IN ARMENIA

On December 7, 1988, an earthquake measuring 6.9 on the Richter scale devastated the Soviet state of Armenia, killing 25,000 people and leaving hundreds of thousands more homeless. Armenia, located between Turkey and Azerbaijan, is densely populated, and many people live in high-rise buildings, which heightened the scale of the disaster. The town of Spitak was entirely destroyed, with no hope to rebuild it. The U.S.S.R. was rocked by the tragedy, pleading for medical aid from the U.S. and pledging that the country would be rebuilt using low-rise buildings. The international community rushed to Armenia's aid, with France and America sending sniffer dogs, which successfully located many survivors in the rubble, India sending clothes and blankets, and Great Britain supplying excavating equipment.

'The U.S.S.R. was rocked by the tragedy, pleading for medical aid from the U.S. and pledging [to rebuild] using low-rise buildings.'

EARTHQUAKE KILLS THOUSANDS

Left: A survivor in the aftermath of the quake.

April 11
The Last Emperor Wins
Bernardo Bertolucci's film *The Last Emperor* wins eight Oscars.

April 30
Eurovision Winner
Celine Dion wins the Eurovision Song Contest, which catapults her to international fame.

May 15
Soviet Withdrawal
The Soviet Union starts its troop withdrawal from Afghanistan, after eight years.

June
Mandela's Birthday Celebrations
Wembley Stadium in London holds a televised 70th birthday celebration for Nelson Mandela, imprisoned leader of South Africa's A.N.C., with celebrities from music, film, and comedy.

1988

TRAIN CRASH IN LONDON

RUSH HOUR DISASTER

It was the peak of the morning rush hour in London on December 12, 1988 when two commuter trains carrying more than a thousand passengers between them collided outside Clapham Junction station, killing 35 people. After the initial crash, a third train, which was empty of passengers, hit the wreckage, killing some of those who had survived the first crash. The accident happened just as the morning commuter train from Basingstoke to London Waterloo was nearing Clapham Junction. It slowed at a signal and the commuter train traveling from Bournemouth on the south coast ran into the back of it, hitting it at a speed of 40 mph (64 kph). Witnesses described carriages flying up into the air before crashing back to the ground. Several passengers with horrific injuries were given emergency surgery on the spot. The enquiry into the crash found that a signaling fault had been to blame, which was itself caused by a wiring error committed by a British Rail employee who had only had one day off in 13 weeks. As a result of the enquiry, British Rail employment practices came under strong attack. It was further recommended that automatic train protection (A.T.P.) systems be fitted to all trains to control their speed and stop them automatically at red lights. However, this recommendation was not implemented due to the prohibitive costs.

> 'The enquiry into the crash found that a signaling fault had been to blame, which was itself caused by a wiring error'

August
The Terminal Man
Mehran Karimi Nasseri, an Iranian refugee, lives at Terminal One in De Gaulle Airport, Paris, from August until July 2006, after his papers are stolen and he is refused entry into Britain.

August 20
Iran-Iraq War Ends
With an estimated 1 million dead, the Iran-Iraq War ends.

October 13
Turin Shroud a Fake
The Turin Shroud is declared a fake.

November 8
Bush Elected
George H.W. Bush is elected President of the United States.

CLEVELAND SCHOOL MASSACRE

On January 17, 1989, Patrick Edward Purdy opened fire with an AK-47 assault rifle, killing five children and wounding 29 others at Cleveland Elementary School in Stockton, California. Purdy, who had exhibited increasing sociopathic and violent behavior, fired more than 100 rounds of ammunition into the school playground before shooting himself in the head with a pistol. All of the children killed were of Southeast Asian background and the majority wounded were also from ethnic minorities. Subsequent police investigation found that the 24-year-old harbored a deep hatred towards immigrants, particularly those from Cambodia, India, Pakistan, and Vietnam, all of whom now lived in Stockton.

'Despite a previous criminal record and alleged mental health problems, Purdy purchased both weapons shortly after being released from jail.'

This incident, one in a long line of school shootings, led journalists and sociologists to question how the current system was dealing with racial hatred and mental health problems as well as how Purdy was able to buy his weapons with ease. Despite a previous criminal record and alleged mental health problems, Purdy purchased both weapons shortly after being released from jail. This attack led to public and political support for tighter gun control in California which, combined with increased media attention, led to the 1989 ban on assault weapons.

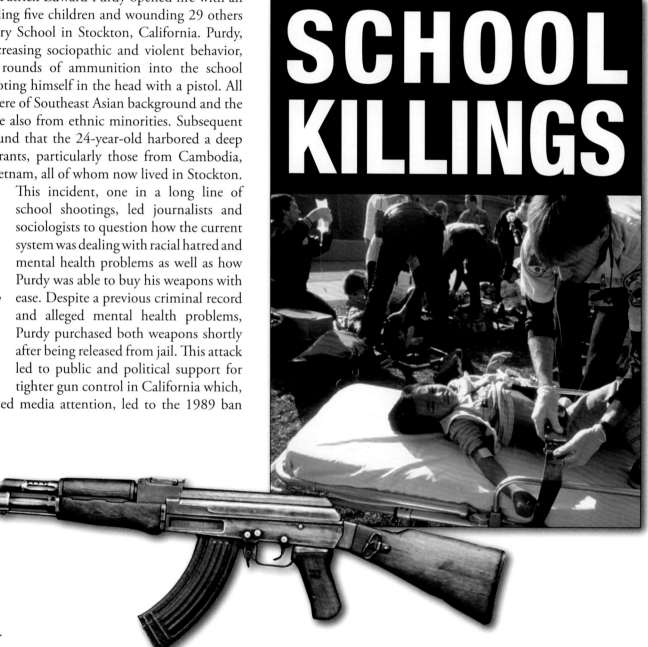

Right: An AK-47 assault rifle, similar to the weapon used by Purdy in the attack.

January 24
Ted Bundy Executed
Serial killer Ted Bundy is electrocuted in the electric chair in Florida, U.S.A. He is thought to have killed at least 30 women.

February 2
Sky T.V.
Sky Television plc is launched in Europe.

February 14
Fatwa Declared
Ayotollah Khomeini declares a fatwa against Salman Rushdie, author of *The Satanic Verses.*

February 15
Soviet Troops Exit
The last Soviet troops leave Afghanistan.

1989

OIL TANKER RUNS AGROUND IN ALASKA

OIL SPILL IN ALASKA

'Around 30 million tons of oil were spilled, which led to the death of about 250,000 seabirds, as well as thousands of otters, seals, and eagles'

On March 24, 1989, the Exxon oil tanker *Valdez* hit a reef in Alaska's Prince William Sound, resulting in a massive oil spill. The environmental disaster caused extensive damage to the coastline, as well as birds and fish. Third Mate Greg Cousins was steering the vessel when a miscommunication over navigation led him to run aground on Bligh Reef, puncturing the hull. The reaction to the spill was far from effective, since there were insufficient chemical dispersants available and the equipment used to clear the oil manually was faulty. In all, around 30 million tons of oil were spilled, which led to the death of about 250,000 seabirds, as well as thousands of otters, seals, and eagles. The captain of the ship was charged with negligence amid rumors that he had been intoxicated. Exxon was forced to pay billions of dollars in damages to the Alaskan communities whose lives had been shattered by the spill, and the *Valdez* was banned from Alaska, even after it underwent a complete overhaul and changed its name.

SOCCER FANS CRUSHED TO DEATH

FANS KILLED IN CRUSH

The 1989 FA Cup semi-final between Liverpool and Nottingham Forest was held at the Hillsborough Stadium in Sheffield, England. It was to become the site of the worst human disaster in soccer's history as 96 Liverpool fans were killed. A series of policing errors led to too many fans being let into a crowded terrace, where they were penned in by fences and crushed to death. The game had been under way for some minutes before the crush was noticed, and an enquiry after the disaster was heavily critical of the police, who were slow to recognize the seriousness of the situation and at first treated the crush as a public order problem. The disaster had a huge emotional impact on the British public, who saw it all unfold live on their TV screens. The Hillsborough tragedy led to a complete redesign of soccer stadiums in England and the removal of fencing around terraced areas.

June
Solidarity
The Polish Solidarity Party is elected to power, the first time in 42 years a non-Communist is elected.

July 5
Seinfeld Premieres
The hit television show *Seinfeld* is first shown.

July 12
I'll Have What She's Having
When Harry Met Sally, a popular film starring Billy Crystal and Meg Ryan, is released.

July 14
Happy Birthday, France
France celebrates the 200th anniversary of the French Revolution.

BERLIN WALL PULLED DOWN AS EAST AND WEST GERMANY REUNITED

After being separated for 28 years by guarded fortifications, in November 1989 East and West Germans were finally reunited. The 27-mile-long (43-km) Berlin Wall had been erected in 1961 by the Communist government of East Germany as a means of preventing East Berliners from escaping to the West. During the years that followed, many would-be refugees had been shot dead attempting to cross it, but a liberalization of governments in Hungary and Czechoslovakia had allowed East Germans to reach West Germany through other borders. In order to call a halt to such 'back door' emigration, on November 9, 1989, the Communist government of East Germany announced that the crossing points would be opened and East Germans would be free to travel to the West. No sooner had the government made the announcement than crowds flocked to the crossing points to be met by cheering supporters on the other side. Still more began to climb the wall itself from both sides, pulling it down piece by piece with their bare hands. The West German Chancellor Helmut Kohl welcomed the move and called for a meeting with East German leader Egon Krenz. Krenz had replaced the Communist hardline leader Erich Honecker and had opened the way for democratic reforms. However, when East and West Germany officially reunited a year later, Egon Krenz was arrested on charges of manslaughter for the deaths of all those who had tried to cross the wall and been shot by guards.

'Crowds flocked to the crossing points to be met by cheering supporters on the other side. Still more began to climb the wall itself from both sides, pulling it down piece by piece.'

TEAR DOWN THE WALL

Right: Germans from East and West Berlin celebrate the end of the divide.

October 17
Quake Kills
An earthquake in San Fransisco kills 63 people.

December 3
Out of the Cold
The end to the Cold War is declared.

December
Chile Elections
Chile holds its first free elections in 16 years.

December 25
Ceausescu Executed
Nicolae Ceausescu, the former dictator of Romania, is executed by firing squad.

1990-1999

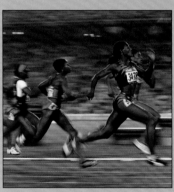

The 1990s brought a measure of unity at last in South Africa, as Nelson Mandela was released from prison and elected the country's first black president. Mandela's support for the 'peace and reconciliation' movement did much to resolve the hatreds that had built up under the apartheid regime.

In Britain, Tony Blair became Prime Minister, with one of the crowning triumphs of his early years being to broker the Northern Ireland peace deal, bringing to an end decades of violence that had only a few years earlier seen the bombing of the Prime Minister's residence, No. 10 Downing Street. Later in the decade he gave his support to America in the decision to bomb Iraq.

During this decade, America was shaken by several apparently pointless mass-killings: first there was the shoot-out and fire in the Branch Davidian cult headquarters in Waco, then the Oklahoma bombing which killed 168 people, and the Columbine High School massacre, which was the first in a line of campus shootings.

In the closing years of the decade, there were momentous events on both a cosmic and a terrestrial level. In 1997, the Hale-Bopp comet was visible from Earth for several days, and in 1999 there was a total eclipse of the Sun. Also in 1999, the euro currency was introduced, uniting the economies of 11 European countries.

1990

IRAQ INVADES KUWAIT

WAR IN THE GULF

Right: Some of the Iraqi troops captured during the war.
Above right: General Norman Schwarzkopf, commander of coalition forces.

On August 2, 1990, Iraqi leader Saddam Hussein ordered his soldiers to invade the Gulf state of Kuwait. A total of 200,000 Iraqi soldiers easily succeeded in taking over Kuwait City, sealing it, and blocking off all lines of communication. The Emir of Kuwait fled to Saudi Arabia, but his brother was killed along with hundreds of others in the first days of fighting. The Iraqi justification for the invasion was that Kuwait had seized an unfair monopoly on the world oil market. Saddam Hussein claimed that Iraq was owed compensation for oil Kuwait had sold that came from a disputed oil field on the border of the two countries. Iraq also owed Kuwait over $60 billion that Kuwait had lent in support of Iraq's eight-year war with Iran, and was reluctant to pay it back. Despite the U.N.'s call for an immediate and unconditional withdrawal from Kuwait, and international condemnation of the invasion, Saddam Hussein refused to back down. The U.S.S.R., Iraq's main arms supplier, immediately stopped the sale of arms to the country but refused to be involved in any military intervention. The U.N. rejected Saddam Hussein's claim that Kuwait was now part of Iraq. Days later, the U.S., under President George Bush Sr., launched Operation Desert Shield. By October 1990, British and French troops had joined U.S. troops in the region, and they were soon also backed by Egypt, Syria, and Morocco. By January 1991, when the Allies launched Operation Desert Storm, there were 580,000 Allied troops against 540,000 Iraqi troops. Several air and land attacks by the U.S. and its allies during January and February eventually succeeded in convincing Saddam Hussein to withdraw his troops from Kuwait. On February 27, 1991, President Bush announced the liberation of Kuwait.

January 31
McDonalds in Moscow
After 14 years of negotiation, the first McDonalds restaurant opens in Pushkin Square, Moscow. It continues to be the busiest McDonalds in the world.

February 14
Solar System Snapped
Following its launch in 1977, *Voyager 1* traveled through the Solar System, taking breathtaking pictures of the entire Solar System in February 1990.

April 1
Prison Riot
Britain's longest prison riot, at Strangeways Prison in Manchester, lasts for 25 days. Two men die.

NELSON MANDELA FREED

MANDELA RELEASED

Nelson Mandela, the anti-apartheid leader and Deputy Chairman of the African National Congress (A.N.C.), was released from prison on February 11, 1990 after 27 years' incarceration at Robben Island prison. His release followed the softening of the apartheid regime under South African President F.W. de Klerk, which had seen the ban lifted on the A.N.C. Following his release, Mandela addressed crowds of supporters in Cape Town, declaring, 'Our march to freedom is irreversible. Now is the time to intensify the struggle on all fronts.' Nelson Mandela had been convicted of treason and sabotage against the apartheid government in 1964 and sentenced to life imprisonment. After his release, he and F.W. de Klerk worked together toward fair, multiracial elections in South Africa.

'Mandela addressed crowds of suppporters in Cape Town, declaring, "Our march to freedom is irreversible."'

RIOTS ON THE STREETS OF LONDON

On March 31, 1990, 100,000 people joined a demonstration in central London against the government's new 'poll tax'. The poll tax had been unpopular ever since it was first introduced, on the grounds that it taxed individuals the same amount regardless of their circumstances. The March demonstration started out as a peaceful protest, but according to police, one group of around 3,000 demonstrators launched a purposefully targeted violent attack on the police. It began when protestors staged a sit-in outside of the governmental offices of Whitehall, near the entrance to Downing Street, and refused to move. The resulting arrests led to placards and cans being thrown at the police. The violence escalated: bricks and other missiles were aimed at police, fires were started and windows were broken, and there was looting of the stores around Trafalgar Square in central London. In all, 113 people were injured and 340 were arrested. The poll tax controversy contributed to Prime Minister Margaret Thatcher's downfall the same year. The following year, the poll tax was replaced by the council tax, which was based on the value of property.

POLL TAX RIOTS

April 9
First Free Elections in Hungary
Decades of Communist rule come to an end with the newly formed Hungarian Democratic Forum forming a new government.

May 20
Hubble Space Telescope Scans the Skies
Within weeks of its launch, a defect in the telescope's mirror is discovered, resulting in blurry images. The problem is not repaired until 1993.

May 22
Microsoft Releases Windows 3.0
The third release of the Windows operating system features more advanced graphics and an improved user interface. It goes on to sell over 10 million copies in the next two years.

June 8
Soccer World Cup Kicks Off in Italy
West Germany meet Argentina in the final, winning 1–0, with Argentina's Pedro Monzon becoming the first player ever to be sent off in a World Cup Final.

1990

CHANNEL TUNNEL COMPLETED

THE FRENCH CONNECTION

In 1981, the French and British governments invited bids from private companies for the construction and maintenance of an undersea tunnel connecting France and Great Britain. By 1986, British Prime Minister Margaret Thatcher and French President François Mitterrand announced that work was ready to begin. Tunneling began from both ends simultaneously. Sophisticated laser surveying techniques meant that, when the two sides met in the middle in December 1990, there was only a $^3/4$-inch (2-cm) error. However, the meeting of the tunnels did not signal the start of under-Channel transportation. The project was supposed to cost $7 billion (£4 billion) at the start, but it ballooned out of proportion and ended up costing $20 billion (£12 billion) by the time it opened for use in 1994. Further problems surfaced for the British rail network when it emerged that Eurostar trains, which could reach 186 mph (300 kph) on the Continent, were limited in their speed by the British system of rails. The required upgrade of the British line was finally completed in 2007, reducing the journey time from London to Paris to 2 hours 15 minutes.

Left: Workers on the British section of the Channel Tunnel.

June 21
Quake Kills Thousands in Iran
An earthquake hits an area northwest of Tehran, causing 40,000 fatalities and making half a million homeless.

October 3
Germany Re-Unified
The former state of Communist East Germany joins the Federal Republic of Germany, and Berlin is re-unified.

November 22
Margaret Thatcher Forced Out
Following an internal leadership contest, the United Kingdom's first female prime minister leaves office after 11 years in charge.

December 25
'World Wide Web' Invented
While working at C.E.R.N. (the European Organization for Nuclear Research), British computer scientist Tim Berners-Lee creates the first hypertext link, the basis for the entire World Wide Web.

FORMER PRIME MINISTER OF INDIA ASSASSINATED

'The assassin had held the basket of flowers out to Rajiv Gandhi, dying herself in the attack.'

On May 21, 1991, Rajiv Gandhi, the former Prime Minister of India, was campaigning for the Indian National Congress (or Congress Party) on the second day of democratic elections in India when a bomb hidden in a basket of flowers exploded inches from his body, killing him instantly. At least 14 others were also killed by the blast. The assassin was a female member of the Tamil Tigers, a guerrilla force fighting for an independent homeland for the Tamil people in Sri Lanka. The assassin had held the basket of flowers out to Rajiv Gandhi, dying herself in the attack. The assassination was presumed to be revenge for India's military intervention in Sri Lanka from 1987 to 1990, which had been initiated by Gandhi in an effort to impose peace. The 1991 election proved to be one of the most violent in India's history, with over 200 people killed in the lead-up. Rajiv Gandhi had become a member of parliament in 1980, taking the seat of his brother Sanjeev, who had been killed in an air crash. Rajiv Gandhi subsequently became Prime Minister after the death of his mother, Indira Gandhi, in 1984. Although he had rejuvenated and modernized the Congress Party, it fell into disgrace under his successor P.V. Narasimha Rao and lost the elections in 1996. Rajiv Gandhi was the grandson of Jawaharlal Nehru, who was the first Prime Minister of an independent India.

RAJIV GANDHI ASSASSINATED

Right: Rajiv Gandhi's family pray at his memorial on the anniversary of his death.

February 26
Iraqi Troops Leave Kuwait
Saddam Hussein orders the withdrawal of Iraqi troops from Kuwait.

March 13
Clean-up Bill
Oil firm Exxon agrees to pay $1 billion to clean up the oil spill from its tanker the *Exxon Valdez* in Alaska.

April 17
Stock Market Milestone
The Dow Jones Industrial Average closes above 3,000 for the first time ever, having recovered from a value of 1,738 following the 1987 crash.

June 12
Yeltsin Elected
Boris Yeltsin becomes the first elected President of Russia, with a 57% share of the vote.

1991

THE END OF THE SOVIET UNION

GORBACHEV RESIGNS

With the creation of the Commonwealth of Independent States (C.I.S.) in December 1991, the former U.S.S.R. (or Soviet Union) was dissolved as 11 Soviet states broke away from the Union. The President of the U.S.S.R., Mikhail Gorbachev, was opposed to the breakup of the Soviet Union because he felt it did not reflect the popular choice. The C.I.S. had been formed by a secret agreement between Russia, Ukraine, and Belarus. On December 25, 1991, Gorbachev announced his resignation. The Soviet red flag depicting the hammer and sickle was lowered over the Kremlin, replaced instead by the Russian Federation's tricolor flag. Boris Yeltsin, as the new President of the Russian Federation, took over leadership of the Kremlin and also took the U.S.S.R.'s permanent seat in the United Nations. Mikhail Gorbachev had transformed the U.S.S.R., distancing it from its Communist roots and introducing democracy. He has been credited with establishing free elections, a free press, freedom of worship, and free enterprise, as well as improving human rights and ending the Cold War with the U.S. His keys words for reform were *perestroika*, meaning restructuring, and *glasnost*, meaning openness.

Right: Boris Yeltsin was Russia's first elected President.

July 11
Lights Out
The longest solar eclipse for 141 years takes place, in which the Moon comes between the Earth and the Sun. Best viewed from the Baja Peninsula in Mexico, it lasts 6 minutes and 52 seconds.

July 22
Milwaukee Murderer Captured
Serial killer Jeffrey Dahmer is arrested, leading to his indictment on 17 murder charges.

July 31
Nuclear Cap
The U.S. and Russia sign the START treaty, reducing the number of nuclear weapons in their stockpiles by a third.

August 25
Schumacher Makes F1 Debut
Michael Schumacher races for the first time in Formula 1 in the Belgian Grand Prix. He retires on the first lap, but goes on to become one of the greatest drivers of all time.

I.R.A. ATTACKS LONDON

MORTAR BOMBS HIT DOWNING STREET

On February 7, 1991, the Provisional Irish Republican Army (I.R.A.) launched three mortar bombs at No. 10 Downing Street, the home and private office of the British Prime Minister. Prime Minister John Major was holding a government cabinet meeting in the Cabinet Room when a white van parked on Whitehall, the street that crosses the end of Downing Street, and launched three mortar bombs at No. 10. One of the bombs exploded in the garden, blowing in the windows of the Cabinet Room, but remarkably no one was hurt. Major had to move to a temporary residence in Admiralty House while Downing Street was repaired, but he made it his priority to carry on business as usual, undeterred by the attack.

Above: Prime Minister John Major survived the attack.

GUNMAN KILLS 22 IN TEXAS DINER

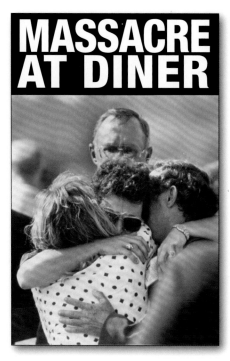

MASSACRE AT DINER

On October 16, 1991, a man named George Jo Hennard drove a pickup truck through the window of Luby's Cafeteria in Killeen, Texas, and began firing at diners. He killed 22 people before turning the gun on himself when police arrived on the scene. The restaurant was unusually full because it was National Boss's Day, and many employees were taking their bosses out for lunch. The surviving witnesses described how Hennard continually reloaded his gun, walked up to his victims, talked to them, and then shot them in the head. The 35-year-old man lived alone in his parents' house in the town of Belton 20 miles (32 km) away. There was no known motive for the massacre, believed to have been driven by delusional psychosis, but in terms of death toll, it was the deadliest rampage in America at the time. Following the tragedy, Texas changed its laws to allow citizens to carry concealed firearms on their person. This move was driven by Suzanna Gratia Hupp, who was at the restaurant with her parents but had left her handgun in the car, as required by law. Both of her parents were shot in the massacre.

'In terms of death toll, it was the deadliest rampage in America at the time.'

September 19
Frozen Find
Two hikers in the European Alps discover a 5,000-year-old frozen, mummified corpse, christened Ötzi, after the Ötztal region in which he is discovered.

November 5
Robert Maxwell Found Dead
The body of newspaper baron Robert Maxwell is found floating in the Atlantic off the coast of Tenerife.

November 24
Farewell Freddie
Queen frontman Freddie Mercury dies, the day after announcing that he is H.I.V. positive. A tribute concert five months later is attended by over 70,000 people and raises money for A.I.D.S. charities.

1992

YUGOSLAVIA BREAKS UP

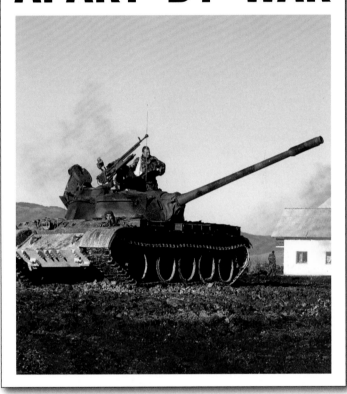

YUGOSLAVIA TORN APART BY WAR

Historically, the area covered by the Socialist Federal Republic of Yugoslavia has been beset by ethnic conflict. President Josip Broz Tito had allowed self-determination among the federal states – Bosnia and Herzegovina, Croatia, Macedonia, Montenegro, Serbia, and Slovenia – as well as for Kosovo and Vojvodina, autonomous regions within Serbia. However, many Serbs were unhappy that the Albanian majority in Kosovo was in control of a region that was felt to be part of Serbia. Before Tito's death in 1980, he had made it a part of the Yugoslavian constitution that each of the eight leaders of the regions should take it in turns to be president for one year. This arrangement weakened and fragmented the government. By the end of the 1980s, Slovenia and Croatia were seeking independence. Meanwhile, Serbia sought to rein in the independent province of Kosovo, and the Albanian majority in Kosovo was looking to become a republic in its own right. Tito had somehow held all the factions together, but since his death, nationalism and separatism had grown. The Serbian leader Slobodan Milošević reduced Kosovan independence so that he himself could choose its representatives. Albanians went on strike in protest, and Slovenia and Croatia supported their calls for republic status. Milošević tried to maintain a united Yugoslavia by force. On June 25, 1991, amid the first rumblings of war, Slovenia and Croatia declared their independence. The Serb population in Croatia formed their own Serbian republic within Croatia. Then, in September 1991, Macedonia declared its independence. In November 1991, the Bosnian Serbs in Bosnia and Herzegovina voted to remain part of Yugoslavia, but the result of a national referendum was the opposite, and the republic declared its independence in April 1992, with Bosnian Serbs forming their own republic within Bosnia. Yugoslavia was tearing itself apart.

> **'Tito had somehow held all the factions together, but since his death, nationalism and separatism had grown.'**

February 7
Maastricht Treaty Signed
The 12 members of the European Community sign the treaty in the Dutch town of Maastricht, creating the European Union and laying out a framework for closer monetary and economic cooperation.

February 20
British Soccer's Premier League Formed
The 22 teams from the existing First Division break away to form the new Premier League, becoming the world's most watched and most lucrative football league.

April 12
Euro Disney Opened
The second Disney theme park outside the U.S.A. opens on a 5,000 acre (20 sq km) site near to Paris. In 1995 the park is renamed Disneyland Paris.

April 29
Los Angeles Race Riots
The acquittal, by an all-white jury, of four white police officers captured on video beating black motorist Rodney King prompts several days of rioting in which 55 people die.

I.R.A. BOMBS LONDON

On April 10, 1992, a truck-bomb exploded outside the Baltic Exchange on St. Mary Axe Street in London's financial district. It was one of several bombs planted by the Provisional Irish Republican Army (I.R.A.) as part of an ongoing campaign in London. The Semtex bomb, planted characteristically in a white van, tore off the front of the building and severely damaged several other buildings nearby. Three people were killed in the blast. In total, the damage cost around $800 million (£500 million) to repair. Originally, English Heritage, the organization responsible for the management of historic buildings in England, insisted that the 1903 Baltic Exchange building should be restored with its facade exactly as it had been. This would have proved too expensive for the Baltic Exchange, and the company was forced to sell the building. When English Heritage realized the full extent of the damage, however, they withdrew the statement. The building was completely destroyed in 1998, and on its site now stands the building commonly referred to by Londoners as the 'Gherkin'.

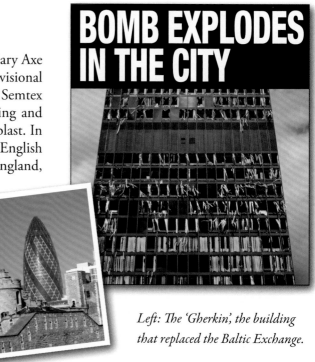

BOMB EXPLODES IN THE CITY

Left: The 'Gherkin', the building that replaced the Baltic Exchange.

EL AL PLANE CRASHES IN AMSTERDAM

On October 4, 1992, El Al cargo flight 1862, traveling from New York to Tel Aviv via Amsterdam, crashed into a nine-story apartment block on the outskirts of Amsterdam, killing 43 people, including three crewmembers, one passenger, and 39 people on the ground. Shortly after takeoff from Amsterdam, the pilot made an emergency radio call reporting that two of his four engines had failed. He attempted to turn back to make an emergency landing, but the plane came down, crashing into the apartment block and hitting 50 apartments. The 114 tons of cargo, reported to include one ingredient used to make up the nerve gas sarin, burst into flames on the ground. The crash occurred at 6.30 p.m. when many of the apartments were occupied. It was the worst air disaster ever in Holland and the first crash in El Al's history. It was initially feared that fatalities would be much higher, causing many newspaper reports to exaggerate the death toll.

PLANE CRASHES ON APARTMENTS

June 3
Rio Earth Summit
The U.N. Conference on Environment and Development is unprecedented in its size and impact, with over 100 governments attending and 10,000 journalists covering the event.

July 25
Barcelona Olympics Starts
Spain hosts the Games of the 25th Olympiad, at which the ban on professional athletes competing is lifted. Gymnast Vitaly Scherbo of Belarus becomes the first athlete to win six gold medals in one Games.

September 16
Black Wednesday
The British pound is forced out of the European Exchange Rate Mechanism following a collapse in its value. The British government increases interest rates from 10% to 15% and spends billions of pounds attempting to prop up the currency, but to no avail.

November 11
Church of England O.K.s Women Priests
The Anglican Church votes (by a very narrow margin) to allow women to become ordained as priests.

1992

PRINCE AND PRINCESS OF WALES SEPARATE

CHARLES AND DIANA SPLIT

After several years of press speculation, the British Prime Minister John Major announced on December 9, 1992 that Prince Charles, the heir to the British throne, and Princess Diana would separate. Major emphasized that the separation was amicable and that the couple would continue to meet over the care of their two sons. There had already been rumors of extramarital affairs on both sides, and the couple were increasingly leading separate lives. They did not divorce until 1996, when the Queen apparently urged them to finish the matter properly. Diana was allowed to retain her title of 'Princess of Wales' and to keep her residence in Kensington Palace, but she had to give up the title 'Her Royal Highness', as well as any claim to the throne. What had initially seemed like a fairy-tale romance before all the secrets began to emerge, turned into a battle fought through the media.

> 'There had already been rumors of extramarital affairs on both sides, and the couple were increasingly leading separate lives.'

November 20
Blaze at Windsor Castle

A fire rages through the Queen's Berkshire residence, damaging 100 rooms and threatening the monarch's priceless art collection. Firefighters battle for 15 hours to bring the blaze under control.

December 9
U.S. Marines Fly into Somalia

A U.S.-led multi-national operation is designed to prevent looting and corruption that was preventing aid supplies from getting through, but ends in failure in 1995 as U.N. forces withdraw, leaving Somalia with no government.

June 23
Yitzhak Rabin Takes Office

Two years after taking power in Israel, Rabin receives the Nobel Peace Prize for his part in the Oslo Accords, which reinvigorate the Middle East peace process.

November 3
Bill Clinton Wins U.S. Presidential Election

Democrat Bill Clinton wins with 43% of the vote, defeating incumbent Republican President George Bush.

75 DIE IN WACO SIEGE

The Branch Davidian Seventh Day Adventists came into existence in 1955 as a separatist branch of the Davidian Seventh Day Adventists, who had themselves broken away from the Seventh Day Adventists. David Koresh was a leader of the breakaway 'Branch', and in 1993, he brought their name to international media attention. On February 28, 1993, a siege began at Mount Carmel, the site of Koresh's Branch Davidian compound just outside of Waco, Texas. The U.S. government's Bureau of Alcohol, Tobacco, and Firearms (A.T.F.) was investigating claims that the Branch Davidians had a store of illegal weapons, and had decided to launch a raid on the compound. Koresh (real name Vernon Wayne Howell) apparently knew that the raid was coming and emerged unarmed to greet the A.T.F. agents, who were coming with a search warrant. A.T.F. agents opened fire as soon as they entered the compound, and in the exchange of fire, four agents and six Branch Davidian members were killed. The raid turned into a 51-day siege by the F.B.I. and A.T.F., with Koresh and his followers refusing to leave their 'Ranch Apocalypse'. Negotiations began via telephone, and Koresh agreed to a peaceful evacuation if his message could be broadcast on national radio. However, he later backtracked on this, saying that God had told him to wait, and releasing only 19 children. It was not known if those who remained inside did so willingly, but the F.B.I. decided to treat it as a hostage situation. One faction of the F.B.I. thought negotiation was the best way forward, while others thought that force was necessary. The F.B.I. used aggressive tactics to drive out the cult members, including playing loud, distorted music and disturbing sounds such as the squeals of a rabbit being slaughtered. They then cut off water and electricity supplies. The F.B.I.'s tactics were later criticized because they could have been part of what drove the sleep-deprived, wounded religious sect to their final act. The F.B.I. did not know how to deal with the Davidians' religious zeal, nor with the apparent willingness of the 21 children left inside to stay. Experts on apocalyptic religious cults tried to convince the F.B.I. that their aggressive siege tactics would only convince cult members that they were facing an end-of-the-world situation, making a violent outcome more likely. On April 19, 1993, the F.B.I. launched an assault on the compound. The agents went in firing tear gas and announcing that no shots would be fired. When the Davidians allegedly opened fire on the F.B.I., however, the agents returned fire. The Davidians had barricaded themselves into a building, and when the F.B.I. began to break in, several Davidians are believed to have set fire to it. In total, 75 Davidians died, 50 adults and 25 children, either buried under the collapsing building, burned alive, or 'mercy' shot by their own people.

SIEGE AT WACO

January 19
I.B.M. Announces Record Loss
I.B.M. reveals a $4.97 billion loss for 1992, which at this point is the largest ever single-year corporate loss in United States history.

February 11
Queen Pays Up
The Queen becomes the first British monarch to pay income tax, although the exact size of her fortune remains a closely guarded secret.

February 17
Haitian Ferry Disaster
The ferry *Neptune*, carrying 1,500 people, sinks 50 miles (80 km) west of Port-au-Prince, drowning over 500 passengers.

February 26
World Trade Center Bombed
A car bomb placed in an underground car park at the Twin Towers in New York explodes, killing six people and injuring hundreds.

1993

I.R.A. TARGETS LONDON AGAIN

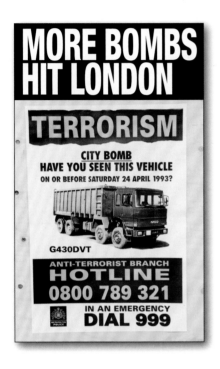

On April 24, 1993, the Provisional Irish Republican Army (I.R.A.) detonated a bomb in a truck in Bishopsgate, at the heart of London's financial district. The explosion killed one person, injured 44, and caused around $1.6 billion (£1 billion) worth of damage. There were fewer casualties than might have been expected because it was a Saturday and police had already spotted the abandoned Ford truck in which the one-ton bomb had been hidden. The police had also received warnings from the I.R.A. to clear the area. The only person killed was a press photographer for the *News of the World*, who ignored warnings to evacuate. The incident, the latest in a string of I.R.A. bomb attacks in London, prompted the City of London to set up a so-called 'ring of steel', involving tight security measures around the square mile of London's 'City' business area, with routes into the City guarded by armed police. By 1993, the peace talks for Northern Ireland were hanging in the balance, with Prime Minister John Major publicly refusing to enter negotiations until the I.R.A. called a ceasefire, arguing that 'those who use violence for political aims exclude themselves by their own actions'. He insisted that business should continue as usual in the City as much as possible, later writing of the event: 'They hardened our attitude, whereas they believed that their actions would soften it.'

JOINT PRIZE FOR SOUTH AFRICAN PEACE

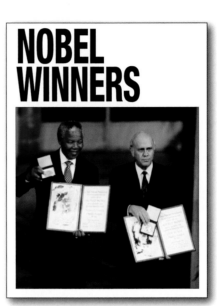

Nelson Mandela and F.W. de Klerk were awarded the Nobel Peace Prize in 1993 for working together to reverse the hatred caused by the apartheid policies of South Africa. They were awarded the prize as recognition of 'their work for the peaceful termination of the apartheid regime, and for laying the foundations for a new democratic South Africa.' As leader of the National Party, F.W. de Klerk became President of South Africa in 1989. He quickly called for an end to racial segregation. It was de Klerk who lifted the ban on the African National Congress (A.N.C.) and authorized Mandela's release. He subsequently entered into negotiations with Mandela and the A.N.C. to create a one-person, one-vote democratic system, which gave black citizens equal rights to whites. Although the two men worked together and created an iconic moment in South Africa's history by presenting a united front that had seemed unimaginable, the process of negotiation after that time was not easy. South Africa was collapsing economically, and de Klerk's historic political decision changed that. The joint actions of Mandela and de Klerk opened the way for a more hopeful future.

March 12
Storm of the Century Batters U.S.
A huge cyclonic snowstorm affects 26 U.S. states along the eastern seaboard, killing over 300 people and causing over $6 billion of damage. Some areas see 3.5 ft (1.1 m) of snow, producing drifts of up to 35 ft (11 m).

March 22
Pentium Chips Launched
Intel Corporation ships the first Pentium microprocessors, giving a speed boost to P.C.s and paving the way for the multimedia capabilities of modern computers.

March 29
Pacino Claims First Oscar
Having been nominated as Best Actor five times previously, Al Pacino finally picks up the coveted statue for his role in *Scent of a Woman*. He is also nominated for a Best Supporting Actor award for his role in *Glengarry Glen Ross*.

April 6
Russian Nuclear Accident
An explosion at the Tomsk-5 Nuclear Plant in Russia spreads nuclear contamination over a 78-mile (125-km) radius.

OIL TANKER DISASTER

The oil tanker *Braer* ran aground on the southern end of the Shetland Islands, which lie north of Scotland, on January 5, 1993. While traveling from Norway to Canada, the *Braer* was hit by hurricane-force winds, causing it to lose power and leaving it to the mercy of a violent sea. When it was clear that a collision was inevitable, the crew was airlifted to safety, while the tanker smashed against rocks in Quendale Bay. The *Braer* was carrying twice as much oil as the *Exxon Valdez* had been when it had run aground in Alaska four years earlier.

'Almost every last drop of the oil spilled out into the North Sea.'

Built in 1975, the ship did not have the double hull of more recent tankers, which might have prevented the spillage of the whole of its 85,000 tons of oil. Almost every last drop of the oil spilled out into the North Sea. Although local authorities had been prepared for such a disaster, fully aware of the rough conditions around their coastline, emergency measures were not enough to prevent an ecological catastrophe. The Shetland Islands are renowned worldwide for their marine and bird life, much of which suffered permanent damage as a result.

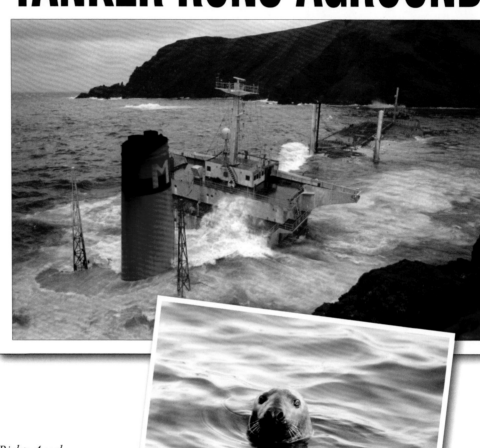

TANKER RUNS AGROUND

Right: A seal struggles in the oily water off the Shetland Islands.

May 27
Florence Bombing
A car bomb parked next to the Uffizi Museum in Florence kills five people, including the museum's curator, and damages many priceless works of art, destroying three Renaissance paintings.

April 30
Tennis Ace Stabbed
Women's number one Monica Seles is stabbed in the back at a match in Hamburg, Germany, by a deranged Steffi Graf fan. She returns to tennis in 1995, winning the Canadian Open.

September 13
Oslo Accords Signed
In a historic photo opportunity, Yasser Arafat and Yitzhak Rabin shake hands on the White House lawn, in the presence of U.S. President Bill Clinton.

October 19
Pakistan Elects Bhutto Again
Benazir Bhutto is elected for a second term as leader of Pakistan. She serves until 1996 before being removed following corruption charges.

1994

U.S. SENDS TROOPS INTO HAITI

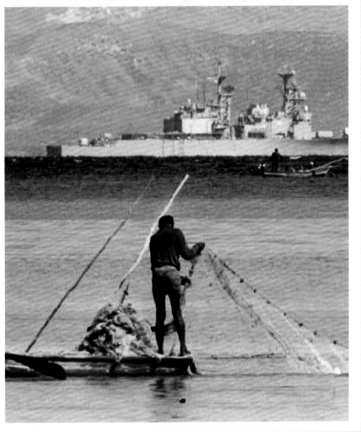

U.S. TROOPS SENT TO HAITI

On September 19, 1994, 20,000 U.S. troops landed in Haiti to oversee the return to power of Jean-Bertrand Aristide. Aristide, a Roman Catholic priest, had become president in Haiti's first free elections in 1991, but in the same year he was removed from power in a military coup. The coup had been supported by many of the country's economic elite, and it prompted a mass exit of many Haitians by boat. For three years, a three-man military junta treated the population with ruthless brutality – it is still not known how many people died – until the U.N. approved the use of force to return the elected leader Aristide. The U.S. responded to the call, and on September 18, 1994, just before the U.S. was preparing to use force against the military dictators, a diplomatic delegation led by former U.S. President Jimmy Carter negotiated a voluntary handover of power. Aristide was returned to power without any bloodshed, although the peace was not to last.

'Former U.S. President Jimmy Carter negotiated a voluntary handover of power.'

January 7
Skating Star Attacked
Top U.S. ice skater Nancy Kerrigan is attacked with a metal crowbar one month before the Winter Olympics. Investigations reveal that rival skater Tonya Harding's ex-husband is behind the attacks. Kerrigan goes on to win a silver medal in the Olympics.

February 12
The Scream Snatched
Thieves break into Oslo's National Art Museum and steal Edvard Munch's iconic painting *The Scream*. A ransom demand for $1 million is received but museum authorities refuse to pay, with the painting finally being recovered on May 7.

March 13
Nessie Photo Faked
The most famous alleged photo of the Loch Ness Monster, dating from 1934, is proved to be a fake after a relative of one of the men involved in creating it confesses. The picture was created by adding a head and neck onto a toy submarine and floating it in the lake.

March 21
Schindler's List Scoops Oscars
Steven Spielberg's film about a German businessman trying to save Jews from the Holocaust cleans up at the Oscars, picking up seven awards, including Best Director, Best Picture, and Best Original Score.

NELSON MANDELA ELECTED PRESIDENT OF SOUTH AFRICA

Despite the lifting of apartheid, violence remained a part of everyday life in South Africa. A new constitution was drafted in November 1993, establishing a timescale for elections in April 1994 and a five-year transitional government. Nelson Mandela and the African National Congress (A.N.C.) tried to encourage new investment in South Africa, but due to the ongoing unrest, foreign investors viewed the country as unstable. A few political parties still demanded a whites-only homeland and declared that they would boycott the elections. The U.N. provided personnel to oversee the elections, which were also being monitored by international mediators. Eventually, on March 31, 1994, President F.W. de Klerk was forced to declare a state of emergency in Natal and Kwazulu, where he deployed 3,000 troops to allow free elections to take place. Elections went ahead on April 26, 1994, with over 22 million voters turning out. Voting was extended to April 29, and tensions remained high, but by May 6, the Independent Electoral Commission gave the result of a 'substantially fair and free' election. The A.N.C. had won 62% of the votes, and Mandela was elected President.

RWANDAN GENOCIDE BEGINS

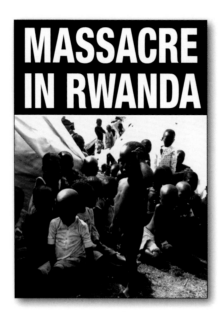

In Rwanda, from April 6, 1994, militia formed of ethnic Hutu began a campaign of brutality against the ethnic Tutsi population, killing 800,000 men, women, and children with machetes and clubs. Historically, the Tutsi, though only accounting for 15% of the population in the small Central African country, had been the aristocratic ruling class. Particularly during the era when Rwanda was a Belgian colony, the Tutsi minority had ruled over an 85% majority of Hutu peasants. However, as soon as the Belgians left in 1962, the Hutu majority took power and began to systematically oppress the Tutsis. Over 200,000 Tutsi fled to neighboring countries and set up a guerrilla force known as the Rwandan Patriotic Front. In 1990, this guerrilla force invaded Rwanda, forcing the Hutu president to sign a power-sharing agreement. Ethnic tensions continued to rise, as a U.N. peacekeeping force watched over the fragile ceasefire. When, on April 6, 1994, two Hutu presidents were shot down in a plane, Hutu militia went on a killing spree, targeting Tutsi civilians. After ten Belgian soldiers were tortured and murdered, the U.N. began to evacuate their personnel. A frenzy of cruelty was unleashed, and the churches and hospitals where Tutsis had taken refuge began to be specifically targeted. The U.N. planned to send forces back in, but they were too late. The genocide only stopped when Tutsi guerrilla groups from neighboring countries defeated the Hutus in July 1994. One tenth of the total population had been killed.

April 8
Kurt Cobain Found Dead
The body of Kurt Cobain, songwriter and lead singer of Nirvana, is discovered at his Lake Washington home. He died from a single gunshot wound to the head. A suicide note is found nearby.

May 1
Ayrton Senna Killed in Race Crash
Three-time Formula 1 champion Ayrton Senna is killed in an accident at the San Marino Grand Prix. His car leaves the track at a speed of 192 mph (309 kph) and crashes into a concrete wall.

May 6
Chunnel Opens
The Channel Tunnel between England and France is officially opened by the Queen and French President François Mitterrand. The tunnel allows trains to travel from London to Paris in 3 hours.

1994

TERRORIST STANDS TRIAL

THE JACKAL IS CAUGHT

Ilich Ramírez Sánchez, the Venezuelan-born international terrorist kwown popularly as 'Carlos the Jackal', was finally captured in Sudan on June 4, 1994 and extradited to France to face trial. Ramírez Sánchez converted to Islam and joined the Popular Front for the Liberation of Palestine, although first and foremost he styled himself as a revolutionary rather than an advocate of one particular cause. He was wanted for several terrorist crimes, ranging from bombings in London and Paris to taking 42 hostages at an Organization of Petroleum Exporting Countries (O.P.E.C.) meeting in Vienna in 1975. He was also thought to have been the mastermind behind the murder of the Israeli athletes at the Munich Olympics in 1972. However, there is no proof of his involvement in all the atrocities attributed to him, and his own almost certainly exaggerated boasts have confused the issue further. During the Cold War, Ramírez Sánchez had found sanctuary in Eastern Europe before settling in Damascus, Syria. By 1990, the Syrians had forced him to become inactive, eventually expelling him in 1991. He moved to Khartoum, Sudan, where he was protected for three years before the Sudanese authorities agreed a deal with France to hand him over. He was given over to French agents after coming into hospital for a routine operation. After three years spent in solitary confinement in a Paris jail, Carlos the Jackal was sentenced to life imprisonment for killing two French intelligence agents. He had always been proud of his notoriety and remained unapologetic to the end.

DEADLY EARTHQUAKE HITS LOS ANGELES

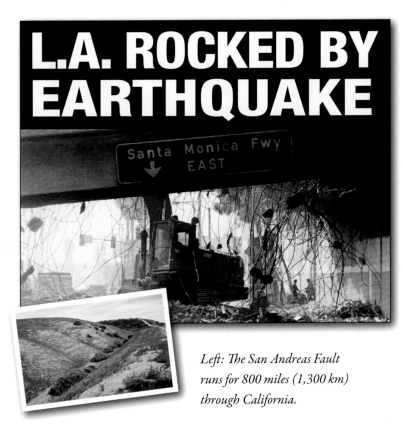

L.A. ROCKED BY EARTHQUAKE

Left: The San Andreas Fault runs for 800 miles (1,300 km) through California.

In the early hours of January 17, 1994, Los Angeles was rocked by a massive earthquake that measured 6.6 on the Richter scale and lasted for 40 seconds. In that short space of time, it caused $30 billion (£18 billion) worth of damage and killed 60 people. The San Fernando Valley was the worst hit, with over 3 million people affected and emergency services working around the clock to rescue people from collapsed buildings. Because of the damage to many hospital buildings, surgeons were forced to operate in the open air. The mayor of Los Angeles declared a state of emergency and imposed an evening curfew. President Clinton visited the city the week after the quake and asked Congress to raise $6 billion (£4 billion) for the relief effort.

July 8
Kim Il Sung Dies
Kim Il Sung, President of North Korea, dies. The longest-serving dictator of the 20th century, he had held power for 46 years and was succeeded by his son Kim Jong Il.

September 28
Baltic Ferry Disaster
The car ferry M.S. *Estonia*, sailing from Estonia to Sweden, sinks in the Baltic Sea, killing 852 people. An inquiry finds the cause of the accident to be crew error and the design of the ferry's doors.

November 5
Reagan Reveals Alzheimer's Diagnosis
Former U.S. President Ronald Reagan announces that he has been diagnosed with Alzheimer's disease, a degenerative form of dementia.

December 11
Chechnya Invaded
Russian President Boris Yeltsin orders troops and tanks into the southern Russian republic of Chechnya. Chechen separatists fight a 20-month war with Russia during which 100,000 people are killed.

BOMBING IN OKLAHOMA CITY KILLS 168 PEOPLE

On the morning of April 19, 1995, a bomb exploded outside the Alfred P. Murrah Federal Building in Oklahoma City. It was 9.05 a.m., and most employees had already arrived at work, many having first dropped off their children at the building's daycare center. The bomb ripped off the front of the building, and by the time rescue workers had finished sifting through the rubble weeks later, the bomb had claimed 168 victims, including 19 children. The bomb had been planted by U.S. citizen Timothy McVeigh, a former army sergeant, who was pulled over by police hours later for driving without a license plate and carrying an unlicensed weapon. It was only when he was about to be released that someone recognized his similarity to the sketch of one of the bomb suspects. Since leaving the army, McVeigh had developed increasingly paranoid political views, and he was convinced that the U.S. government was becoming a controlling dictatorship. He belonged to various white-supremacist groups, and traveled the country attending gun shows and selling bumper stickers that said, 'Fear the Government that Fears your Gun'. The bombing of the Oklahoma City Federal Building, where the Alcohol, Firearms, and Tobacco Agency had offices, had first been suggested to him when he spent time at an anti-government, white-supremacist compound known as Elohim City on the Arkansas-Oklahoma border. Although he was thought to be part of a wider conspiracy and certainly had accomplices, Timothy McVeigh was found guilty of planting and detonating the bomb, and he alone was executed by lethal injection on June 11, 2001.

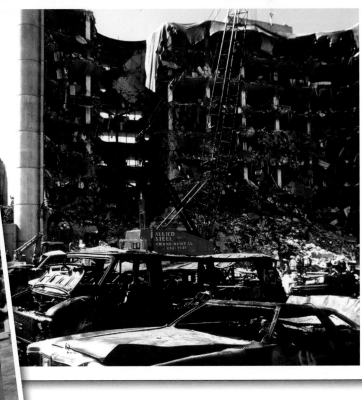

Left: The memorial to victims of the bombing in Oklahoma City.

January 1
World Trade Organization Founded
The W.T.O. is a global body designed to establish rules of trade between nations. It has over 150 members, representing 95% of global trade.

February 21
Solo Balloon Flight Across Pacific
Adventurer Steve Fossett lands his hot air balloon in Saskatchewan, Canada, becoming the first person to make a solo flight across the Pacific Ocean.

May 1
Chirac Elected President of France
Jacques Chirac, the Gaullist candidate, is elected the new President of France, taking over from socialist François Mitterrand.

ROGUE TRADER FELLS BANK

BARINGS BANK COLLAPSES

Nick Leeson, who came from a working-class London background, had first landed a job in the banking industry in the 1980s and, specializing in Far Eastern currency markets, had worked his way up to becoming Barings Bank's star Singapore trader. By 1993, he was working in Singapore and had earned the bank $16 million (£10 million), taking a $220,000 (£130,000) bonus and $80,000 (£50,000) salary. It seemed that nothing could stop this rising star. But in 1994, Leeson's luck began to turn. By the end of the year, his losses for the bank stood at $360 million (£208 million). Then the Kobe earthquake in Japan in January 1995 changed the Far Eastern currency market, and Nick Leeson's star began to fall. He requested more and more money to dig himself out of the crisis, and when the bank did an audit later that year, losses amounted to $1.2 billion (£800 million), which Leeson had managed to conceal by fraud. He went on the run to Borneo and then Frankfurt, but he was eventually extradited by Germany back to Singapore, where he was sentenced to six and a half years in prison. The executives who should have been overseeing him either resigned or were fired. Barings Bank, Great Britain's oldest merchant bank and the personal bank of the Queen, collapsed and was bought for just under $2 (£1) by the Dutch financial group I.N.G.

ISRAELI PREMIER ASSASSINATED

RABIN ASSASSINATED

On November 4, 1995, Israeli Premier Yitzhak Rabin was assassinated by a right-wing Zionist who opposed Rabin's peace negotiations that had resulted in the Oslo Accords. Yitzhak Rabin had been participating in a rally celebrating the Oslo Accords in Tel Aviv when Yigal Amir shot him three times. Rabin had declined to wear a bulletproof vest that day. The Oslo Accords, signed in Washington, D.C. in September 1993 in the presence of Palestine Liberation Organization (P.L.O.) Chairman Yasser Arafat, Israeli Premier Yitzhak Rabin, and U.S. President Bill Clinton, set out a framework for future peaceful relations between Israel and a Palestinian state, allowing territorial trade-offs to a Palestinian Authority. The agreement involved the withdrawal of the Israel Defense Forces (I.D.F.) from parts of the Gaza Strip and the West Bank, and it was the first time a face-to-face agreement had been reached between Israel and the Palestinians. The assassination shocked the people of Israel, who held rallies and renamed parts of the city after their respected leader.

July 13
Chicago Heatwave
The Midwestern U.S.A. experiences a week of record temperatures ranging from 90° to 106°F (32°–41°C), causing 465 deaths.

July 15
Srebrenica Massacre
Bosnian Serbs seize the former safe haven of Srebrenica, where thousands of Muslim refugees are sheltering from the Balkan conflict under the protection of Dutch peacekeepers. Mass graves are later discovered and it is thought that up to 8,000 Muslim men were killed by Serb soldiers.

August 24
Microsoft Launches Windows 95
The successor to Windows 3 is launched with great fanfare, including an advertising campaign built around the Rolling Stones song 'Start Me Up', a reference to the new 'start' button built into the interface.

September 3
Ebay Founded
Computer programmer Pierre Omidyar founds the online auction site, and the first item sold is a broken laser printer. Ebay now boasts over 84 million users worldwide.

EARTHQUAKE HITS KOBE, JAPAN

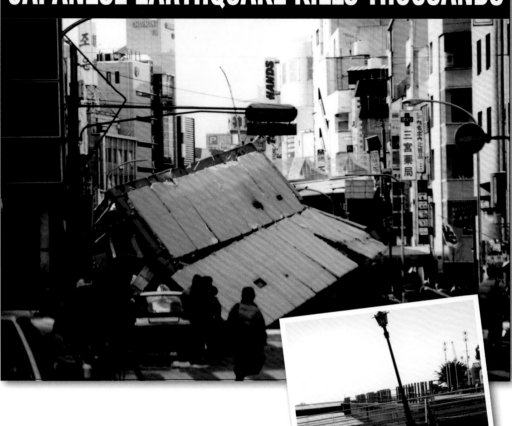

JAPANESE EARTHQUAKE KILLS THOUSANDS

An earthquake with a magnitude of 7.2 on the Richter scale hit Japan on January 17, 1995, devastating entire cities and killing thousands of people. The most powerful earthquake to hit Japan for 47 years struck in the early morning, just as commuters were beginning their journeys to work. The worst-affected city was the port of Kobe, home to around 1.5 million people, where apartment blocks fell to the ground and a raised freeway collapsed, throwing 50 cars off the edge. Damaged water and gas pipes obstructed rescue operations, and electricity was cut off in many areas. At the end of all rescue attempts, it emerged that 6,433 people had died. A further 27,000 had been injured, and 45,000 homes had been destroyed. It was one of the most disastrous earthquakes in Japan's history. Prime Minister Tomiichi Murayama set up an emergency committee and sent troops to help with the rescue operation. The cost of rebuilding Kobe reached the $100 billion (£60 billion) mark, and the city found it difficult to rebuild its population, many of whom left for good after the quake.

Right: the Earthquake Memorial in Meriken Park, Kobe.

'At the end of all rescue attempts, it emerged that 6,433 people had died. A further 27,000 had been injured, and 45,000 homes had been destroyed.'

October 24
Solar Eclipse Over Asia
A total solar eclipse can be seen from Iran, India, Thailand, and Southeast Asia.

November 19
Toy Story Premiered
The first entirely computer-generated animated film is produced by Pixar Animation and features the voices of Tom Hanks and Tim Allen. Since its release it has grossed over $190 million.

December 4
Beatles Release New Single
Fifteen years after the death of John Lennon, The Beatles release a new single, 'Free as a Bird'. Based around a vocal recording of Lennon, the track was created by the surviving three Beatles and producer Jeff Lynne.

December 14
Balkan War Ends
Bosnia, Serbia, and Croatia sign the Dayton Accord in Paris to bring the three-year conflict to an end. The deal is brokered by U.S. President Bill Clinton and is followed by the arrival of a N.A.T.O. peacekeeping force.

1996

I.R.A. BOMBS LONDON

MORE BOMBS HIT LONDON

During 1996, the Provisional Irish Republican Army (I.R.A.) stepped up its bombing campaign on mainland Great Britain. The first target was the Docklands area of London, the redeveloped commercial district, which was hit by a bomb on February 10. This bomb marked the end of a 17-month ceasefire during which British, American, and Irish leaders had failed to reach an agreement on a peaceful end to the Irish 'Troubles'. Two men, both newsagents, were killed, and 39 others were injured by the blast, which brought down a six-story building and damaged several others.

In 1998, James McArdle was jailed for 25 years on the charge of conspiracy to cause an explosion, but he was released under the terms of the Good Friday Agreement in 2000. Just over one week after the first explosion, another bomb went off on a double-decker bus in central London. Only one person was killed, the I.R.A. bomber Edward O'Brien who had been transporting the bomb to another location when it accidentally went off. Then, in June 1996, soon after peace talks had resumed, another I.R.A. bomb went off in a busy shopping district of Manchester. This time there were no fatalities, but many people were seriously injured by the flying glass that resulted. British Prime Minister John Major insisted that peace talks would continue.

> **'This bomb marked the end of a 17-month ceasefire during which British, American, and Irish leaders had failed to reach any agreement on a peaceful end to the Irish "Troubles".'**

Left: Gerry Adams, leader of Sinn Fein.

January 20
First Palestinian Election

Polls open in the first ever election for a Palestinian President and parliament. Yasser Arafat wins the poll for President, taking 88% of the vote.

February 10
Chess Computer Defeats Grand Master

Chess computer Deep Blue defeats world chess champion Garry Kasparov for the first time. Although the I.B.M. machine wins one game, Kasparov wins the overall match.

March 20
British Beef in B.S.E. Panic

The British Government announces that the disease B.S.E. (Bovine Spongiform Encephalopathy, more commonly known as Mad Cow Disease) found in British cattle, could be transmitted to humans.

March 25
'Year of the Independents' at the Oscars

Anthony Minghella's *The English Patient* takes nine awards, making it the third most decorated film in the history of the Oscars.

BOMBING AT 100TH OLYMPICS, ATLANTA

ATTACK AT THE OLYMPICS

Above: The Atlanta Olympics was successfully completed despite the blast.

At the end of the first full week of the 1996 Summer Olympic Games in Atlanta, Georgia, U.S.A., an event that had already been riddled with logistical problems was rocked by a bomb blast. The bomb went off in the early hours of July 27 in Centennial Olympic Park, where tens of thousands of fans were attending an evening rock concert. The explosion killed two people: an American woman and a Turkish cameraman, who suffered a fatal heart attack. America was already feeling vulnerable to the threat of terrorism following the T.W.A. plane explosion that had killed 230 people only ten days earlier. The Centennial Olympic Park bomb blast brought home to the watching world that even a 30,000-strong security presence could not protect people from terrorism, despite the chief organizer's claim before the games that, 'The safest place on this wonderful planet will be Atlanta during the time of our Games.' In April 2005, Eric Robert Rudolph pleaded guilty to planting the bomb.

EVIDENCE OF LIFE FOUND ON MARS

FOSSIL FOUND IN MARTIAN ROCKS

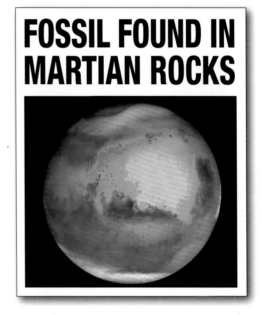

'The complex organic compounds within the rock point toward biological origins'

In August 1996, N.A.S.A. scientists announced that they had discovered evidence of fossil life on the planet Mars. Their claim was based on the discovery of a meteorite in an Antarctic ice field in 1984. According to extensive analysis, this specific chunk of rock had been ejected into space from Mars during an asteroid impact 15 million years ago, and it then orbited as a small planet before being buried in the Antarctic Ocean 13,000 years ago. The complex organic compounds within the rock point toward biological origins, which suggests the existence of life within the rock at one time. The life-forms present in the rock are simple micro-organisms that are similar to bacteria and are believed to be around 3 or 4 billion years old.

Left: the microscopic image of the possible bacteria.

April 3
Unabomber Arrested

Police in the U.S.A. arrest the man behind an 18-year bombing campaign that killed 3 people and injured 23 others. The nickname 'Unabomber' came from the initial letters of his most common targets – universities and airlines.

July 19
Bosnian Serb President Radovan Karadžic Resigns

The President resigns after being indicted on war crimes charges, and the issue of an international arrest warrant. He is not apprehended until 2008, when he is discovered in Belgrade.

July 25
Paris Underground Bombing Campaign

An explosion on the Paris Metro underground rail system marks the start of a bombing campaign by the Armed Islamic Group. The attacks continue until October, killing eight people and wounding hundreds.

1996

GUNMAN MASSACRES PRIMARY SCHOOL CHILDREN

On March 13, 1996, a man entered an elementary school assembly hall in Dunblane, Scotland, firing bullets all around him and killing 16 children and their teacher. It was 9.30 a.m., and the five- and six-year-old children had just started a P.E. class when Thomas Watt Hamilton, a local man, walked in and showered them with bullets before turning the gun on himself. Hamilton had once been a scoutmaster but had been fired after concerns about his behavior around young boys. His suspicious behavior had put him on police registers, and he was known to have a license for six guns. However, an inquiry ruled that his actions on that day in March could not possibly have been predicted. The tragedy shocked and devastated the local tight-knit community. The Snowdrop Campaign, launched after the Dunblane Massacre, as it has come to be known, has since successfully tightened gun control in Great Britain, making it illegal to buy or own a handgun. Campaigners also aimed to set up a centralized database of gun owners in the U.K.

'The tragedy shocked and devastated the local tight-knit community.'

CHILDREN KILLED BY GUNMAN

JET CRASHES AS FUEL TANK EXPLODES

JET CRASHES IN ATLANTIC

On July 1, 1996, T.W.A. flight 800 left New York bound for Rome via Paris, but minutes later the plane exploded in mid-air, killing all 230 people onboard. Although several emergency vehicles reached the spot where the plane had crashed into the Atlantic Ocean within minutes, there were no survivors to be rescued. The first assumption was that the explosion had been caused by terrorist sabotage, and the F.B.I. launched a simultaneous investigation with the aviation authorities. The F.B.I. interviewed several witnesses, many of whom claimed to have seen a streak of light approach the plane before the explosion, and there were suggestions that an external missile had caused the explosion. However, detailed examination of the wreckage could not find any evidence to support this theory, nor the theory that a bomb onboard had caused the explosion. At the end of its investigations, the National Transportation Safety Board concluded that the probable cause was an explosion in the center wing fuel tank.

August 28
Prince Charles and Princess Diana Divorce
The royal couple's marriage officially comes to an end with the granting of a decree nisi. Diana loses her royal title (Her Royal Highness) and is now known as simply Diana, Princess of Wales.

September 7
Tupac Shakur Gunned Down
The 25-year-old American rapper is killed in a drive-by shooting following a feud between East and West Coast gangs and rappers. New York rapper Notorious B.I.G. is shot dead in a revenge attack six months later.

November 6
Bill Clinton Wins Second Term
Incumbent U.S. President Bill Clinton wins a second term after a presidential race against Republican Bob Dole, taking 48% of the vote.

November 7
Huge Cyclone Hits India
The storm hits the eastern coast of India, leaving fishing villages marooned after waves surge as far as 3 miles (5 km) inland, with wind speeds of up to 140 mph (230 kph). Over 1,000 people are thought to die.

COMET HALE-BOPP PASSES EARTH

Referred to as the 'Great Comet', the most spectacular astronomical sight of 1997 was the appearance of the Hale-Bopp comet in the night sky. The comet came closest to Earth on March 22, 1997, and its closest approach to the Sun, when it showed at its brightest, was on April 1, 1997. Amateur astronomers Alan Hale in New Mexico and Thomas Bopp in Arizona separately discovered the comet on the same day in 1995. A comet's head, known as the 'coma', is made up of dust and gas, but at its center is a solid nucleus of rock, dust, and ice. Observations conducted from N.A.S.A. observatories estimated that Hale-Bopp's nucleus is between 19 and 25 miles (30–45 km) in diameter. By comparison, the comet that is thought to have struck Earth 65 million years ago, probably causing the extinction of the dinosaurs, is estimated to have been 6 to 9 miles (10–12 km) in diameter. After the 1997 appearance, it is calculated that the Hale-Bopp comet will disappear from sight again until the year 4397.

'NEW LABOUR' WIN

In May 1997, at the age of 43, Tony Blair became the youngest Prime Minister of Great Britain for 200 years. Following a law degree at Oxford University and several years as a lawyer in London, Blair had entered the House of Commons in 1983 as a Member of Parliament (M.P.) for Sedgefield in County Durham, England. At the age of 30, he was the youngest Labour M.P. in the House of Commons. In the build-up to his election as Prime Minister, Tony Blair had pledged the complete reform of the Labour Party, changing politics in an attempt to broaden the party's appeal beyond its base in the trade union movement. Within the shadow government cabinet, Blair had found a close ally in Gordon Brown, and the two rapidly moved up party ranks together. When the death of Labour leader John Smith in 1994 left the job open, the Labour Party was divided over whether so-called modernizers such as Blair should take over. Blair eventually won and rebranded the party 'New Labour'.

March 26
Heaven's Gate Cult Mass Suicide
The San Diego cult believe that the Hale-Bopp comet is a sign that they should leave their earthly bodies behind to join a spacecraft flying behind the comet. Thirty-nine members of the cult commit suicide by drinking a deadly cocktail of vodka and barbiturates.

April 12
Plot to Kill Pope Foiled
Twenty anti-tank mines are found under a bridge in Sarajevo, Bosnia, on the Pope's planned route around the city. The devices are discovered the day before the Pope is due to arrive, but the visit goes ahead as planned.

April 13
Tiger Woods Becomes Youngest Ever Winner of U.S. Masters
At the age of 21, Tiger Woods also becomes the first black golfer to win a major tournament, with a winning margin of 12 strokes.

1997

PRINCESS KILLED IN HIGH-SPEED CRASH

DIANA KILLED IN CAR CRASH

'The Princess was alive when she was removed from the scene of the crash, but two hours of surgeons' efforts failed to save her life.'

In the early hours of August 31, 1997, Princess Diana was killed in a car crash in Paris. The nation awoke to the news, and there was an unmatched outpouring of public grief, with thousands flocking to Kensington Palace, where she resided, to lay flowers. The Princess had left the Ritz Hotel in Paris with her companion Dodi Fayed, son of the Harrods owner Mohammed al Fayed, when her car was pursued aggressively by paparazzi. This was not unusual, but on this occasion her driver, who was subsequently discovered to have taken both drugs and alcohol, dramatically increased his speed, and the car crashed in a tunnel downtown. The Princess was alive when she was removed from the scene of the crash, but two hours of surgeons' efforts failed to save her life. The Prince of Wales was with the rest of the royal family at Balmoral Castle in Scotland, where he broke the news of their mother's death to his sons, Princes William and Harry. Buckingham Palace issued a statement saying that the Queen and the Prince of Wales were 'deeply shocked and distressed'. Mohammed al Fayed, whose son was also killed in the crash, claimed that Diana had

Above: The Pont d'Alma tunnel in Paris, where the fatal crash took place.

April 22
Embassy Siege In Peru
A four-month siege at the Japanese Embassy in Peru is brought to an end when the building is stormed by security forces. All 12 of the Túpac Amaru rebels inside the embassy are killed, with all but one of the 72 hostages freed.

June 30
First Harry Potter Book Published
London publisher Bloomsbury issues the first of J.K. Rowling's novels for children, entitled *Harry Potter & the Philosopher's Stone*. The series of books has subsequently sold over 400 million copies.

July 1
Hong Kong Handed Back to China
British governor Chris Patten transfers control of Hong Kong back to the Chinese authorities after more than 150 years of British rule.

Left: Mohammed al Fayed, father of Diana's companion Dodi.

been engaged to Dodi, and he was convinced that the royal family had them killed. However, despite a major inquest into the crash, only Henri Paul, the driver, has been found to be at fault. The paparazzi photographers were not officially charged, although their behavior opened up widespread criticism of the increasingly aggressive tactics used by the tabloid press. Princess Diana was given a full state funeral at Westminster Abbey; around 1 million people lined the streets in order to witness the passing of her funeral procession.

'Despite a major inquest into the crash, only Henri Paul, the driver, has been found to be at fault.'

Right: Henri Paul, the driver, who had been drinking.

Above: (From left to right) Earl Spencer, Princess Diana's brother; Princes William and Harry, her two sons; and Prince Charles, her ex-husband, attend the funeral.

July 4
N.A.S.A. Probe Lands on Mars
The Pathfinder probe was launched in December 1996, and arrives on Mars seven months later, delivering a robotic vehicle capable of traveling over the Martian surface to analyze the geology and climate of the red planet.

July 15
Gianni Versace Murdered
The Italian fashion designer is shot dead outside his Miami mansion by Andrew Cunanan. Versace was the fifth victim in a murderous four-month rampage that ended when the gay prostitute shot himself with the same gun used to kill Versace.

September 5
Mother Teresa Dies
After a lifetime caring for the sick and needy, Mother Teresa dies at the headquarters of the order she founded in Calcutta. The Missionaries of Charity forsake all modern conveniences, beg for food, and are allowed home to visit their families once every five years.

1997

MAMMAL CLONED FOR FIRST TIME

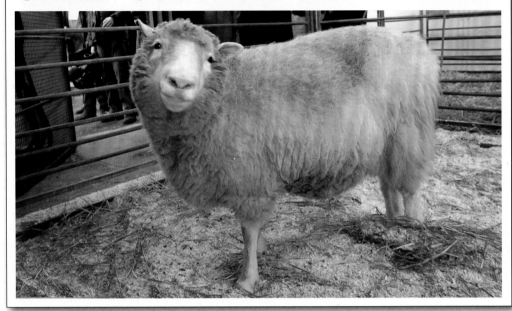

SHEEP SUCCESSFULLY CLONED

'D.N.A. tests revealed that Dolly is identical in every way to the sheep from which she was cloned and shows no genetic similarity to the surrogate mother sheep.'

On February 11, 1997, a group of scientists in Edinburgh announced that they had successfully cloned a ewe using the cell of another adult sheep. Dolly the sheep had actually been born on July 5, 1996, but the announcement was delayed so that her development could be monitored before it was made public. The cloned sheep was created by inserting a single cell from another sheep's udder into an egg, which was then implanted into a surrogate mother sheep. Dolly's birth marked the first time a mammal had successfully been cloned from an adult cell, rather than from an embryo, as with previous experiments. D.N.A. tests revealed that Dolly is identical in every way to the sheep from which she was cloned and shows no genetic similarity to the surrogate mother sheep. The cloning raised ethical questions and sparked fears of human cloning, but Dr. Ian Wilmut, who led the team of scientists, insisted that the cloning of human beings was a 'repugnant' idea, as well as being illegal. P.P.L. Therapeutics, which has bought the rights to the cloning experiments, say that the groundbreaking work will help research into currently incurable genetic diseases. In 2003, Dolly was put down when it was found that she had a fatal lung disease. Her preserved body is on display at the National Museum of Scotland.

September 12
Scotland Votes for own Parliament
A referendum in favor of devolution means that Scotland will have its own parliament for the first time in over 300 years.

September 26
Quake Shakes Italy
A double quake in central Italy badly damages the Basilica of St. Francis in Assisi, killing four people and destroying a priceless series of frescoes by the medieval artist Cimabue. The church is restored at a cost of $50 million and reopens in 1999.

December 17
Landmine Treaty Signed
122 governments sign the treaty banning antipersonnel landmines, known as the Ottawa Treaty. Over 150 countries have now ratified the treaty, but superpowers such as Russia, China, and the United States have not signed.

TALIBAN BANS TELEVISION

15 DAYS TO HAND IN YOUR TV

By 1994, Afghanistan had been divided up by the various conflicting groups within its borders. At the same time, the powerful Mujahideen commanders had established themselves as warlords, and in the southern city of Qandahar, they routinely terrorized the local population. Under former Mujahid Mohammed Omar, a mullah in the Qandahar province, other former Mujahideen opposed to the warlords established a group that called themselves 'taliban', meaning seekers or students. Their aim was to establish Islamic law and order, or at least their own interpretation of it. The Taliban began by attacking the notorious warlords in a series of successful military campaigns. They took control of Qandahar and demilitarized it, before moving on toward Kabul. Pakistan soon made an ally of the Taliban, and Osama bin Laden found a safe haven for his Al-Qaeda troops with them. Their strict, oppressive regime forced women to wear burkas and forbade them to work outside of the home. Every aspect of 'modern' life was banned, including music, dancing, and, in 1998, television. On July 8, 1998, Afghans were given two weeks to hand in their televisions.

U.S. AND U.K. BOMB IRAQ

ATTACK ON IRAQ

On December 16, 1998, the U.S. and Great Britain launched a three-day bombing attack on Iraq known as Operation Desert Fox. Iraqi leader Saddam Hussein was accused of obstructing weapons inspectors, and U.S. President Clinton had threatened the use of force if Saddam's regime did not fall into line with United Nations resolutions. Coalition forces bombed 100 targets with the aim of 'degrading' Saddam's capacity to produce weapons of mass destruction, but as President Clinton acknowledged, 'there will be unintended Iraqi casualties'. Coalition forces blew up various suspected chemical and biological weapons plants, as well as residential sites housing Saddam's secret police. After the three-day attack, the Iraqi Deputy Prime Minister stated that 62 military personnel had been killed, but there were also civilian casualties. Iraq's actual weapons capacity remains a highly disputed question.

Left: U.S. President Bill Clinton, who ordered the bombing.

January 11
Algerian Massacre
Islamic extremists kill over 400 people in an attack on two villages in the northwest of Algeria, as part of an ongoing civil war that claims over 100,000 lives.

February 3
N.A.T.O. Jet Brings Down Cable Car
A low-flying N.A.T.O. jet severs the cable holding a cable car in the Dolomites, causing the deaths of the 20 people inside. The pilot is jailed in 1999 for conducting unauthorized maneuvers.

May 15
Frank Sinatra Dies
Ol' Blue Eyes passes away after a year of ill health following a heart attack in 1997.

1998

AL-QAEDA ATTACKS

U.S. EMBASSIES ATTACKED

On August 7, 1998, bombs exploded outside the U.S. embassies in Nairobi, Kenya, and Dar es Salaam, Tanzania. The terrorist attacks, which killed 224 people, prompted the first military action by the U.S. against Osama bin Laden, who was engaged in a public campaign of violent terrorism against the U.S. From a wealthy family in Saudi Arabia, Osama had first become involved in anti-Western, militant Islamism when he helped to finance the Afghans in resisting the Soviet invasion in 1979. It was there that he formed his own army, known as Al-Qaeda. After his expulsion from Saudi Arabia and Sudan for terrorist activities, Osama bin Laden took refuge in Afghanistan, under the fundamentalist Taliban regime, and issued a fatwah, or religious declaration, calling for the death of Americans. In the 1998 attack on the U.S. Embassy in Nairobi, 213 people were killed and many more were seriously injured when 2,000 lb (900 kg) of T.N.T. explosives were detonated from a van outside the embassy's doors. U.S. President Clinton ordered a military strike against Al-Qaeda training camps in Afghanistan on August 20, 1998. In November, the U.S. charged Osama bin Laden and 21 others with the bombing of the embassies.

PEACE AT LAST FOR NORTHERN IRELAND

PEACE IN IRELAND

After 30 years of bloody conflict and two years of peace talks, on April 10, 1998, Great Britain and Ireland finally reached an agreement over Northern Ireland. The solution, known as the Good Friday Agreement, was seen as a triumph for British Prime Minister Tony Blair and his Irish counterpart Bertie Ahern. The agreement involved the creation of a Northern Ireland Assembly and significant links between Northern Ireland and the Republic of Ireland. The proposals set out in the agreement were sent to every household in Northern Ireland to be voted on in a referendum in May 1998, and the people voted a resounding 'yes'.

April 15
Pol Pot Dies
The former dictator of Cambodia dies of a suspected heart attack, a year after he is deposed as the leader of the Khmer Rouge.

May 6
Apple Launches the iMac
Following the return of founder member Steve Jobs to head up the company, Apple announces the product that is to revolutionize their fortunes over the next five years. Created by British designer Jonathan Ive, the iMac's clean simple lines and iconic design are a huge hit.

May 28
Pakistan Nuclear Tests
Tension between India and Pakistan is heightened when Pakistan tests five nuclear devices under the mountains near its border with Afghanistan.

November 7
New Court of Human Rights
The European Court of Human Rights opens in Strasbourg, France. All 47 member states of the Council of Europe are bound by its judgements.

1999

STUDENTS GO ON ARMED RAMPAGE AT SCHOOL

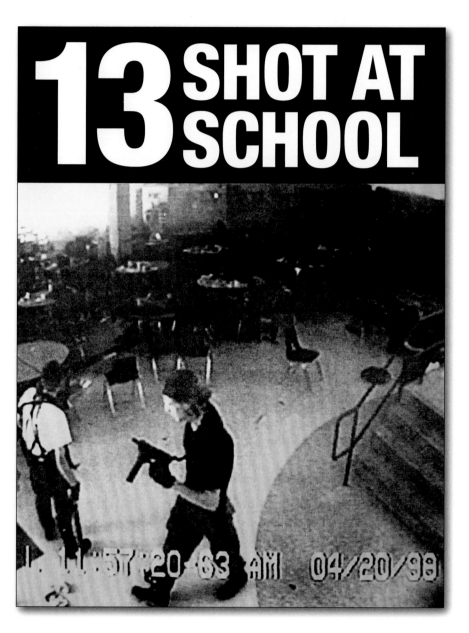

On April 20, 1999, two teenagers, Dylan Klebold and Eric Harris, walked into their high school, their trench coats loaded with guns, knives, and explosives, with the intention of killing as many people as possible before committing suicide. In the end, they killed 12 students and one teacher before killing themselves. The Columbine High School massacre left the suburban Colorado community not only shocked and angry, but also utterly confused. No one could figure out why these two apparently fairly typical teenagers from stable homes had committed such a horrific crime. According to documentary evidence that the boys left behind, Klebold and Harris had been planning the attack, in which they hoped to kill as many as 500 of their peers, for more than a year. Diaries created a confusing image of the two boys downloading recipes for explosives

'In the end, they killed 12 students and one teacher before killing themselves.'

and making them, at the same time as worrying about who they should take to the prom. The two boys had been friends for several years, and although they found it difficult to fit in at their high school, they were not otherwise abnormal. The only clue that could provide any possible motive was a general sense of hatred that they both felt toward the world and toward people in general. The objects of their hatred, however, were often contradictory: they hated both minorities and racists, for example. Even after working on the case for a year, the lead investigator was unable to give any clear-cut answers: 'There's not an easy answer,' she said, 'I can't tell you why it happened.'

January 25
Colombia Quake
One thousand people are killed when an earthquake measuring 6 on the Richter scale hits Colombia. Many older buildings are unable to withstand the tremors, which leave 200,000 homeless.

March 8
Joe DiMaggio Dies
Known as 'The Yankee Clipper,' and one-time husband of Marilyn Monroe, he played baseball in the 1940s and 1950s but latterly became known for his charity work.

April 30
Nail Bombs Hit London
A nail bomb explodes in a busy city center pub in Soho, London's gay district, killing two people. The bomb is the third in a series targeting minority groups. David Copeland, a self-confessed Nazi, is later imprisoned for the attacks.

1999

MONETARY UNION

NEW EUROPEAN CURRENCY

On January 1, 1999, 11 European countries replaced their national currencies with the newly created euro, a single European currency. The previous day, exchange rates between the old currencies and the euro had been permanently fixed. Germany, France, Italy, Spain, Holland, Belgium, Austria, Portugal, Finland, Ireland, and Luxembourg all made the switch. Greece qualified to join the euro two years afterward, with Slovenia (2006), Malta (2007), Cyprus (2007), and Slovakia (2008) joining later. All the participating countries had to meet criteria that had been established by the 1992 Maastricht Treaty. Although the individual national currencies of the first 11 countries remained in circulation for another three years, acting as smaller denominations of the euro, commerce between banks and stock market trading immediately adopted the euro as its sole currency. The actual circulation of euro coins and bills started on January 1, 2002, known as 'E Day', when the old currencies became invalid.

EUROPE AT WAR

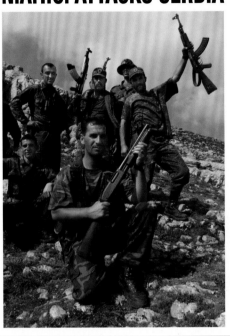

N.A.T.O. ATTACKS SERBIA

On March 24, 1999, N.A.T.O. launched the second military action in its history when it began a bombing campaign against Belgrade, the Yugoslav capital. N.A.T.O. was acting to end the oppressive treatment of Albanians in Kosovo by Serbians under President Slobodan Milošević. Operation Allied Force was carried out entirely from the air to avoid loss of any N.A.T.O. personnel. For several years, Milošević and his Serbian forces had been carrying out a policy of ethnic cleansing, during which 850,000 Albanians were forced from their homes. Some fled into the neighboring countries of Albania and Macedonia, but others were simply displaced within Kosovo, where they were at the mercy of violent Serbian militia. The war ended on June 11, 1999, when the Yugoslav government agreed to withdraw Serbian forces from Kosovo, which nonetheless remained part of Serbia. Milošević saw the outcome as a victory, but he fell from power a year later and was eventually indicted for war crimes.

Above: Prijedor, in Bosnia, an area 'ethnically cleansed' by Serb forces.

June 1
Napster Launched
Shawn Fanning creates software that allows computer users to swap music files across the Internet via a central directory. The service quickly becomes hugely popular, with millions of files shared for free among users.

June 14
Thabo Mbeki Elected President of South Africa
Nelson Mandela's successor is sworn in as head of South Africa's second democratically elected government. The A.N.C. takes two-thirds of the seats in the parliament.

June 19
Horror Writer Stephen King Injured
The bestselling author is hit by a motorist while walking in Maine, U.S.A. Earlier in the year he had been working on a novel in which the protagonist dies after a car accident.

July 23
Woodstock 99 Festival Held
Thirty years after the original Woodstock Festival, an anniversary event takes place. Over 200,000 people attend.

KING HUSSEIN OF JORDAN DIES

King Hussein of Jordan, who had been a stabilizing force for peace in the Middle East during his 46 years of rule, died on February 7, 1999. He had been suffering from lymphatic cancer for some time, and he eventually died of heart failure at the age of 63. His son, Prince Abdullah, was sworn in as his successor, but there were fears about what would happen in the region once the great peacemaker was gone. U.S. President Clinton described King Hussein as 'a man who believed that we are all God's children, bound to live together in mutual respect and tolerance' and that, when peace finally comes to the Middle East, 'his name will be inscribed upon it'.

KING HUSSEIN DIES

TOTAL ECLIPSE OF THE SUN

On August 11, 1999, a total eclipse of the Sun was visible from the U.K., a phenomenon which had not occurred since 1927 and will not do so again until 2090. The eclipse was total along a path stretching from the North Atlantic to India, and in the U.K. it was visible for longest from Cornwall on the southwest tip of the coast of England and in the Scilly Isles off the coast of Cornwall. The partial phase was visible from all over Britain. The total eclipse lasted for around 2 minutes, with the longest visibility in Romania, where it lasted 2 minutes and 23 seconds. The spectacular phenomenon occurs when the Sun, Moon and Earth coincide in a straight line during their orbits around each other. The Sun is about 400 times larger than the Moon, but it is also about 400 times farther away, so when all three lie in a straight line with the Moon at the center, the Moon blocks out the Sun's light to the Earth in certain pathways. All over the world, people flocked to witness this once-in-a-lifetime sight, many traveling great distances to ensure the best possible chance of seeing it.

SOLAR ECLIPSE

May 2
Oliver Reed Dies
Notorious actor Oliver Reed dies during a break in the filming of Ridley Scott's *Gladiator*.

May 28
'Last Supper' Returned to Public View
One of Leonardo da Vinci's most famous paintings is returned to public display in the church of Santa Maria delle Grazie, Milan, after over 20 years of restoration work.

December 30
Beatle Stabbed in his Home
Former Beatle George Harrison and his wife Olivia are attacked in their mansion by an intruder.

December 31
World Welcomes New Millennium
People around the world prepare to celebrate the beginning of a new millennium, with spectacular firework displays and parties planned all over the globe.

2000-2008

The overwhelming crisis of the decade was the Al-Qaeda terrorist attack on the twin towers of the World Trade Center in New York in 2001. It was a tragedy that shook not only the American nation, but the entire world. The 9/11 attacks launched America into war with Afghanistan, whose extremist Taliban regime was known to support and harbor Al-Qaeda terrorists. This marked the start of another phase of America's involvement in the Middle East.

In 2003, British Prime Minister Tony Blair made the unpopular decision to join President Bush in an invasion of Iraq to bring down the potentially dangerous tyrant Saddam Hussein. The terrorist attacks on the London transport network in July 2005 did little to convince the British public that the war in Iraq was justified. When Saddam was captured and eventually sentenced to death by an Iraqi court, the job was still far from over, and the Western invaders were to maintain a presence in Iraq for many years to come.

At the same time, the world's financial markets were heading into what was to be a very difficult global recession, which emerged towards the end of the decade. The glimmer of light in 2008 was the election of America's first black president, Barack Obama.

2000

CROWDS AROUND THE WORLD CELEBRATE A NEW MILLENNIUM

THE NEW MILLENNIUM

'The global computer crash that had been predicted in the years leading up to the millennium eve did not occur, though billions of dollars had been spent in an effort to prevent the potential crisis.'

Right: Crowds watch the London fireworks on December 31, 1999.

The dawn of the new millennium was celebrated across the world by people of all nationalities and all religions. In London, around 2 million people lined the banks of the River Thames to witness a spectacular firework display. Meanwhile, the Queen and the Prime Minister, Tony Blair, celebrated in the newly built Millennium Dome in Greenwich, at a party to which 6,000 members of the public had also been invited. In New York, 4 tons of confetti were dropped on the 3 million party-goers, and in Sydney Harbor, the crowds were treated to what was later agreed to be the most spectacular firework display of all. Among other symbolic moments, Nelson Mandela revisited his former prison cell on Robben Island and handed a candle to a child in a ceremony of hope and resolution. In Bethlehem, the believed site of Christ's birth 2,000 years ago, 2,000 doves of peace were released, and in Rome, the Pope encouraged his audience to work hard for peace over the next 1,000 years. The first dawn of the new millennium broke over the Pacific Islands, in Tonga and Fiji, but the Pacific Island of Samoa was the last place to experience the dawn of the third millennium, around 25 hours later. The global computer crash that had been predicted in the years leading up to the millennium eve did not occur, though billions of dollars had been spent in an effort to prevent the potential crisis.

Left: The Millennium Dome in London was built for the celebrations.

January 31
Doctor Convicted
In the U.K., Dr. Harold Shipman is convicted of murdering 15 patients.

February–March
Mozambique Floods
Devastating floods in Mozambique kill 800 people.

March 26
Putin for President
Vladimir Putin is elected President of Russia, bringing in economic reforms.

April 3
No to Microsoft
U.S. software giant Microsoft is ruled to have violated competition laws.

VOTE COUNTING CONTROVERSY FOR U.S. PRESIDENTIAL ELECTION

BUSH ELECTED PRESIDENT

The 2000 U.S. Presidential election saw the Governor of Texas, George W. Bush, running against Democratic contender Al Gore. The election was close across the states, but when it reached the Florida ballot, which would prove to be the deciding state, the counting ran into problems which buried the outcome in controversy. Early signs prompted news stations to call a victory for Bush in Florida, which made Gore concede defeat, but the final result in Florida was slim enough to require a mandatory recount by machine – and Gore withdrew his concession. The Gore camp now called for a manual recount. When the process was already under way, Bush appealed to the U.S. Supreme Court to stop the recount. On December 12, 2000, the Supreme Court ruled that the recount was unconstitutional and should stop. Florida was called for Bush, who became President. Later detailed analysis uncovered a string of irregularities in the Florida voting process that year, including ambiguous forms that caused many people to vote for another candidate, Pat Buchanan, instead of their intended candidate of Al Gore.

HUMAN GENOME DECODED

In what was declared one of the most important scientific breakthroughs of all time, on June 26, 2000, scientists announced that they had decoded the human genome. The process involved reading the 300 billion 'letters' that are strung out along the spirals of deoxyribonucleic acid (D.N.A.) at the core of human cells. The researchers announced that 85% of the code had been accurately sequenced, and they expected to have completely deciphered the entire code within three years. The discovery had far-reaching consequences for dealing with genetic diseases, as it continues to be the hope that 'faulty' genes will be identified and corrected before causing problems. However, some people fear that the information that will become available about individuals' genetic make-up might prompt genetic discrimination. The ability to read the code of the human genome in effect means that the full instructions for creating a human being will be available for the first time.

HUMAN GENOME PROJECT

May 25
Israeli Withdrawal
Israel withdraws its troops from Southern Lebanon.

July 25
Concorde Crashes
113 people die as Air France flight 4590, a Concorde aircraft, crashes.

August 3
Mob Violence
Rioting erupts about suspected sex offenders in Portsmouth, U.K.

August 12
Submarine Sinks
Russian submarine K-141 *Kursk* sinks. All 118 men on board perish.

September 26
Protests at I.M.F.
Anti-globalization protests take place at the International Monetary Fund (I.M.F.) and World Bank summits.

2000

ENVIRONMENTAL DISASTER FOR KENTUCKY

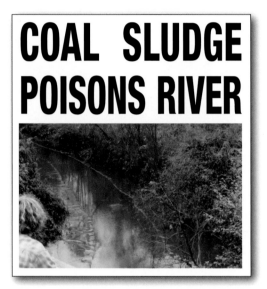

On October 11, 2000, in Martin County, Kentucky, U.S.A., a large-scale environmental disaster occurred when a mass of coal sludge broke through an underground mine and spilled out into the Tug Fork River. A total of 306 gallons of black waste flooded the river, polluting hundreds of miles of waterways and contaminating the water supplies of 27,000 residents. All aquatic life in the river was destroyed. The extent of the pollution was 30 times greater than that of the 1989 *Exxon Valdez* oil tanker spill, and it took years to repair. Fears began to circulate that the same thing would happen with other underground mines in the region, filling local waterways with coal sludge.

Right: Coal sludge wiped out aquatic life in Coldwater Fork and Wolf Creek, Kentucky.

FIRE ON SKI TRAIN KILLS 155 PEOPLE

On November 11, 2000, a ski train was traveling through a tunnel in the Alps when a fire broke out, killing 155 people. The train was preparing to leave a ski resort near Salzburg, Austria, when some drops of oil from the train's cable caused the overheated filament of a faulty fan heater in the rear driver's cabin to catch on fire. The train set off up the mountain and soon entered a tunnel, where the spreading fire caused it to grind to a stop. The doors were firmly shut, preventing the passengers from escaping as the fire moved through the train. Only 12 passengers in the rear car managed to smash a window with their skis and boots and escape down the mountain. The remaining passengers, who were mainly Austrian, but also included Germans, Japanese, British, and Americans, were either burned or suffocated to death. When the doors finally opened, the passengers who were able to climb out soon collapsed from smoke inhalation. Employees of the lift company, its suppliers, and the Austrian Transport Ministry were all charged with negligence.

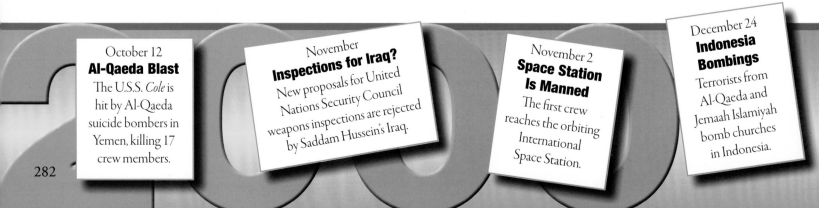

October 12
Al-Qaeda Blast
The U.S.S. *Cole* is hit by Al-Qaeda suicide bombers in Yemen, killing 17 crew members.

November
Inspections for Iraq?
New proposals for United Nations Security Council weapons inspections are rejected by Saddam Hussein's Iraq.

November 2
Space Station Is Manned
The first crew reaches the orbiting International Space Station.

December 24
Indonesia Bombings
Terrorists from Al-Qaeda and Jemaah Islamiyah bomb churches in Indonesia.

TALIBAN REGIME TOPPLED IN AFGHANISTAN

After the September 11, 2001, attacks in New York and Washington, D.C., U.S. President George W. Bush declared a 'War on Terror'. Having identified Osama bin Laden, founder of the terrorist organization Al-Qaeda, as the mastermind of the attacks, the U.S. demanded that the Taliban regime in Afghanistan, which was known to have offered Osama safe haven, turn him over. When the Taliban refused, the U.S. joined with the Northern Alliance, the homegrown resistance forces in Afghanistan, to bring down the Taliban's oppressive, Islamic fundamentalist regime. In October 2001, the U.S. and allies began by targeting Al-Qaeda training camps and Taliban military headquarters. By November, with the suppport of U.S. bombings, the Northern Alliance ground troops had succeeded in capturing the Afghan capital, Kabul. By December, the Taliban had surrendered the major city of Kandahar. The remainder of Taliban and Al-Qaeda troops fled, initially into the Hindu Kush Mountains bordering Pakistan, and then on to hidden retreats within Pakistan. From there, they have maintained a violent revolt against the new Afghan government. U.S. and N.A.T.O. troops remain in Afghanistan.

TALIBAN DEFEATED IN AFGHANISTAN

'The remainder of Taliban and Al-Qaeda troops fled, initially into the Hindu Kush Mountains bordering Pakistan, and then on to hidden retreats within Pakistan.'

Above: Ruined buildings surround a mosque in Kabul.

Left: British soldiers in the Afghan desert, in 2002.

January 15
Information for Everyone
Wikipedia, the free online encyclopedia, is launched.

January 20
George Bush Sworn In
George Walker Bush is sworn in as President of the United States.

January 26
Gujarati Earthquake
More than 12,000 die when an earthquake hits Gujarat in India.

February 12
Getting Near
The Near Earth Asteroid Rendezvous (N.E.A.R.) *Shoemaker* lands on the asteroid 433 Eros.

February 16
Bombing Raids on Iraq
British and U.S. forces bomb Iraq's air defense network.

2001

PLANES HIT TWIN TOWERS

Above: The steel skeleton of the South Tower days after the attacks killed 2,603 people in the towers and on the ground.

Left: Around 17,400 people were in the World Trade Center at the time of the attacks.

February 19
Foot and Mouth Crisis Begins
Foot and mouth disease breaks out among sheep and cattle in the U.K.

April 1
Milošević Surrenders
Former Yugoslavian President Slobodan Milošević is to be tried for war crimes.

April 1
Same-Sex Marriage
Same-sex marriages are legalized in the Netherlands.

June 1
Massacre in Nepal
Prince Dipendra of Nepal kills nine members of his family.

June 19
U.S. Missile Hits Iraq
A U.S. missile kills 23 people when it hits a soccer field in Iraq.

WAR ON THE WORLD

On September 11, 2001, 19 Islamic-extremist terrorists linked to the Al-Qaeda ('The Base') organization hijacked four passenger planes and crashed them all, killing all passengers onboard, as well as thousands of other civilians. The terrorists took control of the commercial planes and crashed two of them into the twin towers of the World Trade Center in downtown New York, bringing down the entire complex, destroying two other buildings nearby, and killing thousands of people inside. Some victims were killed instantly on the planes' impacts; others were trapped inside the buildings, with some leaping to their deaths from the windows to escape the flames. Both towers had collapsed within two hours. A third plane was crashed into the Pentagon, the headquarters of the Department of Defense, located in Arlington, Virginia, killing 125 people working in the building. The fourth plane came down in a field in rural Pennsylvania after its passengers and crew attempted to take control. They prevented the plane from crashing into its intended target in Washington, D.C. America responded to the horrific attacks by declaring war on Afghanistan (see p.283), where the Taliban regime had harbored Al-Qaeda terrorists – specifically, Osama bin Laden, their leader. In 2006, building work began on Freedom Tower on the site of the World Trade Center in Manhattan. It will be joined by three other towers and, when it is completed in 2011, will be one of the tallest buildings in America. In total, 2,974 fatalities resulted from the September 11 attacks (known as '9/11' in the U.S.A.), including 411 emergency workers who were killed in rescue attempts.

'The terrorists took control of the commercial planes and crashed two of them into the twin towers of the World Trade Center in downtown New York'

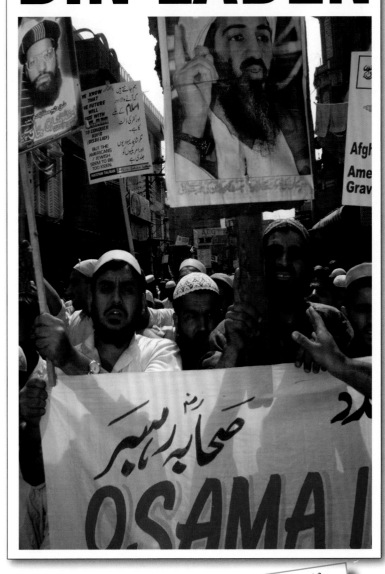

THE HUNT FOR BIN LADEN

July 2
Have a Heart
American Robert Tools receives the world's first self-contained artificial heart in Tennessee.

September 18
Anthrax Attacks
Five people die as letters containing anthrax spores are sent to news media offices in the U.S.

November 10
China Gets Membership
The World Trade Organization admits the People's Republic of China.

November 22
Pope Sends Email!
Pope John Paul II sends the first papal email.

December 13
Attack on Indian Parliament
Tension mounts between India and Pakistan after an attack on the Indian Parliament.

2002

THE U.K.'S QUEEN ELIZABETH THE QUEEN MOTHER DIES

QUEEN MOTHER DIES

Right and far right: The Queen Mother's grandchildren and great-grandchildren attend her funeral.

On March 30, 2002, Queen Elizabeth the Queen Mother died in her sleep at Windsor Castle, England, at the age of 101. The Queen was at her mother's bedside when she passed away. Ten days of national mourning followed before the funeral on April 9. The Queen Mother's body remained at Windsor Castle for three days before being taken to Queen's Chapel at St. James's Palace in London, and then onward, in ceremonial procession, to Westminster Hall before the funeral at Westminster Abbey. The funeral was conducted with full ceremony, creating a majestic spectacle that was viewed by more than 1 million people who had lined the processional route. The Queen Mother's coffin was eventually laid to rest beside that of King George VI, her husband, at St. George's Chapel in Windsor. The Queen Mother's younger daughter, Princess Margaret, had died seven weeks earlier, and her cremated ashes were buried with her mother's coffin. Public sympathy for the Queen was heightened by this double loss in such a short space of time, and by the time of her Golden Jubilee in the summer, nationalistic pride in the royal family was at a peak. The Queen Mother, born Elizabeth Bowes-Lyon, and her husband had been unexpectedly thrust onto the public stage by the abdication of the King's brother, Edward, and they had never expected to be king and queen. The Queen Mother could be credited with making the royal family more accessible, accountable to the nation for their behavior as individuals and as an institution. She invented the now familiar 'walkabout', a way for royals to meet their people face-to-face, and during the wartime Blitz, when many were abandoning London for the country, she insisted that the royal family should remain in the city. She took on public duties fully and was always present to support her shy husband, and later her daughter, Queen Elizabeth II.

January 1
Euro in Europe
Twelve European countries issue euro notes and coins.

February 27
Indian Riots
Hundreds perish in riots in India after 57 Hindus die when their train is burned by a Muslim mob.

May 26
Life on Mars?
The space probe *Mars Odyssey* finds traces of water ice deposits on the surface of Mars.

June 15
Near Miss!
Near Earth Asteroid 2002 MN misses Earth by just 75,000 miles (120,000 km). If it had hit the planet, it could have flattened up to 800 sq miles (2,000 sq km).

ENRON AND WORLDCOM SCANDALS
EXPOSE FRAUDULENT BUSINESS PRACTICES

Two of the world's most successful companies, Enron and WorldCom, collapsed in late 2001 and early 2002, exposing a high level of fraud and corruption at the heart of their management. While Wall Street banks earned millions of dollars in fees and loan interest, hiding the true state of the companies' finances, thousands of investors were conned into sinking money into them by means of fraudulent activity set up by banks and company bosses. Ken Lay (right), the boss of Enron, began by making it look like his company was far more profitable than it actually was in order to boost its share prices. During the 1990s, various banks, including Citibank and J.P. Morgan, staged fake transactions in order to create false income on Enron's accounts. These transactions included pouring $125 million into an offshore company, which then supposedly bought gas from Enron. The scam, however, was that no gas actually changed hands, and the $125 million 'loan' from Citibank appeared as income for Enron. By 2000, Enron was in serious debt, but the banks continued to prop up the company by painting a false picture of its finances. In 1999, the financial services firm Merrill Lynch created a network of fake companies and persuaded investors to pour money into them. This gave Enron an apparent $1 billion profit in 2000, when in fact it made a loss. WorldCom boss Bernie Ebbers managed his fraudulent activity differently. Ebbers convinced the banks to lend money to WorldCom and to employ supposedly unbiased 'star analysts' to hype up WorldCom shares. In this way, as share prices went up, the banks were paid back, plus interest, and WorldCom's shares continued to rise. In 2002, the auditing firm Arthur Anderson uncovered an accounting error in Enron's books that led to further investigations, a fall in share prices – and, ultimately, to bankruptcy. This then led to further thorough corporate investigations, during which WorldCom was also exposed. The companies' bosses were tried, and the bankers responsible were either fired or fined. Meanwhile, thousands of investors lost a total of $240 billion.

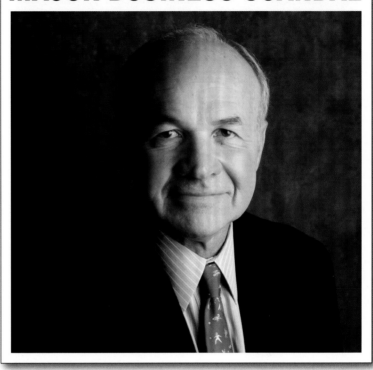

MAJOR BUSINESS SCANDAL

'The scam, however, was that no gas actually changed hands, and the $125 million "loan" from Citibank appeared as income for Enron.'

August
Severe Floods
Dozens are killed and thousands made homeless as floods hit Central Europe.

September 5
Violence Continues in Afghanistan
Interim Afghan President Hamid Karzai escapes an assassination attempt. On the same day, 30 die in a car bomb in Kabul, Afghanistan.

September 26
Joola Capsizes
A Senagalese passenger ferry called the *Joola* capsizes, killing 1,863 people.

October 2
Sniper Attacks
The so-called Beltway Sniper strikes in the U.S. Eleven people are shot in the attacks.

HOSTAGES DIE IN RUSSIAN THEATER SIEGE

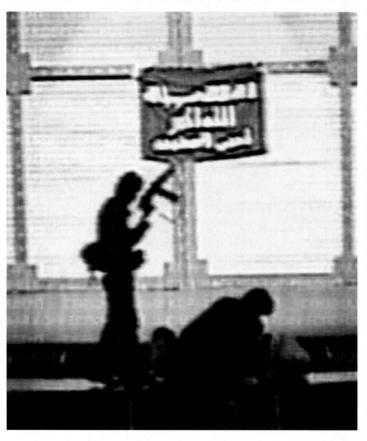

850 TRAPPED IN THEATER

On October 23, 2002, heavily armed Chechen rebels stormed a theater in Moscow just after the start of the second half of a play. The group took 850 people hostage and demanded an end to the Russian military action in the breakaway republic of Chechnya. The terrorists claimed to be 'suicide attackers'; they had explosives strapped to their bodies, and they planted further devices around the theater, threatening to kill ten hostages for every one of their own group killed. Although they released about 100 women, children, and Muslims at the beginning of the standoff, 750 people were still held inside. After no activity for 24 hours, the Chechen terrorists threatened to start executing their hostages if their demand of Russian military withdrawal was not met. On October 26, Russian Special Forces stormed the theater, using a poisonous gas that was intended to stun the terrorists but that also harmed hundreds of hostages. The official Chechen rebel leadership denied any connection with the terrorists, and a Muslim leader appeared on Russian television condemning the attacks, declaring that 'terrorists have no nationality'. At least 129 of the hostages were killed during the rescue attempt, along with 39 of the terrorists. A memorial now stands at the site as a remembrance of the victims. Tens of thousands of Chechens had been killed in two wars with Russia since the predominantly Muslim area declared its independence in 1991.

> 'After no activity for 24 hours, the Chechen terrorists threatened to start executing their hostages if their demand of Russian military withdrawl was not met.'

October 12
Bali Nightclub Bombings
Members of the violent Islamist group Jemaah Islamiyah detonate bombs in the tourist district of Kuta on the Indonesian island of Bali. The attack kills 182 people.

October 16
Iraq War Resolution
The U.S. Congress passes the Iraq War Resolution, authorizing the use of military force against Iraq.

November 18
Inspections in Iraq
United Nations weapons inspectors arrive in Iraq. They are searching for weapons of mass destruction, which Iraq has been banned from producing or possessing since the 1991 Gulf War.

S.A.R.S. SPREADS AROUND THE WORLD

SARS STRIKES

ASTRONAUTS DIE IN SPACE SHUTTLE

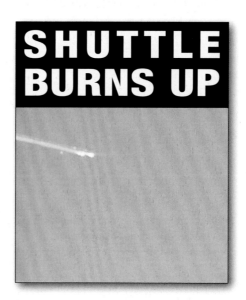

SHUTTLE BURNS UP

'It was the second space shuttle disaster in history, and it shocked and saddened the world as much as the destruction of the Challenger had in 1986.'

In November 2002, a previously unknown infectious disease called S.A.R.S. (Severe Acute Respiratory Syndrome) broke out in the Guangdong province of China. The respiratory disease had a high fatality rate, and in the course of one year it killed 350 people in mainland China, 44 in Ontario, Canada, and around 400 elsewhere, including Singapore and Hong Kong. The disease managed to spread around the globe mostly by air travel. Its apparently selective infection puzzled health officials because the first man known to have contracted the disease infected four other people but did not infect his four grown-up children who lived with him. Eventually, the disease was traced back to civet cats, a Chinese wildcat that is seen as a delicacy, and the Chinese government ordered 10,000 of the animals to be slaughtered. In Canada, Ontario's healthcare system was overwhelmed with the severity of the crisis and did not cope well. Subsequent reports highlighted that more public health spending needed to be directed toward the early identification and control of infectious diseases.

On February 1, 2003, the *Columbia* space shuttle broke up during re-entry into Earth's atmosphere. All seven crewmembers were killed. The *Columbia* crew had just completed a 16-day scientific research mission in space when the tragedy occurred. It was the second space shuttle disaster in history, and it shocked and saddened the world as much as the destruction of the *Challenger* had in 1986. The cause of the shuttle's disintegration was later found to have been sustained during launch. A piece of foam insulation had broken off and hit the left wing, damaging the thermal protection system that was designed to prevent overheating during re-entry. Although some N.A.S.A. officials suspected damage, nothing could be done about it once the shuttle had launched. Shuttle flights were stopped for two years while an investigation took place.

January 25
Human Shield
Volunteers travel to Iraq to act as human shields, hoping to prevent a U.S. invasion.

February 15
Millions Protest
In 800 cities around the world, millions protest against war on Iraq. Rome sees a crowd of 3 million in the largest anti-war rally in history.

March 13
Walking Tall
Some 350,000-year-old upright-walking human footprints are found in Italy.

March 17
No Resolution
U.S.-led efforts fail in securing a U.N. Security Council resolution supporting war on Iraq.

March 17
U.S. Ultimatum
U.S. President George Bush tells Saddam Hussein to leave Iraq or face military action.

COALITION FORCES INVADE IRAQ

IRAQ INVASION

Above: American civil rights activist Jesse Jackson joins the anti-war protest in London.

'The final town to fall was Tikrit, the hometown of Saddam Hussein ... although coalition forces were to remain in Iraq for years to come.'

Above: The bombing of Baghdad.

British Prime Minister Tony Blair had enjoyed a strong relationship with U.S. President Clinton, with whom he shared a center-left political stance, so it was a surprise to many when he formed an even stronger bond with the right-wing U.S. President George W. Bush. The September 11 attacks in New York and Washington, D.C. in 2001 launched the U.S. into a 'War on Terror', which first brought down the Taliban regime in Afghanistan before moving on to Saddam Hussein's Iraq. By linking an invasion of Iraq with the 'War on Terror', President Bush managed to suggest to the American people that Saddam Hussein had some involvement in the 9/11 attacks. Bush

March 19
Baghdad Bombed
Saddam Hussein has not left Iraq. The first U.S. bombs fall on Baghdad.

March 20
Iraq is Invaded
U.S., U.K., Polish, and Australian troops invade Iraq.

April 9
Saddam's Regime is Over
U.S. troops take control of Baghdad, ending Saddam Hussein's 24-year rule.

April 14
Human Genome Sequenced
The Human Genome Project has mapped 99% of the human genome.

THE FALL OF SADDAM

immediately looked to Tony Blair for Great Britain's support in the war against Iraq, but Blair had much more difficulty convincing his people of the war's moral necessity. Blair took the stance that Great Britain and the rest of the world were at risk from Saddam Hussein's 'weapons of mass destruction' and that a 'regime change' was necessary both to liberate the Iraqi people and to remove the global threat of Saddam. United Nations inspectors continued to search for evidence of these weapons, and although Saddam Hussein obstructed their searches, which increased the world's suspicions, none was ever found, and the U.N. refused to support any war. There were several anti-war protests across the United States in January 2003, although the majority of the people still backed their President. On February 16, 2003, millions of British people took to the streets of London to protest against going to war. Despite the protests of the British people, Tony Blair committed Great Britain to an invasion of Iraq, sending tens of thousands of British troops to the aid of the United States. Together, on March 20, 2003, the coalition forces launched the first of many bombing campaigns on Baghdad, killing a number of Saddam's henchmen, as well as innocent civilians. On April 6, Basra became the first city to fall to coalition forces when it came under British control. On April 9, Baghdad itself fell to American forces, and the takeover was greeted by cheers from some Iraqis as the Americans pulled down a statue of Saddam Hussein. The final town to fall was Tikrit, the hometown of Saddam Hussein, and with this, President Bush declared the war effectively over, although coalition forces were to remain in Iraq for years to come.

Right: U.S. tankbuster planes let off anti-missile flares as they fire on Baghdad's presidential compound.

June 26
Landmark Ruling
The U.S. Supreme Court declares that laws against sodomy are unconstitutional.

August 1
Chechen Bomb
A Chechen suicide bomber strikes a Russian military hospital, killing 50 people.

December 13
Saddam Found in Tikrit
Saddam Hussein is captured by U.S. forces.

December 26
Earthquake in Iran
Southeastern Iran is hit by a massive earthquake, which kills 26,000 people.

N.A.S.A.'S SPIRIT LANDS ON MARS

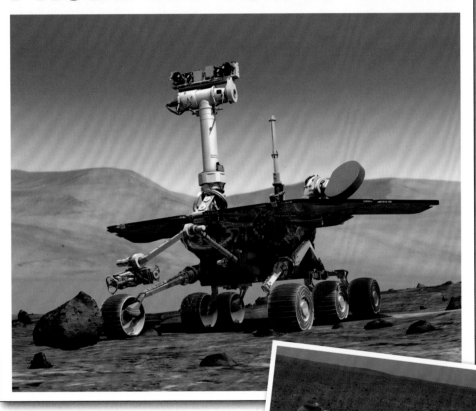

PROBE EXPLORES MARS

Right: Spirit's airbag-protected landing craft on the Martian surface.

On January 4, 2004, N.A.S.A.'s first Mars exploration rover, known as *Spirit* or MER-A (Mars Exploration Rover A), landed safely on Mars. Since that day, the rover has been conducting geological analysis of the planet's surface and communicating effectively with its ground controllers to share invaluable information about the substance of the planet Mars. The specific aims of the MER-A mission are to identify evidence of water on the planet in the past and to determine what geological processes have shaped the current make-up of the terrain. The experiments were designed to add to the ongoing process of determining

'The experiments were designed to add to the ongoing process of determining whether it is possible that life has ever existed on Mars.'

whether it is possible that life has ever existed on Mars. The *Spirit* rover landed on the site of a giant impact crater that is thought could possibly have been a former lake. The landing site was named 'Columbia Memorial Site' in honor of the seven astronauts killed in the 2003 *Columbia* disaster.

February 3
No Weapons
The C.I.A. admits there was no immediate threat from weapons of mass destruction before the 2003 invasion of Iraq.

February 4
Facebook Founded
Social networking website Facebook is launched by Harvard University students.

March 29
Smoking Ban
Ireland is the first country in the world to ban smoking in all enclosed workplaces.

May 1
Union Expands
Ten new member states join the European Union.

RUSH-HOUR TRAINS BOMBED IN MADRID

On March 11, 2004, 191 people were killed when a series of explosions tore through three Madrid train stations during the morning rush hour. In simultaneous blasts, believed to have been remotely detonated by cell phone, the main commuter station of Atocha, in central Madrid, and two smaller suburban stations were targeted. Altogether, there were ten explosions, which ripped trains apart, killing many instantly, injuring thousands, and trapping others inside carriages. A field hospital was set up at Atocha station, and national appeals went out for people to donate blood. A temporary morgue was set up in an exhibition hall, although the busloads of relatives arriving to identify loved ones were warned that it was virtually impossible to match body parts. The attacks came three days before Spain's general election, and the Basque separatist terrorist group Eta was initially suspected to be responsible. However, political parties linked to Eta denied this and suggested that 'Arab resistance' groups could be responsible. Subsequent investigations have pointed toward the possibility of Al-Qaeda involvement. One Syrian-born Spanish citizen has since been extradited to Spain on a charge of recruiting bombers, and seven other suspects blew themselves up in an apartment in Leganés, Spain, to avoid arrest. In all, 27 people were tried regarding the attacks.

BOMBS HIT MADRID

Left: Candles were left at the sites of the attacks, while millions took to the streets to protest.

May 1
Beslan Massacre
At least 335 people are killed when Russian forces end the siege of a school in Beslan, Northern Ossetia, by Chechen terrorists.

November 2
Bush is Back
In the U.S. Presidential Election, President George Bush defeats Senator John Kerry.

December 26
Tsunami
More than 200,000 people die in Southeast Asia when an earthquake generates a devastating tsunami.

2005

SUICIDE BOMBERS SHAKE LONDON

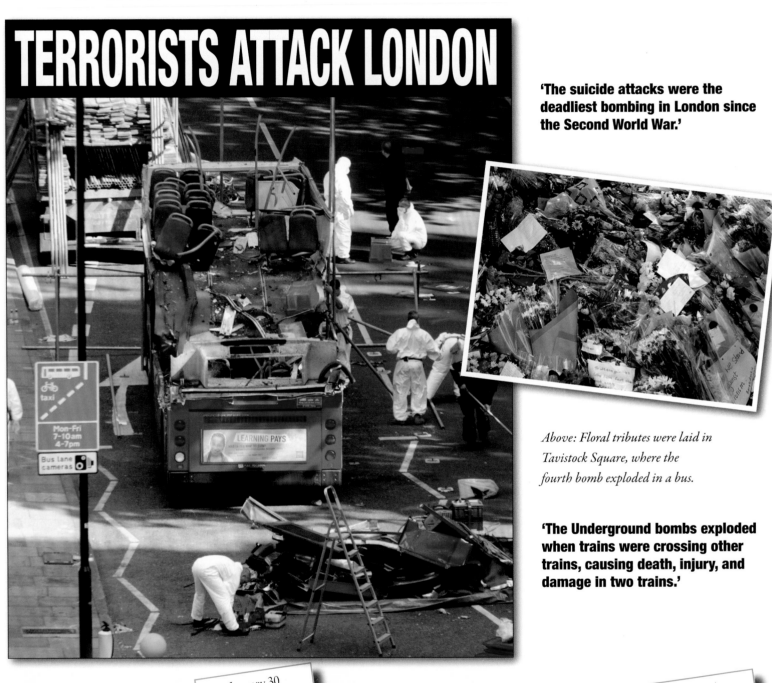

TERRORISTS ATTACK LONDON

'The suicide attacks were the deadliest bombing in London since the Second World War.'

Above: Floral tributes were laid in Tavistock Square, where the fourth bomb exploded in a bus.

'The Underground bombs exploded when trains were crossing other trains, causing death, injury, and damage in two trains.'

January 16
Oldest Mother
Surrogate mother Adriana Iliescu becomes the oldest woman to give birth, at 66 years old.

January 30
Iraqi Elections
For the first time in 47 years, free parliamentary elections take place in Iraq.

February 16
Kyoto Protocol
The Kyoto Protocol international treaty to stabilize greenhouse gas emissions goes into effect.

March 3
Round-the-World Flight
Steve Fossett completes the first non-stop solo flight around the world.

March 4
H.I.V. Crisis
The U.N. warns that, without preventative action, around 90 million Africans could become infected by H.I.V.

During the commuter rush hour on the morning of July 7, 2005, three bombs exploded almost simultaneously on three separate trains in the London Underground, and an hour later a fourth explosion went off on a London bus. The suicide bombings, carried out by extremist British Muslims protesting against British involvement in the Iraq War, represented the first instance of suicide attacks on the London Transport system and the deadliest bombing in London since the Second World War. In total, 56 people were killed, including the four bombers. The force of the explosions, and therefore the number of fatalities, varied according to the tunnel construction within which each of the three trains was traveling. The two bombs on Circle Line trains were in shallow, wide tunnels, which sustained more of the brunt of the explosions, whereas the bomb on the Piccadilly Line train was in a deep, narrow tunnel, making the explosion more concentrated. In all cases, the Underground bombs exploded when trains were near other trains, thus causing death, injury, and damage in two trains. During the initial panic, London Underground thought that an unexpected power surge had caused the blasts, but within hours, the police issued a statement to say that a terrorist attack was the most likely explanation. Evidence found on the bodies of the bombers led the police to a bomb factory in Leeds. However, it is not clear whether the men had planned to commit suicide all along, due to inconsistent details, such as the fact that they bought return train tickets to London.

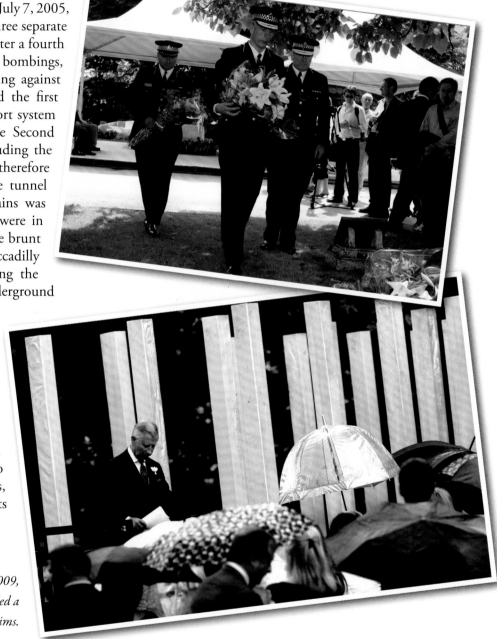

Right: In 2009, Prince Charles unveiled a memorial to the 52 victims.

April 9
Royal Wedding
Prince Charles, Prince of Wales marries Camilla Parker Bowles in Windsor, England.

April 19
New Pope Elected
Pope Benedict XVI succeeds Pope John Paul II, who died on April 2.

July 12
Attack in Israel
Members of Islamic Jihad kill five people in a shopping mall in Netanya, Israel.

July 28
Farewell to Arms
The Provisional Irish Republican Army (I.R.A.) formally ends its 36-year armed campaign.

October 8
Quake in Kashmir
A 7.6-magnitude earthquake in Kashmir kills more than 80,000 people.

HURRICANE KATRINA STRIKES

HURRICANE SWAMPS CITY

In the summer of 2005, Hurricane Katrina became one of the deadliest storms in American history. It first hit the Bahamas then, on August 23, it crossed Florida as a relatively mild storm. But by the time it hit Louisiana on August 29, it had strengthened considerably, resulting in severe damage and loss of life. In New Orleans, the levee system is meant to act as protection against storms, but the fierce hurricane completely destroyed it, causing deadly floods all over the city. By the time Katrina had passed, 1,836 people had lost their lives, either as a result of the hurricane itself or during the floods. Although President Bush had issued a state-of-emergency warning two days before the hurricane hit, it did not include some of the most vulnerable areas on the Louisiana coast. Several evacuation orders went a little way toward saving lives, but it was estimated that around 80% of New Orleans residents were still in the city when the floodwaters broke. There was widespread criticism of the Bush administration, as well as the U.S. Federal Emergency Management Agency, in the aftermath of the New Orleans floods.

'In New Orleans, the fierce hurricane completely destroyed the levee system, causing deadly floods all over the city'

Right: The hurricane totally destroyed many wooden houses in Louisiana.

October 19
Saddam Tried
Saddam Hussein goes on trial in Iraq for crimes against humanity.

November 28
Climate Change Debated
The United Nations Climate Change Conference opens in Montreal.

November 30
First Face Transplant
Surgeons in Amiens, France, carry out the first human face transplant. The patient is Isabelle Dinoire, who had been mauled by her dog.

SADDAM HUSSEIN SENTENCED TO HANG

On November 5, 2006, Saddam Hussein was sentenced to death by an Iraqi court for the 1982 murder of 148 Shia Muslims in Dujail, Iraq. Saddam was due to be tried for further killings of the Kurd peoples, but the death penalty issued in November had to be carried out quickly, so it was never likely that subsequent trials would take place. Human rights groups criticized the inadequacies of the trial. However, the Iraqi court system insisted that no amount of international disapproval would change its decision. Appeals by Saddam's defense lawyers all failed. Iraq's new president, Jalal Talabani, had been an opponent of the death penalty in the past but had been known to have his deputies sign death sentences in his place. Saddam's trial had been beset by problems from the beginning due to the defendant's refusal to cooperate with the court on any level. He shouted abuse at anyone who dared to accuse him and refused to answer any questions. It had been a predictable conclusion, however, that the trial would result in the death penalty. The crime for which he was finally hanged on December 30, 2006 was one of many atrocities that had been committed during Saddam's rule. Video recordings of the noose being placed over his head and tightened were broadcast to the nation; he had refused to wear a black hood. Although the actual hanging was kept off-camera, images of Saddam's dead body in its shroud were also broadcast. It was reported that there was much celebration after his death, including cheering, chanting, and dancing around the dead body, although there were also pockets of protest, particularly in his hometown of Tikrit. The Prime Minister of Iraq, Nouri al-Maliki, said, 'Justice, in the name of the people, has carried out the death sentence against the criminal Saddam.'

'He shouted abuse at anyone who dared to accuse him and refused to answer any questions.'

SADDAM EXECUTED

January 15
Stardust Search
N.A.S.A.'s Stardust mission successfully returns dust from a comet.

February 3
Ferry Sinks
The sinking of Egyptian passenger ferry *al-Salam Boccaccio 98* kills over 1,034 people.

July 11
Mumbai Blasts
Rush-hour commuter trains are bombed in Mumbai, India, by Islamic terrorists. More than 200 people lose their lives.

July 12
Lebanon War
Israel invades Lebanon in response to attacks by Lebanon-based Hezbollah.

2006

YOUNGEST SURVIVOR OF OPEN HEART SURGERY

Owen Smith was born three months early, weighing just 1lb 8oz (0.68 kg), to Stephanie and Alan Smith of Southampton, England. Following his mother's strange premonition that he was about to be born, she went straight to the hospital, and her son was removed from her womb by an emergency caesarean section when it was discovered that he was shrinking rather than growing. In March 2006, still seven weeks before he was even due to have been born, it was found that he had a blood clot on his heart and that his only chance of survival was open-heart surgery. Although such an operation had never before been performed on such a small baby, surgeon Stephen Langley of the Southampton General Hospital knew that, despite the risks, there was no other choice. The operation was successful. Although Owen's heart was only the size of a marble, Dr. Langley managed to open it, remove the clot, sew him back up, and restart his heart.

'Seven weeks before he was even due to have been born, it was found that he had a blood clot on his heart'

MASSIVE ROBBERY

40 MILLION STOLEN IN BIGGEST CASH ROBBERY EVER

On February 21, 2006, an armed gang managed to escape with £53 million (about $80 million) from a Securitas depot in Kent, England. They kidnapped a security manager as he was returning home from work by posing as police in an unmarked car. At the same time, other members of the gang went to his home and kidnapped his wife and son by also posing as police. The security manager was then bundled into a white van and driven at gunpoint to the depot, with threats that his wife and son would be hurt if he did not cooperate. At the depot, where cash is stored to be loaded into A.T.M.s, they tied up staff and spent an hour loading banknotes into the van.

August 23
Kidnapped
Austrian Natascha Kampusch escapes after being held by Wolfgang Priklopil for eight years.

August 24
Pluto Downgraded
Pluto is officially demoted to the status of dwarf planet.

October 15
North Korea Sanctioned
The U.N. sanctions North Korea over its nuclear testing.

November 23
Death Toll in Iraq Mounts
Bombs and mortar attacks kill more than 200 in Baghdad, Iraq.

GUN MASSACRE AT UNIVERSITY IN VIRGINIA

On April 16, 2007, a student at Virginia Tech killed a total of 32 students and professors in the deadliest shooting incident by a single gunman in U.S. history. Seung-Hui Cho, who was from South Korea but had been in America for 15 years, had received therapy for severe anxiety disorder in high school and continued to suffer from mental health problems, including severe depression and selective mutism. His mental illness was not reported to staff at Virginia Tech because of privacy laws, and by then Cho had discontinued his treatment. At the university, staff had first been alerted to his problems when he stalked female students and wrote a hate-fueled essay. Campus police were notified, but the only action taken was to remove Cho from class and teach him separately. Cho's professor described him as the 'loneliest person in the world'. In the early morning of April 16, Cho went to the dormitory of Emily Hilscher, a freshman with whom he may have been infatuated, and shot her dead, along with another student, Ryan Clark. While police and emergency services dealt with the initial shootings, Cho returned to his own dorm room, changed his clothes, logged on to his email, and removed his hard drive. Two hours later, after mailing a package of documents and recordings to N.B.C. News, Cho entered the university building that housed the engineering and mechanics faculty, chained the doors closed, and began shooting into the classrooms. He fired single controlled shots that were apparently random in their intended targets. It was around 15 minutes before police responding to 911 calls were able to break into the building. By then, Cho had killed five professors and 27 students. He then shot himself dead. Inquiries into the massacre found fault with the gun laws that had allowed a psychiatric patient to buy weapons and ammunition. Later that year, a law was passed that allowed educational institutions to ban guns on campus.

'By the time police were able to break into the buildings, Cho had killed five professors and 27 students.'

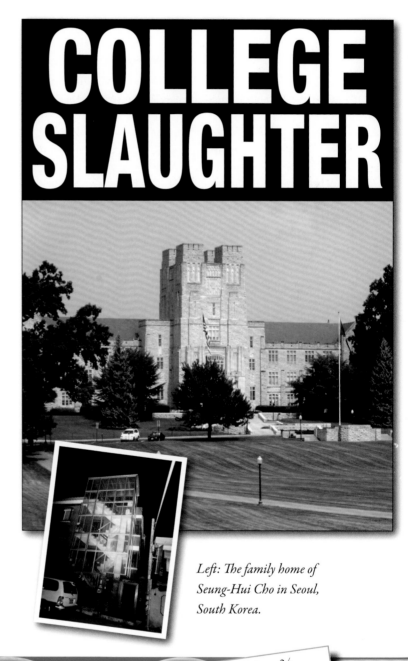

Left: The family home of Seung-Hui Cho in Seoul, South Korea.

February 2
War in Somalia
In the Somalian civil war, eight people are killed in a mortar attack in the capital, Mogadishu.

May 15
Gaza Fighting
Fighting breaks out in the Gaza Strip as the Palestinian National Authority government falls.

June 5
Messenger Mission
N.A.S.A.'s *Messenger* spacecraft makes a fly-by of Venus en route to Mercury.

June 24
Brown for P.M.
Gordon Brown is elected leader of the U.K. Labour Party. He becomes Prime Minister three days later.

2007

BLOW FOR DEMOCRACY IN PAKISTAN

On October 18, 2007, two Al-Qaeda suicide bombers killed 136 people in Karachi, Pakistan, in an assassination attempt on Pakistan's former Prime Minister Benazir Bhutto. Bhutto's truck was sufficiently armored to save her life. She had been aware of the threats that greeted her return from self-imposed exile. Nevertheless, she was determined that extremist terrorists should not destroy the path to democracy in Pakistan, declaring, 'Democracy alone can save Pakistan from disintegration and militant takeover.'

'Benazir Bhutto's support of America in the "War on Terror" made her a constant target of extremist groups.'

Her return to Pakistan signaled a possible power-share between her own Pakistan People's Party and President General Pervez Musharraf, who had seized power in 1999, as a step towards restoring democracy. Benazir Bhutto's support of America in the 'War on Terror' had forced her into exile in Dubai and made her a constant target of extremist groups. On December 26, 2007, just over two months after the failed assassination attempt, Benazir Bhutto was shot dead in another suicide attack, which also killed 14 of her supporters. Al-Qaeda's main commander in Afghanistan claimed responsibility, saying, 'We terminated the most precious American asset.' A U.S. Senator unintentionally upheld this notion with the statement, 'Our foreign policy had relied on her presence as a stabilizing force.'

BHUTTO ASSASSINATED

Left: General Pervez Musharraf, who seized power in a coup in 1999.

June 29
Bombs Defused
Two car bombs are made safe in central London. The plot is linked to extremist Islamist groups.

June 30
Glasgow Terror Alert
In an attack linked to the previous day's London car bombs, a jeep loaded with propane is driven into Glasgow Airport. The attack is foiled.

August 14
Iraq Horror
Suicide bombs in northern Iraq kill 796 people, in the Iraq War's worst car bomb attack.

August 25
Greek Wild Fires
Heatwaves, drought, arson, and negligence cause a series of devastating forest fires in Greece.

September 26
Burma Protests
In Burma (also known as Myanmar), the military cracks down on anti-government protests.

BLIND PATIENTS FITTED WITH ELECTRONIC EYES

In April 2008, surgeons at Moorfields Eye Hospital in London successfully implanted bionic eyes into two blind patients during a four-hour operation. The electronic devices consist of miniature cameras that are mounted in a pair of glasses, which themselves transmit wireless signals into a receiver attached to the patient's retina. The patients are not expected to have clear sight, but they should be able to distinguish light and dark and recognize shapes, as well as being able to navigate sufficiently to walk unaided. Second Sight's Argus II retinal implant works by imitating the eye's action, with the signals received from the camera stimulating the existing nerve endings in the patient's eye. The first patients both had an inherited condition called retinitis pigmentosa, but it is thought that the bionic eye could eventually also by used on people with non-inherited blindness.

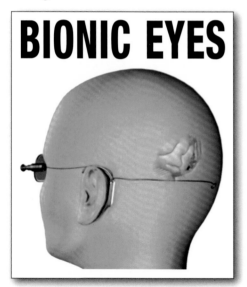

BIONIC EYES

STORM DEVASTATES BURMA

CYCLONE KILLS THOUSANDS

On May 3, 2008, a tropical cyclone hit Burma (also known as Myanmar), leaving around 50,000 people dead and millions homeless. In several townships in the Irrawaddy region, 90–95% of buildings were destroyed and survivors were unable to get food or clean drinking water. As Cyclone Nagris tore through the rice-growing region of the country, winds reached 120 mph (200 kph), sweeping away roads, trees, and buildings. In the main city of Yangon (previously Rangoon), power was lost. The ruling military junta had refused aid in the aftermath of the 2004 tsunami, but the scale of the wreckage from Cyclone Nagris meant that foreign aid was essential. Aid agencies found it difficult to operate in the restricted conditions brought about by the collapsed infrastructure, and many areas were totally cut off.

January 21
Stock Plunge
Fueled by fears of a U.S. recession, stock markets around the world take a plunge.

February 17
Kosovo Declaration
In the Balkans, Kosovo declares its independence from Serbia.

February 22
Rock Falls
In the U.K., Northern Rock is the first bank in Europe to be taken into state control.

March 1
Gaza Strikes
In the ongoing Israeli-Palestinian conflict, Israeli air strikes kill 50 in the Gaza Strip.

March 6
Israeli Dead
Eight Israelis are killed when a Palestinian gunman opens fire in a seminary in Jerusalem.

2008

CREDIT CRUNCH BEGINS

The global financial crisis had been brewing for some time when it began to show its effects in the middle of 2007. Many large financial institutions collapsed when they were unable to call in massive debts, and stock markets fell across the world. After years of economic boom, the financial bubble finally burst at the end of 2007. The first noticeable collapse involved the sub-prime mortgage market in the U.S., in which high-risk individuals had been lent money at high rates of interest. As soon as problems emerged, confidence plummeted, and assets began to drop dramatically in value. Governments poured public money into the banks to prevent them from collapsing, but nothing was sufficient to fill the credit hole. The 'credit crunch' followed, and businesses that relied on credit from failing banks also collapsed. It is estimated that, in the U.S. alone, taxpayers will have paid out $9.7 trillion (£6.5 trillion) to bail out their banks. By the start of 2008, the industrialized world had entered an economic recession.

May 25
Phoenix Lands
N.A.S.A.'s *Phoenix* robotic spacecraft is the first to land on the northern polar region of Mars.

June 27
Elections in Zimbabwe
President Robert Mugabe retains power in a disputed election in Zimbabwe.

August 7
War in South Ossetia
Russia and Georgia launch offensives in the South Ossetia region.

September 9
Thailand Crisis
The Constitutional Court of Thailand orders Prime Minister Samak to resign.

September 15
Mugabe Shares Power
In Zimbabwe, Robert Mugabe signs a power-sharing deal.

FIRST BLACK PRESIDENT OF THE UNITED STATES

OBAMA ELECTED PRESIDENT

Right: Obama supporters celebrate his election in Washington, D.C.

On November 4, 2008, Illinois Senator and Democrat candidate Barack Obama was elected 44th President of the United States of America. He is the first African American in U.S. history to become president, defeating Republican John McCain. At Harvard Law School, Obama had been the first black president of the Harvard Law Review, and he practiced as a civil rights attorney in Chicago before being elected to the Illinois State Senate in 1997. In 2004, he was elected as a Democratic Senator to the U.S. Senate, and in 2008, he beat his rival Hillary Clinton to become the Democratic candidate for the 2008 presidential elections. Then, just 45 years after racial segregation in the United States had come to an end, Barack Obama ascended to the highest office in the land. He came to power during a difficult time in U.S. history, in the middle of a world economic crisis and while the United States military was still tangled in problematic operations in Iraq and Afghanistan. In his acceptance speech, Obama, whose rhetorical powers had been compared to civil rights leader Dr. Martin Luther King, echoed King's speeches by referring to the 'arc of history' that had led to his election. His words, spoken to an audience of 240,000 supporters in Chicago, were broadcast live across the world.

'Just 45 years after racial segregation in the United States had come to an end, Barack Obama ascended to the highest office in the land.'

Left: Michelle Obama, Barack's wife.

September 20
Pakistan Bomb
A suicide truck bomb destroys a hotel in Pakistan, killing at least 60 people.

October 7
Iceland in Trouble
Russia and Iceland begin discussions of a Russian financial bail-out.

October 21
Hadron On
The world's largest particle accelerator, the Large Hadron Collider, is officially inaugurated near Geneva, Switzerland. It will test various propositions of high-energy physics.

November 26
Mumbai Terror
Terrorist attacks by Islamic militants in Mumbai, India, kill 173 people and injure over 300.

Acknowledgements

The publishers would like to thank the following people for their kind permission to reproduce their photographs

Key: a-above; b-bottom/below; c-center; l-left; r-right

All images supplied by Mirrorpix – archives of the Daily Mirror, © Mirrorpix (MGN LTD), except:

1 and 2 NASA, 3b Dirck Halstead/Getty Images, 5tr NASA, 5br istockphoto.com/geopaul, 6r WILLIAM BETSCH/AFP/Getty Images, 7 MPI/Getty Images, 8 NASA, 9 JEAN-PIERRE PREVEL/AFP/Getty Images, 12tl istockphoto.com/duncan1890, 12bc istockphoto.com/Anthony Baggett, 12br istockphoto.com/Peter Spiro, 13cr istokphoto.com/Rob Friedman, 25br Yann Forget, 33bl Charlie Wiederhold, 33br istockphoto.com/Jonatha Borzicchi, 35bl istockphoto.com/Govert Nieuwland, 37b Chicago History Museum/Getty Images, 38b istockphoto.com/Joseph Luoman, 39b istockphoto.com/Daniel Wrench, 40b Roger Viollet Collection/Getty Images, 41b istockphoto.com/Bernhard Weber, 45bc istockphoto.com/Igor Marx, 47bc istockphoto.com/wsfurlan, 48br Pictorial Parade/Getty Images, 51bl MPI/Getty Images, 57bl istockphoto.com/Ian Ilott, 59br Douglas Miller/Getty Images, 60b Picture Post/Hulton Archive/Getty Images, 61bl Topical Press Agency/Getty Images, 61br ostockphoto.com/Alexander Zhiltsov, 63br Keystone/Getty Images, 64bl Topical Press Agency/Getty Images, 65b istokphoto.com/BlaneyPhoto, 69b Fox Photos/Getty Images, 71br istockphoto.com/contour99, 72b istockphoto.com/james steidl, 74b istockphoto.com/james steidl, 79b istockphoto.com/Bill Grove, 80br Popperfoto/Getty Images, 82b Popperfoto/Getty Images, 89b H. F. Davis/Topical Press Agency/Getty Images, 90tr istockphoto.com/John Cairns, 93b FPG/Hulton Archive/Getty Images, 95b Paul Popper/Popperfoto/Getty Images, 96b Time Life Pictures/National Archives/Time Life Pictures/Getty Images, 98b Hulton Archive/Getty Images, 99b istockphoto.com/Brent Bossom, 102b Popperfoto/Getty Images, 105c istockphoto.com/Amanda Udlinek, 108cr Popperfoto/Getty Images, 116tr Monty Fresco/Topical Press Agency/Getty Images, 117cr Yale Joel//Time Life Pictures/Getty Images, 120br istockphoto.com/ayzek, 129bl istockphoto.com/Denis Babenko, 133bl istockphoto.com/clu, 138b Paul Schutzer/Time Life Pictures/Getty Images, 141 br Getty Images, 143b NASA, 144tr Loomis Dean/Time Life Pictures/Getty Images, 146b Howard Sochurek/Time Life Pictures/Getty Images, 147bc istockphoto.com/lara seregni, 149b istockphoto.com/sx70, 150 NASA, 153tr istockphoto.com/Steven Allan, 154br Getty images, 155c istockphoto.com/Alexander Fediachov, 155bl istockphoto.com/jaynemccarthy, 156bl istockphoto.com/woodstock, 156cb istockphoto.com/elmvilla, 157br istockphoto.com/Dave Long, 158l NASA, 158bl istockphoto.com/petestopher, 158bc istockphoto.com/EuToch, 159br istockphoto.com/Dmitry Nikolaev, 160bc istockphoto.com/Kamyshko, 160tc NASA, 161bc istockphoto.com/Chris Reed Photography, 163bc istockphoto.com/infospeed, 163br istockphoto.com/Kaufmann Visual Arts, 164l Time & Life Pictures/Getty Images, 164bc istockphoto.com/joebobbubba, 165r Getty Images, 165br istockphoto.com/Kapstadt, 166b istockphoto.com/Torsten Ståhlberg, 167tr NASA, 167cr istockphoto.com/RFStock, 168tr Time & Life Pictures/Getty Images, 170 istockphoto.com/gprentice, 173tl Time & Life Pictures/Getty Images, 173bl istockphoto.com/stevenallan, 174tr Time & Life Pictures/Getty Images, 178l, 179 all NASA, 181bl istockphoto.com/naes, 182 NASA, 183bl NASA, 184l NASA, 186tr Getty Images, 189br istockphoto.com/Robert Mayne, 191br istockphoto.com/Thomas Hottner, 192l AFP/Getty Images, 193l and cr NASA, 193br istockphoto.com/RUDI TAPPER, 194r istockphoto.com/Richard Gunion, 197br istockphoto.com/Hendrik De Bruyne, 197bc istockphoto.com/Alex de groot, 199cl istockphoto.com/SERDAR YAGCI, 199bc istockphoto.com/alandj, 199br istockphoto.com/alandj, 199tr Getty Images North America, 200tl Getty Images, 202tl Getty Images, 202bc istockphoto.com/Cliff Parnell, 203l courtesy of U.S. Government, 203r Keystone/Hulton Archive/Getty Images, 204cr AFP PHOTO/Getty Images, 204bl abd br NASA, 208tl and bl Getty Images, 209br Time & Life Pictures, 210l AFP/Getty Images, 210bc istockphoto.com/Guillaume Dubé, 212br Getty Images, 214 NASA, 216bc istockphoto.com/Scorpion_PL, 217tr istockphoto.com/creativephoto, 218br istockphoto.com/Steven Allan, 219br itsockphoto.com/Jeremy Voisey, 221bc istockphoto.com/Johan Ramberg, 223tl istockphoto.com/ivan mateev, 223bl AFP/Getty Images, 225tl Time & Life Pictures, 225bc istockphoto.com/SlidePix, 226tl istockphoto.com/dan_prat, 226tr NASA, 226bc istockphoto.com/Mooneydriver, 227 Peter Jordan/Time & Life Pictures/Getty Images, 230tl and cb NASA, 232tl AFP/Getty Images, 232br Code Red, 233r Getty Images, 233bl istockphoto.com/Mateusz Skalski, 234bc istockphoto.com/Sergey Kamshylin, 235r Getty Images, 235bc NASA, 236tr Holger Ellgaard, 236bl Wayne Eastep, 237tl istockphoto.com/Pierre Janssen, 238bl istockphoto.com, 241tl Time & Life Pictures, 243r Michael Chow//Time Life Pictures/Getty Images, 246 Ed Pritchard, 247tc istockphoto.com/Àlex Culla i Viñals, 251 Time & Life Pictures/Getty Images, 253tl istockphoto.com, 253tr Time & Life Pictures/Getty Images, 255tr Ed Pritchard, 255cr istockphoto.com/abbesses, 255br Time & Life Pictures/Getty Images, 258tl Hulton Archive, 258tr Getty Images, 260l AFP/Getty Images, 262tl AFP/Getty Images, 262tr AFP/Getty Images, 262c istockphoto.com/Alan Tobey, 263bc istockphoto.com/John Barnett, 264tl AFP/Getty Images, 264bl Time & Life Pictures/Getty Images, 265bc istockphoto.com/Denis Smith, 267 AFP/AFP/Getty Images, 267tr and bc NASA, 268bl AFP/Getty Images, 269tl istockphoto.com/Scott Orr, 274tl AFP/Getty Images, 275 Getty Images, 276tl istockphoto.com/Àlex Culla i Viñals, 277br istockphoto.com/Simon Podgorsek, 278 istockphoto.com/Terraxplorer, 279tc istockphoto.com/Tomaz Levstek, 279tr istokphoto.com/Joseph Nickischer, 279bc NASA, 281tr istockphoto.com/bluestocking, 281br istockphoto.com/geopaul, 282tr istockphoto.com/nathan winter, 282bl AFP/Getty Images, 284tr istockphoto.com/Terraxplorer, 284bl istockphoto.com/Markus Seidel, 287tr Getty Images, 288l Getty Images, 289tl istockphoto.com/Tomaz Levstek, 289tr CNN/Getty Images, 289bc CNN/Getty Images, 292 all NASA, 293tl istockphoto.com/Jakub Semeniuk, 293r istockphoto.com/harryfn, 293bc istockphoto.com/kelvin wakefield, 296l istockphoto.com/Joseph Nickischer, 296tr istockphoto.com/Parker Deen, 296br istockphoto.com/Joseph Nickischer, 297 Chris Hondros/Getty Images, 298tr Ben Edwards, 299r istockphoto.com/Brian Adams, 301l Mohammed Sawan, 301tr and bc istockphoto.com/Grace Tan, 302l istockphoto.com/JoeClemson, 302r istockphoto.com/Kirby Hamilton, 303tr istockphoto,com/Dan Moore endpapers: front – Getty Images, back – AFP/Getty Images

Page 2: The Earth rises above the Moon in this image taken by the crew of Apollo 8 in December 1968.

Page 3: Journalists and South Vietnamese flee Saigon as communist North Vietnamese troops enter the city in April 1975.

Page 5
Top: Skylab was launched in 1973 and was America's first space station. It remained in orbit until 1979, when it burned up on reentry.

Middle: Concorde made its first supersonic flight on October 1, 1969, and remained in service until October 2003.

Bottom: On June 26, 2000, scientists declared that they had decoded most of the chemical instructions that made up human D.N.A.

Endpapers
Front: The space shuttle Challenger *explodes just 73 seconds after launch from Cape Canaveral, Florida, on January 28, 1986, killing all seven astronauts on board.*

Back: Rescue workers sort through the wreckage of a building in Nairobi, Kenya, following a terrorist attack on the U.S. embassy on August 7, 1998.